Buddhism in the Nordic Countries

This book provides new unprecedented research on Buddhism in the five Nordic countries Denmark, Finland, Iceland, Norway and Sweden. Aiming at comparisons between the different Nordic countries, the chapters identify possible unique characteristics of Nordic Buddhism.

Buddhism in the Nordic Countries contributes to the growing literature on Buddhism in the West. Identifying a number of similar cultural and social trends that have been at work in the Nordic countries, the book shows that these have favoured the growth of Buddhism in northern Europe. The chapters on each of the Nordic countries describe the establishment of the main Buddhist traditions in the country, temple institutions, monasteries, demography, estimation on the number of Buddhists, geography, economy and funding. They discuss tensions between ethnic Buddhist and converts, if any, and controlling mechanisms of who is a proper Buddhist and how Buddhism should be presented in public space. The contributors analyse representation in media and images of Buddhism in popular culture and present relevant scholarly interest in Buddhism. Additionally, the book includes chapters on significant Buddhist individuals in the Nordic countries who have played major roles in the development of Buddhism.

The first book to examine the characteristics of Nordic Buddhism, its connection to the ideology of the Nordic welfare society and to establish if Nordic Buddhism might differ from other forms of Buddhism, this work will be of interest to researchers in the field of religious studies, religion in context and Buddhist studies.

Jørn Borup is Associate Professor at the Department of the Study of Religion in Aarhus University. His research areas include Japanese Buddhism, Buddhism in the West, religious diversity, spirituality, migration and decolonisation. Since 2002, he has conducted research on Buddhism in Denmark for various projects at the Center for Contemporary Religion, Aarhus University. Besides articles for journals and publications in Danish, he is the author of *Japanese Rinzai Zen Buddhism: Myōshinji, a Living Religion* (2008) and *Decolonising the Study of Religion: Who Owns Buddhism?* (Routledge 2023).

Mitra Härkönen is Academy Research Fellow with a master's degree (MSocSc) in social and cultural anthropology and a doctorate degree (PhD) in the study of religions. She also has a degree in university pedagogy and previously worked as a university lecturer. Härkönen's research interests range from Buddhist, Tibetan and migration studies to gender studies. She conducted ethnographic fieldwork among Tibetan Buddhist nuns in India and the Tibetan regions under the Republic of China. She has also extensively studied Buddhism in Finland, conducted ethnographic fieldwork among Thai Buddhist women living in Finland and done research on Thai berry-pickers. Her current research project examines the impact of Thai Buddhism on Finnish-Thai transnational families' decision-making and everyday life and practices. In addition to various articles, she has authored *Power and Agency in the Lives of Contemporary Tibetan Nuns: An Intersectional Study* (2023) and co-edited a book on Buddhism in Finland.

Knut A. Jacobsen is Professor in the Study of Religions at the University of Bergen, Norway, and author of many books and articles in journals and edited volumes on various aspects on religions of South Asia and in the South Asian diasporas. His main fields of research include South Asian transnational religions, religions and public space in South Asia and the South Asian diasporas, sacred geography and pilgrimage in South Asia and Yoga history and theory. He is the author of five monographs, *Prakṛti in Sāṃkhya-Yoga: Material Principle, Religious Experience, Ethical Implications* (1999), *Kapila: Founder of Sāṃkhya and Avatāra of Viṣṇu* (2008), *Pilgrimage in the Hindu Tradition: Salvific Space* (Routledge 2013), *Yoga in Modern Hinduism: Hariharānanda Āraṇya and Sāṃkhyayoga* (Routledge 2018) and *Hinduism in the World: Migrations and Global Presence* (Routledge 2025), and is the editor or co-editor of numerous books, the latest of which are the *Routledge Handbook of South Asian Religions* (2021) and *Hindu Diasporas* (2023).

Katarina Plank is Associate Professor of Religious Studies in Karlstad University, focusing on the lived religious experiences of migrants and on contemporary spirituality in Sweden. She has been conducting research in several projects funded by the Swedish Research Council: her postdoc project (2012–2014) explored Thai Buddhism in Sweden, and two other projects have focused on lived religion and social mobility among migrants (2020–2024) and how COVID affected migrant religious groups in Sweden (2024–2026). Plank led the project "The New Faces of the Folk Church" (funded by Riksbankens jubileumsfond 2021–2025). She has authored and edited several works, including *Mindfulness: Tradition, tolkning och tillämpning* (2014), *Levd religion: det heliga i vardagen* (2018) and *Eastern Practices and Nordic Bodies* (2023).

Routledge Critical Studies in Buddhism
Edited by Stephen C. Berkwitz
Missouri State University, USA

Routledge Critical Studies in Buddhism is a comprehensive study of the Buddhist tradition. The series explores this complex and extensive tradition from a variety of perspectives, using a range of different methodologies.

The series is diverse in its focus, including historical, philological, cultural, and sociological investigations into the manifold features and expressions of Buddhism worldwide. It also presents works of constructive and reflective analysis, including the role of Buddhist thought and scholarship in a contemporary, critical context and in the light of current social issues. The series is expansive and imaginative in scope, spanning more than two and a half millennia of Buddhist history. It is receptive to all research works that are of significance and interest to the broader field of Buddhist Studies.

Editorial Advisory Board:
James A. Benn, McMaster University, Canada; Rupert Gethin, University of Bristol, UK; Peter Harvey, University of Sunderland, UK; Sallie King, James Madison University, USA; Anne Klein, Rice University, USA; Lori Meeks, University of Southern California, USA; Ulrich Pagel, School of Oriental and African Studies, UK; John Powers, Australian National University, Australia; Juliane Schober, Arizona State University, USA; Vesna A. Wallace, University of California, Santa Barbara, USA; Michael Zimmermann, University of Hamburg, Germany

ETHICAL PRACTICE AND RELIGIOUS REFORM IN NEPAL
The Buddhist Art of Living
Lauren Leve

EARLY BUDDHIST MEDITATION
The Four Jhânas as the Actualization of Insight
Keren Arbel

BIRTH IN BUDDHISM
The Suffering Fetus and Female Freedom
Amy Paris Langenberg

THERAVADA BUDDHISM IN COLONIAL CONTEXTS
Edited by Thomas Borchert

BUDDHISM, MEDITATION AND FREE WILL
A Theory of Mental Freedom
Rick Repetti

WOMEN IN BRITISH BUDDHISM
Commitment, Connection, Community
Caroline Starkey

BUDDHIST VISIONS OF THE GOOD LIFE FOR ALL
Sallie B. King

REIMAGINING CHAN BUDDHISM
Sheng Yen and the Creation of the Dharma Drum Lineage of Chan
Jimmy Yu

INDIAN BUDDHIST STUDIES ON NON-BUDDHIST THEORIES OF A SELF
The Studies of Śāntarakṣita and Kamalaśīla on the Nyāya-Vaiśeṣika, Mīmāṃsā, Sāṃkhya, Jain, Vedānta and Vātsīputrīya Theories of a Self
James P. Duerlinger

BUDDHISM, COGNITIVE SCIENCE, AND THE DOCTRINE OF SELFLESSNESS
A Revolution in Our Self-Conception
Hugh Nicholson

BUDDHIST ARCHITECTURE IN AMERICA
Building for Enlightenment
Robert Edward Gordon

BUDDHISM IN THE NORDIC COUNTRIES
Jørn Borup, Mitra Härkönen, Knut A. Jacobsen and Katarina Plank

The following titles are published in association with the *Theravāda Civilizations Project*
    The project supports collaborative exchanges among scholars based in the US, Canada, Britain and Southeast Asia with the aim to undertake a thematic study of Theravāda civilizations in South and Southeast Asia.

THERAVĀDA BUDDHIST ENCOUNTERS WITH MODERNITY
Edited by Juliane Schober and Steven Collins

The following titles are published in association with the *Oxford Centre for Buddhist Studies*

Oxford Centre for Buddhist Studies

a project of The Society for the Wider Understanding of the Buddhist Tradition

The *Oxford Centre for Buddhist Studies* conducts and promotes rigorous teaching and research into all forms of the Buddhist tradition.

EARLY BUDDHIST METAPHYSICS
The Making of a Philosophical Tradition
Noa Ronkin

MIPHAM'S DIALECTICS AND THE DEBATES ON EMPTINESS
To Be, Not to Be or Neither
Karma Phuntsho

HOW BUDDHISM BEGAN
The conditioned genesis of the early teachings
Richard F. Gombrich

BUDDHIST MEDITATION
An Anthology of Texts from the Pāli Canon
Sarah Shaw

REMAKING BUDDHISM FOR MEDIEVAL NEPAL
The fifteenth-century reformation of Newar Buddhism
Will Tuladhar-Douglas

METAPHOR AND LITERALISM IN BUDDHISM
The Doctrinal History of Nirvana
Soonil Hwang

THE BIOGRAPHIES OF RECHUNGPA
The Evolution of a Tibetan Hagiography
Peter Alan Roberts

THE ORIGIN OF BUDDHIST MEDITATION
Alexander Wynne

For more information about this series, please visit: https://www.routledge.com/Routledge-Critical-Studies-in-Buddhism/book-series/RCSB

Buddhism in the Nordic Countries

Edited by Jørn Borup, Mitra Härkönen,
Knut A. Jacobsen and Katarina Plank

Routledge
Taylor & Francis Group
LONDON AND NEW YORK

First published 2025
by Routledge
4 Park Square, Milton Park, Abingdon, Oxon OX14 4RN

and by Routledge
605 Third Avenue, New York, NY 10158

Routledge is an imprint of the Taylor & Francis Group, an informa business

British Library Cataloguing-in-Publication Data
A catalogue record for this book is available from the British Library

Library of Congress Cataloging-in-Publication Data
Names: Borup, Jørn, editor. | Härkönen, Mitra, editor. | Jacobsen, Knut A., 1956– editor. | Plank, Katarina, 1970– editor.
Title: Buddhism in the Nordic countries / edited by Jørn Borup, Mitra Härkönen, Knut A. Jacobsen, Katarina Plank.
Description: Abingdon, Oxon ; New York, NY : Routledge, 2025. | Series: Routledge critical studies in buddhism | Includes bibliographical references and index.
Identifiers: LCCN 2024061572 (print) | LCCN 2024061573 (ebook) | ISBN 9781032868837 (hardback) | ISBN 9781032868844 (paperback) | ISBN 9781003529767 (ebook)
Subjects: LCSH: Buddhism—Scandinavia—History. | Buddhism—Finland—History. | Buddhism—Iceland—History.
Classification: LCC BQ709.S34 B833 2025 (print) | LCC BQ709.S34 (ebook) | DDC 294.30948—dc23/eng/20250312
LC record available at https://lccn.loc.gov/2024061572
LC ebook record available at https://lccn.loc.gov/2024061573

ISBN: 978-1-032-86883-7 (hbk)
ISBN: 978-1-032-86884-4 (pbk)
ISBN: 978-1-003-52976-7 (ebk)

DOI: 10.4324/9781003529767

Typeset in Times New Roman
by Apex CoVantage, LLC

Contents

List of illustrations   *xi*
List of contributors   *xii*
Acknowledgements   *xv*
A note on diacritics   *xvi*

1 **Introduction: Buddhist converts and migrants in a Nordic setting**   1
   JØRN BORUP, MITRA HÄRKÖNEN, KNUT A. JACOBSEN, AND
   KATARINA PLANK

2 **Buddhism in Sweden: religious institutions, secular
   applications and Christian meditations**   25
   KATARINA PLANK

3 **Lama Ngawang and the dissemination of Tibetan Buddhism
   in Sweden**   63
   STEFAN LARSSON

4 **A Thai missionary for the Dhamma in Sweden: ten years
   of a monk in Snowyland**   81
   PREEDEE HONGSATON

5 **Buddhism in Denmark: institutionalised religion,
   mindfulness and cool branding**   101
   JØRN BORUP

6 **Buddhism in Norway: the strange story of the rebirth of the
   Buddha and Sariputra in the early twentieth century and
   other Buddhist histories and developments**   127
   KNUT A. JACOBSEN

7 **Buddhism in Finland: from Kalmyks to engaged activism** 152
MITRA HÄRKÖNEN

8 **Mauno Nordberg and early Buddhism in Finland** 175
JOHANNES CAIRNS

9 **Buddhism in Iceland: an overlooked companion** 189
HARALDUR HREINSSON

10 **Conclusion** 202
JØRN BORUP, MITRA HÄRKÖNEN, KNUT A. JACOBSEN, AND
KATARINA PLANK

Index *207*

Illustrations

Figures

1.1	*A driving force.*	13
2.1	*A special meeting.*	38
3.1	*The nomadic lama that became resident in Sweden.*	72
4.1	*Ten Years of a Thai Monk in Snowy Lands.*	89
5.1	*Protector of the temple.*	120
6.1	*Maitreyya Buddha.*	128
7.1	*Phật Đản (Vesak).*	165
8.1	*Gravestone of Mauno Nordberg.*	179
9.1	*The only stūpa in the North Atlantic.*	196
10.1	*What will the future hold?*	206

Tables

2.1	Swedish demographic patterns in the twenty-first century, with ten-year intervals.	46
2.2	Buddhist groups in Sweden.	54
5.1	Buddhist groups in Denmark.	102
6.1	Buddhist groups in Norway.	146
7.1	Buddhist groups in Finland.	171

Contributors

Jørn Borup is Associate Professor at the Department of the Study of Religion in Aarhus University. His research areas include Japanese Buddhism, Buddhism in the West, religious diversity, spirituality, migration and decolonisation. Since 2002, he has conducted research on Buddhism in Denmark for various projects at the Center for Contemporary Religion, Aarhus University. Besides articles for journals and publications in Danish, he is the author of *Japanese Rinzai Zen Buddhism: Myōshinji, a Living Religion* (2008) and *Decolonising the Study of Religion: Who Owns Buddhism?* (Routledge 2023).

Johannes Cairns has completed Bachelor of Arts (2011) and Master of Arts (2013) degrees at the University of Helsinki in East Asian studies, minoring in Religious Studies. His study focus was always on Buddhism. He currently holds a PhD degree (2018) and postdoctoral position in Environmental Science and is pursuing additional PhD research in religious studies at the University of Helsinki, investigating Buddhist climate activism with an empirical focus. He has also collaborated on numerous other Buddhist-themed research projects, the latest being co-editing and co-writing a comprehensive volume on Buddhism in Finland (2023, Finnish Oriental Society).

Mitra Härkönen is Academy Research Fellow with a master's degree (MSocSc) in social and cultural anthropology and a doctorate degree (PhD) in the study of religions. She also has a degree in university pedagogy and previously worked as a university lecturer. Härkönen's research interests range from Buddhist, Tibetan and migration studies to gender studies. She conducted ethnographic fieldwork among Tibetan Buddhist nuns in India and the Tibetan regions under the Republic of China. She has also extensively studied Buddhism in Finland, conducted ethnographic fieldwork among Thai Buddhist women living in Finland and done research on Thai berry-pickers. Her current research project examines the impact of Thai Buddhism on Finnish-Thai transnational families' decision-making and everyday life and practices. In addition to various articles, she has authored *Power and Agency in the Lives of Contemporary Tibetan Nuns: An Intersectional Study* (2023) and co-edited a book on Buddhism in Finland.

Preedee Hongsaton is a research fellow at Linnaeus University Centre for Concurrences in Colonial and Postcolonial Studies. His research looks at the history of empires and imperialism in Mainland Southeast Asia from the middle of the nineteenth century to the present. Preedee's interest in historical and theoretical aspects of Theravāda Buddhism in Thailand, Myanmar and Sri Lanka results in a co-edited volume *Religion and Violence* (2019, in Thai); *Sri Lankan Civil War* (2019, in Thai); and an edited volume *On Stranger-Kings: Power, Mythology, and Colonialism* (2024, in Thai). Among various publications, he co-edited a volume *New Directions in Thai Studies* (2024). Preedee is currently researching religious and diplomatic aspects of treaty and treaty-making between Siam and European imperial powers from the seventeenth to the early twentieth century.

Haraldur Hreinsson is Assistant Professor in the history of the Christian religion and religious studies at the University of Iceland. He has worked as a research fellow at the Cluster of Excellence: "Religion and Politics," University of Münster and as a senior research fellow at the Centre for Advanced Studies: "Multiple Secularities: Beyond the West, Beyond Modernities," Leipzig University. He is broadly interested in the history of religion but has, in recent years, worked on the cultural history of the political, historical secularities, medieval hagiography, religion and literature, nineteenth-century liberal Protestantism and most recently Buddhism in Iceland. Recent publications include *Force of Words: A Cultural History of Christianity and Politics in Medieval Iceland* (2021).

Knut A. Jacobsen is Professor in the Study of Religions at the University of Bergen, Norway, and author of many books and articles in journals and edited volumes on various aspects on religions of South Asia and in the South Asian diasporas. His main fields of research include South Asian transnational religions, religions and public space in South Asia and the South Asian diasporas, sacred geography and pilgrimage in South Asia and Yoga history and theory. He is the author of five monographs, *Prakṛti in Sāṃkhya-Yoga: Material Principle, Religious Experience, Ethical Implications* (1999), *Kapila: Founder of Sāṃkhya and Avatāra of Viṣṇu* (2008), *Pilgrimage in the Hindu Tradition: Salvific Space* (Routledge 2013), *Yoga in Modern Hinduism: Hariharānanda Āraṇya and Sāṃkhyayoga* (Routledge 2018) and *Hinduism in the World: Migrations and Global Presence* (Routledge 2025), and is the editor or co-editor of numerous books, the latest of which are the *Routledge Handbook of South Asian Religions* (2021) and *Hindu Diasporas* (2023).

Stefan Larsson is Associate Professor of the History of Religions. He works as a senior lecturer and research fellow in religious studies at the University of Gävle. Larsson's research focuses on the non-monastic and practice-oriented aspects of Tibetan Buddhism, particularly as evidenced in Buddhist songs and biographical literature of the fifteenth and sixteenth centuries. Besides articles, Larsson's publications include the book *Crazy for Wisdom: The Making of a Mad Yogin in Fifteenth-Century Tibet* (2012). He is the co-editor of the book *Songs on the Road: Wandering Religious Poets in India, Tibet, and Japan* (2021).

Katarina Plank is Associate Professor of Religious Studies in Karlstad University, focusing on the lived religious experiences of migrants and on contemporary spirituality in Sweden. She has been conducting research in several projects funded by the Swedish Research Council: her postdoc project (2012–2014) explored Thai Buddhism in Sweden, and two other projects have focused on lived religion and social mobility among migrants (2020–2024) and how COVID affected migrant religious groups in Sweden (2024–2026). Plank led the project "The New Faces of the Folk Church" (funded by Riksbankens jubileumsfond 2021–2025). She has authored and edited several works, including *Mindfulness: Tradition, tolkning och tillämpning* (2014), *Levd religion: det heliga i vardagen* (2018) and *Eastern Practices and Nordic Bodies* (2023).

Acknowledgements

The editors want to thank the Margot and Rune Johanssons Stiftelse for generous support. In 2019, we were granted a stipend to hold the symposium *Buddhism in the Nordic Countries* at Sigtunastiftelsen, Sweden. Still, due to the pandemic, we had to wait until September 2022 to meet. This enabled us to start planning for the book and to establish the Network for the academic study of Buddhism in the Nordic countries. In 2023, we were also granted a stipend to conduct fieldwork in Iceland in February 2024. Katarina Plank has also received individual stipends that helped her to conduct fieldwork in Sweden.

We also want to extend a thank-you to Kristina Myrvold and Johan Nilsson for organising the conference *Buddhism and Theosophy in the Nordic Countries*, held at Lund University on 11 May 2022, which enabled several of the authors to meet and take part of ongoing research.

A note on diacritics

Diacritics are used on words from Sanskrit and Pali languages such as *stūpa*, *vihāra*, *nirvāṇa*, Mahāyāna and *vipassanā*. But diacritics are used in names of persons mainly before 1900. For names of temple organisations in the Nordic countries, mostly their own spelling is used.

1 Introduction

Buddhist converts and migrants in a Nordic setting

Jørn Borup, Mitra Härkönen, Knut A. Jacobsen, and Katarina Plank

Ever since the Vikings, the Nordic countries have had extensive contact with the rest of the world. People have travelled, traded and migrated from and to the Nordic countries with intellectual ideas, material goods and bodily practices circulating and leaving mutual impressions on Northlanders, Westerners and Easterners.

The Vikings and the Greenlander Leif Ericson sailed to America long before Christopher Columbus, and the Vikings travelled eastwards and traded along the Silk Road, bringing back a little Buddha figurine later known as the Helgö Buddha, the oldest Buddhist artefact found in the Nordic areas. It would, however, take hundreds of years before the first Buddhists reached Norden ("the North"). In the eighteenth century, some Kalmyks, a small indigenous Buddhist minority belonging to a West Mongolian tribe living in the lower Volga region, arrived alongside Russian Cossacks during the Russian invasion and military occupation of Finland, which was then part of the Swedish Empire. The Kalmyks' burial customs were recorded in Finnish church records as early as the 1740s.

Around 1830 and continuing until the Second World War, mass migration from the Nordic countries led almost three million people to leave their homes and emigrate to Europe, Australia and especially North America. Limits of religious freedom, religious discrimination and other push factors such as population growth, famine, limited job opportunities, low wages and discontent with the political systems made emigrants leave in groups and later as individuals (Nilsson 2004). Among these individuals were also found intellectuals and well-off bourgeoises, some of whom were influenced by the Theosophical currents at the time, who travelled westwards for education and work. Herman Vetterling, born in the landscape of Småland (south Sweden) in 1849, migrated to Minnesota as a 22-year-old and later became one of the first Buddhists in America. Vetterling started his religious career as a "Swedenborgian minister" in a Christian church in Pennsylvania, which, in addition to the Old and New Testaments, was also based on the teachings of the mystic Emmanuel Swedenborg (1688–1772). In 1881, he left the church and trained in homoeopathy in Chicago, later moving to Santa Cruz. There he wrote his first book, *Swedenborg the Buddhist*, published in 1887 under the name Philangi Dasa. The same year, he published the first Buddhist journal, *The Buddhist Ray* (Tweed 1992). When Vetterling gave the epithet "the Buddha of the North"

DOI: 10.4324/9781003529767-1

to Swedenborg, he was not the first to do so. The French writer Honoré de Balzac had already used the expression fifty years earlier when his novel *Séraphita* was published in 1835. Swedenborgianism also influenced D. T. Suzuki, the third to give Swedenborg the epithet "the Buddha of the North" in his work *Swedenborugu*, published in Japan in 1913 (Jansson 2023, Zuber 2010).

Vetterling/Philangi Dasa was not the only one from Norden who propagated Buddhist thoughts in America. Harry Holst, born in Denmark in 1875, also arrived in Chicago as a young man to study homoeopathy. In 1899, *The Chicago Record* wrote about Holst, who made a name for himself as a "Buddhist apostle" and proclaimed Buddhist teachings and philosophy on the streets of Chicago under the name of Tyagananda. Several Swedish newspapers also reported on the event. Harry Holst later settled in Sweden, continuing his interest in Eastern religions, spiritualism and his practice as a homoeopathic doctor.

These are but only a few examples of how the Nordic countries are entangled in the history of Buddhism. Today, the religion is more widespread in Norden than ever before. The number of people identifying as Buddhists or practising Buddhism, as well as the number of different Buddhist associations and communities, has been steadily increasing. In addition, many individuals not affiliated with any Buddhist tradition have personal interests in Buddhism. Wider Buddhist influences are visible in the popularity of various mental training techniques, mindfulness and self-help literature influenced by the religion. The clear majority of Buddhists in the Nordic countries are of Asian backgrounds, and especially migration from Asian countries has reshaped the religious landscapes with the presence of lay and ordained Buddhists and the material presence of their various temples. However, Buddhism is visible not only in temples but also in many other aspects of material culture, illustrated by the ubiquitous Buddha statues in homes, shops and massage parlours, signalling both religious values and secular consumerism. Today, Buddhism thus has a significant presence in all the Nordic countries and is a prominent minority religion in the region. It has made its way through various transnational connections, dating back to the early Middle Ages and continuing through contemporary times. The chapters of the book tell the story of these connections and how Buddhism, brought from different places and in different time periods, has been and still is translocally interpreted, practised and represented in the Nordic context and its five countries.

Despite the relatively long history of Buddhism and its presence today, apart from the individual scholars (whose research is presented in the subsequent country-specific chapters), there has been little – and no comparative – research published on Buddhism in the Nordic countries. Studies of Buddhism outside Asia have been dominated by studies of Buddhism focusing on North America and some countries in Western Europe (and later expanded to all European countries in Baumann et al. forthcoming). This book provides new research on Buddhism in the Nordic countries, contributing to the growing literature on Buddhism in the West and studies of Buddhism in particular regions.

The aim of the book is to compare the different Nordic countries. However, it also aims to identify possible unique characteristics of Nordic Buddhism, having been shaped by its historical roots, contemporary developments and the influence of migration and cultural exchange with Asian countries. It is obvious that the geographic and linguistic closeness, the cultural, political and religious similarities and the historical intertwinement have made the ties of the Nordic countries strong. It is also apparent that such Nordic relations have been the frames of orientation for the Buddhists. Interrelated networks of monks, nuns, lamas and laypeople cross the Nordic borders in "translocative" flows (Tweed 2015) and cross-border ties deepened by transnationalising every day religious practice (Levitt 2004: 2) with Buddhist practices, values and material representations being (often unmistakably) shaped by Nordic culture. While there are common features, it is also clear that diversity is a key characteristic. As will become apparent from the chapters of the book, there are differences across the countries and between the increasingly pluralistic traditions, not least between the "two Buddhisms," the Buddhism of converts and the Buddhism of migrants. In this introductory chapter, the Nordic context is presented, followed by an overview of the history of Buddhism in the region, as well as a discussion of Buddhist organisations and demography.

The Nordic context

Even if not homogenous and in spite of linguistic differences between Finnish and the other Nordic languages, the Nordic countries undoubtedly share many common cultural features and can, in many ways, be considered a common cultural region. The Danish, Norwegian and Swedish languages are mutually intelligible, like dialects of a single language. Icelandic is a development of Old Norse, while Finnish (with Sami) belongs to a completely different Finno-Ugric language group. The five Nordic countries share historical roots and were once united under a monarchy. They still have strong political, cultural and economic cooperation. The countries created the Nordic Council in 1952 and the Council of Ministers in 1971. In the 1950s, they also established a passport union, a common labour market and reciprocal social security benefits for their citizens. This allowed Nordic people to move freely across borders long before the EU adopted similar policies (Syvertsen et al., 2014). Political borders and transnational alliances have varied over the years, and similar political structures have developed. Three of the countries are monarchies (Denmark, Norway and Sweden) and two are republics (Iceland, Finland). The five countries are strong democracies with regular national and local elections and established political party structures placing them among the world's least corrupt countries.

Recognised as developed welfare states known as "the Nordic model," the Nordic countries share similar yet distinct welfare systems. The welfare system encompasses various government programmes that offer financial and social assistance to individuals and families in need. These programmes are intended to help with basic living expenses, healthcare, housing and other essential needs for those who are unable to support themselves. Consistently, the Nordic nations rank highly on the United Nations' Human Development Index,[1] a testament to their high living standards according to UN criteria, with relatively small class, income and gender differences (Hilson 2020: 70; Syvertsen et al., 2014: 1).[2]

Historically, the Nordic countries were religiously homogenous societies, predominantly Lutheran until the 1960s, when the dual forces of pluralisation and secularisation began to emerge. These forces have significantly altered the religious landscape over the past five decades, with all Nordic countries experiencing a shift towards religious complexity (Furseth 2018), diversity and secularisation (Markkola 2015). Initially, the Lutheran churches held a dominant societal role, with their dominance written into the national constitutions. While other religions were permitted, the Lutheran Church enjoyed several monopolies and privileges. The development towards religious freedom in these countries has been marked by both increasing tolerance and a growing apprehension towards other religions.

However, from a Nordic perspective, full religious freedom was established late, and the long history of establishing religious freedom has involved minorities, both migrant and domestic, that have claimed the right to practise their faith outside of the dominant Lutheran evangelical state churches. Sweden was the last country to ensure full religious freedom, achieving this through the Religious Freedom Act of 1951 and its ratification of the European Convention on Human Rights in 1952, which allowed Swedes to leave the State Church and not join any other religious congregation. Previously, unity of state and Church was legislated in the 1634 Constitution and the 1686 Church Law, with restrictions of pietistic movements and Jews being gradually liberated throughout the 1800s, as the Dissenter Acts granted some religious freedom acts in 1860 and 1873. Religious freedom was subsequently enshrined in the 1974 Constitution. When the church and state were separated in 2000, new legislation regarding religious communities came into effect (Svanberg & Karlsson 1997).

Fear of other religions had also been written into the constitutions in the Nordic countries. For example, in Norway, according to the constitution of 1814, the Jews (removed in 1851), monastic orders (removed in 1891) and Jesuits (removed in 1956) were banned. In Denmark, according to the Royal Law of 1665, there was religious coercion. Religious freedom was sanctioned in the Danish Constitution ("Grundloven") in 1849. The Danish National Evangelical Lutheran Church ("Folkekirken") still holds a constitutionally privileged position and the State regulates religious groups outside of the Lutheran Church via the "Act regulating faith communities outside the *Folkekirke*" (*Trossamfundsloven*).[3] In the kingdoms, and according to the constitution, it is mandatory for the king or queen to be a member of the church. In Norway, before 2012, when the Lutheran church ceased to be a state church, half of the ministers of the government had to be members of the Lutheran church since the government was the highest ruler of the church.

Until the 1920s, Finland had relatively restrictive laws regarding religious freedom. The Orthodox Church and the Lutheran Church were considered equal status and people's churches. Institutional Lutheranism was well established until the 1860s when a new Ecclesiastical Act was passed. The first Dissenters' Act was passed in 1889, which allowed the foundation of non-Lutheran Protestant denominations and gave Lutherans the option to join another Protestant denomination.

However, Roman Catholics and non-Christians were not allowed to leave the Orthodox Church. The Constitution of 1919 guaranteed religious freedom, which was more specifically defined in the Freedom of Religion Act of 1922. The introduction of freedom of religion allowed non-Christian denominations to be formally organised in Finland. The Freedom of Religion Act also permitted non-religious choices (Markkola 2015).

As part of Iceland's struggle for independence from the Danish crown, the Icelandic National Assembly of 1851 rejected the Danish constitution from 1849, including its articles on religious freedom. Thus, full religious freedom was not established in Iceland until the country's first constitution in 1874. Up to this point, regulations from 1786 to 1787 were in effect, only allowing for the practice of other forms of Christianity than the prevailing Lutheran one. The Icelandic constitution's articles on religious freedom were, to a large extent, based on the Danish *Grundloven*, allowing for all religious practices which did not endanger the public order. The Lutheran church also received a special position as a national church ("þjóðkirkja") which it still holds to this day. In fact, since 1874, only minor amendments have been made on articles relating to religious freedom, in 1995 and 2014.

Today the Nordic countries are often considered role models for human rights, with relatively liberal welfare systems also granting rights and privileges to minority religions. However, in recent years, regulations impeding religious freedom have re-entered the countries to counter undemocratic teachings and donations, primarily with Islam as a target but with consequences also for other religions. Analysing Pew's Government Restrictions Index, Lene Kühle thus found what she calls the "Nordic freedom of religion paradox" thought-provoking: the Nordic countries were "placed higher than the global median regarding government restrictions since 2017" (Kühle 2024). The paradox relates to the status of being embedded in both religious and secular settings.

While Christianity is occasionally voiced as the defender of cultural values, secular values are more often referred to as guarantors of democratic freedom for even those religious traditions not subscribing to this. Despite the Church's historical authority, the Nordic societies are today generally characterised by their secular nature, evident in the very low church attendance and the minimal influence of religious authority (Enstedt & Plank 2023).[4] A high level of education among the population has further fuelled secularisation trends, although with a traditionally maintained cohesive self-image, rooted in the belief that, despite religious freedom, there is a single, dominant religious institution highly supported by the state. Alternative religious practices or beliefs are often perceived as deviations from this norm, although new spiritual practices such as yoga and meditation have also entered the Lutheran churches (Lundgren et al. 2023; Plank et al. 2023). Thus, a solid Protestant Lutheran tradition pervades these nations, with national churches that maintain close ties to the state. These churches, viewed as public utilities, are involved in social work and cemetery management on their premises. Their pastors are educated at publicly funded universities and serve in state-funded institutions such as the military, healthcare system and prisons (Taira 2019).

Financing of religion differs among the Nordic countries. Religion is considered part of the welfare state in some of the countries. The funding is based on monoreligious identity system; one can be a member only of one registered religious organisation. In Denmark, there is no economic support directly but apart from the blueprint of a "real religion," the official stamp of being a recognised religious organisation also gives tax exemption for donations. The financing of the Evangelical-Lutheran Church in Denmark ("Folkekirken") and in Finland occurs through a church tax from its members. In Denmark, the state also contributes, paying 40 per cent of the clergy's salaries as well as for the preservation of particularly valuable gravestones. In Sweden, the state transfers seven EUR per registered member to religious organisations that have been approved for such support. In Finland, the government provides financial aid to religious communities that apply for assistance on an annual basis based on a number of members and communities. For instance, in 2023, 524,000 EUR were allocated among twenty-nine communities. In recent years, the financial assistance granted has remained steady at around seven EUR, similar to Sweden. Registered religious communities are also exempt from paying transfer taxes. In Iceland, the financial basis of all registered religious communities is the so-called parish fee, membership dues collected by the state as a share of people's income tax. Relative to the income tax base, the amount is collected annually and was around eight EUR per month in 2024. In addition to the "parish fee," the Evangelical-Lutheran Church of Iceland receives significant additional payments every year based on a contract about the state's recompensation for the church estates it formally took over at the beginning of the twentieth century.

In Norway, religious groups receive support from the state equal per member to the total state's support of the Lutheran Church (Den Norske Kirke, DNK) divided by the number of its members. Economic support from the Norwegian state in 2024 was NOK 1419 (125 EUR) per member. This system encourages organisation and registration and, for people, to organise religious groups instead of cultural groups. The number of registered members of Buddhist organisations in 2023 was 22,126. This means that the state in 2024 transferred more than 31 million NOK (2.7 million EUR) to Buddhist organisations, which is significantly higher than in the other Nordic countries. The number of Buddhist "display" temples built from the ground is much higher in Norway than in the other Nordic countries, and the reason for this is probably the generous public funding.

The Lutheran churches have lost their earlier dominant roles, and the view that the Nordic countries are and were homogenous societies is now a mistaken perception. Lutheranism is still the dominant Christian denomination. However, current statistics show that only 53 per cent of Swedes were members of the Lutheran Church, 54 per cent in Iceland, 63 per cent in Norway, 64 per cent in Finland and 71 per cent in Denmark in 2023. State church membership numbers have declined for years in all the Nordic countries. The changes started accelerating in the 1960s, and the fall in membership is stable and systematic. In Norway, for example, in 1970, 94 per cent were members; in 1980, 87 per cent; in 2008, 80 per cent; in 2012, 75 per cent; and ten years later, 63 per cent. Processes for withdrawal from church membership were simplified, which is one significant reason for the sharp decline in the last ten years. In Denmark, the membership rate has declined from 90 per cent in 1990 to 71 per cent in 2024, and in Finland, from over 90 per cent in the 1980s to 62 per cent in 2024. This decrease in the percentage of members is primarily attributed to withdrawals and an increase in immigration of citizens not belonging to the Lutheran Church.

People in the Nordic countries are generally less inclined to identify themselves as religious as compared to the rest of Europe and the world. In addition, they tend to have a lower belief in God as compared to other countries, are less active in participating in religious events, and do not consider religion as an important aspect of their lives. Attendance at religious services has also declined steadily in the Nordic countries (Taira 2019; Taira et al., 2021; PEW 2018a). According to a Pew Research survey (2018b), religion is also considered less important to national identity in the Nordic countries compared to the rest of Europe. In Denmark, "Culture Christian" is a term many members use about themselves: very low levels of belief and church attendance, but with institutional belonging based on identifying with religion as a cultural tradition.[5]

Secularisation also characterises the teaching of religion in schools. The ideal in schools in the Nordic countries of Sweden, Denmark, Norway and Finland is currently neutral religious education. Pupils learn about religions as cultural phenomena, whereas apologetic teaching and practice of religion are offered in churches and religious communities. Buddhism, for example, is mostly presented as a philosophical tradition in schoolbooks and as a species of "Modern Buddhism." In high schools, Buddhism is often covered as one of the "world religions." In universities, Buddhism is typically covered as a historical and contemporary religion, and some universities still offer studies in Sanskrit (e.g., Uppsala). However, only a few PhDs with competencies in Buddhism are educated at Nordic universities.

In Finland, Religious Education (RE) is non-confessional but mandatory in basic (grades one to nine) and secondary education. Pupils are eligible to receive religious education of their own faith if their religious community is registered in Finland, and if at least three students request it. Buddhism is among the fourteen religious groups that currently have a national curriculum for RE developed. Secular Ethics, also known as Life Stance Education, is also available for those who wish to take part (Hannikainen and Hannikainen, 2021).

Parallel to the development of secularisation is the increasing pluralisation due to immigration. The Nordic countries have been influenced by waves of refugees and migrants, particularly since the 1970s and 1980s. This has impacted cultural and religious aspects, resulting in a variety of Christian denominations, Muslim groups and religious communities with people of Asian origins. Religious diversity has become a reality visible to varying degrees in all countries and analysed by scholars as important change in the religious landscapes.[6] Immigrants from Asian countries such as Thailand and Vietnam have contributed significantly to the Buddhist landscape with various forms of religiosities being transported and adapted to the Nordic context.

The history of Buddhism in the Nordic countries

The common Nordic historiography often begins with the Vikings, and it is also from this time that the oldest Buddhist artefact found in the Nordic countries is preserved. The small Helgö Buddha, discovered during archaeological excavations in 1954, is only 8.4 cm high and was most likely made in the sixth century in the Swat Valley, in present-day Pakistan (Gyllensvärd 2004). It was found on the small island of Helgö in Lake Mälaren, not far from Birka, Sweden's first city. Archaeological analyses of the Helgö Buddha, along with findings of Chinese silk and Arabic silver coins that have been found in Birka, show that the Vikings' trade network was extensive. Helgö held a central place in the Nordic region during the period 200–900 CE, as the island had many religious functions, and there was also knowledge of advanced metalwork. It is not possible to determine with certainty when the small Buddha reached Helgö; however, the site on Helgö where the artefact was found together with other religious symbols, indicates that

> [a]lthough it is unlikely that the residents of Helgö were knowledgeable about Buddhism, the presence of several highly potent religious symbols, representing different religious convictions, nevertheless indicates that they were aware of the power that the objects were thought to possess. (Hedenstierna-Jonsson 2020: 55–56)

Many centuries later, another small Buddha statue was brought to the Westcoast of Sweden. This time, the small ivory statue travelled with a woman, Hilma Svedal (born Wounsch, 1870–1965), who, like a million of other Swedes and Norwegians, had travelled westwards to America at the turn of the twentieth century in connection with the largest migration flow from Europe to the United States. Hilma Svedal ended up in Alaska during the gold rush, where she cooked for miners. Somewhere along her travels in America, she met with a Chinese who gave her the small white ivory Buddha that she kept close in a pocket during the days and at her bedtable at nights.[7] Hilma Svedal did not keep a diary and never recorded a biography; the stories about her relationship with the small Buddha statue have been passed down within the family and are often highlighted in relation to her tombstone, where her life motto is summed up in the words "Don't worry." Hilma Svedal's relationship to the Buddha statue indicates two things: on the one hand, she attributed some form of religious power to it – although it is not possible to determine to what extent this also affected her lifestyle and way of thinking – and on the other hand, that she probably is the first Swede who was affected by lived Buddhism of laypeople, as she did not learn about Buddhism through texts, temples or practices taught by ordained teachers, nor by Theosophical texts or ideas.

Nevertheless, persons from the Nordic countries have also for several centuries had encounters with the "real Buddhists" in Asia. Trading companies, like the Swedish East India company, *Svenska Ost-Indiska Companiet* (est. 1731), facilitated a Nordic exposure to Chinese culture through the import of goods, and travelogues contained representations of Buddhism, Confucianism and Daoism

(Offermanns 2015). Denmark was a colonial power for 300 years (1620–1920) and did have both trading companies (like East Asiatic Company, *Østasiatisk Kompagni*) and administrative presence in also Southern India, paving the way for the linguist Rasmus Rask (1787–1832), who already in 1821 went to Ceylon to study Pali and collect palm-leaf manuscripts. Several Norwegians worked for the military in China, the most famous being General Johan Wilhelm Normann Munthe (1864–1935), who was a general in the Chinese Emperor's army and after the fall of the empire, in the early years of the republic an adviser to the Chinese Ministry of War. He amassed a massive collection of art and Buddhist artefacts, which are now housed in several museums, with the majority located in Bergen, Norway (Haakestad 2018).

Many Nordic Christian missionaries also set out to Asia. Christianising the world was inherent in the Foreign Missions' raison d'être, substantiated by narratives of Buddhism's apparent nihilism and idolatry. Some missionaries were not doubting their God-given role in converting Asians from primitive to perfect religion, while others followed a more dialogue-oriented approach in their missionising. Norwegian Karl Ludvig Reichelt (1877–1952) was one such Lutheran missionary of the latter type who worked in China and was important for the founding of the Nordic Buddhist Christian Mission (Den Nordiske Kristne Buddhistmisjon/Den nordiske Østasia-misjon), still existing under the name of Areopagos (Thelle 2022).

The first group of Buddhists to enter the Nordic area were probably the Kalmyks, an ethnic Mongol group. In the eighteenth century, some Kalmyks, who predominantly lived in Russia, came to Finland along with Russian Cossacks during the Russian invasion and military occupation of Finland, which was then part of the Swedish Empire. The Kalmyks and their religion are mentioned, for example, in Finnish church records, newspapers and dictionaries, but it is uncertain how much interaction they had with Finnish people and whether their religion had any influence on the Finns (Tolvanen 2023).

Buddhism was introduced to the other Nordic countries mainly through individuals reading about the religion through scholarly or popular books entering the market already in the middle of the nineteenth century. Apart from the aforementioned Rasmus Rask going to Ceylon to study Pali and collect palm-leaf manuscripts, later Indologists such as Michael Viggo Fausbøll (1821–1908) from Copenhagen University, who translated *Dhammapada* in 1855, paved the way for textual studies of early Buddhism. The Norwegian C.A. Holmboe (1796–1882), who was a professor at the University of Oslo (called Royal Frederik University until 1939), was one of the first to show the Buddhist origin of the Christian narrative of Barlaam and Josaphat (Kværne 2022). Intellectuals were reading translations and descriptions of Buddhist teachings, and some authors wrote popular novels with Buddhist themes, more or less inspired by Edwin Arnold's famous book *Light of Asia*, also appearing in Nordic translations.

Theosophy was another important channel of reception. In varying degrees, Theosophist ideas of "Eastern mysticism" influenced individual seekers, and the often-highlighted correspondence between Buddhism and the Theosophical Society was also seen in some Nordic contexts. One of the first self-proclaimed

Buddhists influenced by Theosophy was the Swedish agitator Kata Dalström (1858–1923), who, in 1907, during a political debate, publicly announced that she was both a Social democrat and a Buddhist. The public debate thus highlighted the need for religious freedom and a reform of the Swedish Dissenter Acts (Plank 2004). Other intellectuals, like the pedagogy reformer Ellen Key (1849–1926), also held an interest in Buddhism and Theosophy (Jansson 2023).

It is likely that the first Swedish Buddhist nun, Amita Nisatta (Ingrid Wagner, 1910–2001), who promoted a unified form of Buddhism, was also influenced by Theosophical thoughts. Similarly, the French-born Marcel Sirander (1912–1983), who was ordained in China in 1933, came to Sweden as a married layperson in 1948. There, he started teaching Buddhism under the title of ācārya Śūnyatā. In 1954 he established a Buddhist society that became a regional centre for the World Fellowship of Buddhism (Hultberg 1971; Plank 2004). Both Marcel Sirander and Amita Nisatta promoted a Buddhism that incorporated all the three main vehicles, including an adaptation "that highlight a culturally stripped-down Buddhism which fits in the West" (Fredriksson 2013: 56). In 1964, Amita Nisatta became responsible for the religious teaching of a group of thirty-three of Tibetan girls that had travelled from India to Småland for their education, while a similar group of boys was sent to Norway. This was the first time a group of Asian Buddhists arrived in the Nordic countries.

In Iceland, The Theosophical Society – the fifth largest in Europe – was influential in introducing Buddhism. Books, articles and lectures often touched upon Buddhism, and President Grétar Fells (1896–1968) was an active proponent of the religion. Also, in Finland, the first Buddhists operated under the Theosophical Association at the beginning of the twentieth century. However, it was not until 1947 that some like-minded members of the society founded the first Buddhist association. The association mainly followed the Theravāda tradition of Buddhism, which involved studying, discussing and translating texts related to it. Also, early efforts made to distinguish Buddhism from Theosophy. The most central figure in the birth of the first Buddhist association, a Finnish cosmopolitan Mauno Nordberg (1844–1956), sought to separate Buddhism from Theosophy, which he considered to have misunderstood Buddhism. In Denmark, too, the founder of the first Buddhist group, Christian Frederik Melbye (1881–1961), was highly critical of the Theosophists. He was closely connected to Anagarika Dharmapala, who had already visited the country in 1904 to give lectures at Askov Højskole and who encouraged and financially supported Melbye to establish the *Buddhist Society in Denmark*. Melbye, however, was not impressed by Danish Theosophists whom he thought (just like the too theoretically minded scholars) were not able to authentically comprehend the religion.

Grasping "authentic" Buddhism as an intellectual project was typical for Nordic scholars, authors, intellectuals and spiritual seekers in the early phases of Buddhism reception from the mid-nineteenth century. The popularisation of Zen Buddhism (and ingenious use of "Zen") from the 1950s, with inspiration from D. T. Suzuki and the American groups of "beat Zen" authors, in a way, was a continuation of this "intellectualised Buddhism." Nevertheless, with the post-war economic recovery and (also economically) available travel means, a new generation of Buddhists, especially from the late 1960s onwards, initiated a new phase of "practised Buddhism." Many youngsters went to Asia for leisure, spiritual self-exploration and work, like Swedish Marie Ericsson (b. 1948), who already in 1970 learnt meditation from S. N. Goenka. Some stayed in Sri Lankan or Thai forest monasteries, like Finnish Martti Anttila (b.1954), who lived as a novice monk in Sri Lanka from 1975 to 1978 and the French–Danish Denys Jeune, who lived as a solitary monk on the same island from 1969 until his death in 2020. Others went to Japanese Zen temples for shorter or longer periods. Some of those finding and practising Buddhism "over there" brought it back and initiated the first organised Buddhist groups. In Denmark, the first Buddhist group began in 1972, following Ole and Hannah Nydahl's travels in the Himalayas, where they had met influential Tibetan lamas. Buddhist organisations were spread in the Nordic countries in the following decades, giving the general positive image of the religion also an institutional appearance.

In Norway, Buddhism began in 1928 when an Indian guru from Bengal declared himself to be a rebirth of the Buddha called Maitreyya Buddha and his disciple a rebirth of Buddha's disciple Sariputra. In 1964, forty Tibetan Buddhist boys arrived and lived for several years in a camp school in Gjøvik in eastern Norway that had been bought for this purpose. The first Buddhist organisation was a Zen Buddhist group established in the early 1970s and based on encounters with books. At the same time, a charismatic Tibetan lama who visited Oslo played an important role in establishing Tibetan Buddhism. At end of the same decade, the Buddhist umbrella organisation in Norway, Buddhistforbundet, was established, which signalled that there were already a few Buddhists and more than one Buddhist organisation. Indicative of the successful transplantation of Buddhism to Norway is the new phenomenon of confirmation of Buddhist youth as a parallel to the Christian confirmation, which is economically supported by the state.

Importing Buddhist ideas and practices has been an important "push factor" for Buddhism as part of Nordic cultural and religious history. However, in recent decades, the "pull factor" with the arrival of Asian Buddhists has contributed to a more prominent presence of Buddhism as a lived and visible religion and, not least, as a religion centred around temple worship. Migration flows have continued, and today, the Nordic countries are characterised as multicultural and multireligious societies, where Buddhists from different Asian countries have settled and thus brought with them the religious traditions of their cultures.

Migrant and convert Buddhism in the Nordic context

Buddhism in the Nordic countries can analytically be divided between "migrant Buddhism" and "convert Buddhism" (as proposed in an American context by, for instance, Prebish 1979, and Numrich 1996). Migrant Buddhism is the Buddhist teachings and practices of migrants, mostly from Asian countries with Buddhist populations who attempt to continue their inherited Buddhist practices in new countries. Convert Buddhism is the Buddhist teachings and practices of new followers of Buddhism. These categories are, of course, fluid and empirically dynamic. For instance, later generations of migrants – "descendants" – might not follow or agree to their parents' religiosity or religious identity, and convert Buddhists also migrate and establish centres in the new place for their practice and attract other migrants.

Migrants from Asian countries with Buddhist populations often establish Buddhist institutions in the new countries based on maintaining a relationship with their ancestral country. The material objects of their Buddhist religion, such as statues and other ritual equipment and sacred texts, are brought from the country of origin, and monks and nuns will mainly be recruited from that country. The temples serve as places for celebrating the culture through language, clothing, food and their country of origin's sounds, sights, tastes and smells. In the temples, national holidays of the migrants' country of origin are often celebrated, and the temple might provide services and networks for new arrivals. The temples become particularly important as they become localities that reproduce the sacred spaces of the country of origin as much as possible. Temples thus typically function equally as religious, cultural and community centres (e.g., Härkönen 2024), where laywomen are central in supporting the temples (see Figure 1.1).

As Thomas Tweed has noted (1997), religion in a migration context operates at different levels: locative, translocative and supralocative levels. Establishing a religion in a new context leads to sacred sites being established in the local landscapes. This is visible not only in the temples but also in spirit houses that are put up in front of a house, in statues of the bodhisattva Quan Yin and other guardian deities outside of temples, as well with *stūpas* and Buddhist graves at cemeteries. We also find processions and rituals taking place in the local landscapes. The food offerings that take place daily in many temples aid in creating a translocative dimension where eating and tasting food create horizontal links to the home country, but there is also vertical and cosmical linking to a suprahuman dimension where food is given not only to monks but to other beings in the samsaric world: to Buddha statues, to place-bound spirits or deities, to animals. Food creates social relationships, not only with other Buddhists but also with other beings (Plank 2015).

The material religion of Buddhism also has a significant presence in private homes, as many people have brought Buddhist artefacts from vacation travel in Buddhist-majority countries such as Thailand, Sri Lanka and Japan to decorate or 'Buddhicize' their homes. For some, the Buddha image is merely a decoration, a beautiful image that they have brought from Thailand or have received from someone special. For others, the statue has religious value and functions as a focal point for meditation, chanting or prayers. For yet others, the Buddha image might serve as a psychological tool that brings a sense of calming and some kind of relief for anxiety or complicated feelings (*Bastubacka & Härkönen 2023*). The Buddha statues highlight several methodological difficulties when depicting the history of Buddhism in the Nordic countries: without written sources or direct access to individuals, it is difficult to deduce anything about how people think, live and relate to Buddhist material culture. When we have access to textual sources, these are often written by men (or by people around male teachers or religious personalities). We also lack historical documentation of lived Buddhism in the Nordic countries that

Figure 1.1 A driving force. Laywomen are often the driving forces in the associations that enable the temples to function. This woman is called an angel by her Swedish husband. She coordinates hospital visits for the monks meeting with sick and dying people, sits on the board and ensures that the temple activities run smoothly during the year. She has also invited a tattoo artist skilled in protective Sak Yant tattoos. Photo: Katarina Plank.

show how laypeople in their everyday lives have related to Buddhist culture and Buddhist authorities in the form of teachings, teachers and practices.

Religion has thus the power to sacralise culture, which is an important dimension of the Buddhist religious traditions of migrants also in the Nordic countries. In the 1980s and 1990s, the Vietnamese were the most prominent Buddhist community.

However, because of the migration of tens of thousands of Thai women, Thai Buddhists have since replaced the Vietnamese as the most numerous Buddhist community in the Nordic countries. Buddhist temples in the Nordic region are manifold. Most temples belong to Thai and Vietnamese traditions, but there are also Khmer, Sri Lankan and Burmese temples. Unlike these, the Tibetan Buddhist temples and centres mainly serve to convert Buddhists. However, the temples may have a resident Tibetan lama and some Tibetan immigrants' participation.

Convert Buddhism typically adopts Buddhist practices of mediation whereas migrant Buddhism is typically more temple-oriented. While this is a general trend that is also found in the Nordic countries, it can be noted that, for example, Tibetan Buddhist groups whose members are mainly converts also emphasise joint rituals, and there is a growing interest in meditation, for example, among Thai migrant women. The popularity of mindfulness in the West illustrates this general trend of utilising Buddhism. However, while mindfulness has removed meditation almost completely from Buddhist worship practices, the early convert groups were eager to adopt Buddhist cultural forms but often limited to the meditation environment. Some convert Buddhist groups have adopted and offered mindfulness in its modern version as a traditional form of Buddhist meditation.

Except for Sweden, where the Zen and the Goenka *vipassanā* are the largest, the biggest convert Buddhist temples and centres in the Nordic countries belong to Tibetan Buddhist traditions. Soka Gakkai Denmark's main centre in Copenhagen is situated in a large house, but like most other convert groups, their local branches have smaller meeting places in apartments or spaces in office buildings. Since the focus in convert Buddhism is on meditation (and for Soka Gakkai, chanting) and not on temple worship, several retreat centres have been established. It is also common to rent places in the mountains or at other places of natural beauty for weekend or weeklong meditation retreats.

Since there are significant migrations within Europe, especially from the eastern parts of Europe to the western parts, convert Buddhism can also be migrant Buddhism. An example is some Diamond Way Buddhism centres in the Nordic countries that are, in many cases, constituted by converts who come from Eastern Europe and have settled in the Nordic countries because of work and study opportunities. This is significantly the case in Iceland, where the members of the Diamond Way Buddhism centre in Reykjavik are primarily Eastern European migrants. Other centres similarly have many of the features of migrant Buddhism, organising immigrants and providing meditation, a community of like-minded persons, meeting places and social relations. Some groups also experience changes in structures and compositions of ethnicity. For example, Soka Gakkai in Denmark and Sweden originally began as religious communities for Japanese migrants. Later, they attracted people from diverse origins, also in the Nordic countries, perhaps being the most multicultural and -ethnic Buddhist groups. While both Diamond Way and Soka Gakkai are thus globally minded in terms of ethnicity and culture, they are typically also the two Buddhist groups insisting most intensely on their sectarian exclusivity.

Buddhist umbrella organisations are found in Finland, Norway and Sweden and are all represented in the European Buddhist Union (EBU).[8] In Denmark, the "Buddhist Forum" previously functioned as a trans-sectarian organisation, and in 2014, it was shortly attempted to revive. There is no such organisation in Iceland. There are annual ecumenical Buddhist events organised by the Buddhist umbrella organisations such as Buddhistforbundet in Norway or Suomen Buddhalainen Unioni ("Finnish Buddhist Union"), but commonly, the migrant Buddhist temples are not visited or used by convert Buddhists. This is not least because of the language barrier and because they primarily serve as gathering places for the ethnic group that established the temples.

Beyond the Buddhist umbrella organisations and their organised meetings, hardly any ecumenical Buddhist worship groups are found in the Nordic countries. In Denmark, two groups, Phendeling (Copenhagen) and Øsal Ling (Aarhus), see themselves as ecumenical centres for all Buddhist traditions, but the diversity of Buddhisms also here only occasionally crosses or meets. Mostly all worship and meditation groups are limited to certain inherited traditions. They belong to Buddhist lineages of teachers or ethnic and national traditions. It seems particularly important for most Buddhist persons and groups in the Nordic countries to trace their belonging to a lineage of Buddhist teachers or ethnic or national traditions. No new Buddhist groups have developed in the Nordic countries that do not claim lineage back to Asia. Individuals practising or studying Buddhism apart from organised religiosity or beyond Buddhist lineage divisions as "private Buddhists" are also known but difficult to identify.

Counting Buddhists in the Nordic countries

How many Buddhists, Buddhist temples and Buddhist religious specialists are there in the Nordic countries? According to our calculations, there are around 200,000 Buddhists. In addition, there are "private" Buddhists whom we have no available method to count. According to the same calculations, there are around 200 Buddhist monks and nuns residing in the Nordic countries, the majority of whom are from Thailand. The total population in the Nordic countries is around 28 million, which means that around 0.7 per cent of the population in the Nordic countries are Buddhists.

In Denmark, there are around 36,000 Buddhists (nearly 90 per cent of these being immigrant Buddhists), constituting 0.6 per cent of the population. Such numbers are naturally highly problematic and based on estimates combining statistics, reports and talks with representatives from the Buddhist groups (for detailed methodological reflection, see Borup 2016). Twenty groups have an official stamp as "Recognised religious organisations," which is given by the Ministry of Ecclesiastical Affairs to the applying groups who comply with certain criteria. Not all Buddhist groups in the country qualify for – or are interested in – this official approval, and there are approximately twenty groups without this status, several of which only consist of handfuls of practitioners. There are thirteen Theravāda temples – ten

Thai temples (from Mahā Nikāya, Dhammayuttika Nikāya and Dhammakāya tra-ditions), two Burmese temples and one Sri Lankan temple – and nine Mahāyāna temples – six Vietnamese and three Chinese temples. Although not all affiliated with the temples are equally active, the number of members and participants is typically much higher than that of the convert groups. Compared to the mainly urban centres of the convert groups, the migrant temples are furthermore situated in rural areas. Among the convert groups, there are six small Zen groups and sev-enty local Soka Gakkai groups related to the main centre in Copenhagen. Fifteen groups affiliated with Tibetan Buddhism are primarily centred in cities, with two main centres in Copenhagen and Aarhus and six local groups of the Karma Kagyu School (Diamond Way Buddhism) in some of the larger cities. As religious special-ists serving the Buddhist groups, there are approximately thirty monks and nuns, a handful of Tibetan Buddhist lamas, one Zen priest and a number of lay teachers. As meditation is a key practice of the convert groups, *vipassanā* and mindfulness are often included in the groups' activities and provided also by individual teachers beyond institutionalised Buddhism.

In Norway, it is estimated that there are between 40,000 and 50,000 per-sons (between 0.8 and 0.9 per cent of the total population) who are identifying with, or being identified with one of the many different Buddhist traditions and organisations established or are Buddhist individuals without any affiliation. Prob-ably around 90 per cent of the Buddhists are immigrants from Asian countries or their descendants. The largest groups are Buddhists from Thailand and Vietnam. Migration started in the 1960s with a group of Tibetan refugees and continued in the 1970s and 1980s with Vietnamese refugees. The earliest Buddhist organised groups were convert followers of Zen and Tibetan Buddhist traditions. Buddhist organisations in Norway can thus be divided between migrant groups and convert groups. Migrant groups are mainly temple organisations: at least twenty Theravāda organisations (Thai, Khmer, Burmese and Sri Lankan) and four Mahāyāna organi-sations (Vietnamese and Chinese). Convert groups are mainly meditation groups divided between Mahāyāna, Theravāda and Western Buddhism, fifteen in all. The total number of monks and nuns is around eighty-five, and in addition, there are some Tibetan Buddhist lamas and several Zen priests.

In Sweden, as in the other Nordic countries, there are no valid statistics on religious belonging. Statistical estimates suggest that 0.8 per cent of the total population of 10.5 million inhabitants are Buddhists, which would suggest that there are approximately some 80,000 Buddhists living in Sweden (Weissenbilder 2019). The majority are Buddhists with Asian background, and the largest groups are Thai, Vietnamese and Chinese. Close to forty Thai temples (including Mahā Nikāya, Dhammayuttika Nikāya and Dhammakāya) have been established from the south (Eslöv) to the north (Morjärv), spanning over a distance of 1,462 km. A handful of other Theravāda temples have also been established: four Sri Lankan and one Burmese. There are a total of 124 registered monks at the temples. How-ever, since mobility is high, it is more likely that there are around eighty active monks. Within the Mahāyāna traditions, three main Vietnamese temples have been established in Gothenburg, Bjuv and Malmö, and they have together five branches, with approximately fifteen to twenty monks and nuns. There is only one Chinese temple in the Stockholm area (Rosersberg) belonging to the International Buddhist Progress Society, with two nuns. The convert Buddhists are numerically smaller; however, they have established some thirty meditation groups (city temples or city meditation centres) in the major university cities, as well as seven retreat centres in the country side (The Nordic Vipassana Center Dhamma Sobhana; Zengården, which is the main temple and retreat facility of the Swedish Zen Buddhist Society; Enekulla Zendo run by Christian priest Pelle Bengtsson; Dharmagiri Retreat centre belonging to Triratana; Byvalla retreat centre and collective housing; Karma Dechen Ösel Ling which since 1980 has held three-year retreats as well as shorter retreats in the tradition of Karma Kagyu School and where the first Scandinavian *stūpa* was built in 1988; and Tyresö retreat centre established by the Diamond Way Buddhists in 2018).

It is estimated that up to 30,000 Buddhists (0.55 per cent of the total population) reside in Finland. People of Buddhist backgrounds consisted of 4.6–4.8 per cent of the total immigrant population of Finland in 2019 (Pauha & Martikainen 2022) which means that there are over 20,000 immigrant Buddhists in the country. Thailand and Vietnam are the primary countries of origin for most immigrant Buddhists. Apart from the Kalmykian Mongols, a group of Vietnamese boat refugees were the first immigrant Buddhists to settle in the country in the 1970s. Thai Buddhists have mainly arrived through marriage migration since the 1990s. A small number of Burmese Buddhists and a growing Sri Lankan Buddhist community also reside in Finland. While there are no Buddhist temples serving the Chinese Buddhist residents in the country, there are three Thai Buddhist and three Vietnamese Buddhist temples, one Burmese temple, and one Sri Lankan temple. These temples are home to approximately twelve monks, although not all of them live in the temples permanently due to lack of a permanent residence permit. There is also a Tibetan Buddhist temple with a Tibetan lama living in the centre, and two Tibetan Buddhist nuns and one Vietnamese nun. Additionally, there are some Zen priests and teachers in the country. Despite the relatively small number of temples and monastics, there are around forty Buddhist communities with varying numbers of members.

Of Iceland's 390,000 inhabitants, around 1,500 people (around 0.4 per cent of the total population) are registered as members of a Buddhist organisation. No study has been done on the number of unregistered people identifying as Buddhists in the country. There are six formally registered Buddhist organisations, the most significant being a Thai temple, Wat Thai Iceland, in Reykjavík with several residing monks. Founded in 1995, this group has approximately 950 registered members, which amounts to a bit more than half of the entire Buddhist population in Iceland. Larger Thai Buddhist communities outside the Capital area, for example, in Akureyri in the North of Iceland and Hella in the South are served by this temple. Another Thai temple of the Dhammakāya tradition has been operating in Reykjanesbær since 2022, smaller in numbers, counting around 130 members.

Vietnamese Buddhists in Iceland do not have an organised centre of worship and use private homes and connections to Vietnamese Buddhists in Britain when ritual experts are needed. Converts to Zen, Soka Gakkai and Tibetan Buddhist traditions have organised centres of worship in owned or rented apartments in Reykjavík. Of these, the Zen group is the largest, counting around 200 members.

While there are still no Buddhist groups in Faroe Island and Greenland, statistics from the former list sixty-six Buddhists,[9] the majority of whom are probably Thais married to locals.

In the last fifty years, Buddhism in the Nordic countries has been growing steadily in terms of the number of temples, institutions, monks and nuns, lamas and Zen priests, texts, statues and *stūpa*s, and people who consider themselves Buddhists. Convert monks have been returning from training in Asia and migrants have transferred their religion to be revised by their descendants. Also, beyond institutionalised Buddhism, ideas, symbols and practices have significantly impacted the Nordic countries. Buddhism has emerged in new secular contexts such as mindfulness being taught in workplaces and meditation apps giving private Buddhists tools for developing their private Buddhist practices. Buddha has become an icon for branding, and Buddhist terms have become part of everyday language, suggesting accommodation and domestication of a previously exotic religion.

The chapters

The book has chapters on each of the Nordic countries and, in addition, a few separate chapters on some particularly significant Buddhist individuals in the Nordic countries. These are persons who have played significant roles in the development of Buddhism and have, because of that, received robust research interest. The first of the county chapters covers Sweden. In her chapter, Katarina Plank, drawing on data from several research projects, focuses on how Buddhist groups and teachers have been active in Sweden since the 1950s and the distinct developments that can be discerned within the two groups of Asian and converted Buddhists. The first Asian temple-monasteries were established in Sweden in the 1980s (a Sri Lankan *vihāra* and a Thai Buddhist temple), and for a long time, two monks catered for the religious needs of Sri Lankan and Thai Buddhists in all the Nordic countries. As Asian migration began to increase, so did the number of established temples. Most of the Vietnamese temples are concentrated in the geographical areas of the main three cities of Stockholm, Göteborg and Malmö. However, Thai temples have been established from north to south in sparsely populated areas, giving rise to special challenges regarding food offerings and maintaining a temple in a colder climate. The chapter discusses some societal tensions that have arisen through the establishment of the Asian temples and, in particular, the Swedish tax authority's difficulties in dealing with the religious status of monks and the food offerings given daily in the temples. In 2021, the case was decided in the Administrative Court in favour of the Buddhist congregations. As in the other Nordic countries, several convert groups and some convert training centres have been established that mainly focus on longer meditation courses and community living (*vipassanā*, Tibetan, Zen,

Triratna). The interaction between convert and Asian Buddhists is relatively low; however, there is one specific convert group, the "Svensson Buddhists" connected to the Thai temples that are becoming more of "cultural Buddhists," not necessarily focusing on meditation as most other convert Buddhists tend to.

In Sweden, secular forms of mindfulness meditation have had a strong establishment in many institutions where religion is not expected to be found: schools, health care and organisational development. However, another development seems to be even stronger, where Buddhist convert teachers and Buddhist meditations are integrated into other religious and spiritual settings such as yoga training or in Christian churches.

The following two chapters deal with two significant persons in the development of Buddhism in Sweden, the Tibetan teacher Lama Ngawang[10] (1929–2011) and Phra Chamnong Chutinattharo (1938–2003), who was the first Buddhist missionary monk in Sweden and the Nordic countries. In Chapter 3, Stefan Larsson analyses the Tibetan teacher Lama Ngawang, who became the resident lama in a recently founded Tibetan Buddhist centre in Mälarhöjden, Sweden, in 1976. His chapter examines what happened when this unconventional and charismatic lama, who was born and raised in traditional Tibet, tried to teach people in secular Sweden how to understand and practise Buddhism. Based on interviews, informal conversations, personal experiences and memories, the chapter describes the challenges Lama Ngawang faced and the impact he had upon the people who met him during the thirty-five years he spent in Sweden. In Chapter 4, Preedee Hongsaton discusses the life and career of Phra Chamnong Chutinattharo (1938–2003). The activities of Thai Buddhist missionary monks are usually understood as explicitly spreading the words of the Buddha to the non-Buddhists abroad. This view overlooks the role of the Thai state in coordinating religion with state ideology and the voices of Thai Buddhist migrants whose active roles are neglected in the history of official Thai Buddhism. The article shows that central to the task of Phra Chamnong Chutinattharo was to facilitate the folk Buddhism that Thai migrants, mostly women, carried with them from their home country. Without any support from the Thai authority, Phra Chamnong witnessed various forms of migrants' lives and struggles and managed to help establish several Buddhist institutions. The chapter tells stories of Thai Buddhist lives in Scandinavia towards the end of the last century through the eyes of the Thai monk and it also focuses on how the Thai state and the perception of Buddhism in the West intersected.

In the next chapter, Jørn Borup presents central aspects of Buddhism in Denmark. When Christian Frederik Melbye (1881–1961), in 1921, created the first Buddhist group in Denmark as basically a one-man project, he could not anticipate its future success as a vibrant, living religion. Although Buddhists constitute only about half a per cent of the Danish population, Buddhism has thrived as a minority religion with monks, lamas and dharma teachers guiding a variety of an estimated number of 36,000 Danish converts and migrant Buddhists from mainly Vietnam, Thailand, Sri Lanka and Myanmar. Buddhism in Denmark has undergone periods of cultural accommodation, evolving from a focus on texts to practised religion, from Theravāda to Zen and Tibetan Buddhism, and from monoethnic to the plural agency in a contemporary tradition of "Danish dharma" characterised by diversity. Beyond its institutionalised formations, Buddhism has influenced spiritual seekers, intellectuals, mindfulness instructors and new-age spiritualists. Its impact probably exceeds the numerical practitioners with its general brand value as a popular narrative and symbol of cool branding. The chapter describes the history and changes of Buddhism in Denmark, including the demography and characteristics of individuals and groups and their relation to society.

In Chapter 6, Knut A. Jacobsen analyses central histories and developments of Buddhism in Norway. Buddhism arrived in Norway in 1928 when an Indian Hindu guru from Bengal who had settled in Norway in 1915 declared himself to be a rebirth of the Buddha and his main Norwegian follower to be a rebirth of one of the disciples of the Buddha, Sariputra. The Indian guru passed away in Norway in 1945, but as late as the 1960s, the only surviving follower was known as the only Buddhist in Norway. It was only in the late 1960s and the 1970s that Buddhist converts and immigrants started creating Buddhist communities in Norway belonging to well-known forms and schools of Buddhism. The chapter first analyses the understanding of Buddhism of the Indian Buddha in Norway and his Buddhist disciple and, second, describes the growth of Buddhism and gives an overview of the significant plurality of Buddhist traditions in the country, and third, analyses a conflict between convert and migrant Buddhism about the interpretation and representation of Buddhism in public space.

In her chapter, Mitra Härkönen analyses Buddhism in Finland. Although Buddhism is still clearly a minority religion in Finland, its popularity has increased in recent years, as evidenced by the sharp rise in Buddhist communities and practitioners. While most Buddhists in Finland are of Asian origin, the increase in the popularity of Buddhism cannot be solely attributed to immigrants. Many Finns have also turned to Buddhism for ethical, philosophical and mental guidance. As in many other Western countries, Tibetan and Zen Buddhism are particularly popular among Finnish people. These practice communities may be small, but they are diverse due to the variety of schools, lineages and masters that their practitioners follow. Additionally, other Buddhist-based meditation techniques such as *vipassanā* and mindfulness are becoming more prevalent. Compared to many other European countries, Buddhism has taken longer to develop in Finland. Despite this fact, it is worth recognising that Buddhism was present in Finland from an early stage. In the eighteenth century, the Mongolian Kalmyks became the first group of Buddhists in the country. In the nineteenth century, Finnish explorers, linguists and missionaries were known to encounter Buddhist peoples but it was not until the advent of theosophy that Buddhism began to take root locally. The first Buddhist association in Finland was established relatively early, in 1947, and for a brief period in the late 1940s and early 1950s, Helsinki was an international centre for Buddhism. The chapter provides a historical overview of Buddhism in Finland, from its early presence to the present. Furthermore, it presents the growing diversity of Buddhism in contemporary Finland and discusses Buddhism in Finnish society and the future of Buddhism in the country.

In the next chapter, Johannes Cairns presents an analysis of Mauno Nordberg (1884–1956) and early Buddhism in Finland. Mauno Nordberg was a founding member and early president of the first Buddhist society in Finland, Buddhismin ystävät ry – Buddhismens Vänner r.f. ("Friends of Buddhism"), founded in 1947. During Nordberg's presidentship, the society assumed centre stage in the modernisation and westernisation of Buddhism, including its spread to other Nordic countries and the chapter explores his efforts to promote Buddhism from his return to Finland from Paris in 1944 to his death in 1956.

In Chapter 9, Haraldur Hreinsson presents an overview of Buddhism in Iceland. The story of Buddhism in Iceland as an officially registered religious affiliation dates from 1980, the year when Soka Gakkai in Iceland was founded. Nevertheless, since the early twentieth century Icelanders had been introduced to Buddhism mainly through the publication activities of the Theosophical Society, through the writings of interreligiously oriented Lutheran pastors and later also Zen converts. The Buddhist Association of Iceland was officially founded in 1995 by Thai immigrants who had moved to the country either to work in its fast-growing fishing industry or because of the marriage relationship to Icelanders. Hreinsson shows that the history of Buddhism constitutes an intriguing chapter in Iceland's rapid modernisation process in the twentieth century.

The concluding chapter summarises some of the general characteristics of Buddhism in the Nordic countries. The historical role of the Evangelical Lutheran Church as well as a high level of secularity and welfare give Sweden, Norway, Finland, Denmark and Iceland a common cultural frame in which the religious landscape including Buddhism has been formed. A high degree of diversity is predominant in all countries, where also the authority of umbrella organisations varies. The chapter concludes by suggesting some topics for future research, asking for reflections on the new generation of Buddhists in the Nordic countries.

Buddhism has received a solid but not always acknowledged presence in the Nordic countries. It is present but not always visible. The book represents the first attempt to analyse Buddhism in the Nordic region as a whole. A number of similar cultural and social trends have been at work in these countries, which have favoured the growth of Buddhism. Pluralisation of religion is currently going on throughout Europe, and in this book, we investigate one little-known part of this pan-European phenomenon: the characteristics of Buddhism in the Nordic countries.

Notes

1 "Human Development Index (HDI) by Country 2024," available at https://worldpopulationreview.com/country-rankings/hdi-by-country, accessed March 10, 2024.
2 The Nordic countries are the most gender equal in the world (*Global Gender Gap Report* 2023: 11).
3 Betænkning 1564/2017. A religious community is defined as a community whose members gather around a belief in powers that are above humans and the laws of nature, following formulated doctrines and rituals.
4 The American sociologist of religion Phil Zuckerman investigated how Scandinavian (Danish and Swedish) societies are "societies without God" (Zuckerman 2008).

5 On "culture Christianity" and "culture religion" in Denmark, see Mauritsen et al. 2023.
6 Centre for Contemporary Religion at Aarhus University has since the first Pluralism Project in 2002 (e.g. Ahlin et al. 2012) continuously mapped different aspects of the changing religious landscape in Denmark (Centre for Contemporary Religion n.d). On Finland, see Illman et al., 2017. On religion and immigration in Sweden, see Nordin 2023. On Norway, see Jacobsen 2018.
7 *Göteborgs-Posten* 2017-07-15.
8 "ebu: European Buddhist Union," available at https://europeanbuddhistunion.org/, accessed 17 November 2014.
9 "MT10.1.1 Religion by age, sex and district," available at https://statbank.hagstova.fo/pxweb/en/H2/H2__MT__MT10__MT1001/MT321.px/table/tableViewLayout2/, accessed 17 November 2024.
10 According to his passport, Lama Ngawang was born in 1927, but his actual birth year was 1929.

References

Ahlin, Lars, Jørn Borup, Marianne Qvortrup Fibiger, Lene Kühle, Viggo Mortensen, and René Dybdal Pedersen. 2012. "Religious Diversity and Pluralism: Empirical Data and Theoretical Reflections from the Danish Pluralism Project." *Journal of Contemporary Religion*, 27(3), 403–418.

Bastubacka, Johan and Mitra Härkönen. 2023. "Buddha-kuvat kotona: Buddhalaiset sisustuselementit suomalaisissa kodeissa." In *Buddhalaisuus Suomessa*, edited by Mitra Härkönen and Johannes Cairns, 363–378. Helsinki: Finnish Oriental Society.

Baumann, Martin, Jørn Borup and Knut A. Jacobsen (eds.) (Forthcoming). *Handbook of Buddhism in Europe* (Two volumes). Leiden: Brill.

Betænkning 1564/2017. *En samlet lovregulering om andre trossamfund end folkekirken. Betænkning fra Trossamfundsudvalget*. Available at: (https://www.km.dk/fileadmin/share/nyheder/En_samlet_lovregulering_om_andre_trossamfund_end_folkekirken.pdf).

Borup, Jørn. 2016. "Who are these Buddhists and How Many of Them are There? Theoretical and Methodological Challenges in Counting Immigrant Buddhists: A Danish Case Study." *Journal of Contemporary Religion*, 31, 85–100.

Centre for Contemporary Religion. n.d. *Centre for Contemporary Religion*. https://samtidsreligion.au.dk/en/.

Enstedt, Daniel and Plank, Katarina. 2023. "Introducing Eastern Practices and Nordic Bodies." In *Eastern Practices and Nordic Bodies: Lived Religion, Spirituality and Healing in the Nordic Countries,* edited by Daniel Enstedt and Katarina Plank, 1–26. Cham: Palgrave Macmillan.

Fredriksson, Trudy. 2013. *Uppvaknandets vägar: Från buddhistisk historia till nutidens utövning och gemenskapsliv*. Stockholm: Nämnden för statligt stöd till trossamfund.

Furseth, Inger (ed.). 2018. *Religious Complexity in the Public Sphere: Comparing Nordic Countries*. Palgrave Macmillan.

Gyllensvärd, Bo. 2004. "The Buddha found at Helgö." In *Excavations at Helgö XVI. Exotic and Sacral Finds from Helgö,* 10–27. Stockholm: Kungl. vitterhets-, historie-och antikitetsakad.

Hedenstierna-Jonsson, Charlotte. 2020. "With Asia as Neighbour." *The Museum of Far Eastern Antiquities*, Bulletin No 81, 43–64.

Hilson, Mary. 2020. "The Nordic Welfare Model" In *Introduction to Nordic Cultures,* edited by Annika Lindskog and Jakob Stougaard-Nielsen, 70–83. UCL Press.

Hultberg, Thomas. 1971. "Hinduism, Buddhism, Islam i Sverige." *Utblick*, no. 3.

Haakestad, Jorunn. 2018. *Porcelain and Revolution: Johan Munthe and the Chinese Collection in Bergen*. Bergen: Fagbokforlaget.

Hannikainen, Pietari, and Meri Hannikainen. 2021. Finland: Religious education in accordance with one's own religion. In G Amati, A Clerx and M Scott-Cracknell (eds.), Education and Religion in Europe: A dossier by EARS on the role of religion in education in 17 European countries. European Academy of Religion and Society, Amsterdam, 21–23.

Härkönen, Mitra. 2024. "'A mini home far away from home.' The Thai temple and women's sense of safety in Finland." *Frontiers in Psychology, Sec. Gender, Sex and Sexualities*, 15, 1–14, 1354068. https://doi.org/10.3389/fpsyg.2024.1354068.

Illman, Ruth, Kimmo Ketola, Riitta Latvio, and Jussi Sohlberg (eds.). 2017. *De många religionernas och åskådningarnas Finland.* Kyrkans forskningscentrals webbpublikationer.

Jacobsen, Knut A. (ed.). 2018. *Verdensreligioner i Norge*, 4th edition. Oslo: Universitetsforlaget.

Jansson, Hedda. 2023. *Solbadets Buddha: Buddhism och teosofi i Ellen Keys livstro.* Stockholm University [dissertation].

Kühle, Lene. 2024. "Religious Freedom and Restrictions in the Nordic countries." *Nordics Info.* Available at: https://nordics.info/show/artikel/religious-freedom-and-restrictions-in-the-nordic-countries (accessed Sept 2024).

Kværne, Per. 2022. "C.A. Holmboe. 1796–1882. "The First Norwegian Scholar of Buddhism." *Revue d'Etudes Tibétaines*, 64, 344–351.

Levitt, Peggy. 2004. "Redefining the Boundaries of Belonging: The Institutional Character of Transnational Religious Life." *Sociology of Religion*, 35(1), 174–196.

Lundgren, Linnea, Katarina Plank, and Helene Egnell. 2023. "Nya andliga praktiker i Svenska kyrkan: Från exklusiva retreatmiljöer till kyrklig vardagspraktik." *Svensk teologisk kvartalskrift*, 99, 229–248.

Markkola, Pirjo. 2015. "The Long History of Lutheranism in Scandinavia. From State Religion to the People's Church." *Perichoresis*, 13(2), 3–15. https://doi.org/10.1515/perc-2015–0007 (accessed 12 Nov 2024).

Mauritsen, Anne L., Jørn Borup, Marie Vejrup and Benjamin Grant Purzycki. 2023. "Cultural Religion: Patterns of Contemporary Majority Religion in Denmark." *Journal of Contemporary Religion,* 38(2), 261–281.

Nilsson, Åke. 2004. *Efterkrigstidens invandring och utvandring.* Stockholm: Statistiska centralbyrån.

Nordin, Magdalena. 2023. *Migration, religion och integration.* Stockholm: Delegationen för migrationsstudier. https://gup.ub.gu.se/publication/324997 (accessed 12 Nov 2024).

Numrich, Paul David. 1996. *Old Wisdom in the New World: Americanization in Two Immigrant Theravada Buddhist Temples.* The University of Tennessee Press.

Offermanns, Jürgen. 2015. "Debates on Atheism, Quietism, and Sodomy: The Initial Reception of Buddhism in Europe." *Journal of Global Buddhism*, 6, 16–35.

Pauha, Teemu and Tuomas Martikainen. 2022. "Arvio maahanmuuttotaustaisen väestön uskonnollisesta jakaumasta Suomessa vuosina 1990–2019." *Teologinen Aikakauskirja*, 127(1), 3–23.

Pew Research Center. 2018a. "Being Christian in Western Europe." https://www.pewresearch.org/religion/2018/05/29/being-christian-in-western-europe/ (accessed 29 Feb 2024).

Pew Research Center. 2018b. "Eastern and Western Europeans Differ on Importance of Religion, Views of Minorities, and Key Social Issues." https://www.pewresearch.org/religion/2018/10/29/eastern-and-western-europeans-differ-on-importance-of-religion-views-of-minorities-and-key-social-issues/ (accessed 29 Feb 2024).

Plank, Katarina. 2004. "Buddhism i Sverige." In *Det mångreligiösa Sverige: ett landskap i förändring,* edited by Daniel Andersson and Åke Sander, 217–284. Lund: Studentlitteratur.

Plank, Katarina. 2015. "The Sacred Foodscapes of Thai Buddhist Temples in Sweden." *Religion and Food, Scripta Instituti Donneriani Aboensis*, 26(2015), 201–224.

Plank, Katarina, Linnea Lundgren and Helene Egnell. 2023. "Meditation and Other New Spiritual Practices in the Church of Sweden." In *Eastern Practices and Nordic Bodies: Lived Religion, Spirituality and Healing in the Nordic Countries.* Cham: Palgrave Macmillan.

Prebish, Charles S. 1979. *American Buddhism*. North Scituate, Mass.: Duxbury Press.

Svanberg, Ingvar and Pia Karlsson. 1997. *Religionsfrihet i Sverige: Om möjligheten att leva som troende*. Lund: Studentlitteratur.

Syvertsen, Trine, Gunn Enli, Ole J. Mjøs, and Hallvard Moe. 2014. "The Nordic Model and the Media Welfare State." In *The Media Welfare State: Nordic Media in the Digital Era*, edited by Trine Syvertsen, Gunn Enli, Ole J. Mjøs and Hallvard Moe, 1–23. University of Michigan Press. https://doi.org/10.2307/j.ctv65swsg.4 (accessed 12 Nov 2024).

Taira, Teemu. 2019. "Studying Religion in Nordic Newspapers: An Introduction." *Temenos – Nordic Journal for the Study of Religion*, 55(2), 175–99. https://doi.org/10.33356/temenos.87824 (accessed 12 Nov 2024).

Taira, Teemu, Atko Remmel and Anton Jansson. 2021. "The Nordic and Baltic Countries" In *The Cambridge History of Atheism*, edited by Stephen Bullivant and Michael Ruse, 898–917. Cambridge: Cambridge University Press. https://doi.org/10.1017/9781108562324.049 (accessed 12 Nov 2024)

Thelle, Notto R. 2022. *Karl Ludvig Reichelt: Misjonær mellom øst og vest*. Oslo: Cappelen Damm.

Tolvanen, Kaisa. 2023. "Buddhalaisuuden varhaisvaiheet Suomessa" In *Buddhalaisuus Suomessa*, edited by Mitra Härkönen and Johannes Cairns, 27–40. Helsinki: Finnish Oriental Society.

Tweed, Thomas. 1992. *The American Encounter with Buddhism, 1844–1912: Victorian Culture and the Limits of Dissent*. Bloomington: Indiana University Press.

Tweed, Thomas. 1997. *Our Lady of the Exile: Diasporic Religion at a Cuban Catholic Shrine in Miami*. New York: Oxford University Press.

Tweed, Thomas A. 2015. "Theory and Method in the Study of Buddhism: Toward 'Translocative' Analysis." *Journal of Global Buddhism*, 12, 17–32.

Weissenbilder, Marcus. 2019. *Svenska religionstrender*. Göteborg: SOM-institutet. https://www.gu.se/sites/default/files/2020–09/26.%20Svenska%20religiontrender.pdf (accessed 12 Nov 2024).

World Economic Forum. 2022. *Global Gender Gap Report 2023*. Cologny/Geneve: World Economic Forum.

Zuber, Devin. 2010. "The Buddha of the North: Swedenborg and Transpacific Zen." *Religion and the Arts*, 14(1–2), 1–33.

Zuckerman, Phil. 2008. *Society without God*. New York: New York University Press.

2 Buddhism in Sweden

Religious institutions, secular applications and Christian meditations

Katarina Plank

Introduction

Interest in Buddhism and Eastern thought began to fascinate Swedish intellectuals around the turn of the nineteenth century (1800–1900). However, it was only after the Second World War that the first Buddhist teachers, often converts themselves, began teaching in Sweden. In 1980, the first retreat facility was established at Solbo, near Fellingsbro, founded by Kalu Rinpoche and the Sixteenth Karmapa to enable full-time training in the Tibetan tradition, including several three-year retreats. In 1988, the fourteenth Dalai Lama inaugurated the first *stūpa* in northern Europe here. Increasing migration, primarily following a European pattern, has shaped the Buddhist landscape in Sweden. However, the Buddhist groups vary in their internal composition, mainly due to the different types of migration. Vietnamese Buddhists, who arrived as refugees, have since established viable communities in Scania and Gothenburg, with several Pure Land temples. In Malmö, the large and aging community of Vietnamese refugees contributed to establishing a Buddhist cemetery in 1989, the first of its kind in Sweden. The Chinese community came early on, primarily to work in the restaurant industry, and although many are secular, there is a Chinese temple in Rosersberg, Stockholm. More recently, Thai Buddhism has become the most widespread Buddhist tradition in Sweden, with temples in more than thirty localities from south to north. Other Asian Buddhist traditions represented include those of Sri Lanka and Burma. The mobility of ordained monks and nuns makes it difficult to estimate how many reside in Sweden, though it is likely that around a hundred monks and nuns serve Buddhist communities. Regular Buddhist practices are estimated to occur at over a hundred locations, including convert Buddhists and their retreat centres. However, only half of the temples are members of the Swedish Buddhist Community and thus receive state funding.

This chapter will provide an overview of the reception of Buddhism, focusing on religious thought and practices, including early converts and Asian Buddhists. It will also discuss religious and Buddhist demographics in Sweden and how Swedish legislation shapes how faith communities organise themselves. The chapter will also discuss new emerging frontiers, where practices like meditation and yoga have not only been secularised and used in the healthcare sector but are now re-sacralised in new religious settings, such as the Church of Sweden.

DOI: 10.4324/9781003529767-2

The data on which the following chapter is based (document analyses, fieldwork including interviews and observations, netnographic observations of homepages, and archive studies) has been collected within the framework of four different research projects conducted between 2020 and 2025. By mainly using a methodological perspective of lived religion, where the lived experiences of individuals are highlighted, the interplay between individual and institutionalised forms of religion can be considered (Enstedt & Plank 2018). The chapter prioritises individual stories that, to different degrees, have contributed to or shaped Buddhism in Sweden, thus giving precedence to the lived aspects of religion. Micro-histories of people and places do not aim to give a full biography but to point to a cultural context (Lepore 2001). Thus, it is through the lives of individuals that Nordic and international intersections become visible, sometimes in surprising ways. Buddhism in Sweden has never existed in a vacuum, and influences have come from Asia and Western countries.

As this chapter is based on data that deals with lived Buddhism, including insights into people's religious affiliation and practice, sensitive personal data has been handled. The different research projects have all undergone rigorous ethical reviews and have been approved, ensuring the integrity and ethical conduct of the research.[1]

The early reception of Buddhism

The oldest preserved Buddhist artefact found in the Nordic countries is the Helgö Buddha, which was discovered during archaeological excavations in 1954. The 8.4-cm-tall Buddha statue was probably made in the sixth century in the Swat Valley in present-day Pakistan (Gyllensvärd 2004). The small island of Helgö is situated in Lake Mälaren, not far from Birka, an important Viking centre, which was the hub for trade in Northern Europe during the 700s–900s. Viking trade networks were extensive, and archaeological analyses of the Helgö Buddha, along with finds of Chinese silk and Arabic silver coins found in Birka, suggest that the Vikings travelled far eastward along the Silk Road and thus had contact with several different cultures. Helgö held a central role in the region and was used during a period spanning from 200 to 900 CE, which extends from the Roman Iron Age up into the Viking Age. Helgö had many religious functions and knowledge of advanced metalwork. It is impossible to determine with certainty when the Helgö Buddha reached Sweden. However, the archaeological site on Helgö, where the Buddha statue was found together with other religious symbols, indicates that the Vikings "were aware of the power that the objects were thought to possess" (Hedenstierna-Jonsson 2020: 56). It is, however, unlikely that residents of Helgö had any knowledge of Buddhism.

Several hundred years would pass before early knowledge of Eastern and Asian religions reached Swedes in various ways, such as through Jesuit travel letters that circulated in Europe during the sixteenth century, reporting on the religion of Fo. In 1731, the Swedish East India Company was established to trade with South and East Asia, fostering growing enthusiasm for China during the Age of

Enlightenment, with imported goods like porcelain, silk, cotton, paper, tea, spices and art becoming part of cultural life. This laid the foundation for the later reception of Buddhism in Sweden during the seventeenth and eighteenth centuries. Swedish travelogues from China contained representations of Confucianism, Buddhism and Daoism, where Buddhism were portrayed as superstitious paganism (Spence 1999: 98–100; Nyberg 2001: 83–89; Gregory 2002: 36–49, 116–128). Offermanns notes that these early representations focused more on lived traditions than on religious texts, which later became the subject of academic work (Offermanns 2002, 2005). For an overview of the scholarly study of Buddhism in Sweden, see Myrvold, Plank, and Sardella (2024).

The growing interest in Eastern goods and thought contributed to the so-called Oriental Renaissance that Hedda Jansson (2023) suggests influenced the Swedish mystic, mathematician and scientist Emanuel Swedenborg (1688–1772). Swedenborg was later given the epithet "the Buddha of the North" by various authors from different continents who were inspired by his teachings: in 1835 by the French author Honoré de Balzac (1799–1850) in his novel *Séraphita*; in 1887 by one of the first American Buddhists, Philangi Dasa, who was born in Sweden; and in 1913 by D.T. Suzuki in Japan (Jansson 2023). Today, Swedenborg's works may be largely unfamiliar; however, he had a broad impact on the late eighteenth and early nineteenth centuries. Devin Zuber argues that elements of Swedenborgian doctrine "enabled certain Western authors to approach and adumbrate Zen concepts . . . [while on] the other hand, Swedenborg's ideas can be seen to ferry in the other direction, from the East towards the West . . . where Zen authors . . . adapted and translated Buddhist concerns into a Western Judeo-Christian framework" (Zuber 2010: 4). To some extent, this mention of the Buddha of the North may also have contributed to the favourable reception of Buddhism in the Swedish alternative and esoteric milieus (Faxneld, Plank & Nilsson 2024).

Swedenborg and the later Theosophical currents influenced several Swedish intellectuals at the turn of the century, 1800–1900. The Swedish Theosophical Society was founded in 1889, the same year as the eighth International Orientalist Conference took place in Stockholm and Christiania (Sweden and Norway were in union at this time). Leading Theosophists like Henry Steel Olcott, Annie Besant and Katherine Tingley visited Sweden during the 1890s. Swedish newspapers also reported on the World's Parliament of Religion held in Chicago in 1893, which contributed to an interest in Eastern religions. At this time, the term *Buddhist* could apply to either a "free-thinker, truth seeker, theosophist or a plain agnostic" (Jansson 2023: 169), as Theosophy and Buddhism were intertwined. Like their European and American counterparts, Swedish Theosophists were interested in South Asian religious traditions and esoteric interpretations of Christianity. Theosophical ideas influenced several prominent Swedish intellectuals. Hedda Jansson (2023) has written extensively about the life of the educational reformer Ellen Key (1849–1926) and traced how Buddhist and Theosophical teachings influenced Key's *Life Faith* (*Livstro*). Key read, for instance, Max Müller, Paul Carus, Schopenhauer, Nietzsche and Tolstoy, who may have influenced her thinking. She also had a strong interest in Japan during the 1890s and read, for instance, Lafcadio Hearn's book *Exotica*

(Jansson 2023: 171–177). Another prominent exponent of Theosophy in Sweden was the author Viktor Rydberg (1828–1895), who, in 1888, translated Sir Edwin Arnold's *The Light of Asia* and also wrote a preface in which he identified Christ as Maitreya, the coming Buddha. Among other intellectuals with an interest in Theosophy were the author August Strindberg (1849–1912), the Social Democrat Kata Dalström (1858–1923), the artist Hilma af Klint (1862–1944) and the poet Dan Andersson (1888–1920), all of whose works have had an impact on Swedish society (Almqvist & Passmark 2023).

Thomas Tweed (1992) identified two proponents with strong Scandinavian connections as part of the early Buddhist developments in North America. As mentioned earlier and in the introduction, one of them was Philangi Dasa (1849–1931). He was born as Herman Vetterling in Småland, southern Sweden, and migrated to America, where he, after several years as a Swedenborgian minister in a church in Philadelphia, trained as a homoeopathic doctor and later established the first Buddhist journal. Vetterling took the pseudonym Philangi Dasa, meaning "Western devotee." The other was the Danish-born Harry Holst (1875–1932), who, like Vetterling/Philangi Dasa, trained as a homoeopathic doctor in Chicago. In his book *The American Encounter with Buddhism* (1992), Thomas Tweed mentions that, in 1899, the newspaper *Chicago Record* reported on Harry Holst as he taught about Buddhism in the streets of Chicago. This was also mentioned about two weeks later in *Chicago Bladet*, a Swedish Christian newspaper providing "Christian and Political News for Swedes in America."[2] On 22 August 1899, under a heading featuring reports from "the mission field," a short article mentions "a Danish Buddhist" named Harry Holst. This raises questions about the impact these two might have had on the early reception of Buddhism in the Nordic countries.

A search in the digitised archive of the Royal Library, where Swedish newspapers from 1645 to today are available, shows no indication that the Swedish press ever mentioned Vetterling/Philangi Dasa during his lifetime. However, there are several reports on Harry Holst, the first mention appearing in September 1899. Thus, the story of the Danish "Buddhist apostle" continues on the other side of the Atlantic. Since transatlantic news was of interest to many due to the great migration from Sweden and the Nordic countries, several Swedish newspapers, such as *Aftonbladet* (1899-09-08), *Öresundsposten* (1899-09-15), and *Sundsvalls Dagblad* (1899-09-15), picked up on the reports from *Chicago Record* and *Chicago Bladet*, and they also informed their readers that Harry Holst had used the name Tyagananda. However, according to the newspapers, Holst never claimed to be a Buddhist. Instead, he saw himself as a disciple of Buddhist philosophy and spoke about reincarnation and karma. A review of other digitised archives and newspaper archives[3] illuminates the global dimensions of Harry Holst's life and provides insights into his extraordinary life as a non-Christian. His Nordic roots included his birth and christening in Skovby, Denmark; Christian confirmation in the parish of Helsingør Cathedral; and marriage to his Norwegian wife, Ane Marie Lai Hansine Laursen. This marriage took place in London in 1905, and later that year, their daughter, Radha Sakuntala, named after the consort of Krishna, was born in Östersund, in the province of Jämtland, where Holst also worked at Sweden's largest homoeopathic institute, founded by O. T. Axell (Ellert 2009). Holst and his family moved several times, as he practised homoeopathic medicine in Stockholm and Småland. Harry Holst published two books on homoeopathy (Holst 1909, 1914) and one on vaccination (1912).

Holst's interest in spiritualism, Eastern philosophy and religion took him and his family on several extended tours. Holst had the financial means to travel (at least) three times to America, twice to London, and to take the family with him to India and Ceylon. Together with his wife, his close friend Sigurd Trier and his colleague O.T. Axell, Holst undertook a "spiritistic journey" to London in 1907. A lengthy travel report was published in the journal *Efteråt – Tidskrift för spiritism och dermed beslägtade ämnen* (no 6, 1907), where it was revealed that Holst was given a greeting from his late teacher Swami Vivekananda (1863–1902) during a séance. During one of Holst's early stays in America, he appears to have met Swami Vivekananda and become his disciple. A small advertisement published in December 1912 in *Svenska Dagbladet* confirms this. In the ad, Holst sold stenographically (shorthand) reproduced lectures by his teacher on the topic of Vedanta, and more specifically "The Idea of a Universal Religion. Bhakti Yoga. Man – What She Is and How She Presents. Atman" (*Svenska Dagbladet* 1912-12-16). Meeting Vivekananda and becoming his disciple under the name Tyagananda are probably what led him to propagate Buddhist philosophy in Chicago. However, it is not clear from the sources if he also followed his teacher's unified view on religion, in which Buddhism was considered to be the fulfilment of Hinduism.

During his life in Sweden, Holst seems to have kept an interest in religion as well as a distance to Christianity and the Lutheran Evangelical Church. His daughter Radha was never baptised, and in the 1910 Census, it is stated that Harry and his wife, Marie, professed Hinduism. Around 1911, Harry Holst also created an Ex Libris,[4] where he drew books and manuscripts to frame a map of India. The Ex Libris also contains the text *Ex Oriente Lux* (the light comes from the East) and a verse from *Bhagavad-gītā* 4.11.[5] In later church records from when the Holst family was living in Jönköping, a priest notes that he cannot attest to their knowledge of Christianity and that they did not take communion.

Harry Holst and his colleague O.T. Axell were charged multiple times with quackery, and both Swedish and transatlantic newspapers reported on the trials. In 1916, the legislation regulating the medical profession was tightened, making it more difficult for Holst to continue his practice. This prompted the family to travel to India, though they returned to Sweden a year later, in 1917. The couple divorced in 1925, after which Harry Holst remarried, this time to Maria Cecilia Jeppesen, a Danish woman. They lived in Gothenburg until Harry Holst's death in 1932 at the age of 57. Based on the available source material, Harry Holst was a seeker rather than a spiritual teacher and was primarily known to the public for his profession in homeopathy. If we can conclude that Harry Holst affiliated himself with Hinduism rather than Buddhism, then it was the Social Democrat and agitator Kata Dalström (1958–1923), who was the first in Sweden to declare herself a Buddhist. This took place during a public debate in 1907 when Kata Dahlström was in Vansäter, in the Gävleborg region, to debate with a theologian on the role of religion in politics. At the beginning of the twentieth century, as Sweden experienced industrialisation, women's liberation and mass migration, people began to look for other religious alternatives, as exemplified in the life of Harry Holst. During the discussion, attended by an audience of over 1,000 people, Kata Dalström advocated for complete religious freedom. At that time, the Dissenter Acts of 1860 and 1873 permitted individuals to leave the Church of Sweden only if they joined another denomination approved by the state, which limited alternatives to becoming a Methodist or a Catholic. Thus, the debate also highlights how Christian doctrine was publicly challenged as Kata Dalström declared herself a Buddhist and a Social Democrat at the same time (Plank 2009b).

It is unlikely that Swedish intellectuals at the turn of the century had any direct contact with Asian Buddhists. However, there is a possible exception in the remarkable life story of Hilma Svedal, née Wounsch (1870–1965). She was never part of the Swedish intellectual scene; instead, she was born into a fishing family on the West Coast. As noted in the introduction, she was a Swedish gold digger who took part in the Klondike Gold Rush. She migrated to New York in 1897, where she worked as a maid for a few years before travelling to California and Alaska. There, she met and married Norwegian John Svedal in 1912. The couple returned to Sweden in 1925, when Hilma inherited the island of Nord Långön in the northern archipelago of Strömstad on the West Coast from her deceased father. (This was around the same time that Belgian-French explorer Alexandra David Néel travelled to Tibet.) Hilma Svedal's husband did not settle well, and he returned to America the same year. Hilma, however, started planning and constructing a stone and cement garden filled with exotic flowers, creating her own Alaska in the Swedish archipelago, with a temple dedicated to the wind and an igloo, to name a few of her buildings. She was in her 60s when she began building her Alaska, and the island soon became a major tourist attraction, featuring music, dance and moonlight tours (Dave 2018; Jägerbrand 2011). Her family recounts how Hilma Svedal met a Chinese cook during her time in America, who gifted her a small ivory Buddha that she kept close to her, day and night. They claim she had a Buddhist outlook on life, encapsulated by the words "Don't worry," which are inscribed on her gravestone (Haglund 2017).

It was, however, not only Swedes who travelled westwards and eastwards. A notable event occurred in 1897 when King Chulalongkorn, Rama V of Siam, visited Sweden. He had been invited by King Oscar II of Sweden to visit the Stockholm Exhibition, which highlighted art and industry. During his visit to Sweden, he went on an excursion to Norrland. King Chulalongkorn, a moderniser of Siam, was interested in the Swedish sawmill industry, and they therefore visited Bispgården and Utanede in the Ragunda area of Jämtland to observe timber rafting on the river Indalsälven. The visit was considered exotic at the time, and large crowds came to greet the King of Siam. The event lived on in the memories of local residents, and some fifty years after the visit, the small gravel road the king had travelled was named Kung Chulalongkorns väg [King Chulalongkorn's Road]. In 1992, a Thai dance group visited this road when they came to the Ragunda area to perform. The group was excited to learn about the road's history and formed an association to honour the memory of their beloved King Chulalongkorn. In 1997, one hundred years after the royal visit, a royal pavilion was built with support from both Thai and Swedish sponsors. The pavilion is the only one of its kind outside of Thailand. Inside, a statue of King Chulalongkorn was placed, and his memory is honoured there on 19 July of every year, a celebration organised by the Royal Thai Embassy, the Thai communities in Ragunda and Ragunda Municipality. The royal pavilion is not a religious site. However, it has become a significant attraction for both Thais and Swedes. In 2007, a meditation centre and temple, Wat Piyadhammaram, was established a few kilometres away, and it also houses a small museum commemorating King Chulalongkorn's visit. King Chulalongkorn also gifted Sweden three complete copies of the Theravāda canon, the *Tipiṭaka*, printed in 1893. These copies were given to the Uppsala and Lund University libraries and the Stockholm Royal Library.

The early reception of Buddhism in Sweden contains several elements that influenced the later development of lived Buddhism. Theosophy and eastward travels would continue to be important for the early converts who started to practise and teach Buddhism, and westward travels, whether through forced or voluntary migration, would shape when and how Asian Buddhists established their traditions in Sweden. Today, Buddhism in Sweden is interconnected with both Western and Asian teachers and traditions, and Sweden plays a vital role for other Nordic Buddhists since many retreat facilities have been established there.

Convert Buddhism: from unity to diversity

In the 1950s, when full religious freedom was granted, Buddhism attracted converts, many of whom were still influenced by Theosophy. From this time, Buddhism can be recognised as a lived religion with identifiable elements from Asian traditions where meditation, puja, teacher-disciple relations and the study of texts were central. Thus, when Buddhism began to be practised as a religion in Sweden, it was by and through Swedes. This led the author and translator Gunnar Gällmo (1946–2023) to somewhat provocatively argue that Buddhism is the most Swedish of all religions, contending that Christianity arrived with foreign missionaries, while Islam came with migrants from outside Europe. However, by the time migration from Buddhist countries began, Buddhism had already established a foothold in Sweden (Gällmo 1999a: 4). This argument is echoed by Trudy Fredriksson, Chairwoman of the Swedish Buddhist Community, who states that this made Sweden unique in that Swedish Buddhists early on formed networks and a joint Buddhist union together with Asian Buddhists who had migrated to Sweden. In regard to similar Buddhist unions in Europe and the United States, Fredriksson observes that most members are converts, with limited interactions with Asian Buddhists (Fredriksson 2013: 95).

Two early converts were instrumental in establishing and domesticating Buddhism in Sweden: Ingrid Wagner, née Svensson (1910–2001), and Marcel Sirander (1912–1983).[6] Both promoted a unified view of Buddhism, Ekayāna. However, it was not until the 1970s that more organised teachings began to emerge. Marcel

Sirander, born in Nice, France, travelled to China in the 1930s and was ordained as a *bhikshu* in 1933 at Tsz Shan Monastery near Nánjīng (belonging to the Tiāntái tradition). He left China in 1936 and arrived in Sweden as a married layperson in 1948. He settled on the West Coast near Gothenburg, and as he began teaching Buddhism in the 1950s, he became known as Acarya Shunyata. In 1954, he established a Buddhist society that became a regional centre for the World Fellowship of Buddhism. Sirander became an influential teacher for a group of ten to fifteen Buddhists who met with him regularly (Hultberg 1971; Plank 2004).

In 1955, four years after full religious freedom was granted in Sweden, the artist Ingrid Wagner was the first Swedish woman to take renunciant vows. This occurred in Nepal during a Theravāda ordination. According to Annakarin Svedberg, one of her close disciples, it took place at the Swayambhunath *stūpa* in Kathmandu, where Wagner received the ten precepts as *dasasīlamātā* and the name Amita Nisatta (Svedberg 2011: 242). Two years earlier, Ingrid Wagner had travelled to India with her then-husband, Karl-Henrik Wagner, to study art and Buddhist religion. The couple had been involved with the Theosophical Society for several years and had thus become acquainted with Buddhism. Six months after Ingrid Wagner had taken the ten precepts, Karl-Henrik Wagner received an anagarika-ordination, committing to a celibate and ascetic lay life and adopting a homeless existence without formally joining the monastic community. Even though neither spouse took full ordination, they still viewed the ceremonies as the beginning of a new life, one in which they would live as a nun and a monk.

When Amita Nisatta returned to Sweden, she wore robes that she kept for the rest of her life and maintained a shaved head. She also considered it appropriate to be called Sister Amita, in keeping with the way Catholic nuns are addressed. In the late 1950s, Amita Nisatta was invited to Burma to learn meditation from Mahasi Sayadaw. Upon her return, Anagarika Sugata moved to Norway to teach Buddhism, while Amita Nisatta remained in Sweden. Her apartment on Södermalm in Stockholm became a gathering place for a growing group of interested people who adopted the name Friends of Buddhism (Buddhismens Vänner). Starting in 1969, she also frequently taught in the Chinese temple room at the Ethnographic Museum in Stockholm on Saturdays. Between eight and ten people would attend her teaching and meditation sessions. On an altar made of red lacquer stood a Buddha statue, along with candlesticks, vases and offering bowls. Seated on the floor in front of the altar, with her shaved head and yellow robes, Amita Nisatta exuded a concentration and austerity during meditation that contrasted with her otherwise lively demeanour, and her teachings included puja, meditation and dharma talks (Plank 2004, 2009a).

Later, Sister Amita took two additional ordinations: one in the Tibetan tradition and another in the Chinese tradition. Svedberg recalls how Amita Nisatta once showed her lower arm, where she had received three small burn marks during the Chinese ordination ceremony as part of the bodhisattva ceremony (Svedberg 2011: 242). Amita Nisatta received several dharma names through her ordinations. At the Tibetan ordination, she was given the name Tin Lei, and as a fully ordained nun in the Chinese tradition, she was given the name Kwang Liu. The additional ordinations she undertook within the various Buddhist traditions were likely an expression of the ecumenical and unified view of Buddhism that seems to have permeated her teaching. Her theosophical background likely influenced her view of Buddhism as a fundamentally unified religion. Also important was the recognition of becoming a fully ordained nun (Svedberg 2011: 96), as taking full ordination in the Chinese tradition follows a path that other Asian nuns have taken (Lindberg Falk 2004).

Marcel Sirander was reordained in 1975. According to one of his disciples, the reordination took place in the same temple where Amita Nisatta was ordained as a bhikshuni nun in the Tiantai tradition in Hong Kong. Sirander was given the name Tao Wei Kwong Wu and permitted to establish the Lotus Buddhist Order in Sweden, a branch of the Lotus Buddhist Association in Hong Kong.[7] He passed away in 1983 and was buried at Nolby Cemetery, Alingsås.[8]

Both Sirander and Amita Nisatta represented an approach that included the centrality of Theravāda and Mahāyāna Buddhism, and they made efforts to find ways "to highlight a culturally stripped-down Buddhism that fits in the West" (Fredriksson 2013: 56).

During her lifetime, Amita Nisatta maintained a Buddhist network of national and international contacts, connecting with other convert monastics in Sri Lanka, such as Piadassi Thera and Narada Thera (Svedberg 2011: 96–97). She also brought together both Asian and convert Buddhists in Sweden to form the Swedish Buddhist Union around 1980, which the newly formed Thai, Sri Lankan and Zen organisations joined (Fredriksson 2013).

After Amita Nisatta died in 2001, her ashes were enshrined in a *stūpa* in Nepal (Gardell 2001; Almqvist 2009).

For a long time, Marcel Sirander and Amita Nisatta were the only Buddhist teachers in Sweden, and they came to play a crucial role in the early development of Buddhism there. Neither would establish a Swedish tradition of their own. However, their legacy can be seen in the networks of Buddhists who have cooperated and celebrated Vesak in the Malmö and Stockholm areas. In Malmö, where Marcel Sirander had several disciples, the Ekayana group was founded in the 1970s. The group later became Föreningen Malmö Buddhistcentrum, where several Buddhist groups, both converts and Asian, cooperated and held joint Vesak celebrations. Malmö Buddhistcentrum was dissolved in 2006. Another group promoting a broader, non-sectarian practice without a clear lineage is the association for Tibetan Buddhism in Gothenburg, established in 1994, which invites teachers from several Tibetan traditions.

In Stockholm, the Buddhist Union, formed in 1980, was followed by Sveriges Buddhistiska Samarbetsråd (SBS) in 1993, which in 2020 became a faith community called Sveriges Buddhistiska Gemenskap (the Swedish Buddhist Community, SBC). Today, the SBC serves as an umbrella organisation for both Asian and convert groups and facilitates state grants to faith communities. The SBC currently has twenty-four-member organisations that collectively serve around 11,000 registered individuals.[9]

In 1974, the Sixteenth Karmapa visited Sweden and performed the Black Crown Ceremony at Kulturhuset in Stockholm in front of a large audience. In 1976, the crganisation Karme Tenpe Gyaltsen was established, and Dorje Lopön lama Nga-wang[10] (1927–2011) was responsible for the Karma Kagyu tradition in Sweden until his death (see also the chapter by Stefan Larsson). In September 1980, the first traditional three-year retreat in Sweden began; six out of eight participants (all converts) completed the entire retreat, with some later becoming active as teachers. The retreat centre Karma Dechen Ösel Ling, located at Solbo, north of Fellings-bro, also houses the first Scandinavian *stūpa*, built in 1988 and inaugurated by the Dalai Lama. The official name of the *stūpa* is Du Khor Djangchub Chöten Töndröl Chenmo. The retreat centre also has an ash cemetery called the Mandala Grove, where memorial ceremonies and funerals are held. In Hägersten, Stockholm, the society also operates a meditation centre called Karma Shedrup Dargye Ling, where meditation sessions, sadhanas, dharma teaching and study circles are organ-ised throughout the year.[11] Karma Tenpe Gyaltsen is also represented in Örebro.

Several other Tibetan groups have also been established in Sweden. Another organisation which was founded early, in 1979, is Sakya Changchub Chöling, by Khenchen Sherab Gyaltsen Amipa Rinpoche. They offer study and meditation in accordance with the Tibetan Buddhist Sakya tradition. Since 2014, when Khenchen passed away, Khenpo Tashi Sangpo Amipa has served as the head teacher of the centre. He resides in Switzerland at the Thubten Changchub Ling centre and travels to Sweden several times a year to teach.[12]

Other Tibetan groups include Karma Yönten Ling in Scania; the Yeshin Norbu meditation centre in Stockholm, which is part of the Foundation for the Preserva-tion of Mahāyāna Tradition (FPMT); the New Kadampa, with meditation centres in Stockholm and Gothenburg; and Diamond Way Buddhism in Stockholm.

The growing interest in meditation during the 1970s and 1980s led to Swed-ish meditators inviting prominent *vipassanā* teachers to visit Sweden. Since the mid-1980s, the Vipassana group in Stockholm has regularly organised meditation retreats, and since the early 1990s, Swedish representatives in S.N. Goenka's med-itation tradition have arranged intensive ten-day courses. Since 2007, Dhamma Sobhana in Ödeshög has served as the Nordic centre for *vipassanā* meditation in the tradition of S.N. Goenka, offering 20–25 courses every year, attended by around 2,000 meditators.[13]

Triratana (formerly Friends of the Western Buddhist Order) has been active in Sweden since the early 1980s, with a centre in Stockholm (Stockholms buddhist-center) and a retreat facility, Dharmagiri, located north of Sala. In Sweden, there are about thirty ordained members (mitras), who also lead local groups in Gothen-burg, Linköping, and Hudiksvall.[14]

In 2004, one of Marcel Sirander's disciples in southern Sweden founded a Chan temple in Malmö, the Tao Zen temple, which caters to converts and focuses on puja, meditation and studies. It also conducts naming ceremonies, weddings and funerals.[15] Another of Sirander's disciples became involved with the Arya Maitreya Mandala, AMM and was appointed dharmacarya[16] (teacher and priest). He later left the AMM and continued teaching independently, including teaching meditation at the state prison in Malmö.[17]

Several traditions of Zen Buddhism have become established as convert groups in Sweden:

The Zenbuddhistiska Samfundet, established in 1982, stemming from Sanbō Kyōdan through the tradition of the American teacher Philip Kapleu, operates a training temple, Zengården, in Fellingsbro, as well as city centres for meditation in Stockholm, Göteborg, Lund, Tampere (Finland), Cologne (Germany) and Glasgow (Scotland). At Zengården, full-time training and retreats are offered. The teachers, Sante Poromaa and Kanja Odland, trained with Philip Kapleau and later with his successor Bodhin Kjolhede. The have been teaching full-time since 1998 and 2001, respectively.[18]

The Swedish Soto-Zen Association, in the tradition of Taisen Deshimaru and closely connected to the main temple La Gendronnière in France, was established in 1984. In Sweden, the Soto-Zen Association has *dōjō*s in Uppsala, Göteborg, Lund and Stockholm.[19]

In Gothenburg, the So Gyo Zen Dojo is part of the international Kosen sangha and is led by Rei Kiku Femenias, who received dharma transmission in 2015.[20]

In Umeå, in northern Sweden, Ordinary Mind is connected to Tavallinen Mieli Zendo in Tampere, Finland.

Svalornas sangha is part of the Zen Peacemaker tradition of Bernie Glassman, focusing on socially engaged Buddhism and interreligious work. Pake Hall, who received dharma transmission from Barbara Salaam Wegemüller in 2023, has also been involved with interfaith pilgrim walks, teaching meditation in prisons and the Books Behind Bars project (where inmates can borrow books on Buddhism and meditation), and ordaining trees in order to help preserve old forests.[21]

Another association of converts consists of meditators connected to the Order of Interbeing and students of the late Vietnamese monk Thích Nhất Hạnh, practising in the Plum Village Tradition (Fredriksson 2013). The association was founded in 2021 and promotes mindfulness and Zen meditation.[22]

Asian Buddhists in Sweden

The Asian Buddhist groups are very diverse; their internal compositions vary, as do their immigration backgrounds. Asian immigration to Sweden dates back to the first decades of the twentieth century, when some Chinese peddlers travelled around Sweden, but it was only in connection with the Second World War that Asian immigration to Sweden truly began. Among the first to settle in Sweden were Asian sailors from Hong Kong and Indonesia who had served in the Swedish merchant navy (Hübinette 2024: 42).

The first group of Asian Buddhists came to Sweden in the 1960s. In 1964, thirty-three Tibetan girls, aged 14 to 19, were sent from India to Småland to receive an education, while a corresponding group of boys was sent to Norway. The Swedish NGO, IM (Individuell människohjälp, Eng: Swedish Development Partner), guided by the principle of religious freedom, had responded to the Dalai Lama's appeal to support Tibetans in exile through education. The girls were accommodated at the IM home, Strand, in Småland, along with an elderly Tibetan couple who were responsible for the girls' language lessons. Sister Amita Nisatta oversaw their religious education, and, occasionally, lamas from Copenhagen visited (Davidsson 2000). The thirty-three Tibetan girls were trained in healthcare and agriculture and were eventually able to return to India. Some of them, however, stayed and started families in Sweden (Svanberg 1988b: 424). Today, the Tibetan exile community consists of a small handful of individuals, primarily concentrated in the Jönköping area. To support education back in the homeland, the Swedish-Tibetan School and Culture Association was established in 1988 and works to build schools in Tibet (Plank 2015a).

During the 1960s and 1970s, several left-wing students from Japan and other Asian countries came to Sweden, including guest students on Sida scholarships from South Korea, Thailand, Singapore, Vietnam and Malaysia. Some of these students stayed in Sweden after completing their studies. Additionally, several Japanese women came to Sweden to marry Swedish men, and Nichiren Buddhism came with them. Thus, Soka Gakkai has had members in Sweden since the late 1960s. The organisation was formally established in 1981, and in 1989, the Villa Baggås in Saltsjöbaden, outside Stockholm, was purchased and became the Swedish centre for Nichiren Buddhism. According to the organisation, the Swedish branch of Soka Gakkai has approximately 600 members and is organised in three districts, focused on Stockholm, West Sweden and South Sweden.[23]

In the 1970s, a larger group of Cantonese- and Hakka-speaking Chinese came to Sweden, primarily from Hong Kong. Many established themselves in the restaurant industry and thus became concentrated in the major cities (Svanberg 1988a: 222). With financial support from Taiwan, the Chinese community established a temple in Rosersberg, outside Stockholm, in 1996: the International Buddhist Progress Society (IBPS) Sweden.[24] It is a branch of the main temple Fó guāng shān, promoting the Humanistic Buddhism of Xīng Yún.

When refugees from Vietnam began arriving in 1979, it marked the first time that a larger Asian group immigrated to Sweden, totalling around 5,000 individuals. The Vietnamese refugee group was one of the most homogeneous refugee groups that came to Sweden. This homogeneity resulted from specific humanitarian selection criteria: refugees were required to speak Cantonese (to facilitate interpretation, as Cantonese-speaking Chinese were already in Sweden); entire families were selected; priority was given to those whom other countries could not accommodate; and preference was also given to those who were disabled or ill. Subsequent family immigration has been encouraged to support reunification (Ragvald 1982; Beach 1988; Londos 2004). Many belonging to the Sino-Vietnamese group had lived in Vietnam for several generations, and some children spoke Vietnamese more fluently than Chinese. Due to the high concentration of Vietnamese Buddhists in Scania, Sweden's first Buddhist burial site was established at Fosie Cemetery in Malmö in 1989.

One of the main Vietnamese temples is Phật Quang Temple in Gothenburg (Pure Land-tradition), with three branches in Stockholm, Kalmar and Gävle. They are organised under a joint association, the Vietnamesiskt Buddhistförbund i Sverige, to qualify for grants for faith communities in Sweden. Another Vietnamese temple, Đại Bi Tâm in Bjuv, is seemingly not part of the SBC, although it has previously received state grants for faith communities. This temple also has a branch in Gnosjö.

During the 1980s and 1990s, female immigration from Asia to Sweden increased, as women from the Philippines, Thailand, Japan, South Korea, Hong Kong, Singapore and Taiwan married Swedish men. The Asian population in Sweden doubled during this period, reaching approximately 32,000 people of East or Southeast Asian origin. This period also marked the shift when adoptees became a minority among Asians living in Sweden (Hübinette 2024: 45–46).

Unlike other Buddhist diaspora groups, which are typically based on family immigration, the demographic profile of the Thai group in Sweden is distinct: eight out of ten Thais who come to Sweden through family immigration are women, and their temples are spread across the country, not only concentrated around major cities like Gothenburg, Stockholm, and Malmö as with other Buddhist groups (Plank 2004, 2015a, 2015b). The Thais are therefore one of the few immigrant groups that are widely distributed throughout Sweden, in both sparsely populated areas and large cities (Hübinette 2009). Additionally, in recent years, since 2006, Thais have formed one of the largest groups of labour immigrants, with the majority coming to work seasonally in agriculture and forestry, especially as berry pickers.

The institutionalisation of Thai Buddhism in Sweden started in 1984, when Phra P. J. Chutinattharo Thera was invited by Buddhists of Thai, Sri Lankan and Chinese origin to establish the country's first Buddhist temple. This was made possible after several years of donations and savings, which allowed for the purchase of an older house in a summer cottage area on the island of Värmdö, some 20 kilometres east of Stockholm. Here, the Buddharama Temple was established as a branch of the Mahānikāya order. As the only Thai monk with Swedish residency, he became well known as Luang Ta among the gradually growing diaspora in the Scandinavian countries (Plank 2004: 251–252; Chutinattharo n.d.). (See also Chapter 4 by Preedee Hongsaton.) With the exception of two temples (in Bispgården and Fredrika), all Thai temples in Sweden have been established due to the efforts and religious needs of the Thai Buddhist women living in a particular geographical area (Plank 2015b). Supporting the sangha sometimes also occurs in remote areas and at unexpected places (see Figure 2.1).

The establishment of a temple typically follows a pattern. (1) A group of Buddhists in a locality comes together and invites a monk from a nearby temple, which may be located in another Scandinavian country. (2) The monk then begins making regular visits to the congregation, and a discussion is initiated about the desire to house a monk on a permanent basis. The monk assesses whether the congregation is robust enough to assume the responsibilities (expenses and food logistics) required to operate a temple association. (3) If so, the next step is to register an association and rent an apartment or house where a monk is invited to reside. The temple association then usually corresponds to a *samnak song*. (4) To achieve the status of a *wat*, at least three monks need to live there permanently, and the association must also obtain official authorisation from the Mahathera Samagom, the

Figure 2.1 A special meeting. When migrating to a new country, supporting the sangha sometimes occurs at unexpected places and in new material forms. The Thai Buddhist nun has lived in south Sweden for twenty years and has regularly received packages with food gifts from the laywoman. This is the first time they meet in person, in a parking lot in Mora, where the self-employed woman has her food truck. The picture was used with permission from the nun. Editing: Kristian Niemi.

highest Buddhist council in Thailand. The Department of Religious Affairs, the governmental body that oversees all activities between the Thai state and the Thai sangha, is responsible for missionary monks who travel abroad, and requests for new monks to a locality are sent to this department (Payutto 2009). Occasionally, a monk from a nearby temple relocates to the new locality. As mentioned, two exceptions to this general pattern are notable: in Bispgården in Jämtland, where the royal pavilion was built in commemoration of King Chulalongkorn's visit, there was a need for representation from the monastic sangha; and in Fredrika in Lappland, the successor at the Värmdö temple had a vision in 2004 to establish a large-scale retreat facility, raising hopes for religious tourism and economic growth in an area heavily affected by depopulation. Known as the "Temple Mount," it remains, some twenty years later, one of the most widely reported topics on Buddhism in Swedish newspapers, with both national documentaries and local coverage, due to the extraordinary financial liabilities and attempts of fraud by outsiders (Plank, Raddock & Selander 2016).

Today, the Thai temples belong to either the Mahā Nikāya or Dhammayuttika Nikāya orders and function as nodes for the Thai diaspora in Sweden, with their catchment area often extending over several regions. It is not uncommon for lay-people to drive one to three hours to reach a temple on weekends. The temples also function as transnational arenas for Thai Buddhism, especially visible during major holidays and festivals celebrated in Swedish temples – monks can travel from neighbouring countries to participate (primarily from the larger temples in Norway, Denmark and Finland), as do also other Theravāda monks of various Asian nationalities. Most importantly, groups of laypeople also travel to different temple locations to make merit by offering financial support during major celebrations. A temple typically needs to organise two or three such celebrations a year to secure funding for heat, rent, and other expenses.

In addition, the new Buddhist religious movement Dhammakāya has been present in Sweden since 2010, with its main temple in Borås and branches in Stockholm and Gävle.

The first Sri Lankan Buddhist temple, Stockholm Buddhist Vihara, was established in 1985 with assistance from the Sri Lankan Embassy. It belongs to the Siam Nikaya order. The *vihāra* has housed several prominent Sri Lankan monks who learned Swedish and taught in many places in Sweden. The community consists mostly of families who immigrated from Sri Lanka. Bhante K. Sri Dhammaratana Maha Thera, who arrived in 1989, is the Chief Prelate (Sangha Nayake) of Sri Lankan Buddhist temples in Scandinavia, and the longest staying monk in Sweden.

There is also a Burmese Buddhist Association (BBFSE), formed in 2007. In 2012, Sweden's first Burmese Buddhist temple, Tiratana, was inaugurated in Hjortkvarn in Örebro County, where the association is based. It has approximately 170 members from ethnic groups from Burma/Myanmar.

There can be significant differences between the Buddhist groups in terms of segregation and integration, even though they might be situated in the same city. In our research project *Lived Religion and Social Mobility among Migrants in Sweden*, we conducted fieldwork in Gothenburg among Mahāyāna Buddhists connected to the Vietnamese temple and Theravāda Buddhists associated with the Thai temple. We observed that these communities face different challenges. The Vietnamese community, located in Angered, tends to be quite segregated in terms of language, culture, and religion. They have minimal interaction with other religious groups in the area but maintain strong transnational connections with other Vietnamese temples, including one in France, which they occasionally visit. Many community members struggle with the Swedish language, and for some, interactions with Swedes remain limited even after living in Sweden for many years, especially among first-generation immigrants.

In contrast, the Thai temple on Hisingen demonstrates higher levels of language proficiency and civic literacy, particularly among women who moved to Sweden after marrying Swedish men and having children. This difference is also reflected in the temples' organisational structures. The Thai temple benefits from the support of Swedish-born and raised men who are knowledgeable about managing nonprofit associations and navigating building permit applications.

Both temples have a strong presence of and active participation from women, who often describe their temples as a small part of Vietnam or Thailand within Sweden. Many laypersons, primarily women, assist with tasks such as cooking in the temple. Both temples host cultural events, including the dragon dance at the Vietnamese temple and various musical performances and dances at both locations. These temples serve as important social and cultural hubs, especially during holidays like New Year's celebrations. They offer overnight accommodations during holidays and other occasions, often used for short weekend retreats. Extended stays, typically lasting up to a month, are also possible, especially during times of distress or for meditation purposes. Many interviewees have shared personal experiences of finding solace and refuge in Buddha within the temple, particularly during periods of depression, burnout or domestic problems. The Thai temple has also provided support to women needing to return to Thailand after divorcing their husbands, and the monks can also provide assistance with various everyday matters.

Sociologist Erika Willander (2019) notes that there over 100 localities in Sweden where Buddhists meet and practise together, and she is likely correct if all smaller and informal groups are counted. However, when considering only organisations and groups with an address and a physical meeting place, either their own or shared with another group, the number is approximately seventy-five (see complete list in Table 2.2). The Theravāda groups encompass more than thirty Thai temples established across the country, from south to north, as well as four Sri Lankan and one Burmese temple. These temples have 124 registered monks, but probably around 80 are actively serving. The Mahāyāna groups encompass one Chinese temple in the Stockholm area with two nuns, and eight Vietnamese temples, with the main ones located in Gothenburg, Bjuv, and Malmö. Approximately fifteen to twenty monks and nuns are associated with these temples. Although converts are fewer in number, they have established around thirty city temples and city meditation centres, along with five retreat centres in rural areas.

Since there are few second-generation Buddhists born to native Swedes, the use of convert and Asian Buddhists as analytical categories is still applicable to distinguish between those who have taken up a Buddhist practice as adults and those who have migrated to Sweden or are born to migrant parents and thus have a relation to Buddhism as a culturally transmitted heritage through their families. This is in line with what Prebish (1979) identified as two distinct lines of development for Buddhism in America, which he later (1993) typified as "ethnic Asian-American Buddhist groups" and "mostly members of European origin" (Prebish 1993: 189). Other scholars, such as Numrich (1996), Fields (1998) and Seager (1999), have referred to these as immigrant and convert groups. As in other Nordic countries, convert Buddhists mainly focus on meditation and reading as religious practices, whereas Asian Buddhists mainly engage in devotional practices centred on merit-making. However, several of the Asian temples include meditation either as part of the daily rituals in the temple or as part of training during larger celebrations or lunar observance days. Baumann (2002), like McMahan (2008), argues that the significant difference in interpretations of Buddhist doctrine and practice is about traditional or modernist branches that affect both Asian Buddhists and converts.

Stefan Larsson has argued that the boundaries between convert and Asian groups may not be that distinct. He has also noted that "diaspora Buddhists can be modernists and convert Buddhists can be traditionalists" and that they may also influence each other (Larsson 2020: 86). This is especially true regarding a particular subcategory of convert Buddhists that I have termed the "Svensson-Buddhists" (Plank 2004), named after one of the most common Swedish surnames. One informant used this term to describe himself as a non-practising Buddhist who wants to support the temples as cultural institutions in the same way that many Swedes continue to pay church tax to support the activities of the Church of Sweden. This could be understood as "belonging without believing" (Marchisio & Pisati 1999; McIntosh 2015; Oakes 2015). As a gendered category, with predominately Swedish men in relationships with Thai partners, the Svensson-Buddhists can relate to the Buddhist tradition in many different ways. Not only do they take part in rituals and social interactions in the temples, thus learning traditional forms of Buddhism, they also help out in various practical ways by running temple boards, managing finances, filling in forms, driving monks, doing carpentry and more. In short, their support helps the temples function as religious institutions, and their involvement may also facilitate their partners' connections to a temple. They might have different ways of relating to religion and to Buddhist practice, where some might be meditation oriented, others might be devotionally oriented, while still others might have no interest in religion.

However, most Asian Buddhists in Sweden are not members of a temple, nor do they visit the temple regularly. Instead, they might come to the temple for New Year celebrations, birthdays, national holidays or other festivities, or when a loved one is ill or has died. There is a knowledge gap concerning the role religion plays in their everyday lives and the extent to which their self-understanding also includes a secular outlook. A recent study by Thurfjell and Willander (2023) on secularity in a multireligious Sweden shows that men are generally more secular than women. This aligns with what many other researchers have noted: that women tend to be more religious than men across most religious cultures and traditions (Trzebiatowska & Bruce 2012). However, another observation made by Thurfjell and Willander is that the most important factor determining if one views oneself as secular is close relationships – if a mother, father or partner is secular. This raises questions about how the intermarriages between Thai women and Swedish men might affect the development of Buddhism in Sweden in the coming decades. What does Buddhist secularity look like for those born into families with a Buddhist background? And how might this affect their affiliation with Buddhist temples? Could these mixed marriages contribute to the secularisation of Buddhism and to the next generation becoming post-Buddhists, that is, individuals born into a family with a Buddhist background but who do not necessarily identify as Buddhist?

Translations and publications by Swedish Buddhists

Converts have come to fill an essential role as translators and interpreters of Buddhist teachings. In Sweden, however, few female Buddhist teachers have written or received assistance writing their biographies or publishing their teachings. Therefore, reading the history of Buddhism in Sweden through published books tends to be done through an overrepresentation of male Buddhist voices. Male teachers have been assisted in publishing their life stories, anecdotes or Buddhist teachings. As a telling example, the teachings of Marcel Sirander were published in two books: *Buddha, Dharma, Sangha* (Sirander 1973) and *Den buddhistiska livsåskådningen* (Sirander [Tao Wei] 2000). The teachings of Amita Nisatta, however, have not been collected or printed.

Early books written in Swedish included short introductory texts and translations of the *Dhammapada* from Pāli. Several were written by Gunnar Gällmo (1946–2023), an author of science fiction and translator of Pāli and Esperanto: *Praktisk buddhism* (*Practical Buddhism*) (Gällmo 1986), *Några fakta om buddhismen* (*Some Facts on Buddhism*) (Gällmo 1997) and *Buddhas liv* (*The Life of Buddha*) (Gällmo 1999a). Gällmo also translated the *Dhammapada* from Pāli (Gällmo 1999b).

However, the first translation of the *Dhammapada* directly from Pāli to Swedish was completed in 1967 by Rune E. A. Johansson (1918–1981). Neither a historian of religion nor a classically trained philologist, he held a Lic Phil in Psychology. Johansson became an internationally recognised scholarly voice. His exceptional knowledge of languages, particularly Pāli, combined with a deep personal interest in Buddhism, enabled him to bring fresh interpretations to Buddhist texts, using psychological perspectives to explore central Buddhist concepts. In doing so, he also broadened the academic discipline of Psychology, which until then had primarily focused on studying the human psyche based on a Judeo-Christian cultural context. Johansson worked for a period as a university lecturer at Lund University, conducted research at Tel Aviv University, and studied Sanskrit at the University of Calcutta and Pāli at the University of Ceylon. He also spent some time working at the Norwegian Defense Research Institute. In addition to directly translating both the *Dhammapada* (1967) and the *Sutta Nipāta* (1976) from Pāli into Swedish, he published a teaching aid for learning Pāli that came to be used internationally (1973), as well as three books in English: *Citta, Mano, Vinnana: a Psychosemantic Investigation* (1967), *The Psychology of Nirvana* (1969) and *The Dynamic Psychology of Early Buddhism* (1979). In 1972, Rune E. A. Johansson, together with his wife Margot, established a scholarship foundation aimed at promoting scientific research that sheds light on the development of Buddhism and its ideological content. Over the years, the foundation has supported researchers in the fields of the History of Religions and Philology at Swedish universities. The foundation is managed by Uppsala University.[25]

Several contemporary Swedish Buddhist teachers have published books: the Zen Buddhist priest Sante Poromaa (b. 1958), who lives at Zengården and oversees several Zen centres in Sweden, Finland and Scotland, has authored several books on topics including Buddhist practice (1997), science and rebirth (2008) and the climate challenge (2019). His wife, Kanja Odland (b. 1963), also a priest and teacher, has published a collection of notes on Zen practice (2013).

Another female author is Marie Ericsson (b 1948), a *vipassanā* teacher who learned to meditate with Goenka in India in the early 1970s. She has trained with several Western and Asian *vipassanā* teachers and is active in Vipassanagruppen in Stockholm. Ericsson has written a commentary on the central meditation text the *Satipaṭṭhāna Sutta* (Ericsson 2011a) and a book introducing meditation and Theravāda Buddhism (Ericsson 2011b).

Several Buddhist groups have translated and published texts specific to their tradition. Triratana has its own bookstore at their Stockholms Buddhistcenter, where various translations of Sangharakshita's texts are sold, along with puja texts for recitations and Jataka stories in Swedish.[26]

Humanistic Buddhism, as taught by the Fó guāng shān order, has been translated into Swedish by Buddhists affiliated with the Buddha's Light International Association at the temple in Rosersberg, Stockholm (e.g., Hsing Yun 2003, 2016, 2019).

Also among the male voices are several celebrity Buddhists who have gained public recognition. The first of these was Henning Sjöström (1922–2011). Born in Burträsk, in the northern region of Västerbotten, he came from a poor farming family and was one of twelve siblings. Sjöström moved to Stockholm, where he worked as a defence attorney and became known in connection with the "Haijby scandal" when he defended Kurt Haijby, who was accused of blackmailing King Gustav V of Sweden. Sjöström was also a disciple of Marcel Sirander, and together they published *Vägen till Buddha* (The Path to Buddha) in 1967. In this book, Sjöström, in a dialogical format, asks his teacher the classical question that also preoccupied the Greco-Bactrian King Menander I (Pāli: Milinda) in his dialogue with the monk Nāgasena: What is it that identifies as "I," and how can the doctrine of *anatta* be understood?

> However. I, Henning Sjöström, say – this is me! My body is mine. My mind functions are mine. /---/ Would I then all of a sudden deny my own body. Not recognise it? Impossible! [my translation]
>
> (Sjöström & Shunyata 1967: 80–81)

Henning Sjöström continued to be involved with high-profile cases and converted from Christianity to Buddhism during a stay in Sri Lanka, which he wrote about in his autobiography *Dagbok från Djungelklostret* (Diary from the Jungle Monastery) (Sjöström 1968).

Another celebrity Buddhist is comedian and actor Claes Malmberg (b. 1961), who, in two books, has described his controversial life, marked by fame, drug and alcohol abuse, incarceration, and his journey to finding the Tibetan temple in Stockholm, where he learned to meditate with Lama Wangchuck (Malmberg & Ohlson 2008; Malmberg & Karlsson 2016).

However, the most loved and appreciated public Buddhist was Björn Natthiko Lindeblad (1961–2022), who, in 1992, took up the ordained life as a Thai monk and lived at the Wat Pah Nanachat monastery in northeastern Thailand. After facing several health issues, he disrobed in 2008, keeping his monk's name as his middle name. Upon returning to lay life, he experienced a life crisis and deep depression, eventually redirecting his path to become a lay spiritual teacher. He married, taught meditation, gave lectures and shared his life wisdom on social platforms and through Swedish media. Twice he spoke on the Swedish radio show *Summer*: the first time in 2012, when he was chosen as the listener's summer host, and in 2020, when he was marked by the disease ALS and addressed, in a deeply personal way, questions about facing difficulties and suffering in life and how to approach death and leaving loved ones behind. His autobiography, *Jag kan ha fel* (Lindeblad et al. 2020) was translated into more than twenty languages and, in 2022, it was published in English as *I May Be Wrong and Other Wisdoms from Life as a Forest Monk,* thus making Björn Natthiko Lindeblad widely known internationally.[27]

Natthiko Lindeblad initiated a public discussion on the right to euthanasia. In his last post on Instagram, after his death, he wrote: "If you think, like me, that everyone, under certain circumstances, should receive society's help for a dignified and safe death, then make yourself heard. Lex Natthiko, I wouldn't mind [my translation]."[28] He died peacefully at his own chosen time, around noon on 17 January 2022 at age 60.

Figuring out the Buddhist demographics of Sweden

Estimating religious demographics in Sweden is a challenge due to the absence of public data on religious affiliation. Since the last government religion census in 1930, Sweden has not maintained public data sets specifying individuals' religious affiliations. As a result, there is a lack of registered data on religious affiliation. Instead, the Swedish system relies on religious communities to register their members. This data is then utilised by the Swedish Agency for Support for Faith Communities, which plays a crucial role in administering grants to these communities, thereby supporting their activities and initiatives.

Since no reliable statistics exist on religious affiliation, various estimates have been made to approximate the number of Buddhists. Additional data on religious affiliation is generated via the SOM institute (Society, Opinion, Media) at Gothenburg University, which has conducted an annual survey since 1986 on issues related to politics, media and lifestyle. The survey is based on responses from approximately 20,000 randomly selected Swedes. Other research institutes, such as Novus and Kantar Sifo, also conduct surveys based on voluntary and anonymous survey responses.

In the 1930 census, the last time religious affiliation was recorded, 99.7 per cent of all residents in Sweden reported that they were members of the Church of Sweden, that is, Lutheran Christians belonging to the state church (Willander 2019). At that time, only fifteen individuals answered that they belonged to Asian religious traditions, such as Bramaism, Buddhism, Confucianism and Taoism, as well as Sufism, Islam and Muhammedanism (Sorgenfrei 2018).

Almost a hundred years later, in 2024, Sweden had a population of 10.5 million, of which more than 2 million, or 20 per cent, were born abroad (Statistics Sweden 2024-02-22). Sweden has been identified as one of the world's most secular countries and also one of the most multireligious in Europe (Thurfjell & Willander 2022), alongside Great Britain, France and the Netherlands. Membership in the Church of Sweden has almost halved since the 1930 Census, dropping to 52.1 per cent in 2023 (Svenska kyrkan 2023). The Muslim minority constitutes the largest non-Christian group in Sweden, with several hundred local congregations across the country. The Jewish and Buddhist minorities have been regarded as roughly equal in size. However, the Jewish congregations are primarily concentrated in Stockholm, Gothenburg and Malmö, whereas Buddhists meet regularly at more than a hundred locations nationwide (Willander 2019: 22).

According to the Swedish Buddhist Community (SBC), they serve more than 11,000 registered members, which is 0.1 per cent of the total population (SBC no date). However, this figure reflects only a smaller portion of the Buddhist population. The SOM Institute, in their 2019 survey, estimates that 0.8 per cent of the population identifies as Buddhist, which would correspond to approximately 80,000 Buddhists (Weissenbilder 2019). The SOM surveys are representative of the entire population, and the statistics are not dependent on the administration of governmental grants and membership fees and are thus "not limited to those eligible for grants" (Willander 2019: 42). However, another research institute, Novus, using their "Swedish Panel," a public opinion panel consisting of approximately 50,000 randomly recruited members and claiming to provide a representative picture of Sweden's population, argues that the proportion of Buddhists is 0.3 per cent (approximately 31,500 individuals). Novus claims that the public space in Sweden is too inclusive and that minorities have been given a disproportionally large space, leading to a picture of a society that is not representative: "the focus on minorities leads to a delusion about what Sweden looks like . . . [the adults are not] particularly religious, regardless of skin colour or origin. Sweden is a very secularised country, and a tiny group consider themselves to be very religious [my translation]" (Novus 2023-11-05).

Demographic data from Statistics Sweden can also give an indication regarding the largest Asian groups in Sweden and some of their distinct features (see Table 2.1). However, the statistics are difficult to interpret in terms of religious belonging, as some migrant groups are not representative of the religious majority of home countries. For example, many Sri Lankans in Sweden are part of the Tamil diaspora. Similarly, many Chinese migrants may have a secular outlook on life and no religious affiliation. These statistics also include adopted children and Swedes born in Asia.

Swedish legislation and faith communities

The Swedish constitution regulates religious freedom, and the legislation in place stipulates certain conditions for faith communities. A religious community can apply to be registered; however, practising religion is neither dependent on community membership nor on the community being officially registered. The Instrument of Government (SFS 1974: 152) emphasises the freedom to "practice one's religion alone or together with others" as an absolute right (ch. 2, § 1). Additionally,

Table 2.1 Swedish demographic patterns in the twenty-first century, with ten-year intervals. The statistics show the number of people born in foreign countries, categorised by gender. The Asian countries selected in the table all have potential Buddhist populations that may have migrated to Sweden. However, there are many objections that could be made, since it does not account for adopted individuals, or Swedes born abroad. The three largest groups with Asian origins are those born in Thailand (total: 45,109), China (total: 37,172) and Vietnam (total: 21,528).

		2001	*2011*	*2021*
Cambodia	male	149	207	295
	female	184	313	477
China	male	3,589	10,155	15,284
	female	5,370	15,502	21,888
Japan	male	915	957	1,116
	female	1,393	2,140	2,681
Laos	male	182	202	188
	female	196	284	323
Mongolia	male	15	550	2,388
	female	33	800	2,923
Myanmar	male	81	754	798
	female	48	682	767
Singapore	male	220	314	435
	female	272	440	623
Sri Lanka	male	2,592	2,981	3,564
	female	3,372	3,809	4,378
South Korea	male	3,379	4,086	4,666
	female	5,941	6,413	7,129
Taiwan	male	233	411	760
	female	432	770	1,295
Thailand	male	2,820	7,352	9,732
	female	8,365	26,261	35,377
Vietnam	male	5,288	6,973	9,811
	female	5,928	8,202	11,717

Source: Statistics Sweden, born in a foreign country.

Sweden has ratified the European Convention on Human Rights, and the convention has been part of Swedish domestic law since 1995.

When the Church of Sweden was separated from the state at the turn of the millennium, a law (SFS 1988: 1593) on faith communities was added, which regulates how faith communities can be registered and outlines their rights and obligations. At the time, the definition of faith communities was based on a Christian understanding as "a community for religious activity, which includes organising worship." In 2025, this law will be updated to better reflect a multireligious society, adopting a broader understanding of what activities can take place. A faith community will now be defined as "a community that practices religious activities in which worship, prayer, meditation or other rituals are included" [my translation].

Support to faith communities is regulated by law (SFS 1999: 932), which stipulates in Section 3 that such support may only be given if a faith community "1. contributes to maintaining and strengthening the fundamental values on which society rests, and 2. is stable and has its own vitality." A planned update to this law is expected to specify minimum requirements. Under the proposed changes, an association must serve at least 2,500 individuals who are residents of Sweden and have been operating in the country for at least five years to qualify for support. A further condition is that the community must derive its primary funding from residents of Sweden. The many Buddhist temples and organisations are primarily local, and very few, if any, would individually meet the criteria of serving 2,500 people. Thus, the umbrella organisation, the Swedish Buddhist Cooperation Council, decided to change its name to Sweden's Buddhist Community, the SBC, and register as a religious community in 2020, enabling individual temples and associations to become members of the SBC. In § 1 of the SBC's statutes, it is made clear that the member organisations retain their independent activities and distinctiveness "with the Buddha's teaching and practice common to all." To qualify for state grants and state fee assistance (Buddhist dāna), § 2 of the statutes clarifies the democratic principles guiding the SBC's operations: opposing racism, discrimination and violence; promoting equality; and advocating for basic democratic values, including gender equality. In addition, it is made clear that the member associations must "promote Buddhist principles and ways of life in theory and practice that are based on the Buddha's teachings on the Three Jewels, the Four Noble Truths and the Eightfold Path" [my translation]. The SBC's activities also aim to support the development of Buddhist activities in Sweden, foster peaceful coexistence regardless of cultural and religious backgrounds, advocate for environmental sustainability, and promote humanity and compassion in Sweden and the rest of the world. The SBC has two types of membership: an ordinary membership for Buddhist organisations that want to operate based on the SBC's purpose, and a membership called friends of the SBC, consisting of private individuals or organisations that sympathise with the community's activities as well as so-called dāna members, which allows one to contribute Buddhist dāna through the tax bill.

Buddhist dāna, administered through the tax system, is a form of state fee assistance that has its basis in how the Church of Sweden has been financed via the so-called church tax. Religious communities can thus receive government assistance in administering membership fees determined by income. In addition to these membership fees, all residents of Sweden pay a funeral fee, regardless of religious affiliation. This fee finances funeral services and goes to the Church of Sweden, which has a state mandate to ensure that funerals can take place. The funeral fee covers expenses for crematoria, funeral chapels, burial grounds and funeral staff. "Simply put, the funeral fee is used to ensure that all people, regardless of faith and denomination, receive dignified treatment when they die" (Svenska kyrkan 2024). The Church of Sweden thus administers the Buddhist burial sites in Sweden as they are part of existing cemeteries.

The first Buddhist burial site in Sweden was established in Malmö at Fosie Cemetery to meet the needs of an aging Vietnamese community. Quarter number 9 was put into use in 1989 and included approximately 140 graves. In 2022, the Buddhist burial sites were expanded by another block, Quarter number 8, which provided 104 new graves expected to suffice for another twenty years (Svenska kyrkan 2022). In Stockholm, the cemetery administration, in collaboration with the SBC, has developed a Buddhist burial section at Strandkyrkogården, where a *stūpa* has been erected. The site has room for 130 coffin burials, 225 urn burials and anonymous ash burials (Stockholms stad Kyrkogårdsförvaltningen, n.d).

As noted, Swedish legislation emphasises the absolute right to "practice one's religion alone or together with others." However, the United Nation's Special Rapporteur Nazila Ghanea has pointed out that the Swedish formulations are narrow and that international conventions recognise the right to express one's religion more comprehensively in ways that also include religious holidays and clothing and view religion as more than just a private matter: the "historical homogeneity of Swedish society and its secular model has informed an understanding of 'religion' as being individual and private. However, societal structures have significantly changed, including as a result of recent migration. The reality is that religiosity is now far more diverse within society."[29]

The Special Rapporteur has also commented on the consequences of viewing religion primarily as a private matter, noting that this perspective can impede equal access to rights. Additionally, lack of data on religious belonging was also identified as an obstacle to working with human rights issues. Ghanea called for improved statistical data and research on the situations of different religious groups. The Special Rapporteur also noted that there are regional and local differences that must be taken into account, as these can affect how individuals exercise their right to freedom of religion and belief.[30]

Although no hate crimes targeting Buddhist temples were reported in the 2023 report from the Swedish National Council for Crime Prevention (BRÅ 2023), there have been several examples of how societal norms and legislation have struggled to accommodate an ordained lifestyle and understand the material aspects of religious practice. A narrow understanding of religion led the Swedish Tax Authority to question *piṇḍapāta* (almsround/food gifts) as a religious practice and argue that food and living at a temple should be considered taxable benefits for monks, classifying them as food and housing allowances. In 2020, Swedish local media reported that monks at Wat Pah Sokjai in Brunflo, Jämtland, left the temple because the temple organisation lacked sufficient funds to cover the additional taxes. This was not the first such case. In a series of tax disputes, dating back to 2013, the Tax Authority maintained that food gifts constituted taxable fringe benefits and that living in a Buddhist temple should be understood as a taxable housing allowance and that the monks' activities should therefore be taxed. The tax authority argued that food and lodging could be understood as compensation for the services provided by the monks. Not only did this have devastating economic consequences for the affected Buddhist associations, which did not have the finances for this and were consequently forced to reduce their activities, but the SBC also viewed the interpretation as a threat to the entire Buddhist community in Sweden. It also, the SBC argued, violated the principle of equal treatment, as Christian monasteries have been exempted from tax under a praxis of "free vivre." The SBC raised funds to challenge the decision in court and was assisted by a defence lawyer. In 2021, the case was decided in the Administrative Court, which ruled in favour of the Buddhist congregations. The court recognised that Buddhists temples were part of an ancient religious tradition and determined that living in a temple should be treated equivalently to the practice of "free vivre" granted to Christian monasteries.

Buddhist associations have significantly contributed to civic engagement across local, regional, and national levels, both in regard to crisis preparedness and in providing spiritual care within healthcare institutions. In Sweden, religious communities can be viewed both as a resource but also as a risk; they can be seen as a resource when included in welfare provision but, at the same time, also as a potential problem that needs to be regulated and controlled, thus an emphasis on adhering to democratic principles to be eligible for state grants (Lundgren 2021).

The Swedish Buddhist Community as well as individual temples is engaged in the work of emergency preparedness and spiritual care. This work is done both on a national level through the coordinating work of the Swedish Agency for Support to Faith Communities and on local and regional levels in several parts of Sweden, where the cooperation around crises and emergencies is organised through interfaith and intercultural councils, or through hospitals.

Here, Jönköping is a forerunner, where spiritual care can be asked for on the platform 1177, the national web-based communication platform for information and services regarding healthcare.[31] Spiritual care is a collective term for interventions carried out in health care by representatives of different life views and beliefs. Those who participate in spiritual care have a duty of confidentiality and do not keep records. The services are free of charge. The Swedish spiritual care is based on a model from Great Britain.

New emerging frontiers

The presence of Buddhism in Sweden is not limited to the numerous groups of Asian and convert Buddhists. It can also be observed in secular applications within the healthcare sector (Plank 2010) as well as in neo-spiritual contexts (Hedenborg White 2023) and the commercial sector (Plank 2014). Additionally, influences are evident in Christian spiritual practices, where Zen meditation was introduced during the 1970s and where secularised practices are currently undergoing a process of resacralisation (Plank, Lundgren & Egnell 2023). In the therapeutic sector, healthcare centres and licensed healthcare professionals (e.g., psychologists and psychotherapists) increasingly offer mindfulness-based treatments, usually within the framework of cognitive behavioural therapy (CBT) aimed at addressing anxiety, depression and pain. Here, the Center for Mindfulness Sweden and Camilla Sköld, a physiotherapist with a doctorate in neuroscience, have, since 2007, been instrumental in developing university-level courses on mindfulness at Karolinska Institute, Stockholm's medical university, as well as providing teacher training in MBSR and MBCT. That same year, Mindfulnesscenter was founded by Ola Schenström, a medical doctor who has also trained many Swedish mindfulness teachers.

In the neo-spiritual sector, where mindfulness is commercially framed, coaches, meditation teachers and yoga teachers target private individuals and companies that offer mindfulness training focusing on the private and public sectors (see also

Hornborg 2012). In a mapping study conducted in 2016 (Stålnacke & Plank 2016) where we examined mindfulness producers in Gothenburg, we found 122 producers, of which 82 were women and 17 were men, while 24 were made up of organisations, companies, institutions or Buddhist centres. Around 60 per cent were identified as working with mindfulness for self-development and optimisation purposes, 25 per cent for therapeutic purposes, and the remaining were unspecified or a mix of both.[32] In an American context, sociologist Jaime Kucinskas has observed that distancing from both traditional Buddhism and the new spiritual landscape is a critical factor in the legitimisation of mindfulness in healthcare, schools and businesses (2019). In Sweden, such a double distancing is apparent when mindfulness is used in the healthcare sector; however, whether this is the case in schools or businesses needs to be explored further.

Another way to distinguish between "religious" and "therapeutic" mindfulness is by examining the extent to which a practice is promoted with salvific (liberating) or salvetive (healing) qualities, or a combination of both (Schlieter 2017). The emphasis on health and healing plays a vital role in understanding how meditation practices have entered the Church of Sweden and how they are now part of holistic practices that are framed within a culture of care that focuses on bodily and spiritual well-being.

Buddhist influences on Christianity in Sweden can be traced back to the 1970s. Two Christian meditation centres founded by priests from the Church of Sweden teach Zen-inspired meditation: Berget in Dalarna, and Enekulla Zendo in Höör. Both are strongly influenced by the Sanbō Kyōdan tradition.

The priest and professor of Philosophy of Religion Hans Hof (1922–2011) introduced Zen Buddhism to Sweden through his close relationship with the German Jesuit priest Hugo Enomiya-Lasalle, who had studied Zen meditation in Japan under the Sanbō Kyōdan tradition.

Hans Hof (1922–2011) grew up in a Chartauan environment on Sweden's West Coast. He was ordained in the Church of Sweden in 1946 and served as a priest in Luleå Diocese during the 1950s. He earned his doctorate in theoretical philosophy with a thesis on Master Eckhart, whose theology came to shape his own. In 1969, he was appointed professor of Philosophy of Religion at Uppsala University. In 1972, he co-founded Rättvik's Meditation Centre, in connection with St Davidsgården, where he taught Zen meditation. The construction of the centre was described in an article in *Svenska Dagbladet* as one of "the newest and most remarkable signs of the times within our Swedish ecclesiastical province" (Ekman 1973). When he was in his 20s, Hans Hof had been taught a contemplative relaxation method to alleviate nervous stomach problems. In addition to the physical benefits, the exercises led to a mystical experience, convincing him that "the way to a changed state of consciousness can go through the body." This realisation transformed his understanding of religious practice: "I was freed from the compulsion to suspend my faith in formulations. I had been given a path to a personal experience of God" (Hof 1983: 39). This experience later led him to establish contact with Catholic priests who incorporated Zen meditation into their theology and practice, as well as with the Zen master Taisen Deshimaru. Hans Hof regarded Zen meditation as a religiously neutral practice, with a particular emphasis on bodily posture. In his book *Bli mer människa*, a central theme is that Zen meditation can contribute to physical and mental well-being. That Zen meditation is a bodily practice was emphasised by the inclusion of eutony exercises, led by Gun Kronberg, in the courses offered at the meditation centre and St Davidsgården. Eutony is a physical education and therapeutic method developed by the Dane Gerda Alexander. Eutony means "good tension," and Hans Hof found the method helpful when teaching the sitting posture in zazen. It became an integral part of the practice in both Rättvik and Sigtuna. Additionally, courses in Tai Chi were offered. Hof also collaborated with the Catholic nun Sr Monica Bexell, OP, who used meditation and relaxation in her work as a psychotherapist.

Criticism also arose within the Church regarding the activities at Rättvik's Meditation Centre, where Hof was accused of syncretism. When the Zen Buddhist teacher Philip Kapleau was invited to Rättvik in 1982, tensions surfaced between the management of St Davidsgården and Hans Hof and the circle around him. This led the latter to establish the Association Zenvägen in 1984, which continued to practise and teach a religiously unbound form of meditation. At St Davidsgården, meditation activities continued but took on a more explicitly Christian confessional interpretation under the leadership of the Carmelite Wilfrid Stinissen, who had previously collaborated with Hans Hof, and eutony pedagogue Gun Kronberg. The meditation practice was rebranded as "Christian deep meditation," which was also introduced at the Refugiet in Sigtuna and at Stiftsgården in Båstad (Karlsson 2011: 15).

Disappointed by what he perceived as a betrayal of spiritually seeking individuals, Hans Hof resigned from the priesthood and left the Church of Sweden in 1982. Over the following years, he expressed his criticism of the Church in a number of articles and lectures. He argued that a gap exists between institutional religion and people's lived realities. Church representatives, he contended, did not understand the "spiritual paradigm shift" that was taking place and that Hof had come into contact with in those who applied to the meditation courses. He wrote: "[When] the church in its representatives does not understand and therefore rejects the many expressions of new spirituality for border-crossing, and authentically religious, experience, then the church shows that it has lost contact with an important part of its true identity" (Hof 1983: 18, translation by Helene Egnell). However, he returned to the priesthood five years later when he felt that openness had increased within the Church.

Priest Pelle Bengtsson (b. 1951) introduced Zen meditation into the activities of the Student Priests at Liberiet in Lund's cathedral parish. He began meditating in the mid-1970s and, in 2003, was appointed a teacher by his teacher, the German Lutheran priest and Zen master Gundula Meyer. Today, he runs the meditation centre Enekulla Zendo in Höör. Although the practice of meditation continues at Liberiet under the Student Priests, it is not explicitly advertised as Zen meditation.

Over the past fifty years, many new spiritual practices have emerged within the Church of Sweden that fall under holistic practices that engage the body, soul and spirit. These practices are no longer taught exclusively in retreat settings but have become an integral part of daily church activities. In the Diocese of Stockholm, eight out of ten parishes now offer meditation and movement-based bodily practices such as yoga, qigong and dance (Lundgren, Plank & Egnell, 2023). These activities are framed within a culture of care that emphasises both bodily and spiritual well-being (Plank, Egnell & Lundgren 2024). The new spiritual practices in the Church of Sweden have not been standardised in the same way as Borup (2016) has noted is the case in Danish churches where a special brand of "Christfulness" has been implemented. Instead, individual teachers, including ordained priests and deacons as well as lay persons, have more freely developed and taught holistic practices (Plank, Egnell & Lundgren 2024).

Another strand of development outside of the Church is the merging of yoga and Buddhist practices. Several individual (Buddhist) meditation teachers, many of whom many are connected to a broad *vipassanā* community, lead retreats at yoga-based retreat facilities such as Shambala Gatherings and Oshofors, where courses in Advaita Vedanta, nondual meditation, Tantra, various yoga traditions and qigong are held. Here, Buddhism and neo-spirituality intermingle, as the practices have an emphasis not only on bodily health but also on personal and spiritual development. Using Schlieter's distinction salvific and salvetive, the Christian use of body-mind-practices puts emphasis on the healing qualities, the salvetive aspects of meditation, and the neo-spiritual use of meditation tends to focus on a combination of both liberating and healing qualities. Hence, this indicates the importance of contextual field studies to understand future developments.

Conclusion

Although there are early examples of Swedish teachers emphasising a unified presentation of Buddhism that have left traces in the form of intra-Buddhist collaboration, there is no indication today of a distinct kind of "Swedish" Buddhism or a "Swedish Buddhist tradition" developing. However, the Swedish Buddhist Community has been registered as an intra-Buddhist faith community. Swedish legislation is based on an understanding of religious communities as nationally organised entities, whereas Buddhist groups operate locally and regionally and thus do not individually reach the required 2,500 members to qualify for state grants and state fee assistance (Buddhist dāna through the tax system). This necessitates that, particularly for Asian Buddhist communities, groups have strong Swedish language skills, master administrative procedures, and, most importantly, are able to cooperate with other Buddhist groups belonging to different traditions than their own through the Swedish Buddhist Community.

One of the major challenges that Asian Buddhist temples are likely to face in the future stems from changing Buddhist demographics. As the first generation of migrant Buddhists ages and with second-generation Buddhists increasingly marry outside their ethnic groups, there is a growing trend towards secularisation among individuals with Buddhist family backgrounds. This may make it difficult for Buddhist groups to maintain their membership numbers and influence. Since the strongest predictor of developing a secular outlook is having close relationships with a parent or a partner who is secular, the high incidence of mixed marriages between Thai women and Swedish men suggests that it is within this group that we will first be able to find "post-Buddhists," individuals born into families with Buddhist background but who no longer identify as Buddhist. On the other hand, "Buddhist dāna" via the tax system makes it possible and easier for individuals who want to support Buddhist temples, that is, "belonging without believing."

Although there are some studies on Asian Buddhism in Sweden and mindfulness and convert Buddhism, there is still a lack of in-depth research on specific communities and traditions, particularly among Vietnamese, Chinese and Sri Lankan groups. The outskirts of Buddhism, where Buddhist practices merge with yoga, Christian and neo-spiritual traditions, or become post-Buddhism, also need to be explored further.

Acknowledgement

This work was supported by the Swedish Research Council grant numbers 2019–02173_VR, 2022–06311_VR; and the Riksbankens Jubileumsfond grant number P20–0606_RJ.

Appendix

Table 2.2 Buddhist groups in Sweden.

Buddhist establishments in Sweden (as of February 2024)

Name of facility	Location	Specific tradition
Meditation centres in Sweden		
Byvalla retreat centre and Buddhist collective housing	Horndal	Nondenominational
Dhamma Sobhana	Ödeshög	Nordic Vipassana Center in the tradition of S.N. Goenka
Dharmagiri retreat center	Sala	Triratana
Enekulla zendo	Höör	Sanbō Kyōdan
Karma Dechen Osel Ling	Fellingsbro	Buddhistiska gemenskapen – Karme Tenpe Gyaltsen (Karma Kagyu)
Tyresö Retreat center	Tyresö	Diamond Way
Zengården	Fellingsbro	Zenbuddhistiska samfundet

Umbrella organisation and its membership organisations
Sveriges Buddhistiska Gemenskap (Swedish Buddhist Community)

Groups of mainly migrants and migrants' children
Thai

Buddharama Tempel Fredrika	Fredrika, Lappland	Mahā Nikāya
Buddharama Temple, Värmdö	Värmdö	Mahā Nikāya
Dhammangalarama tempel	Sundsvall	Mahā Nikāya
Wat Buddhabhavana	Västerås	Mahā Nikāya
Wat Buddhasothorn	Uppsala	Mahā Nikāya
Thaiföreningen Prakatbuddhakon	Borlänge	Dhammayuttika Nikāya
Sam Naksong Ludvika	Ludvika	Dhammayuttika Nikāya
Wat Pha	Göteborg	Dhammayuttika Nikāya
Wat Pah Sokjai	Brunflo	Dhammayuttika Nikāya
Wat Santinivas	Haninge	Dhammayuttika Nikāya
Wat Sanghabaramee	Eslöv	Dhammayuttika Nikāya
Wat Thai Karlstad	Skattkärr	Dhammayuttika Nikāya
Burmese		
Tiratana Buddhist Temple	Hjortkvarn	Theravāda
Chinese		

(Continued)

Table 2.2 (Continued)

Buddhist establishments in Sweden (as of February 2024)

Name of facility	Location	Specific tradition
International Buddhist Progress Society, Sweden	Rosersberg	Fó guāng shān
Sri Lankan		
Stockholm Buddhist Vihara	Järfälla	Theravāda
Vietnamese		
Vietnamesiskt buddhistförbund i Sverige		Pure Land
Chùa Phât Quang	Göteborg	
Ngoc Dien	Gävle	
	Stockholm	
	Kalmar	
Groups of mainly converts		
Buddhistiska gemenskapen – Karme Tenpe Gyaltsen		Tibetan/Karma Kagyu
Karma Shedrup Dargye Ling	Stockholm	
Karma Dechen Ösel Ling	Fellingsbro	
Karma Machik Chöling	Örebro	
Buddhistiska gemenskapen Triratana		Triratana Buddhist Community
Stockholm buddhistcenter	Stockholm	
Dharmagiri	Sala	
	Malmö	
	Göteborg	
	Linköping	
	Hudiksvall	
	Östersund	
Föreningen 3Juveler	Stockholm	Insight meditation
Föreningen för tibetansk buddhism i Göteborg	Göteborg	Tibetan/Nondenominational
Karma Yönten Ling	Malmö, Lund	Tibetan/Nondenominational
Sakya Changchub Chöling	Stockholm & Uppsala	Tibetan/Sakya
Svenska Soto-Zenföreningen		Association Zen Internationale (Soto-shu)
Sanbodojo	Göteborg	
So Gyo Zendojo	Göteborg	
Lunds zendojo	Lund	
Uppsala Soto-Zendojo	Uppsala	
Stockholms Zengrupp	Stockholm	
Vipassanagruppen	Stockholm	Insight meditation
Yeshin Norbu meditationscenter	Stockholm	Foundation for preservation of the Mahayana tradition (FPMT)
Zenbuddhistiska samfundet		The Cloud Water Sangha (Philip Kapleau/Bodhin Kjolhede)
Zengården	Fellingsbro	
Stockholm Zen Center	Stockholm	
Göteborg Zen Center	Göteborg	
Lund Zen Center	Lund	

(*Continued*)

Table 2.2 (Continued)

Buddhist establishments in Sweden (as of February 2024)

Name of facility	Location	Specific tradition
Other Buddhist groups (not affiliated to SBC)		
Groups of mainly migrants and migrants' children		
Thai		
Buddharam Temple	Boden	Mahā Nikāya
Buddharam Temple	Grums	Mahā Nikāya
Buddharam Temple	Ragunda	Mahā Nikāya
Wat Buddhabhavana	Västerås	Mahā Nikāya
Wat Buddhasothorn	Uppsala	Mahā Nikāya
Wat Piyadhammaram	Utanede	Mahā Nikāya
Wat Siammin Mangkalaram	Norrköping	Mahā Nikāya
Wat Thai Norrtälje	Muskö	Mahā Nikāya
Wat Thai Uppsala	Uppsala	Mahā Nikāya
Mae chii/Nun retreat	Blentarp	Dhammayuttika Nikāya
Phoyhitham Meditation Center	Morjärv	Dhammayuttika Nikāya
Prakatsanghkhakhun	Jönköping	Dhammayuttika Nikāya
Prakatsatjatam	Eskilstuna	Dhammayuttika Nikāya
Prakas Santidham	Umeå	Dhammayuttika Nikāya
Tipaksong Watpha Dhammara-tana Förening	Halmstad	Dhammayuttika Nikāya
Thailändska föreningen Santidham	Sandviken	Dhammayuttika Nikāya
Wat Buddha Udayana	Landvetter	Dhammayuttika Nikāya
Wat Dhammarangse	Sollentuna	Dhammayuttika Nikāya
Wat Pha Buddhabucha	Kyrkhult	Dhammayuttika Nikāya
Wat Khemago	Månkarbo	Dhammayuttika Nikāya
Wat Thai Eskilstuna	Eskilstuna	Dhammayuttika Nikāya
Buddhawajana Sweden	Knivsta	Buddhawajana
Wat Dalarnavanaram	Ulvshyttan	Buddhawajana
Wat Pha Boabocha	Unnaryd	Buddhawajana
Wat Pha Dhammakāya	Borås	Dhammakāya
Wat Pha Dhammakāya	Stockholm	Dhammakāya
Wat Pha Dhammakāya	Gävle	Dhammakāya
Vietnamese		
Chùa Dai Bi Tam	Bjuv	Pure Land
Chùa Trúc Lâm	Malmö	Pure Land
Katrineholm Viet Buddhistisk förening	Katrineholm	Pure Land
Sri Lankan		
Helsingborg Buddhist Vihara	Helsingborg	Theravāda
Skåne Pansala	Ljungbyhed	Theravāda
Tapovanarama Buddhist Vihara	Norsborg	Theravāda
Groups of mainly converts		
Diamond Way		Tibetan/Ole Nydahl
Tyresö Meditation Retreat Center	Tyresö	
Stockholm Buddhist Group	Stockholm	

(*Continued*)

Table 2.2 (Continued)

Buddhist establishments in Sweden (as of February 2024)

Name of facility	Location	Specific tradition
Göteborg Buddhist Group	Göteborg	
Malmö Chan Buddhist Temple	Malmö	Chinese Línjì-lineage/Jǐng Huì
New Kadampa Tradition		Tibetan/Geshe Kelsang Gyatso
Hjärtjuvel Kadampa Buddhiscenter	Göteborg	
Kadampa Meditation center	Stockholm	
Ordinary Mind	Umeå	Ordinary Mind/Charlotte Joko Beck
Rosensanghan	Göteborg	Thích Nhất Hạnh
SGI Sverige	Saltsjöbaden	Nichiren
Zenvägen	Lund	Nondenominational

Notes

1 *The Ethical Review Act* (SFS 2003:460) mandates an ethical review of all research, including the humanities, that involves sensitive personal data in Sweden. Data was collected as part of the following research projects with approval from the Swedish Ethical Review Authority (EPM): Buddhism in the Nordic Countries, EPM: Dnr 2023-01308-01; Religion in Times of Crises (Swedish Research Council), EPM: Dnr 2023-03992-01; Lived Religion and Social Mobility among Migrants in Sweden (Swedish Research Council), EPM: Dnr 2021-02719; The New Faces of the Swedish Folk Church (Riksbankens Jubileumsfond), EPM: Dnr 2021-05807-01. (Note that the Act is under revision and may be amended in 2025, potentially allowing research in the humanities and social sciences to conduct fieldwork and interviews without EPM approval.)
2 CARLI digital collections, *Chicago-Bladet (Trinity International University)* https://collections.carli.illinois.edu/digital/collection/tiu_bladet (accessed 16 Nov 2024).
3 Digitised archives include Arkivdigital, Befolkningen i Sverige; Riksarkivets specialsökningar: Medicinalstyrelsen 1876–1915, Folkräkningar 1910, 1930; Libris, Kungliga biblioteket; Bebyggelseregistret at Riksantikvarieämbetet; Carlotta; Jamtli; Ancestry; FamilySearch; parish and church records; Rotemansarkivet; Swedish America Newspapers (Minnesota Historical Society). Special thanks to my colleague, historian Kristin Mikalsen, for guiding me!
4 The Ex Libris is part of a collection from Nils Rosén, a bequest to Malmö Museum in 1928. http://carlotta.malmo.se/carlotta-mmus/web/object/84267 (accessed 16 Nov 2024).
5 The verse, written in Devanagari script, reads: "In whatever way they approach me, I reward them accordingly. People follow my path in every way, oh son of Pṛthā (Arjuna)." The translation was provided by my colleague Pawel Odyniec, a trained Indologist.
6 The presentations of the two teachers are based on my early research on Buddhism in Sweden (Plank 2004).
7 https://buddhaways.wordpress.com/2010/10/10/tao-wei-kwong-wu/ (accessed 16 Nov 2024).
8 https://svenskagravar.se/gravsatt/a63a510e-a945-4c2d-9e02-8fc048ee64da (accessed 16 Nov 2024).
9 https://www.sverigesbuddhister.se/about-sbc/ (accessed 16 Nov 2024).

10 According to his passport, Lama Ngawang was born in 1927, but his actual birth year was 1929.
11 https://tibetanbuddhism.se/ (accessed 16 Nov 2024).
12 https://www.sakya.se (accessed 16 Nov 2024).
13 https://www.dhamma.org/sv/schedules/schsobhana (accessed 16 Nov 2024).
14 https://stockholmsbuddhistcenter.se/ (accessed 16 Nov 2024).
15 https://www.taozen.se/ (accessed 16 Nov 2024).
16 The AMM-movement uses this spelling.
17 https://buddhaways.wordpress.com/ (accessed 16 Nov 2024).
18 https://www.zazen.se/index_en.php (accessed 16 Nov 2024).
19 https://www.soto-zen.se/ (accessed 16 Nov 2024).
20 http://www.zen-goteborg.se/ (accessed 16 Nov 2024).
21 https://www.svalornassangha.org/ (accessed 16 Nov 2024).
22 https://plumvillage-traditionen.se/om/ (accessed 16 Nov 2024).
23 https://www.ssgi.se/sgi-i-sverige (accessed 16 Nov 2024).
24 https://en.ibpssweden.se/ (accessed 16 Nov 2024).
25 This book results from several generous stipends provided by the foundation that enabled the authors to meet at workshops and conduct fieldwork together.
26 https://stockholmsbuddhistcenter.se/bokaffar (accessed 16 Nov 2024).
27 A 12-minute video with English subtitles was published on his Instagram account on September 25, 2021. https://www.instagram.com/natthiko/p/CWsQYtHD-0O/ (accessed 16 Nov 2024).
28 https://www.instagram.com/natthiko/p/CY2146oIpqi/ (accessed 16 Nov 2024).
29 https://www.ohchr.org/en/press-releases/2023/10/sweden-must-strengthen-dialogue-faith-communities-combat-religious-or-belief (accessed 16 Nov 2024).
30 https://mrinstitutet.se/nyheter/flera-utmaningar-for-religions-och-trosfrihet-i-sverige/ (accessed 16 Nov 2024).
31 https://folkhalsaochsjukvard.rjl.se/vardstod/omvardnad/andlig-vard/?accordionAnchor=69316
32 Producers were classed into six groups to capture differences and similarities in their professions, mindfulness training and how, and for what purpose, they use mindfulness. Psychologists and healthcare professionals (doctors, nurses, physiotherapists and psychotherapists) are producers with a protected professional licence from the Swedish National Board of Healthcare and Welfare. The wellness instructors and the body-oriented instructors, such as yoga instructors and coaches, are also producers who possess knowledge in healthcare but who do not hold such a license. The group of Buddhist and mindfulness meditators draws knowledge primarily from Buddhist traditions or mindfulness. The group creative professions encompass producers engaged in different creative activities.

References

Aftonbladet. 1899-09-08.
Almqvist, Erik Eje. 2009. "Johann Neumanns vidunderliga historia." *Magasin Filter.* 2009-06-05.
Almqvist, Kjell and Passmark, Carl Philip (eds.). 2023. *Det esoteriska Sverige – från Swedenborg till Strindberg.* Stockholm: Bokförlaget Stolpe.
Chicago Bladet. 1899-08-22.
Chutintharo, Phra (Rajaratanarangsi). n.d. *Buddha och hans lära* [stencil].
Baumann, Martin. 2002. "Buddhism in Europe – Past, Present, Prospects." In *Westward Dharma – Buddhism Beyond Asia*, edited by Charles Prebish and Martin Baumann, 85–105. Berkley: University of California Press.

Beach, Hugh. 1988. "Sinovietnameser." In *Det mångkulturella Sverige – en handbok om etniska grupper och minoriteter,* edited by Ingvar Svanberg and Harald Runblom, 360–367. Stockholm: Gidlunds Bokförlag.

Borup, Jørn. 2016. "Mindfulness as a Booming, Diverse and (Non) Religious Phenomena: Mapping and Analyzing Mindfulness in the City of Aarhus." *Religion i Danmark* 7(2), 1–16.

BRÅ. 2023. *Polisanmälda Hatbrott 2022 – En Sammanställning av de ärenden som Hatbrottsmarkerats av Polisen.* Rapport 2023: 16. Stockholm.

Dave, Göran. 2018. "Hilma Svedal." *Svenskt kvinnobiografiskt lexikon.*

Davidsson, A. 2000. "Smålands 'Lilla Tibet'." IM:s Tidskrift, 3:2000.

Efteråt – Tidskrift för Spiritism och Dermed Beslägtade ämnen. 1907. 6.

Ekman, Nils Gösta. 1973. "Sinnesändring genom Meditation." *Svenska Dagbladet.* 1973-03-31.

Ellert, Kerstin. 2009. "Homöopatiska Institutet i Östersund och Homeopaten Olof Theodor Axell." *Gamla Östersund Årsskrift,* 30–34.

Enstedt, Daniel and Plank, KatarinaKatarina. 2018. *Levd Religion: Det Heliga i Vardagen,* Lund: Nordic Academic Press.

Ericsson, Marie. 2011a. *Här och Nu: Om Sathipatthana Sutta och Buddhas Väg till Upplysning.* Stockholm: Vipassanagruppen.

Ericsson, Marie. 2011b. *Kom och se: Om Meditation och Theravadabuddhism.* Stockholm: Vipassanagruppen.

Faxneld, Per, Katarina Plank and Johan Nilsson. 2024. "Sweden" In *East Asian Religiosities in the European Union: Globalisation, Migration, and Hybridity,* edited by Laurence Cox, Ugo Dessì & Lukas K. Pokorny, 321–320 Leiden: Brill.

Fields, Rick. 1998. "Divided Dharma: White Buddhists, Ethnic Buddhists, and Racism." In *The Faces of Buddhism in America,* edited by Charles Prebish and Kenneth Tanaka, 196–206. Berkley: University of California Press.

Fredriksson, Trudy. 2013. *Uppvaknandet vägar.* Stockholm: Nämnden för statligt stöd till trossamfund.

Gardell, Karl G. 2001. "Amita Nisatta." *Svenska Dagbladet,* 2001-07-16.

Gregory, John. 2002. *The West and China Since 1500.* New York: Palgrave.

Gyllensvärd, Bo. 2004. "The Buddha found at Helgö." In *Exavations at Helgö XVI. Exotic and Sacral Finds from Helgö,* 10–27. Stockholm: Kungl. Vitterhets-, Historie-och Antikitetsakad.

Gällmo, Gunnar. 1986. *Praktisk Buddhism.* Delsbo: Åsak.

Gällmo, Gunnar. 1997. *Några Fakta om Buddhismen,* Stockholm: Buddhasasanaförlaget.

Gällmo, Gunnar. 1999a. *Buddhas Liv.* Stockholm: Buddhasasanaförlaget.

Gällmo, Gunnar. 1999b. *Dhammapada.* Stockholm: Buddhasasanaförlaget.

Haglund, Magnus. 2017. "Alaska Ligger I Bohuslän." *Göteborgs-Posten.* 2017-07-15.

Hedenborg White, Manon. 2023. *Mindfulness som Historiskt och Kulturellt Fenomen.* Malmö Universitet.

Hedenstierna-Jonsson, Charlotte. 2020. "With Asia as Neighbour." *The Museum of Far Eastern Antiquities.* Bulletin No. 81, 43–64.

Hof, Hans. 1983. *Var Finns Gud. Tankas om Andlighetens Villkor Idag.* Åsak: Hudiksvall.

Holst, Harry. 1909. *Framstående läkare som öfvergått till Homöopatien.* Östersund.

Holst, Harry. 1912. *Om Vaccinationstvånget.* Stockholm.

Holst, Harry. 1914. *Homöopatien och Medicinska Fakulteten.* Värnamo.

Hornborg, Anne-Christine. 2012. Coaching och Lekmannaterapi: En Modern Väckelse? Stockholm: Dialogos.

Hsing Yun. 2003. *Att Vara God: Buddhistisk Etik i Vardagslivet.* [Printed in Sweden]

Hsing Yun. 2016. *Humanistisk Buddhism.* [Printed in Taiwan].

Hsing Yun. 2019. *Buddha Dharma: Klart och Enkelt.* Norrköping: Tellotryck.

Hübinette, Tobias. 2009. *Demografisk översikt över de 32 Största Invandrargrupperna i de 24 Största Kommunerna.* Mångkulturellt Centrum & Stockholm: Konstnärsnämnden.

Hübinette, Tobias. 2024. *Svenska Asiater – Antiasiatisk Rasism och Framväxten av en Ny Minoritet.* Stockholm: Verbal Förlag.

Hultberg, Thomas. 1971. "Hinduism, Buddhism, Islam i Sverige." *Utblick,* no 3.

Jansson, Hedda. 2023. *Solbadets Buddha: Buddhism och Teosofi i Ellen Keys livstro.* Stockholm: Institutionen för Etnologi, Religionshistoria och Genusvetenskap [diss.]

Johansson, Rune E. A. 1967. *Citta, Mano, Vinnana: A Psychosemantic Investigation.* Peradeniya: Univ. of Ceylon.

Johansson, Rune E. A. 1967. *Dhammapada.* Stockholm: Natur och Kultur.

Johansson, Rune E. A. 1969. *The Psychology of Nirvana.* London: George Allen and Unwin.

Johansson, Rune E. A. 1973. *Pali Buddhist Texts: Explained to the Beginner.* Lund: Scandinavian Institute of Asian Studies.

Johansson, Rune E. A. 1976. *Sutta Nipata.* Stockholm: Forum.

Johansson, Rune E. A. 1979. *The Dynamic Psychology of Early Buddhism.* London: Scandinavian Institute of Asian Studies.

Jägerbrand, Mikael. 2011. *Hilmas Alaska: Guidebook om Guldgräverskan och Trädgården av Cement.* Lysekil: Virvelvind Förlag.

Karlsson, Henrik. 2011. "Hur Zen Kom till Sverige." *Zenvägen,* no. 127/March.

Kucinskas, Jamie. 2019. *The Mindful Elite: Mobilizing from the Inside Out.* New York: Oxford University Press.

Larsson, Stefan. 2020. "Svenska buddhister och buddhisminfluerade svenskar." In: *Människan i en existentiell kultur,* edited by Olov Dahlin, Sara Duppils and Jari Ristiniemi, 75–92. Gävle: Gävle University Press.

Lepore, Jill. 2001. "Historians who Love Too Much: Reflections on Microhistory and Biography." *The Journal of American History,* 88(1), 129–144.

Lindberg Falk, Monica. 2004. "Thailändsk Bhikkhuni-sangha: Mor och dotter förändrar den monastiska ordningen." *Chakra,* 1, 21–35.

Lindeblad, Björn Natthiko, B ankler, Caroline and Modiri, Navid. 2020. *Jag kan ha fel: och andra visdomar från mitt liv som buddhistmunk.* Stockholm: Bonnier fakta.

Londos, Eva. 2004. "Båtflyktingar i Gnosjö" In: *I skuggan av Gnosjöandan,* edited by Eva Londos, 101–115. Jönköping: Jönköpings läns museum,

Lundgren, Linnea. 2021. *A Risk or a Resource? A Study of the Swedish State's Shifting Perception and Handling of Minority Religious Communities between 1952–2019.* Stockholm: Esta Sköndal Bräcke Högskola (dissertation).

Lundgren, Linnea, Katarina Plank and Helene Egnell. 2023. "Nya andliga praktiker i Svenska kyrkan – från exklusiva retreatmiljöer till kyrklig vardagspraktik." *Svensk teologisk kvartalskrift.* 99(3), 229–248.

Malmberg, Claes and Johan Ohlson. 2008. *Konsten att undvika nirvana.* Stockholm: ICA Bokförlag.

Malmberg, Claes and Petter Karlsson. 2016. *Mysteriet Claes Malmberg: Mina ocensurerade memoarer.* Stockholm: Ekerlids förlag.

Marchisio, Roberto and Maurizio Pisati. 1999. "Belonging without Believing: Catholics in Contemporary Italy." *Journal of Modern Italian Studies,* 4, 236–255.

McIntosh, Esther. 2015. "Belonging without Believing – Church as Community in an Age of Digital Media." *International Journal of Public Theology,* 9(2), 131–155.

McMahan, David. 2008. *The Making of Modern Buddhism.* New York: Oxford University Press.

Myrvold, Kristina, Plank, Katarina and Sardella, Ferdinando. 2024. "Indian Religions." In *The Study of Religion in Sweden: Past, Present and Future,* edited by Henrik Bogdan and Göran Larsson, (eds.), 95–112. London: Bloomsbury.

Novus. 2023. *Rapport: Ursprung, språkkunskap och religion.* 2023-11-05.

Numrich, Paul. 1996. *Old Wisdom in the New World.* Knoxville: University of Tennessee Press.

Nyberg, Kenneth. 2001. *Bilder av Mittens rike.* Gothenburg: Historiska institutionen.

Oakes, Kaya. 2015. "Belonging without Believing." *CrossCurrents,* 65(2), 229–238.

Odland, Kanja. 2013. *Vandring på spårlös stig: en zenutövares anteckningar.* Fellingsbro: Zendo.

Offermanns, Jürgen. 2002. *Der lange Weg des Zen-Buddhismus nach Deutschland: Vom 16. Jahrhundert bis Rudolf Otto.* Lund: KFS.

Offermanns, Jürgen. 2005. "Debates on Atheism, Quietism, and Sodomy: The Initial Reception of Buddhism in Europe." *Journal of Global Buddhism,* 6, 16–35.

Östersundsposten. 1899-09-15.

Payutto, P. A. 2009. *Thai Buddhism in the Buddhist World.* Bangkok: Sahadhammika Co. Ltd.

Plank, Katarina. 2004. "Buddhism i Sverige – om asiatiska buddhister, konvertitbuddhister, kristna zenmeditatörer och sympatisörer." In *Det mångreligiösa Sverige – ett landskap i förändring,* edited by Daniel Andersson & Åke Sander, 217–284. Lund: Studentlitteratur.

Plank, Katarina. 2009a. "Syster Amita Nisatta – pionjär och traditionsöverskridare." *Buddhism-nu.* 2009:2.

Plank, Katarina. 2009b. "Kata Dalström – Sveriges första buddhist." *Buddhism-nu.* 2009:1.

Plank, Katarina. 2010. "Mindful Medicine: The Growing Trend of Mindfulness-Based Therapies in the Swedish Health Care System." *Finnish Journal of Ethnicity and Migration,* 5(2), 47–55-

Plank, Katarina. 2014. "Mindfulness i svenska kontexter." *Religionsvidenskabeligt Tidskrift,* 61, 35–54.

Plank, Katarina. 2015a. "Buddhister och buddhism: asiatisk migration, konvertiter och sekulär meditation." In *Det mångreligiösa Sverige – ett landskap i förändring,* edited by Daniel Andersson & Åke Sander, 203–262. (3rd revised edition.). Lund: Studentlitteratur.

Plank, Katarina. 2015b. "Sacred Foodscapes in Thai Buddhist Temples in Sweden." *Religion and Food. Scripta Insituti Donneriani Aboensis,* 26, 201–224.

Plank, Katarina, Helene Egnell and Linnea Lundgren. 2024. "Caring for Health, Bodies, and Development: Teaching New Spiritual Practices in the Church of Sweden." *Approaching Religion,* 14(2), 113–131.

Plank, Katarina, Linnea Lundgren and Helene Egnell. 2023. "Meditation and Other New Spiritual Practices in the Church of Sweden." In *Eastern Practices and Nordic Bodies: Lived Religion, Spirituality and Healing in the Nordic Countries.* Cham: Palgrave Macmillan.

Plank, Katarina, Elisabeth Raddock and Peter Selander. 2016. "The Temple Mount of Fredrika – Translocality and Fractured Transnationalism of a Visionary Thai Buddhist Retreat Centre." *Contemporary Buddhism,* 17(2), 405–426.

Poromaa, Sante. 1997. *Bortom alla begrepp: Buddhas väg till frihet.* Hägersten: Red Dot Publ.

Poromaa, Sante. 2008. *Varandets väv: Zen, vetenskap och återfödelse.* Fellingsbro: Zendo.

Poromaa, Sante. 2019. *It's never too late – to give up.* Fellingsbro: Zendo.

Prebish, Charles. 1979. *American Buddhism.* North Scituate, MA: Duxbury Press.

Prebish, Charles. 1993. "Two Buddhisms Reconsidered." *Buddhist Studies Review,* 10(2), 187–206.

Ragvald, Lars. 1982. *Vietnamflyktingarna: deras första år i Sverige.* Statens invandrarverk: Rapport 5.

SFS 1974:152. *Regeringsformen.* https://www.riksdagen.se/sv/dokument-och-lagar/dokument/svensk-forfattningssamling/kungorelse-1974152-om-beslutad-ny-regeringsform_sfs-1974–152/ (accessed 16 Nov 2024).

SFS 1988:1593. *Lag om trossamfund.* https://www.riksdagen.se/sv/dokument-och-lagar/dokument/svensk-forfattningssamling/lag-19981593-om-trossamfund_sfs-1998–1593/ (accessed 16 Nov 2024).

SFS 1999:932. *Lag om stöd till trossamfund.* https://www.riksdagen.se/sv/dokument-och-lagar/dokument/svensk-forfattningssamling/lag-1999932-om-stod-till-trossamfund_sfs-1999–932/ (accessed 16 Nov 2024).

SFS 2003:460. *Ethical Review Act.* https://www.riksdagen.se/sv/dokument-och-lagar/dokument/svensk-forfattningssamling/lag-2003460-om-etikprovning-av-forskning-som_sfs-2003-460/ (accessed 16 Nov 2024)

SBC. n.d. *About Swedish Buddhist Community.* https://www.sverigesbuddhister.se/about-sbc/ (accessed 16 Nov 2024).

Schlieter, Jens. 2017. Buddhist insight meditation (Vipassana) and Jon Kabat-Zinn's "Mindfulness-based Stress Reduction": An Example of Dediffrerentiation of Religion and Medicine? *Journal of Contemporary Religion,* 32, 447–463.

Seager, Richard. 1999. *Buddhism in America.* New York: Columbia University Press.

Sirander, Marcel. 1973. *Buddha, Dharma, Sangha.* Strömstad: Buddhistiska förlaget.

Sirander, Marcel. (Tào Wei). 2000. *Den buddhistiska livsåskådningen.* Malmö: Tao Food/Buddhist publikation.

Sjöström, Henning & Acarja Sunyata (Marcel Sirander). 1967. *Vägen till Buddha,* Stockholm: Bokförlaget Sjöström & Sjöström.

Sjöström, Henning. 1968. *Dagbok från Djungelklostret.* Stockholm: Sjöström & Sjöström.

Sorgenfrei, Simon. 2018. *Islam i Sverige de första 1300 åren.* Stockholm: Swedish Agency for Support to Faith Communities.

Spence, Jonathan. 1999. *The Chan's Great Continent: China in Western Minds.* New York: Norton.

Statistics Sweden. 2024. *Utrikes födda i Sverige,* https://www.scb.se/hitta-statistik/sverige-i-siffror/manniskorna-i-sverige/utrikes-fodda-i-sverige/ (accessed 24 Nov 2016).

Stockholms stad Kyrkogårdsförvaltningen. n.d. *Buddhistiskt gravkvarter.*

Stålnacke, Jacob and Plank, Katarina. 2016. *Mindfulness in Gothenburg.* Poster presentation. University of Gothenburg.

Sundsvalls Dagblad. 1899. September 15.

Svanberg, Ingvar. 1988a. "Kineser." In *Det mångkulturella Sverige – en handbok om etniska grupper och minoriteter,* edited by Ingvar Svanberg and Hans Runblom, 222–223. Stockholm: Gidlunds bokförlag.

Svanberg, Ingvar. 1988b. "Tibetaner." In *Det mångkulturella Sverige – en handbok om etniska grupper och minoriteter,* edited by Ingvar Svanberg and Hans Runblom, 423–424. Stockholm: Gidlunds bokförlag.

Svedberg, Annakarin. 2011. *Andlighet och kärlek – ett kunskapsäventyr.* Borås: Recito Förlag.

Svenska Dagbladet. 1912. December 16.

Svenska kyrkan. 2022. *Nytt kvarter för buddhistiska begravningsplatser,* https://www.svenskakyrkan.se/malmokyrkogard/nyheter/nytt-kvarter-for-buddhistiska-gravplatser (accessed 24 Nov 2016).

Svenska kyrkan. 2023. *Svenska kyrkans medlemsutveckling år 1972-2023,* https://www.svenskakyrkan.se/statistik (accessed 24 Nov 2016).

Svenska kyrkan. 2024. *Begravningsavgiften,* https://www.svenskakyrkan.se/begravning/begravningsavgiften (accessed 24 Nov 2016).

Thurfjell, David and Willander, Erika. 2022. "Ärvd eller erövrad sekularitet? Sekulär identitet bland postmuslimer och postkristna i Sverige." *Sociologisk forskning,* 59(4), 417–446.

Thurfjell, David and Willander, Erika. 2023. *Postmuslimer. Om sekularitet i ett mångreligiöst Sverige.* Stockholm: IMS & Swedish Agency for Support to Faith Communities.

Trzebiatowska, Marta and Bruce, Steve. 2012. *Why are Women more religious than Men?* Oxford: Oxford University Press.

Tweed, Thomas. 1992. *The American Encounter with Buddhism 1844–1912.* Bloomington: Indiana University Press.

Weissenbilder, Marcus. 2019. *Svenska religionstrender.* SOM-institutet.

Willander, Erika. 2019. *The Religious Landscape of Sweden – Affinity, Affiliation and Diversity in the 21st Century.* Stockholm: Swedish Agency for Support to Faith Communities.

Zuber, Devin. 2010. "The Buddha of the North: Swedenborg and Transpacific Zen." *Religion and the Arts,* 14, 1–33.

3 Lama Ngawang and the dissemination of Tibetan Buddhism in Sweden

Stefan Larsson

> I did not travel the long way to Sweden to convert people to Buddhism. I came here to be of benefit. Everyone must choose their own path.
>
> Lama Ngawang[1]

Introduction

In December 1976, following his spiritual teachers' – the Sixteenth Karmapa's (1924–1981) and Kalu Rinpoche's (1905–1989) – command, Lama Ngawang (1929–2011) (see Figure 3.1) moved to Sweden to become the resident lama in a recently founded Buddhist centre named Karma Shedrub Dargye Ling (KSDL), located in a red house in Mälarhöjden, a wealthy suburban area south of Stockholm. Coming from a simple nomadic background, with little exposure of modern western culture, this was quite a challenge, both for Lama Ngawang and for the people in Sweden who needed guidance in their attempts to practise and understand Buddhism. Lama Ngawang had studied and practised Buddhism since childhood, but he had no formal education. Since he only spoke Tibetan and knew little about western culture, it is quite astonishing that he not only managed to inspire people in Sweden to practise and study Buddhism but also created an infrastructure for practising and studying Buddhism in Sweden, thus setting the ground for the dissemination of Buddhism in the country. Lama Ngawang's legacy, achievements and influence in Sweden and beyond are, I will argue, pervasive, yet sometimes overlooked. As this essay will show, he was not alone in his undertaking; however, many people participated, and the initiative to establish Tibetan Buddhism[2] in Sweden came from the country's own citizens.

In this chapter, I will summarise Lama Ngawang's long and eventful life, with special emphasis on the thirty-five years he spent in Sweden. I will investigate what happened when Lama Ngawang encountered modern secular Swedes and describe his attempts to transmit the Buddhist teachings to people with an entirely different background than he himself had. Moreover, I will explore Lama Ngawang's role when Buddhism was introduced in Sweden and examine the impact that he had on some of the people who met him. I will also describe how the foundation of Tibetan Buddhism was established in Sweden a few years before Lama Ngawang arrived.

DOI: 10.4324/9781003529767-3

Since there are few written sources about Lama Ngawang, most of the information presented in this essay comes from interviews with people who participated in the centres which Lama Ngawang supervised, and from numerous informal conversations with people who are, or have been active in these centres.[3] Moreover, many years of interaction with Lama Ngawang and participation in various activities in the centres he oversaw have enabled me to incorporate my personal memories and experiences into the essay.[4] While striving to be unbiased and focus on facts, I hope that the close relationship that both I and the interviewees had with Lama Ngawang will contribute to bring some life and intimacy into this study.

To understand who Lama Ngawang was and recognise his role when Buddhism came to Sweden, it is necessary to know something both about his background and about the background of the centre in Sweden to which he came.

Tibetan Buddhism comes to Sweden[5]

Before 1959, when thousands of Tibetans left Tibet due to the Chinese invasion, information about Tibetan culture and religion were mainly accessible in Sweden through books. These books were written by the few adventurers who had succeeded in travelling in Tibet and tended to present Tibetan Buddhism in an exotic and mystical way.[6] One of the first direct contacts between Swedes and Tibetans occurred in the mid-1960s when a group of female Tibetan refugees from India received nursing and agriculture education in Sweden (Svanberg & Runblom (eds) 1988: 424). These Tibetan girls also received Buddhist teachings from the Swedish Buddhist nun Sister Amita Nisatta (Ingrid Wagner, 1910–2001) (Plank 2015: 232). Sister Amita became a nun in the 1950s and remained a nun until her passing in 2001. She had an ecumenical approach to Buddhism and received teachings and ordinations from Theravāda, Mahāyāna and Tibetan traditions.[7]

In the late 1960s and early 1970s, eastern religions, meditation and yoga became popular in Sweden and other western countries. In the eyes of many of the spiritual seekers who were interested in Buddhism and other eastern philosophies, Tibet was a mysterious and spiritual place where, as they saw it, ancient wisdom that had been lost or distorted in the West had been preserved (cf. Lopez 1998). When these westerners, some of them hippies, travelled to Nepal and India in search for a meaningful life, they met Tibetan refugees, lamas and monks who had escaped from Tibet. A few of these westerners took refuge to the Triple Gem (Buddha, Dharma and Sangha) and became disciples of Tibetan lamas.[8] These parallel situations, Tibetans who had lost their country and tried to preserve their religion and culture on one hand and westerners who were interested to know more about Tibetan religion and culture on the other, created a fertile meeting ground for these two different peoples and cultures. A situation where Tibetan Buddhism could be disseminated in the West had arisen.

In October 1973, the Dalai Lama visited Sweden for the first time (Goldstein-Kyaga 2008: 89). The following year, a group named the Swedish Lama Society (Svenska lama föreningen) invited one of Lama Ngawang's teachers, Kalu Rinpoche, to Sweden.[9] When Kalu Rinpoche gave teachings in Stockholm, in

June 1974, a group of Swedish people who were eager to practise and study Buddhism asked him if they could start a Buddhist centre.[10] Kalu Rinpoche granted his permission and named the new centre Karma Shedrub Dargye Ling – "A Centre where the Study and Practice [of the] Karma [Kagyu Teachings][11] Flourishes and Expands." This small group began to meet regularly in an apartment in Stockholm, where two of the members lived.[12] They performed basic Buddhist practices together, such as taking refuge to the Triple Gem and Chenrezig meditation (Sanskrit: Avalokiteśvara), a meditation designed to develop compassion.[13] During the visit, Kalu Rinpoche also asked Jan Bärmark to assist in establishing a centre in Gothenburg.[14] He named this centre Karma Shenpen Kunchap but it eventually dissolved (Bärmark 2010: 134–135).[15]

About the same time, two Swedish siblings, who were interested in practising and studying Tibetan Buddhism, bought a small farm in the southern part of Sweden (Småland) where a Tibetan Buddhist centre named Karma Ling was established.[16] One of the siblings received nun's ordination from the Karmapa in Denmark. The Danish couple Ole (b. 1941) and Hannah Nydahl (1946–2007) were also involved in establishing Karma Ling and in organising the round trips of the Karma-Kagyu lamas (Nydahl 2011).[17]

The same year, in December 1974, the head of the Karma-Kagyu tradition, the Sixteenth Karmapa, visited Sweden for the first time. When the Karmapa visited Stockholm, he performed the so-called Black Crown Ceremony at Kulturhuset in Stockholm. One of my informants recalls that the 1,500-capacity hall was completely full and a line of people who could not get in were waiting outside. The Karmapa then visited Karma Ling in Småland where he once again performed the Black Crown Ceremony.[18]

After Karmapa's visit, Lama Lodru (b. 1942) from Sikkim moved from a newly founded Tibetan Buddhist centre in Copenhagen to Stockholm. He apparently did not find his stay at the centre in Copenhagen meaningful. In an interview he said the following about his time in Denmark: "In those days [I] did not know the language to teach. And there was none that knew Tibetan. So, there was not much teaching to do. In Denmark I was like an animal in the zoo."[19] In Sweden, Lama Lodru lived together with a couple of Swedish Buddhist converts[20] in temporary borrowed apartments and houses. One of the converts had recently received monk's vows from the Karmapa. In May 1975, Nikita (1902–1992) and Diana Tolstoy (b. 1937) made a donation which enabled the small group to buy a house in Mälarhöjden, south of Stockholm.[21] Lama Lodru and the aforementioned Swedish Buddhists moved in there, and soon they were joined by Trudy Fredriksson from Holland.

In only a few years, Tibetan Buddhism had spread rapidly in Sweden: The Dalai Lama, Kalu Rinpoche and the Karmapa had visited; many people had met them and received teachings and empowerments (Tibetan: *dbang*). A nice house had been bought, daily rituals were performed, and a Tibetan Lama was giving teachings on a regular basis. Several devoted practitioners, including a Swedish monk, lived together with the lama. There was also a retreat centre in the countryside in Småland, where one Swedish nun and several people from different Nordic countries lived.

However, it was not easy to establish Tibetan Buddhism in Sweden. Many of the people who came to the centres in Småland and Mälarhöjden had personal issues of various sorts. Being westerners, brought up in a completely different culture, they knew little about Buddhism. Moreover, the people who were active in the centres had different ideas concerning what type of activities should be performed there. While some wanted to practise and study Tibetan Buddhism according to the Karma-Kagyu tradition, others were just fascinated by Tibet and spirituality in general. When the centres began to grow and more people became engaged, it became necessary to decide what their purpose were and what kind of activities the centres should engage in. The Swedish nun in Småland eventually sold Karma Ling, much to the Sixteenth Karmapa's dismay. Meanwhile the people who disliked that Karma Shedrub Dargye Ling in Mälarhöjden had turned into a traditional Tibetan Karma-Kagyu centre, led by a Tibetan lama, left the centre. This created a more stable situation, but the troubles continued. After about a year in Sweden, Lama Lodru decided to leave as well. He had worked hard and been important for establishing Tibetan Buddhism in Sweden, but he faced difficulties and was transferred to a centre in San Francisco, where he remains.[22] At this critical point, Nikita and Diana Tolstoy once again became important. The autumn 1975 Diana Tolstoy went to the Karmapa's main seat, Rumtek in India, where she met the Karmapa and asked for a new lama. The Karmapa's choice fell on Lama Ngawang, and it was also decided that an umbrella organisation should be established. The Karmapa named the umbrella organisation Karme Tenpe Gyaltsen (KTG) – "The Victory Banner of the Karma [Kagyu] Teachings," anticipating further growth of Buddhism in Sweden. Nikita and Diana Tolstoy also assisted in creating a non-profit organisation. The association statutes outlined what kind of activities the Swedish Kagyu centres should engage in. It was now clearly stated that the centre (KSDL) and the umbrella organisation (KTG) should facilitate the study and practice of Buddhism, and that the centre belonged to the Karma-Kagyu tradition guided by the Karmapa or his representatives.

Lama Ngawang's life before he came to Sweden

Tibet (1929–1959)[23]

Lama Ngawang was born in Yangpachen, a nomadic area situated about 85 kilometres northwest of Lhasa, in 1929.[24] Before he received his Buddhist name – Ngawang – and before he became a lama, he was called Yulgyel (g.Yul rgyal).[25] As a young child he became interested in Buddhism, and when he was around 8 years old, he learned to read and write at a nunnery named Galo Gonpa (rGwa lo dgon pa), situated on the mountain slopes, a few kilometres above his family's home base in the valley below. The former consort of the Fifteenth Karmapa (Khakyab Dorje, 1871–1922), Urgyen Tsomo (1897–1961), also known as "The Great Dakini of Tsurpu" (Tsurpu Khandro Chenmo), regularly resided at the nunnery. Lama Ngawang formed a strong connection with the nuns at Galo Gonpa and with Urgyen Tsomo.

As a young teenager Lama Ngawang's parents had arranged a marriage for him, but since he did not want to marry, he ran away from home when he was around fourteen. He travelled to a relative who was a monk in the large and famous Drepung monastery in Lhasa. Drepung belonged to the Gelugpa tradition and his relative was a famous chant leader (*dbu mdzad*) at Drepung, known as Tamgo Omdze (rTa mgo dBu mdzad). After having served Tamgo Omdze for some months, Lama Ngawang left Drepung. He joined some nuns from Yangpachen who were going to Shugseb nunnery (Shug gseb dgon) near Kangri Tökar (Gangs ri thod dkar), about 68 kilometres south of Lhasa where the famous female master Jetsun Lochen Rigdzin Chöying Zangmo (1853/1865–1951), also known as Shugseb Khandro, resided.[26] He stayed with Jetsun Lochen for about a year and received complete teachings about how to cut off clinging to a self (pronounced: *chö*, spelled: *gcod*) from her.[27] After this, in the autumn, he returned to his home in Yangpachen. He helped his family to cut grass for the animals during the days, while cutting clinging to a self (*chö*) during the nights.

After this, at age 16, Lama Ngawang went to Tsurpu Monastery (mTshur phu mgon), the main seat of the Karmapa-incarnation lineage, where one of his relatives, the monk Zimka Yeshe Pembar (gZim 'gag ye shes dpal 'bar), lived. On his way to Tsurpu, he encountered the Second Jamgön Kongtrul, Palden Khyentse Öser (1902–1952), the son of the Fifteenth Karmapa, who gave him his name: Karma Ngawang Chöpel (Ka rma Ngag dbang Chos spel).[28]

The Sixteenth Karmapa Rangjung Rigpe Dorje lived in Tsurpu at the time, and Lama Ngawang became a devout disciple of the Karmapa and began practising in accordance with the Karma-Kagyu tradition.[29] Lama Ngawang had now found the tradition to which he felt affiliated and he became a fervent follower of the Karma-Kagyu tradition from this day onward.[30] He wanted to become a resident monk in Tsurpu but, coming from a poor family, he lacked the financial backing that was needed for such an endeavour.

For the sake of collecting offerings that would enable him to fulfil his wish to become a monk at Tsurpu, he served a lama named Chödar (Chos dar) for about six years.[31] Lama Chödar lived in a small monastery named Kuyul Gönpa (Gu yul mgon pa) situated in southwestern Tibet, near Saga. He was the brother of the aforementioned Urgyen Tsomo and had been sent to the monastery after having completed a three-year retreat. During his time in Kuyul Gönpa, Lama Ngawang worked hard and encountered many difficulties. Lama Ngawang explains his time in Kuyul Gönpa as follows in the book *Solens hjärta* (*Heart of the Sun*): "In those years I sometimes had no time to change clothes for a whole month, I fell asleep as soon as I had laid down, exhausted from heavy work" (Ngawang 2011: 17).[32] During this period, Lama Ngawang made a long pilgrimage trip to India. He wandered through Mustang in Northern Nepal, and then to Bodhgaya in India, the place where the Buddha became enlightened. He also visited holy places in the Kathmandu valley before returning to Lama Chödar and Kuyul Gönpa. Lama Chödar became glad to see him again and Lama Ngawang continued to serve him.

Before, during, and after his stay in Kuyul Gönpa, Lama Ngawang went by foot to the holy Kailash Mountain, far away in western Tibet. He circumambulated the mountain clockwise several times and one time he performed the arduous task of circumambulating around Kailash while performing full-length prostrations. On one of his trips to Kailash, he befriended a Bonpo practitioner whom he helped and later visited.

On these journeys, Lama Ngawang walked for months, slept out in the open and withstood many hardships. Then, rich in experience, but still without worldly wealth, Lama Ngawang went back to Tsurpu monastery. Having failed to obtain the necessary offerings that was needed to become a resident monk, he decided to become a mountain hermit. After having received instructions from the meditation master of Tsurpu, Drubpön Tenzin (sGrub dpon bsTan 'dzin), also known as Teja Drubpön (Di g.yag sGrub dpon),[33] he practised the preliminary practices (pronounced: *ngöndro*, spelled: *sngon 'gro*)[34] in a simple dwelling beneath stone blocks, on the mountain slopes above Tsurpu Monastery.

While he was doing his contemplative practices, Lama Ngawang heard that the Karmapa and many of his followers were planning to leave Tibet. Chinese communist troops had begun to invade Tibet, claiming that Tibet was a part of China. Rumours of destroyed monasteries and various forms of suppression spread. Powerful lamas and political leaders were especially threatened by the approaching Chinese armies and thus particularly keen on escaping. In 1959, the Karmapa, the Dalai Lama and thousands of other Tibetans fled from Tibet. Lama Ngawang decided to leave as well and a long dramatic journey on foot over the Himalayan Mountain range began. On his way out of Tibet, he met a monk from Tsurpu named Tönsang (1934–2023), who became one of his closest friends. He also met with the aforementioned female master, Urgyen Tsomo, during his escape. They walked day and night, and after two dramatic weeks of constant fear for being discovered by Chinese troops, they arrived in Bhutan, where Lama Ngawang stayed for two months (Ngawang 2011: 19). Then he went to India, where he remained for seventeen years.

India (1959–1976)

In India, Lama Ngawang often stayed in the vicinity of the Rumtek Monastery in Sikkim, where the Sixteenth Karmapa and other dignitaries of the Kagyu tradition had settled down.[35] He alternated between receiving teachings,[36] performing rituals, pilgrimage[37] and extensive periods of retreat. For about a year, he lived as a hermit in caves above the holy lake Tso Pema (mTsho padma) in India, a place connected with Padmasambhava (Guru Rinpoche), a central figure when Buddhism was brought to Tibet in the eighth and ninth centuries. He also did long fasting retreats (pronounced: *nyungne*, spelled: *smyung gnas*) (Ngawang 2011: 19).[38] He eventually performed the traditional three-year retreat under the guidance of Kalu Rinpoche in Sonada in the Darjeeling district of West Bengal (Ngawang 2011: 20; cf. Fields 2022: 386).

Lama Ngawang was now in his late forties. After a life dedicated to the practice and study of Buddhism, his teachers recognised him as a Buddhist master – a lama – and he became authorised to teach and guide others.[39] Lama Ngawang had experienced great hardships in his life; however, one of his most demanding and difficult tasks, to teach Buddhism in Sweden, was yet to come. Throughout his life he had been a wandering yogi of sorts, not belonging to any monastery; he was something of an outsider. However, his stable personality, unshakable devotion to Buddhism, and his profound trust in his lamas, the Karmapa in particular, had made him respected by the authorities in the Karma-Kagyu tradition to which he belonged. His teachers therefore found him to be a suitable candidate for taking on the huge responsibility of representing Buddhism and the Karma-Kagyu lineage in the West, where a demand for Tibetan lamas began to arise (cf. Baumann 2002: 92).

Lama Ngawang in Sweden (1976–2011)

In 1976, Lama Ngawang and around twenty-five other lamas were sent from India to Kagyu Ling, a Karma-Kagyu centre in La Boulaye, France, where they stayed while waiting to be transported to centres in different countries all over the world. Among these lamas were Lama Ngawang's close friend Lama Tönsang, who became the resident lama of Karma Migyur Ling in France; and Lama Talo (1917–1994), who became the resident lama of Karma Tashi Ling in Norway.[40] Kalu Rinpoche and the Karmapa trusted that these chosen individuals were able to act as their representatives in the Karma-Kagyu centres that recently had been established. After several months of waiting, Lama Ngawang received permission to enter Sweden. In December 1976, he arrived at Arlanda airport and saw Sweden for the first time.

When settling down in the Buddhist centre in Mälarhöjden, Lama Ngawang's life changed dramatically. For the first time in his life, he settled down for a longer period, and the place where he now lived was unlike the places he had stayed at previously. Sweden, one of the most modern and secular countries in the world, was entirely different from nomadic Yangpachen where he was born and raised and from the monasteries and retreat centres in India where he had spent his last seventeen years. It is difficult to imagine what it must have been like for a mature lama from Tibet to adjust himself to this dramatic change.

Lama Ngawang appeared to be unimpressed by western civilisation; he continued to eat roasted barley flour (*tsampa*) and drink salted butter tea, the Tibetan staple food he was used to eating and drinking since childhood. He found no meaning in sightseeing or luxury but kept on with his simple life. He bought his clothes second hand and continued to carry out his daily contemplative ritual practices. However, to be able to teach and communicate with the people at the centre, he needed a translator. Only a few months after Lama Ngawang's arrival at the centre, he was joined by Soenam Jamyangling, an enthusiastic exile Tibetan in his thirties. Soenam had been cured from tuberculosis in Denmark, and he knew Kalu Rinpoche and Lama Ngawang from India. He helped Lama Ngawang, not only with translating but also with bridging the cultural gap between him and his western disciples and sorting out various misunderstandings between them.[41] One of the informants told me that "it was a great relief when Soenam came, he helped a lot and was always happy and easy going."

With a translator at hand, Lama Ngawang began to teach at the centre. He also travelled around to assist at funerals and to help people in need of spiritual guidance in different parts of Sweden. Many school classes and groups of various types visited the centre. Lama Ngawang found it especially important to talk with young people. He told the pupils of visiting school classes that their human lives were precious, and he encouraged them to avoid things that harmed their minds and bodies (cf. Jamyangling 2021: 160; Lagerkvist & Fredriksson 2011: 362).

Lama Ngawang woke up early every morning, performed contemplative rituals by himself, and then went down to the main shrine room at the centre, where a Tārā-ritual which lasted for about an hour was performed.[42] Throughout the day, he did his meditations and ritual practices, and in the evenings, a Chenrezig ritual which lasted for almost an hour was carried out. The morning and evening rituals were open to the public, and the people who lived at the centre were obliged to participate. Besides teaching, Lama Ngawang also served as a living example for people to emulate and be inspired by. He not only talked about Dharma but also practised and lived Dharma. Regardless of what happened around him, he continued his practices, and these daily rituals became the backbone of the centres he supervised.

In the autumn 1977, the head of the Karma-Kagyu tradition, the Sixteenth Karmapa, visited the centre.[43] Numerous other high-ranking lamas visited the centre while Lama Ngawang was the resident lama, for example, the Dalai Lama, Sakya Trizin (the head of the Sakya tradition), Situ Rinpoche, the Third Jamgön Kongtrul Rinpoche (1954–1992), Gyaltsab Rinpoche, Bokar Rinpoche, Kalu Rinpoche, Beru Khyentse Rinpoche, Sangye Nyenpa Rinpoche, Thrangu Rinpoche, Khandro Rinpoche, Jigme Rinpoche (Karmapa's representative in Europe), Khenpo Chödrag Rinpoche and Khenpo Könchog Gyaltsen Rinpoche.[44] Lama Ngawang knew many of these lamas both from Tibet and from his time in India, and in some cases (i.e., Kongtrul Rinpoche and Khandro Rinpoche), he had also met and received instructions from their previous incarnations. Besides these famous visitors, many other lamas, who were not as well known, visited, gave teachings and contributed to spreading Buddhism in Sweden. Some of them were old friends of his who served as resident lamas in other centres in the West. Others came from monasteries in India or Nepal and made teaching tours in Europe.

These visiting lamas stayed for a few days, sometimes for a week or two; they gave teachings (*khrid*), transmissions (*lung*) and empowerments (*dbang*), enabling the people who attended to practise on their own. Then the lamas continued their travelling and went to other centres. Although inspiring people to become Buddhists and to practise Buddhism, they could not see the results that their teachings had when people put them into practice. Lama Ngawang, on the other hand, remained in Sweden, day after day, year after year, and had to deal with difficult situations and obstacles that arose when people attempted to practise Tibetan Buddhism. This enabled him to get to know his disciples and provide long-term guidance, but it also made him realise that it was not an easy task to transmit Buddhism in Sweden.

Lama Ngawang also contributed to creating an organisation where Buddhists in Sweden who belong to different traditions could meet and cooperate. Together with Buddhists from Thailand and Sri Lanka, Lama Ngawang, Sister Amita Nisatta and Trudy Fredriksson began to meet in the late 1970s. These informal meetings became the seed that later grew into the Swedish Buddhist Council (SBC) (Fredriksson 2013: 95).[45] Lama Ngawang also participated in many interfaith meetings with representatives from other religions, and he is remembered for his sincere respect for other religions.

In 1979, Lama Ngawang and group of his students went to India. During the trip, they purchased *Kangyur* and *Tengyur* a collection of canonical scriptures where Tibetan translations of the Buddhist teachings are gathered. He also bought many other important Buddhist texts and ritual objects, thus further establishing Buddhism in the Swedish soil.

The same year another Tibetan Buddhist centre was established in Sweden by the Tibetan lama Khenchen Sherab Gyaltsen Amipa Rinpoche (1931–2014). This centre follows the Sakya tradition and is named Sakya Changchub Chöling.[46] The Sakya centre never has had a resident lama but instead invites lamas to Sweden regularly.

Another important step for the dissemination of Buddhism in Sweden and beyond was the establishment of a retreat centre. In 1980, an old farm was bought in Fellingsbro, a remote place in the countryside, about 169 kilometres west of Stockholm. Once again, Nikita and Diana Tolstoy provided the down payment for purchasing the place, which was named Karma Dechen Ösel Ling (KDÖL) – "Karma [Kagyu] Garden of Great Bliss [and] Luminosity." The retreat centre enabled people to engage in intense long-time Buddhist study and practice. The traditional three-year retreat was carried out three times in Sweden (cf. Masuda 2000: 83). Lama Ngawang now became a retreat master and divided his time between the centre in Mälarhöjden and the retreat centre in Fellingsbro. His own retreat experiences from Tibet and India came to good use when guiding the retreatants. In 1980, in the presence of Kalu Rinpoche, the first Swedish three-year retreat began. This was one of the first three-year retreats in Europe and people came from different countries to participate (cf. Fields 2022: 386–390).[47] In each three-year retreat, a group of people practised together without leaving the retreat area. The main idea behind these intense esoteric practices in isolation from the outside world is that the practitioner should realise the nature of his or her mind and develop wisdom and compassion, enabling him or her to help others. Several of the people participating in the three-year retreat became lamas and acted as such, thus contributing to spreading Tibetan Buddhism in Sweden and beyond.[48] The three-year retreats in Sweden were unusual in so far that both women and men participated in the same retreat. This surprised some people, since men and women usually make such retreats separated. Besides these long retreats, many shorter retreats were done in KDÖL. When Lama Ngawang became older, he was no longer able to be responsible for the three-year retreat and those who wanted to do such a retreat had to do so abroad.[49] However, shorter retreats continued to be performed at KDÖL.

Figure 3.1　The nomadic lama that became resident in Sweden. Lama Ngawang at the retreat
centre Karma Dechen Ösel Ling, Fellingsbro, mid-1980s (Karme Tenpe Gyaltsen's photo collection).

Lama Ngawang also took the initiative of inviting the Dalai Lama to Sweden in
the 1980s (Lagerkvist & Fredriksson 2011: 261). Since then, the Dalai Lama has
visited Sweden many times and he has played an important role in popularising
Tibetan Buddhism in Sweden. Several of his books have been translated to Swedish and many people have attended his talks (cf. Larsson 2021: 81).

In the mid-1980s, the first Swedish *stūpa* was built in front of the three-year
retreat in KDÖL. This was another important step in establishing Buddhism in
Sweden. Although emphasising practice, Lama Ngawang realised the importance
of building something concrete that people could relate to and experience. The
Dalai Lama and representatives from different religions performed the consecra-
tion ceremonies in 1988 (cf. Masuda 2000: 83). Thousands of people have travelled

all the way to this remote area in an unknown part of Sweden to see the *stūpa* over the years. Many people have reported that they, although not being Buddhists, have found it meaningful and inspiring to see the *stūpa* (Fredriksson 2013: 89–91).

In 1988, before the *stūpa* was consecrated, Lama Ngawang, Soenam and several other people participated in a Swedish Buddhist delegation to Tibet.[50] Having returned from the Tibet trip, Soenam gradually became less engaged in the centre's activities, and after a few years as a "general director," he left the centre and never returned (Jamyangling 2021: 209). Instead Soenam devoted his time and energy to a cultural organisation which built schools in Tibet: The Swedish Tibetan School and Culture Society.[51] Many members of the centre joined Soenam and became engaged in this organisation.

Around the same time as Soenam left the centre, a dispute arose within the Karma-Kagyu tradition concerning the identification of the Seventeenth Karmapa – the successor of the Sixteenth Karmapa who passed away in 1981. This must have been tremendously difficult for Lama Ngawang, who was sent to Sweden as a representative of the Karmapa and his tradition. He needed to know which one of the two Karmapa candidates he was representing. Lama Ngawang initially told those who remained at the centre to be neutral and not take sides in the Karmapa controversy. He gradually gained confidence in the Karmapa candidate that one of the regents of the Karma-Kagyu tradition, the Fourteenth Shamar Rinpoche (1952–2014), had installed: Karmapa Thaye Dorje. Around this time, Lama Ngawang was diagnosed with diabetes and he had other health issues as well. Despite all these troubles, the people who remained close to him witness that the atmosphere at the centres was peaceful and serene, and the activities continued like before. However, Lama Ngawang was getting old, and the need for an assisting lama became increasingly urgent. The board of directors at KTG contacted the leading representatives of the Karma-Kagyu tradition in Europe and India and asked for an assisting lama. A lama from Yangpachen named Lama Ngedön Wangchuk was chosen for the task, but he left after a few years.[52]

Despite his age and bad health, Lama Ngawang continued his practices and although many people had left the centres, he remained, demonstrating that the Karmapa and Kalu Rinpoche had chosen the right man for the position. Again and again, he proved that he had a strong, almost unstoppable, will power. During this period, he regularly visited the many centres in Hungary that were flourishing under his disciple Lama Chöpel's supervision, and despite being old and fragile, he also made several trips to Tibet.[53]

The situation at the Karma-Kagyu centres in Sweden improved significantly when a relative of Lama Ngawang, Lama Tsultim Rinpoche, an incarnated lama (*sprul sku*) from Yangpachen, came to the centre. He visited the centre for the first time in 2000, and after a few years, he became a resident lama at the centre.

After Lama Ngawang's last trip to Tibet in 2007, his health gradually became worse. He spent his last years at the centre in Mälarhöjden where he passed away in his room on 9 April 2011. Lama Tsultim Rinpoche remained with Lama Ngawang until his passing and became his successor as the main lama of the centre. Together with Lama Chöpel in Hungary, he is now one of the main upholders of the centres, and he visits the centres in Hungary regularly.

Impressions of Lama Ngawang

Nomadic people in Tibet are known for being straightforward and direct in their way of acting and speaking, and Lama Ngawang was no exception. Besides being direct and spontaneous, he was also charismatic and funny. One of my informants remarked that if he had not become a lama, he would probably have been an actor or comedian. He was exceptionally good at imitating people and animals.

Lama Ngawang was an unconventional and uncontrived person, who surprised and sometimes chocked people who encountered him. They did not expect a religious authority to behave as he sometimes did, and people often did not know what to think of him. What Swedish people initially thought was due to him being from a different culture, surprised Tibetans who met him just as much that it had surprised the Swedes: Lama Ngawang apparently transgressed not only western customs but Tibetan customs as well. While some people found his acts incomprehensible, others were inspired by him and claimed that his actions were profound and meaningful.

A former member of the centre, who was active from the mid-1980s to the mid-1990s, describes Lama Ngawang as follows: "He was one of the most genuine and present persons I have met. Always himself, but people who met him perceived him very differently."[54]

Lama Ngawang did not seem to care what others thought of him and he never tried to become popular. One of my informants mentions that Lama Ngawang could be quite rough: "it was a way for him to teach. But he had no clinging, he said something and acted, and then it was all gone."[55]

Lama Ngawang is also remembered for his confidence in women's ability to practise Buddhism (cf. Lagerkvist & Fredriksson 2011: 261). He often gave donations to nuns and was received with great respect when he visited the nunneries Galo Gönpa in Tibet and Tilokpur in India.

Lama Ngawang's kindness could manifest in odd ways. His former translator, Soenam, writes how Lama Ngawang, when travelling by bus in Nepal towards Tibet together with a Buddhist delegation from Sweden in 1988, had to walk for hours in the heat because of a landslide. "Lama Ngawang wore three or four hats, one on top of the other and he was very warm in the three coats he was wearing in the hot climate of Nepal. His reason was to give them as presents to the needy in Tibet. He was a warm and compassionate lama." (Jamyangling 2021: 176).

Lama Ngawang's compassion was not only directed towards human beings; Elin Lagerkvist and Trudy Fredriksson write about his concern for animals, including fishes and insects: "His leftover food, every tiny piece of rice, was used to feed the innumerable ants at the ant-hills and the birds around the centre" (Lagerkvist & Fredriksson 2011: 261).

One of my informants said the following about Lama Ngawang:

Whatever Lama Ngawang did, had the effect that I looked at myself. While many teachers and lamas that I have met have been inspiring, and have given me wonderful teachings, these teachings have not been as direct as the teachings that Lama Ngawang gave me. He did not even need to say anything; it was enough that you just saw him or that he did something. To teach through signs and examples is a way to teach in Tibetan Buddhism, and this is how he often taught. That is what Lama Ngawang was for me, but that does not mean that others perceived him that way, that is understandable.

When asked about what Lama Ngawang has meant for her, she answered: "It is difficult to express. He is probably the person who have been most important for me, in my life."

Final thoughts

When Buddhism in the West is described in western scholarship, a distinction between traditional Buddhism and Buddhist modernism is often made (cf. McMahan 2008). Another common way of categorising western Buddhism among scholars is that between immigrant/diaspora Buddhism and convert Buddhism (cf. Baumann 2002: 85; Nelson 2017). Lama Ngawang and the centres he oversaw defy such categorisations. Although being a Tibetan, born and raised in a traditional society, Lama Ngawang did not shy away from adapting and adjusting the practices and teachings to the new situation he faced in modern secular Sweden. His way of teaching could be unorthodox and norm-overturning but at the same time very traditional. A meeting between traditional and modern Buddhism thus occurred at the centres he oversaw. The boundaries between diaspora and convert Buddhism were also crossed. He was a traditional Tibetan lama who tried to teach modern western converts what Buddhism, in his opinion, was about. Although there was plenty of room for misunderstanding on both parts, a dynamic and unique learning situation also arose. The Swedish people who met Lama Ngawang became deeply affected by him, and learned something, not only about Buddhism but also, and perhaps most importantly, about themselves.

Notes

1 "Jag har inte kommit den långa vägen till Sverige för att omvända människor till buddhismen. Jag har kommit för att vara till hjälp. Var och en måste välja sin egen väg." (Ngawang 2011: 22). My translation from Swedish.
2 Lama Ngawang disliked the term "Tibetan Buddhism." The Tibetan term for Buddhism is "inner religion" (*nang pa'i chos*). This term does not differentiate between different forms of Buddhism.
3 Among the interviewees, Lama Ngawang's successor, Lama Tsultim Rinpoche, has been particularly helpful. I have had many conversations about Lama Ngawang with him over the years. I have also interviewed the chair of the Swedish Buddhist Community (SBC), Trudy Fredriksson. She was present when Lama Ngawang arrived in Sweden and has been a member of the board of Karma Shedrub Dargye Ling since that time. Moreover, I have interviewed the man who brought Lama Ngawang to Sweden from France in 1976. He was a central figure when Tibetan Buddhism was established in Sweden and has spent much time with Lama Ngawang. I have also interviewed a female member of the centre who was close to Lama Ngawang from the late 1980s up to Lama Ngawang's passing.

4 I met Lama Ngawang for the first time in 1985, served as his assistant and translator in the 1990s, and remained close to him until his passing, but I was not present when he passed away.

5 The information in this section is primarily derived from one of my informants and from Trudy Fredriksson, both were actively involved when Tibetan Buddhism came to Sweden. There is also some information about the centre and its history on the web-page of Karme Tenpe Gyaltsen (KTG) www.ktg.nu; a short description is also found in Masuda 2000.

6 See, for example, Hedin 1909; David-Néel 1933. Other examples of books that were translated to Swedish are Lama Anagarika Govinda's (Ernst Lothar Hoffmann, 1898–1985) *The Way of the White Clouds* (*De vita molnens väg* 1975); *The Life of Milarepa* (*Milarepas liv*, Rechung 1954; Lagerkvist 1986); and *The Tibetan Book of the Dead* (*Den tibetanska dödsboken*, Evans-Wentz & Dawa-Samdup (eds) 1974). Besides these books the Swedish translation of *Tintin in Tibet* (*Tintin i Tibet*) by the Belgian cartoonist Hergé (1969) contributed to make Tibet and Tibetan Buddhism known in Sweden.

7 Being the first Buddhist nun of Swedish origin makes her historically important. Sister Amita founded a small organization called "Buddhismens vänner" (Friends of Buddhism) and she was an honorary member of the board of KTG/KSDL for a while.

8 One of my informants travelled to India before he met the lamas in Sweden and so did Ole and Hannah Nydahl who also were important when Tibetan Buddhism came to Sweden (Nydahl 2011). To take refuge to the Buddha, Dharma and Sangha is what makes a person a Buddhist (cf. Larsson 2021: 82–84).

9 Among the members of the Swedish Lama Society, we find Elin Lagerkvist (1918–2009), daughter of the famous Swedish author Pär Lagerkvist (1891–1974) and Gudrun Hegardt (1922–2014). Elin Lagerkvist remained an important member of KSDL until her passing.

10 He gave teachings at Strindbergsmuséet in Stockholm, Drottninggatan 85.

11 Karma can also stand for Karma Kagyu Teachings.

12 Both members later participated in the first three-year retreat in Sweden.

13 For more on this practice, see Bokar 1991; Gyatso 1997.

14 Jan Bärmark later pursued an academic career and became professor in theory of science (vetenskapsteori) at Gothenburg University.

15 Before the centre dissolved, the Tibetan lama Khenpo Tsultrim Gyatso visited Gothenburg. Later, in 1994, the Association for Tibetan Buddhism in Gothenburg (Föreningen för Tibetansk Buddhism i Göteborg) was founded (this association is still active). Jan Bärmark served as the chair of the association for a while. For more information, see their homepage: https://www.tibetanskbuddhism.se/.

16 According to one of my informants, Karma Ling was situated in the village Språxhult, in Markaryd, Småland.

17 A picture of Karma Ling is found in Nydahl (2011: 13).

18 For a description of the Black Crown Ceremony and the impact it had on those who attended it during the Karmapa's visit to the United States the same year, see Fields (2022: 381–383).

19 "Tibet Oral History Project," interview with Lama Lodru Rinpoche, 17 June 2013.

20 I use the term converts for people who were not born into Buddhism but became Buddhists later in life. It should be held in mind, however, that many of these so-called converts do not like the designation. They do not necessarily perceive Buddhism as a religion and many of them do not feel that they have belonged to any specific religious tradition before they became Buddhists, thus no conversion has occurred.

21 Nikita Tolstoy was the grandchild of the famous Russian author Leo Tolstoy (1828–1910).

22 Kagyu Droden Kunchab, http://www.kdk.org/lama-lodru-rinpoche.html.

23 The information about Lama Ngawang's life in Tibet is primarily derived from a talk that Lama Tsultim Rinpoche gave at KSDL, 9 April 2022, and from interviews with Lama Tsultim Rinpoche. Lama Ngawang's life is also described in the book *Solens hjärta* (Ngawang 2011: 13–23). For an English translation, see "Lama Ngawang Rinpoche" https://buddha-tar.hu/en/lama-ngawang-rinpoche/.

24 According to Lama Ngawang's passport, he was born in 1927, but when asked about his birth year, he said that he was born in an Earth Snake Year (*sa sprul*), which would mean that he was born in 1929.

25 To avoid confusion, I will call him Lama Ngawang throughout this essay. I have chosen to write Tibetan as pronounced and not as spelt. I have, nevertheless, provided the spelling of certain names and words that are uncommon and therefore likely difficult to identify in brackets (and some technical terms as well). The spellings of some of these names are tentative.

26 For more information about Jetsun Lochen, see, for example, Havnevik (1999); Chhosphel & Tsuji (2018). For a short description of Shugseb nunnery, see Gyurme Dorje (2004: 161–162).

27 It is noteworthy that Jetsun Lochen is believed to be the reincarnation/emanation of Machik Labdrön (1055–1149), the female master from whom the lineage of *gcod* originated. For more on Machik Labdrön and this practice, see, for example, Edou (1996).

28 It is a bit unclear what type of ordination he received from the Second Jamgön Kongtrul. For stories about, and a picture of, the Second Jamgön Kongtrul, see Kunsang & Schmidt (2005: 193–203; 264–265). Bear in mind that Lama Ngawang was not yet a lama and, therefore, not yet known as "Lama Ngawang," but from this day, he got his Buddhist name: Ngawang.

29 For more about the Karmapa and other incarnations in the lineage, see, for example, Douglas & White (1976).

30 He was, however, impartial in his approach toward other religions and other Buddhist traditions.

31 He was twenty-two when he began assisting Lama Chödar, and stayed for seven years, according to *Solens hjärta* (Ngawang 2011: 17).

32 "Under de åren hade jag ibland under en hel månad inte tid att ta av mig kläderna. Jag kastade mig ned på bädden och somnade ifrån allt, uttröttat av tungt arbete" (Ngawang 2011: 17). My translation from Swedish.

33 A photo of Drubpön Tenzin is reproduced in *Solens hjärta* (Ngawang 2011: 18).

34 For more on this practice, see Kongtrul (1986).

35 According to *Solens hjärta*, he stayed in Rumtek for six years (Ngawang 2011: 19).

36 He received teachings and empowerments from distinguished lamas, such as the Karmapa, the Dalai Lama and Dilgo Khyentse Rinpoche (c. 1910–1991) (Ngawang 2011: 20).

37 He visited Bodhgaya and other holy places connected with the historical Buddha in India. He also went to sacred places in and around the Kathmandu valley.

38 Lama Ngawang's *nyungne* teacher was Tulku Lodru Rabzel (sPrul sku bLo gros Rab gsal). This practice is said to have been created by the fully ordained Indian nun Gelongma Palmo (b.10th cent. – d.11th cent). For more on Gelongma Palmo, see for example Stenzel (2023); for more on *nyungne*, see Wangchen Rinpoche (2009).

39 A letter of authorization written by Kalu Rinpoche is included in *Solens Hjärta* (Ngawang 2011: 9).

40 Both of them were friends with Lama Ngawang and they visited each other several times.

41 Soenam describes the seventeen years he worked for the centre in his memoirs, *My Son of Tibet Never Give Up!* (Jamyangling 2021).

42 For more on this practice, see Beyer (1973); Bokar (1999).

43 The Karmapa brought along many prominent lamas when he visited.

44 Before Lama Ngawang arrived, in 1976, the head of the Nyingma tradition, Dilgo Khyentse, visited KSDL.
45 SBC was a national union for Buddhist associations of various Buddhist traditions. In 2019, the SBC reorganised into a registered religious community named Swedish Buddhist Community, currently having twenty-four Buddhist member organisations, collectively serving more than 11,000 registered individuals ("Swedish Buddhist Community," accessed 2023-04-05, https://www.sverigesbuddhister.se/about-sbc/).
46 Sakya Changchub Chöling, accessed 2023-04-09, https://www.sakya.se/index.html.
47 It is noteworthy that two Swedish women participated in the first three-year retreat in France. This retreat began in 1976. One of these women became a translator for lamas after the retreat. She visits the Karma-Kagyu centres in Sweden regularly translating for a learned Tibetan lama (*khenpo*).
48 Most notable among them: Lama Chöpel (Ferenc Füzeskuti) who served as a lama in Sweden many years and nowadays is the main lama of several centres in Hungary; Lama Lodru (Allan Fotheringham) who after having served as a lama at KDÖL for many years, became the general secretary of the Swedish Tibetan School and Culture Society where he also teaches; the late Jetsunma Wangyel (Britt Lindhe, 1947–2018) who taught in several centres in Sweden; Lama Roar (Roar Vestre) who is teaching in the Karma-Kagyu centres in Norway (Karma Tashi Ling buddhistsamfunn, Oslo) and the United States (Mindrolling Lotus Garden, Virginia).
49 Three Swedes have made three-year retreats in France more recently. All three of them were disciples of Lama Ngawang and are participating in the Swedish centres. One of them, a woman, did her three-year retreat at Karma Migyur Ling in Montchardon, and two of them, a man and woman, did their three-year retreats in Dhagpo Kundreul Ling, a Karma Kagyu centre in Auvergne, France.
50 This was the second time Lama Ngawang returned to Tibet after he left in 1959. He also visited Tibet in 1986 together with Britt Lindhe (Ani Wangyel) who participated in the first three-year retreat.
51 Svensk-tibetanska skol-och kulturföreningen, https://tibet-school.org/EN-homepage/about-us/background.
52 Lama Ngedön Wangchuk served as assisting lama from 1996 to 1998.
53 He visited Tibet in 1986, 1988, 2002, 2003 and 2007.
54 "Lama Ngawang. En av de mest genuina och närvarande personer jag har mött. Alltid sig själv men ändå uppfattades han väldigt olika av de personer som träffade honom." Buddhism i Sverige, public Facebook page, accessed 2023-02-10, https://www.facebook.com/groups/662538120487021/search/?q=sven%20tobrand. My translation to Swedish.
55 Throughout this essay, I have edited my informants' answers and translated them to English.

Bibliography and sources

Baumann, Martin. 2002. "Buddhism in Europe: Past, Present, Prospects." In *Westward Dharma: Buddhism Beyond Asia*, edited by Prebish, Charles S. and Baumann, Martin, 85–105. Berkeley: University of California Press.
Beyer, Stephan. 1973. *The Cult of Tārā: Magic and Ritual in Tibet*. Berkeley: University of California Press.
Bokar Rinpoche. 1991. *Chenrezig Lord of Love: Principles and Methods of Deity Meditation*. San Francisco: Clear Point Press.
Bokar Rinpoche. 1999. *Tara: The Feminine Divine*. Clear Point Press: San Francisco.
Bärmark, Jan. 2010. *Jag vet inte: självkännedom genom humor, buddhism och psykoterapi*. Stockholm: Carlsson.

Chhosphel, Samten and Catherine Tsuji. 2018. "Shukseb Jetsun Choying Zangmo." *Treasury of Lives*, accessed March 27, 2023. https://treasuryoflives.org/biographies/view/Shukseb-Jetsun-Choying-Zangmo/3152.

David-Néel, Alexandra. 1933. *Bland mystiker och magiker i Tibet*. Stockholm: Geber.

Douglas, Nik and Meryl White. 1976. *Karmapa: The Black Hat Lama of Tibet*. London: Luzac.

Edou, Jérôme. 1996. *Machig Labdron and the Foundations of Chod*. Ithaca: Shambhala Publications.

Evans-Wentz, Walter Yeeling and Dawa-Samdup, Kazi (eds.). 1974. *Den tibetanska dödsboken eller Upplevelserna efter döden på Bardo-planet enligt lama Kazi Dawa-Samdups återgivning*. Stockholm.

Fields, Rick. 2022. *How the Swans Came to the Lake: A Narrative History of Buddhism in America*. Boulder: Shambhala Publications.

Fredriksson, Trudy. 2013. *Uppvaknandets vägar: från buddhistisk historia till nutidens utövning och gemenskapsliv*. Bromma: Nämnden för statligt stöd till trossamfund. Tillgänglig på Internet: http://www.sst.a.se/download/18.6e8d553514f5d72fdf7286f5/1440485848904/Uppvaknandets+v%C3%A4gar_komplett.pdf.

Goldstein-Kyaga, Katrin. 2008. *Tibet och den svenska tystnaden: Tibets politiska status och Sveriges ståndpunkt*. Stockholm: Amaryllis.

Govinda, Anagarika. 1975. *De vita molnens väg: en buddhistisk pilgrims upplevelser i Tibet*. Stockholm: Bergh.

Gyatso, Janet. 1997. "An Avalokiteśvara Sādhana." In Donald S. Lopez, Jr. (ed.) *Religions of Tibet in Practice*, 266–270. Princeton: Princeton University Press.

Gyurme Dorje. 2004. *Tibet*. Third edition. Bath: Footprints Handbooks.

Havnevik, Hanna. 1999. *The Life of Jetsun Lochen Rinpoche (1865–1951) as Told in Her Autobiography*, Vols. 1 & 2. Ph.D. Dissertation. Oslo: Faculty of Arts.

Hedin, Sven. 1909. *Transhimalaya: upptäckter och äfventyr i Tibet*. Stockholm: Bonnier.

Hergé. 1969. *Tintin i Tibet*. Stockholm: Illustrationsförlaget.

Jamyangling, Soenam T. 2021. *My Son of Tibet: Never Give Up!* Stockholm: Vulkan.

Kongtrul, Jamgön (The First Kongtrul Lodru Thaye, 1813–1899). 1986. *The Torch of Certainty*. Translated by Judith Hanson. Boston: Shambhala Publications.

Kunsang, Erik Pema and Schmidt, Marcia Binder. 2005. *Blazing Splendor: The Memoirs of the Dzogchen Yogi Tulku Urgyen Rinpoche, as Told to Erik Pema Kunsang and Marcia Binder Schmidt*. 1st ed. Kathmandu, Nepal: Rangjung Yeshe Publications.

Lagerkvist, Elin, translator. 1986. *Milarepas liv*. Stockholm: Natur och kultur.

Lagerkvist, Elin and Fredriksson, Trudy. 2011. "Vördade Lama Ngawangs verksamhet." In *Solens hjärta: hur man tränar sitt sinne – spegeln som klargör allt*. edited by Elin Lagerkvist, 260–262. Johanneshov: Larson.

Larsson, Stefan. 2021. "Svenska buddhister och buddhisminfluerade svenskar." In *Människan i en existentiell kultur: En antologi om Människa-Kultur-Religionsprogrammet vid Högskolan i Gävle*, edited by Olov Dahlin, Sara Duppils and Jari Ristiniemi, 71–88. Gävle: Gävle University Press.

Lopez, Donald S. 1998. *Prisoners of Shangri-La: Tibetan Buddhism and the West*. Chicago: University of Chicago Press.

Masuda, Monica. 2000. "Buddhismen i Sverige." *Orientaliska Studier*, no 103–104, 81–88.

McMahan, David L. 2008. *The Making of Buddhist Modernism*. New York: Oxford University Press.

Nelson, John. 2017. "Diasporic Buddhisms and Convert Communities." In *The Oxford Handbook of Contemporary Buddhism*, edited by Michael Jerryson. Oxford Handbooks (2017; online edn, Oxford Academic, 5 Dec. 2016), https://doi.org/10.1093/oxfordhb/9780199362387.013.21, (accessed 10 Feb. 2023).

Ngawang, Lama. 2011. *Solens hjärta: hur man tränar sitt sinne – spegeln som klargör allt*. edited by Elin Lagerkvist. Johanneshov: Larson.

Nydahl, Lama Ole. 2011. *Riding the Tiger: Twenty Years on the Road: The Risks and Joys of Bringing Tibetan Buddhism to the West*. Third printing. Nevada: Blue Dolphin Publishing.

Plank, Katarina. 2015. "Buddhister och buddhism: Asiatisk migration, konvertiter och sekulär meditation." In *Det mångreligiösa Sverige: ett landskap i förändring*, edited by Andersson, Daniel and Sander, Åke, 203–262. Lund: Studentlitteratur.

Rechung. 1954. *Milarepa, Tibets store yogi*. Translated to Swedish by Daniel Andreae. Stockholm: Natur och Kultur.

Stenzel, Julia. 2023. "Gelongma Pelmo." *Treasury of Lives*, (accessed Mar 17, 2023), http://treasuryoflives.org/biographies/view/dge-slong-ma-dpal-mo/13773.

Svanberg, Ingvar and Runblom, Harald (eds). 1988. *Det mångkulturella Sverige: en handbok om etniska grupper och minoriteter*. Stockholm: Gidlund.

Wangchen Rinpoche. 2009. *Buddhist Fasting Practice: The Nyungne Method of Thousand-Armed Chenrezig*. Ithaca: Snow Lion Publications.

Interviews

Lama Tsultim Rinpoche 2023-02-03, 2023-03-26
Trudy Fredriksson 2023-02-20
Male informant 2023-02-13
Female informant 2023-02-23

Talks

Talk by Lama Tsultim Rinpoche at the Buddhist centre Karma Shedrub Dargye Ling, 9 April 2022.

Websites

"Buddhism i Sverige," public Facebook page, accessed 2023-02-10, https://www.facebook.com/groups/BuddhismISverige.

"Föreningen för tibetansk buddhism i Göteborg," accessed 2023-02-02, https://www.tibetanskbuddhism.se/.

"The Hungarian Karma-Kagyüpa Buddhist Community," accessed 2023-02-20, https://buddha-tar.hu/en/about-us/.

"Kagyu Droden Kunchab," accessed 2023-02-18, http://www.kdk.org/lama-lodru-rinpoche.html.

"Karma Migyur Ling," accessed 2023-04-04, https://www.montchardon.fr/.

"Karma Tashi Ling buddhistsamfunn," accessed 2023-02-02, https://www.ktl.no/.

"Karme Tenpe Gyaltsen (KTG)," accessed 2023-02-02, www.ktg.nu.

"Karma Yönten Ling," accessed 2023-02-02, https://buddhism.se/larare.html.

"Lama Ngawang Rinpoche," accessed 2023-04-11, https://buddha-tar.hu/en/lama-ngawang-rinpoche/.

"The Swedish-Tibetan School- and Culture Society," accessed 2023-02-02, https://tibet-school.org/EN-homepage/.

"Tibet Oral History Project," Interview #8C – Lama Lodu Rinpoche, 17 June 2013, accessed 2023-04-09, https://www.tibetoralhistory.org/interview_details.php?id=202

"Sakya Changchub Chöling," accessed 2023-04-09, https://www.sakya.se/index.html.

"Summary of the Life of Lama Ngawang (1927–2011) in Sweden," accessed 2023-04-11, Karmapa-News.org, accessed 2023-02-20, https://www.karmapa-news.org/summary-life-lama-ngawang-1927-2011-sweden/.

"Swedish Buddhist Community (SBC)," accessed 2023-04-05, https://www.sverigesbuddhister.se/about-sbc/.

"Treasury of lives," http://treasuryoflives.org.

4 A Thai missionary for the Dhamma in Sweden

Ten years of a monk in Snowyland

Preedee Hongsaton

Introduction

Thai Buddhism was in the process of institutionalisation in Sweden at a historical conjunction between the 1980s and 2000s. This process began with the contestation between, on the one hand, folk Buddhism and, on the other hand, Official Thai Buddhism as espoused by the Thai state. I will elaborate this through the life and works of Phra Chamnong Chutinattharo (1938–2003), the first Buddhist missionary monk in Sweden and Scandinavia.

With a humble background, the recognition that Phra Chamnong posthumously received from the Thai monkhood and the public imagination about him are an achievement. We do not know much about his life before monkhood, but we know that he was born in a remote Southern Thai village in the Phatthalung province. His career path did not show a quick rise like intellectual monks of his contemporary,[1] and he only slowly rose into the middle ecclesiastical rank and moved to the Saket Temple in Bangkok at the end of 1970s. During this time, he was a teacher to novices and taught high school students at the Buddhist Sunday School (Chamnong Chuttinattharo 1993). There was nothing remarkable in his career at this stage. But by the time that he entered his forties, his connection to the transnational Buddhist world began. In the early 1980s he received support to continue his study in philosophy in India. Once he finished and with sufficient knowledge of English, he was sent to the Netherlands, and from there he entered Sweden in 1983. He spent the last decades of his life there until his unexpected death in 2003. After his death, he was entitled officially the Thai Buddhist Missionary in Sweden (The Sangha Supreme Council of Thailand, 30 July 2003).

His posthumous recognition as the Thai missionary monk in Sweden represents only a limited understanding of Phra Chamnong himself and the understanding of Thai Buddhism in Sweden in general. In 1993, Phra Chamnong published a memoir titled *sip pi phra thai nai daen hima* [*Ten Years of a Thai Monk in Snowy Lands*]. Flipping through the pages of the memoir for the first time, I expected to find the conceptualisation of a missionary and how the words of the Buddha were being spread during the decades Phra Chamnong was living as a monk in the "snowyland." But I was struck by how little he mentioned the *dhamma*, and instead

DOI: 10.4324/9781003529767-4

the pages are filled with unguarded lived experience and a sense of humour. His was the life of a humble diaspora, with the Buddhist community as his only company. This memoir adds the story of folk Buddhism in the understanding of Thai migrant lives in Sweden in the last two decades of the twentieth century.

With this in mind, I question the use of the "missionary intent" argument (notably Kitiarsa, 2010) at this particular historical point and invites a closer look at the sociopolitical context. According to Kitiarsa, Thai Buddhism meets the criteria for being a transnational religion or one among many "world religions" which carry with it an "expansive aspiration" by default (Kitiarsa, 2010: 113). But we come to a contradiction here: how can this form of Buddhism be "Thai," in other words "national," while at the same time being "trans" national? If Buddhism ought to be universal, then how can it be Thai at the same time? How can we understand this contradiction?

Meditating on inquiries in this vein, Gananath Obeyesekere proposes to distinguish the two terms which might be useful as a point of departure, *sāsana* and *Buddhasāsana*, two terms of which, in my view, Kitiarsa's reading is too limited (Kitiarsa 2010: 113–114). For Obeyesekere, in the history of Buddhism's establishment in South and Southeast Asia, "the idea of *sasana* took on a purely local meaning as the religion of the 'nation,' as it were . . . as the community of the faithful and the beliefs and symbols associated with an imagined sense of communal unity." The other term, *Buddhasāsana*, expresses "Buddhism's translocal, indeed global outreach . . . the large Buddhist order that knows no ethnic or national bounds and represents the universal Buddhist church." What underlines Obeyesekere's proposal is a necessary contradiction – in his words "interplay" – of the two in the process of Buddhism becoming global (Obeyesekere 2006: 69–70). This interplay is essential to understanding the role of Phra Chamnong.

Here Obeyesekere's awareness is pronounced: although Buddhism is a universal religion, it is not a world religion "in any obvious sense. Buddhism did not penetrate fully even the then-known world of Asia; neither did Islam. It was the discovery of the new world and European imperialism that saw one universal religion, Christianity, began to take root in virtually every part of the world and in this sense it becomes the world religion, and perhaps remains the only one" (Obeyesekere 2006: 70).

To consider the experiences of Phra Chamnong, I will read Thai Buddhism in Sweden for "concurrences" (Fur 2017), showing the entanglements between Thai migrants' folk Buddhism and Official Thai Buddhism, which the Thai monkhood wished to promote. The two Buddhisms manifested themselves *at the same time* and were often in tension with each other. The "missionary intent" thus will be re-evaluated and it will take into account the actual experience of a missionary monk Phra Chamnong through his own writings which will be set against a historical background.

According to Gunlög Fur, concurrences are a method of studying life "as lived in different realms that at times interfere with and influence one another, while at other times appearing as completely separate and incommensurable." More importantly, as a concurrence emphasises a sense of competition and conflict, it "signals contestation over interpretations and harbours different, divergent, and at times competing claims . . . The task is to account for intersections, contentions, imbalances, and bridge-building as part of the manner in which human beings narrate and engage with their world(s)" (Fur 2017: 33, 40). These descriptions of concurrences accommodate the Buddhisms that I investigate, not only because they co-existed simultaneously, albeit by centring different narratives, but also because they remained contradictory.

The Thai migrants' Buddhism that Phra Chamnong experienced took a form that has usually been criticised by Official Thai Buddhism. It is pejoratively called ignorant blind faith (*khwam ngom ngai*) consisting of supernaturalism, superstition and rituals and, hence, does not represent true Buddhist teachings. For educated Buddhist intellectuals, monks and laymen, these are the reasons for Thai social problems (Jackson 2022: 20–22). It is therefore not surprising that the official recognition of Phra Chamnong's missions mentions nothing about his work on the ground, connecting with the ordinary Thai migrant lives in Sweden. To take into account the different and competing claims about Buddhism in Sweden towards the end of the last century, it is necessary to listen to the voices of the Thai migrants that he encountered throughout his career there.

The arguments are twofold. First, by studying the role of Phra Chamnong in Sweden from the 1980s until his death there in 2003, I propose that he saw his role as to facilitating Buddhist migrant lives in Sweden more than as a missionary mission: his focus was more on *sāsana* than *Buddhasāsana*, to use Obeyesekere's distinction. His tasks were very ritualistic, repetitive, spiritual, superstitious and received no support from the Thai state. These are repeated again and again in his own account. He was aware of the role of a missionary monk, that is, to spread the word of the Buddha as understood by educated Buddhist intellectuals (Chamnong Chutinattharo 1993: 36). But he found himself most of the time servicing the unity of an imagined local community. This concurrent narrative was rarely recognised in the official story of Thai Buddhism bolstered by the Thai state.

Buddhism at this particular conjunction in Thai lives in Sweden – that is, in the mid-1980s – manifests not Official Thai Buddhism alone, but also its concurrences with "Thai supernaturalism" which characterised the lives of Thai peasants and urban workers (Jackson 1989: 40–62). Looking at Phra Chamnong's activities in his memoir *Ten Years,* his Buddhism was not so much about the "religions of expansion," but he prioritised folk Buddhism and focused on the lives of Thai commoners in the Nordic countries and Europe. These migrant lives, in turn, determined the ways in which Phra Chamnong reflected his mission. His memoir expresses how connecting and facilitating Buddhist lives were at the forefront of his tasks.

It was only after Phra Chamnong's death in 2003 that the Thai state and the Thai monkhood capitalised on Phra Chamnong's success, turning him posthumously into the Official Thai Missionary Monk. His colloquial name, *Luang Ta* (venerable grandfather), would be officially recognised, and he would be represented as central to the Thai Buddhist lives in Sweden. Two developments made this possible: support from the Thai state and a growing global recognition of Buddhism as a world religion. The narrative about Phra Chamnong from this point on would be elaborated from Bangkok and heavily tainted with nationalism: the Nation-Religion-King pillars that bolstered the Thai state through the twentieth century (Murashima 1988). The mission for the Thai monkhood was not only to spread Buddhism but also to spread "Thai" Buddhism. In short, the universal vision has been espoused by the nationally bounded entity.

The second argument follows that when we insist on reading Thai Buddhisms in Sweden as concurrences, we will be able to hear the voices of migrant Thais, which were peripheral to the story of Official Thai Buddhism. While the Thai monkhood kept on promoting its expansion activities, we hear at the same time the voices of migrants, who spearheaded the establishment of Thai temples in Sweden in the first place. These voices confirm that "non-Western polities and cultural organisations possessed socially recognised and validated collections of information and facts . . . pertaining to such things as historic/al events and processes, law, and religion" (Fur 2017: 41). While Buddhism in the West was being promoted as a philosophy, an alternative way of living from the material Western religion,[2] we also hear that rituals were central to the lives of migrants in Sweden. It follows that if we see Phra Chamnong's work as connected to the common people's lives, we will begin to see the roles of Thai and Buddhist migrants and start putting them at the centre of the narrative. That is what Phra Chamnong did in his memoirs.

Official Thai Buddhism

To understand the role ascribed to Phra Chamnong, one must first look at the growing role of Buddhism as part of the official state ideology in Thailand since the turn of the last century. The transformation of the Thai state between the 1890s through to the 1930s marked the beginning of such a process. This very process was part and parcel of the emergence of the absolutist state, which consisted of a number of strands. King Chulalongkorn (r.1868–1910) of the Chakri Dynasty was central to this manoeuvring. Administratively, a premodern conception of the polity based on the traditional Traiphum cosmology shifted over the course of the late nineteenth century towards a modern conception of Siam as a nation-state, centred on the monarch. These moves included the redefinitions of sources of governing authority, the unification of central, provincial and judicial administration and, importantly, the introduction of modern geography through mapping which rendered the emergence of Siam's "geo-body" (Winichakul, 1994). Economically, the feudal mode of production shifted towards a capitalist one. The centuries-old manpower (*phrai*) system, with power distributed among various individual nobles and elites, was replaced by a reformed taxation system overseen by the new Ministry of Finance, which provided revenue for the state-building process (Chaiyan 1994: 85–92; Mead 2004: 38–65). Ideologically, the foundation for the idea of Thai nationhood was formed around three core institutions: nation, religion and king. These transformations stemmed from both the external pressure of European colonialism in the region and the internal political moves of Siamese elites themselves. This formation of official state ideology was "founded on the traditional Thai concept of Buddhist monarchy, on a conception of *chat* [nation] as a national political community, and on the firm belief of the significance of the Thai national traditions" (Murashima 1988: 88)

Central to our focus is the transformation of the Thai monkhood during this period, marked especially by the establishment of a centralised Buddhist authority – one of several campaigns to build an absolute monarchy under King Chulalongkorn (r. 1868–1910). While thousands of Theravāda Buddhist monks and monasteries had been involved with the lives of Thais for centuries, during this period, the reformation put them under one organisational structure, whether they agreed or not. The figures at the centre of this were Prince Wachirayan (1860–1921) and Prince Damrong Rajanubhab (1862–1943), Chulalongkorn's younger half-brothers, whose work on ecclesiastical reform culminated in the 1902 Sangha Act. The code was perhaps the first to codify an official Thai Buddhism. The Act established a governing body for the monkhood, reorganised the ecclesiastical hierarchy, and defined the ways in which Thai Buddhism related to monarchy. It went as far as to penalise those without an officially-recognised monastic affiliation. These "vagrant" monks would now be arrested and forced to disrobe. From this point on, those who were outside of the official recognition would not be recognised as monks (Ishii 1986: 69–71). Through these monastic reforms, Buddhism in Thailand was transformed into "Thai" Buddhism. The king stepped into the role of the "defender" of a national religion, while the latter in turn provided the monarch with the ideological legitimation to rule.

A few decades on, Official Thai Buddhism would itself be increasingly seen as the defender of Thai nationhood, with the support of the United States. From the 1950s on, Washington recognised Official Thai Buddhism as an indispensable force for its anti-communist activities, a move which the Thai government and the Thai monkhood facilitated (Ford, 2017). This included the establishment of the Dhamma Missionary project.

The Thai Dhamma Missionary

The history of the figure of the Thai Dhamma Missionary (*Thammathut*) emerged with the Cold War in Thailand, or "the American Era" (Anderson and Mendiones, 1985). With the support of the government's Department of Religious Affairs, the state-sponsored Buddhist missionary effort was first initiated in 1963 (Ford 2017: 196) with plans to send monks who were experienced in meditation training and living in rural areas out to politically sensitive areas to combat the encroachment of communism, especially the northern and northeastern Thailand. Accordingly, the Thai Monkhood (Sangha) came to take over the programme in 1966 and initiate various missions, playing a part in national integration during the Cold War (Keyes 1971: 560–562).

By 1965, despite various shortcomings, the programme was evaluated as successful (Suksamran 1979: 188). From a mere 180 missionary monks who participated in the 1964 missions, a year later the number had risen to 818 (Ford, 2017: 196, 198). The Thai Monkhood moved actively into anti-communist roles and the Thammathut monks were important to these efforts. From 1966 to 1975, the number of monks included in the programme grew to 2,196 and served in 70 provinces (Suksamran 1979: 190).

The history of the Dhamma Missionary Programme's overseas expansion paralleled these anti-communist activities. As early as 1957, the first Thai temple abroad was built in Bodhgaya, India, to mark the 2,500 years of Buddhism. In the mid-1960s, the first Thai temple in Europe, Buddhapadipa Temple, was built in Wimbledon, England (Kitiarsa, 2010: 116).

The decline of communism worldwide and the collapse of the Communist Party of Thailand (CPT) during the late 1970s and early 1980s ushered the Dhamma Missionary Programme into a second, transnational phase. Its energy and resources were redirected towards Thai communities abroad. In Thailand, the Dhammaduta College restarted its preparation programme in answer to this challenge (Dhammaduta College, 2022).[3] During this period, the history of the programme corresponded with the transnational migrations of Thais to Western countries. The biggest Thai community outside of Thailand was in the United States, which became the destination where the Dhamma Missionary Programme was most clearly pronounced. The Wat Thai of Los Angeles was built around 1971 followed by Vajiradhammapadip Temple in New York (est. 1972), Dhammaram Temple in Chicago (est. 1976) and Buddhawararam Temple (around late 1970s). These were among the largest Thai Buddhist activities abroad; together they established the Thai Sangha Council in the United States in 1975 (Sriboonhung 2007: 40–41). From that decade onwards, the number of Thai temples around the world multiplied in response to the growing Thai communities abroad. From the current official numbers, there are 596 Thai temples overseas, with 149 in Europe. For the Nordic region, there are currently five Thai temples in Denmark, seventeen in Sweden, thirteen in Norway, two in Finland and one in Iceland (National Office of Buddhism, 2021).

The life and career of the Dhamma Missionary in Sweden

The story of Phra Chamnong Chutinattharo is part of this transnational phase of Thai Buddhism, which Kitiarsa describes as "the venue of and venue for reconfiguring, negotiating, and expression of diasporic religio-cultural identities involving sets of actors, structured regulations, and processes of cross-border religious globalization" (Kitiarsa 2010: 111). He was born in 1938 in Phatthalung Province in Southern Thailand. There has been relatively little recorded about his time prior to Sweden, but we know that he went to study for his master's degree in India during the early 1980s. He continued to live in the subcontinent and was stationed in Sri Lanka for a few years. After Sri Lanka, he moved back to his home province for about six months. We can surmise from his short bio that he became the assistant to the Head Abbot at Saket Temple in Bangkok. It was Saket Temple that was responsible for the selection of monks to be sent abroad. Between 1983 and 1984, he was sent by the Head Abbot at Saket Temple to the Netherlands. After about half a year and some visits, Phra Chamnong moved to Sweden in late 1985, while holding the ecclesiastical title Phra Visutthisophon (Chamnong Chutinattharo 1993: [7]).

Phra Chamnong was one of the major figures in establishing the first Thai temple in Sweden in 1984, which was also the first in Scandinavia (Buddharama Temple 2021). By that year, the Thai community in Sweden had already taken the initiative to establish a place in the Stockholm region for Sweden's growing Thai community, which by that time numbered 1,534 (SCB, 2021). They contacted Phra Chamnong while he was in the Netherlands. The attempt to establish a Thai Buddhist temple was quite unorthodox, as he and the Thai and Buddhist community in Sweden had to first collect enough donations to rent a flat in Alby in the suburbs of Stockholm. Using a flat for a temple was unusual for Thai Buddhists, but it helped shift the conventional understanding that Thai temples could only be established in traditional settings such as with a main temple building and traditional architecture. The temple was named Buddharama following the temple established earlier in the Netherlands, where Phra Chamnong had stayed for a period of time. The first temple in Sweden was inaugurated with Phra Chamnong as the chair on 2 June 1984, initiating the institutionalisation of Thai Buddhism in Sweden (Buddharama Temple 2021; Plank 2005).

Buddharama Temple began its life as the centre for all Theravāda Buddhist activities and not only for Thais. Activities such as birth ceremonies, marriage, the tonsure ceremony and funeral chanting became major services provided by the temple to the Buddhists in the region. There were also major Buddhist events all year round, such as for Vesak Day, Buddhist Lent, Kathin Ceremony and Songkran, the traditional Thai New Year (Buddharama Temple 2021). The Temple became an institution for Buddhists in the Stockholm region and was not exclusively for Thais.

After Phra Chamnong moved to Sweden, he did not stay put. He was asked to visit Thai communities in various northern European countries. He travelled to chair Buddhist activities in Norway, Finland, Denmark, the Netherlands, Germany and France. Travelling in Northern Europe as a Buddhist monk was challenging for him, whether by plane, train, car or ferry due to the limited financial resources and transportations available (Chamnong Chutinattharo 1993, [3]).

During the first five years of Phra Chamnong's ecclesiastical activities, the number of participants and donations to the temple grew quickly. By late 1987, Buddhists from various origins including Thai, Swedish, Sri Lankan, Vietnamese, Cambodian, Laotian, Chinese and Tibetan contributed enough money so that the temple could buy a 3,000 -square-metre plot of land in Värmdö Kommun, and the building of the temple began. It was completed in 1989, with Phra Chamnong as the head abbot. The temple did not rely on any financial support from the Thai government (Chamnong Chutinattharo 1993, [7]). In the following decade, the temple was able to buy another plot of land nearby and became one of the most important Buddhist temples in Sweden. From the last decade of the twentieth century, Thai temples in Sweden would grow correspondingly with the increase in Thai migration. Since 2000, the number of temples has grown from two to fourteen (Plank et al. 2016: 407).

Although he did not possess high official ecclesiastical rank, Phra Chamnong was held in high respect among the Thai community in Sweden and the Nordic countries. They gave him the beloved name *Luang Ta* (venerable grandfather), which has become the name by which he is still referred to today. It will be shown later, however, that this beloved name was only made official by Thai monkhood and the Thai state, through its embassy, after he passed away.

After arriving in Sweden in 1984, Phra Chamnong spent the rest of his time in the country until dying unexpectedly of asthma and pulmonary oedema on 17 June 2003. He was posthumously announced by the Thai monkhood as a Dhamma Missionary (*Thammathut*) in Sweden, a recognition which he was the first to receive (Sangkhatikan 2021).

Katarina Plank et al. (2016) have put the career of Phra Chamnong against the larger context of the transnationalisation of Buddhism in Europe, and in particular Sweden, at the turn of the century. Towards the last decades of the past century, Buddhism became part of the plural religious landscape of Sweden, as Thai Buddhists grew to at least 37,000 in 2013. The actual number should be higher, if the children of mixed marriages/relationships and adopted children are included. It is also noted that Thais, mostly female, are among only a few migrant groups to have spread all over the country (Plank et al. 2016: 408).[4]

Ten Years of a Thai Monk in Snowy Lands[5]

During his time in Sweden, Phra Chamnong wrote a memoir titled *Sip pi phra thai nai daen hima* (*Ten Years of a Thai Monk in Snowy Lands* [1993]) (see Figure 4.1). It is a compilation of notes he made of his service to the Buddhist community while he was in Sweden and Scandinavia. These scattered notes include both his own written records and his recollections. In the winter of 1991, he thought they were sufficient to put together as a book. "The reason for this," he declares, "is because I watched an interview of an elderly Swedish man who lived in the northern part of the country . . . he said that because the extreme cold weather lasts so long, a man his age could not go out much. So he preferred to sit in front of the fireplace and write. After a winter had passed, he could have written a book . . . I am like this elderly Swedish man" (5). As a starting point in the preface, he humbly says that "I must first apologise to the readers. I am not a man of knowledge and I am from the countryside, so if there are any mistakes I must beg for your forgiveness" (5). Reading his memoir against the historical context, we shall see that his humble enterprise actually reveals the concurrences in the transnational lives of Buddhism in general, and in the lives of Thai migrants in particular.

There are at least three significant themes in *Ten Years*. The first is the record of Phra Chamnong's encounters with various ordinary Thais and Buddhists living in Sweden. These are voices previously unheard as they have not entered public narratives either in Sweden or in Thailand. They are names, mostly female, that otherwise would have been forgotten in the history of Thai Buddhism if this memoir had not brought them to life.

Secondly, by recording encounters with ordinary lives, *Ten Years* helps disentangle discourses relating to the study of Thai Buddhism in Sweden. Here I follow Peter Jackson's typologies from his study of forms of Thai Buddhism, which he divides into three: the metaphysical form of Buddhism emphasised by the

Figure 4.1 Ten Years of a Thai Monk in Snowy Lands (Chamnong Chutinattharo 1993). Cover of the memoirs of Phra Chamnong Chutinattharo, the first monk to establish a Thai temple in Sweden and the Nordic countries. Facsimile.

establishment; the rationalist and doctrinal form espoused by the middle class and the magical and supernatural form of the religion adhered to by many peasants and urban workers (Jackson 1989: 40–62). The three forms exist as concurrences, and as we shall see, Phra Chamnong's memoir reflects this throughout.

The last theme but not the least is that while Phra Chamnong emphasises that he did not want to make readers feel uncomfortable, he often adds criticisms of both the Thai monkhood and Swedish society through his eyes. This is possible because of his peripheral position to both the Thai monkhood – a monk dispatched abroad and not holding a high ecclesiastical rank – and to Swedish society, in which he was a minority. Being outside of the extremely hierarchical structure of the Thai monkhood enabled Phra Chamnong to give opinions otherwise rarely heard from a monk during the time. By the same token, while communicating in a minority language in Sweden, he could present the "snowy lands" through his lenses and with his prejudices for the specific audience literate in his small language.

Voices from the ordinary

Phra Chamnong opens his memoir with a captivating experience. One autumn in the mid-1980s, while he was stationed in Stockholm in his first year, he received a phone call from a hospital in Göteborg. On the other end of the line was a doctor, calling on him to make an emergency visit to a critically ill patient in the hospital. The patient was a Buddhist. He prepared his journey and rushed to the train station. It was going to be a long and demanding journey, but he did not feel discouraged. "I like to do this service, for at least I can give the patient moral support" (6), he writes. It was part of his vocation. Throughout Phra Chamnong's early years in Sweden, when there were seriously ill Buddhists in hospitals in both Sweden and Norway, hospitals would call to ask him to visit, and he never refused. If the hospitals were located in the Stockholm region, no matter how late in the night, he would be there. There were instances of fatal road accidents during the night and the patients needed to see a monk for the last time (6–7).

That was also the case in that hospital in Göteborg. He arrived at 23.00 and went straight to visit the patient. She was a Thai woman suffering from tonsil cancer in its terminal phase. He describes what he saw:

> The patient's room was rather large and she was the only patient there. It was airy and did not smell of medicine although one could smell blood. I saw that her neck bled continuously . . . I sat down beside the bed and the nurse whispered to the patient that a monk had arrived for her. She opened her eyes and tried to put her hands together weakly to greet me, her eyes begging for help. If I could perform miracles, I would take her pain away right at that moment. But I could only pray for her not to suffer any more than she already had . . . She said she was in so much pain, and please help her.
>
> (9–10)

Phra Chamnong commented with resignation: "I could only sympathise with the lives of Thais abroad. There were no relatives or family to look after them" (10). He was there for about twenty minutes and performed the ritual chanting.

During his brief time in Göteborg, he also mentions the lives of a Thai-Swedish family, Narin, Cecilia and their daughter. Narin offered him a place to stay overnight and transport. He observed their lives and how they tried to facilitate his visit in the middle of their busy weekday schedule. Both were working full-time but offered to drop him off at the hospital the next day (11).

Phra Chamnong paid his second visit to the patient the next morning. She appeared better and calm. At the hospital he also met another Thai woman who worked as a cleaner at the hospital. She wanted to offer him lunch, but he informed her that he did not eat more than once a day. Then he came back to the patient to bid farewell as he had to attend a ceremony in Stockholm. He promised to visit her again in a few days. She wished to make merit by donating 200 SEK to the Buddharama Temple. They performed a water-pouring ceremony, and he left Göteborg that afternoon. On the train, he pondered with sarcasm, "I pitied the patient. She did not have anybody. The husband came to visit once every few days, but only stayed outside, fearing infection. This was not just between husbands and wives; people here don't even want to be close to their parents. This is European generosity" (14). He did not know that it would be the last time he would see her alive.

The life of a Thai migrant woman dying a lonely death in a hospital in Göteborg during the mid-1980s bursts to the fore in the opening pages of *Ten Years*. We do not know her name, and that was probably deliberate on the part of Phra Chamnong. What we *hear*, in his description of his encounter with the terminally ill patient, corresponds with what Fur describes succinctly as the possibility of listening to "complementary or conflicting occurrences at the same time and in the same place," while also considering "whether this plurality can be communicated further in one and the same narrative, and how we account for the complexity of lived experience" (Fur 2017: 39). There were concurrent histories in these passages in the memoir. On the one hand, Phra Chamnong was a monk dispatched from the central authority of Thailand's monkhood, whose task was to spread the word of the Buddha. But sitting by that deathbed, on the other hand, he was just a companion to her, wishing to perform a miracle. "I am happy to do this task, for at least I can give moral support to the patient. Even the doctors at the hospital were glad that a monk was there, performing a duty like a psychologist" (6).

The concurrent histories, furthermore, extended to include the lives of non-Thai Buddhists, whose rituals were not necessarily the same as Thais. As major Buddhist activities in Sweden in the 1980s revolved around Buddharama Temple, Buddhist lives in Sweden depended on Phra Chamnong for various services. One winter morning in February 1986, Phra Chamnong received a phone call from an ex-police captain who had migrated from South Vietnam many years ago. He was asked to help perform an ancestor worship ceremony. Phra Chamnong was acquainted with the captain's family and knew that the family left for Sweden because of the war (15). He followed the captain to the cemetery – not easily as he fell many times on the icy path – to chant in front of the tombstone of the captain's brother. The captain told him that his brother died a year before "from suffering over having lost everything in Vietnam" (17). The history of Vietnamese war refugees in Sweden appears here, with Phra Chamnong as the medium.

Rituals and supernatural Buddhism

The ritualistic routine that Phra Chamnong performed throughout his time in Sweden highlights the second theme of *Ten Years*. Being a Dhamma Missionary abroad, his priority was less in being a missionary than in performing magical and supernatural forms of the religion. "I voluntarily abandoned my [scriptural] Buddhist studies because I was occupied with social and religious events. For the first three years I had to chair everything [ceremonies and rituals] by myself, and went to all the events by myself" (20). This passage juxtaposes uneasily with the Buddhist missionary intent which is based on the "Sangha's assiduous efforts to send personnel to engage in evangelical and humanitarian missions abroad" (Kitiarsa 2010: 115). Phra Chamnong's mission was humanitarian indeed, but humanitarian in the sense that it stemmed from the needs of ordinary Buddhist migrants in Sweden, whose form of Buddhism was based heavily on spirits, mediumship and magic – *saiyasart*. It includes the belief in the protective spiritual power of material objects such as amulets, the propitiation of local spirits or ghosts, astrology and the practice of spirit mediumship, among others. This form of Buddhism has been criticised by educated Buddhist monks and laymen as irrational and supernatural, contrasting with the rational and empirical Buddhism which is the central gravitational force of Official Thai Buddhism (Jackson 1989: 57–61). However, what appears in *Ten Years* shows the concurrent histories of Buddhist lives in Sweden: Phra Chamnong, who was supposed to represent Official Thai Buddhism as a missionary monk, instead performed a central role in practices that the Official Thai Buddhism criticised. This subtle conflict echoes in his assertion that "[performing rituals] is a duty of a missionary monk abroad. A missionary monk is just like a Thai worker who takes a pilgrimage to sell his labour in the Middle East" (71). For instance, he tells how Thai migrants came to worship the Buddha statue at Buddharama Temple and prayed to pass their driving licence test, an ordeal known for its difficulty (115).

This theme becomes clearer when he talks about ghosts (*phi*). When he recently arrived in Sweden, he was called to chant at a Buddhist funeral which took place in a Christian church. It was his first time in such a setting (72). He comments that Buddhists had to depend on Christian graveyards and churches. Keeping bodies at the temple, which is a normal practice in Thailand, was not permitted. "When a person dies in Sweden," he writes, in a display of his sense of humour, "the body is kept in a hospital to prevent infections. So Western ghosts cannot come out to wander around, going into folks' houses like Thai ghosts do. Western ghosts are not allowed to go out of the hospitals because it is illegal. Any ghosts who can be seen outside, we can surmise that they definitely escaped from a hospital" (19).

In 1992, Phra Chamnong was called by a Thai woman named Noi for a tonsure ceremony for her child in a mixed marriage household in Borås. He describes a ceremony he performed at the house where:

> . . . there was something strange and scary which disturbed them even during the day time. I was told that after I had performed a water-blessing ceremony, that thing did not appear again . . . Many might wonder if there are ghosts in Western countries, as Westerners do not believe in ghosts. I want to clarify here that the story of Dracula came even before the story of our Lovelorn Ghost [*Mae Nak*]. How could Westerners not believe in ghosts?
>
> (86)

Phra Chamnong substantiates his story that Swedish people had believed in Dracula for a long time by pointing out that Swedish parents thought their babies died because of Dracula's bites. This was due to the fact that knowledge about Sudden Infant Death Syndrome (SIDS) was not yet widespread. He mentions talking to a psychologist at S:t Göran Child Hospital in Stockholm. "But now the doctors have discovered the cause of death" (87–88).

His ghost stories are not confined only to Thais and Buddhists. Phra Chamnong also records an intriguing story about a Swedish man who had gastritis and was scheduled for an operation. The night before the operation, he dreamt of his deceased wife who wanted to take him with her. The next day he rushed to Phra Chamnong, who performed for him a robe ceremony dedicated to the deceased (*suat bangsukun*). When he went back to the hospital, the x-ray showed that there was no wound in his stomach anymore. So he did not need to go through the operation (86–87). Perhaps his wish to perform a miracle came true on that occasion.

The story of *saiyasat* Buddhism enters its transnational form in the following entry of *Ten Years*. On his way to Borås, he met a young Greek-Swedish medical student. They introduced themselves and the student, while studying orthopaedics at Uppsala University, showed how his grandmother on the Greek side taught him bone-healing magic. He asked Phra Chamnong if there was such a thing in Buddhism. In reply, the latter wrote down a Romanised chanting for bone healing in exchange for contacts. "The Greeks believe in *saiyasart* as much as we Asians do," he remarks in the memoir (91).

He continues the story by recalling another incident in the summer of 1988. He received a phone call from a young Swedish woman. She told him that she got his contact information from a Lutheran pastor and that she needed help. When they met,

> she looked exhausted, like a drug addict or an alcoholic. Her face was very sad. I asked how I could help. She told me her story. She had gone for a holiday in Greece many months before. There she met a Greek man. He loved her very much and wanted to marry her. But she did not love him so she refused. After she got back to Sweden, she could not sleep at night as she would hear his voice asking for her love all the time. When she refused she was reprimanded and scolded by the voice. She believed that the man cast a spell on her. First she went to the hospital. They only gave her sleeping pills and she did not get any better . . . So she called a local pastor, who said that it could not be helped. The pastor then gave her a Thai monk's contact information.
>
> (92)

Phra Chamnong listened carefully and said he would help. In the memoir, he describes a forty-five-minute-long ceremony involving holy thread and chanting and giving her blessed water for her to bathe with. He asked her to return to repeat the ceremony three times. "Now she is better, and does not hear that voice again" (93).

The last story on this theme involves a hot-air balloon. In January 1985, a Chinese-Malay entrepreneur called Phra Chamnong to bless the balloon which was used for his tourism business. This was not the first time he had called the Thai monk, as on earlier occasions he asked the monk to bless his car and his newly opened restaurant. Indeed, he was satisfied with Phra Chamnong's services, so the businessman was row requesting more help. That January morning he took passengers up in the hot-air balloon for sightseeing over Stockholm city. Everything went well until, as they were about to land, the balloon's basket flipped and injured one of the passengers. This had never happened before, so he requested the monk to bless the balloon for good luck.

But Phra Chamnong was not informed how exactly he was expected to perform the ceremony. It was suggested that he wear winter clothes as it was a windy day, and it would be a lot colder up in the air. "After I hung up the phone," he worried, "I regretted that I did not suggest he take the balloon to the temple instead. There was no need to perform it up in the air . . . I am not afraid to die, but if an accident happens, the Thai Buddhist community would not be happy about it" (111).

That afternoon, Phra Chamnong found himself looking down over Stockholm, along the Södertälje rivers. He pondered that during the Buddha's time, the major disciples (*phra arahats*) of the Buddha flew by themselves to spread the Buddha's words in faraway lands. "I am not a *phra arahat*, I am a *phra balloon* [balloon monk]. I have an opportunity to float in the air to wherever the winds carry me, and I do not know where I will end up" (120–121).

Critiques from the periphery

The third salient theme in *Ten Years* involves Phra Chamnong's critiques of the Thai monkhood and Swedish society. This was possible given his doubly peripheral positions vis-à-vis the two institutions: first, he held a relatively middling rank in the Thai monkhood and was dispatched abroad, and, second, in Sweden, he was part of a minority community with its own distinct language. This position paradoxically enabled him to express contrasts and criticisms from the margins, which were rarely heard from a Thai monk in his times.

We can begin with his views on electoral democracy. In 1988, Sweden held its first general election since the murder of Olof Palme two years earlier. Phra Chamnong received a ballot for a municipality election. It was the first time in his life that he had a right to vote. "I am a Thai national and I never had the right [to vote] according to Thai law, but I have it in a foreign country" (25). Indeed, monks in Thailand have no legal right to vote, as they are expected to distance themselves from secular politics. Phra Chamnong wonders why monks are obliged to report for military conscription yet possess no right to vote (25). Apart from his criticism of the Thai monkhood's lack of financial support for Buddhism (56), he asks further: "Why is it that a monk who wants to vote for good, moral representatives to govern the country is seen as gravely violating the rules and regulations of the monkhood?" (25). He continues his criticism:

[In the past,] Thai elected representatives were a lot more moral and virtuous, but they could not govern the country as they wanted, because there were bayonets forcing them from behind. They had to follow what the people holding the bayonets wanted. Today [1988] there are no bayonets anymore, but the politicians lack morality and *dhamma*. They only have greed and lust for their own interests, regardless of the damage they do to mankind.

(25–26)

Indeed, Thailand in the 1980s had transitioned from a long and tumultuous period of military rule the decade before. It was a period when the Communist Party of Thailand (CPT) was in decline and the new government under General Prem Tinsulanonda (PM from 1980–1988) ushered the country into another political era. The military and the monarch successfully "refashioned" themselves into being a stronghold for Thai national ideology against the big businesses who turned themselves into politicians (Ferrara: 2015, 190–194). Phra Chamnong's view was a product of this refashioning, as politicians were to be seen to be greedy, only entering politics for their own interests – a common political conception that continues to present day Thailand.

However, his intention was not to celebrate the right to vote. "I am like an amphibian," he says. On the one hand, he wanted to go out to vote because he had the right, but, on the other, he was at best indifferent. He notes that "[I don't want to go out to vote] because I do not have any knowledge in voting . . . .politics should belong to the laymen, and monks should stay out of it. This thought echoed in my feelings all the time. I came to Sweden as a missionary monk, not to seek political rights. I am here in Sweden to serve Thais who share the same heart as I" (28).

This "amphibious" (*krueng bok krueng narm* – half on land, half in water) position is central to our understanding of Phra Chamnong's role as a missionary monk abroad, a manifestation of his divided self. Being an amphibian positions him neither on the land nor in the water, but peripheral to both. The situation for Phra Chamnong was "the question of an individual's loss of his communal identity and his struggle to find another . . . these are precisely what make it hard for him to find a toehold in that living present where a communal identity renews itself as incessantly in the day-to-day transactions between people as it is promptly reinforced by a common code of belonging" (Guha 2002: 646).

This struggle to find an identity is shown in his attempt to portray Swedish society through his eyes, often with a sense of dark humour. Take his observation of drinking behaviour in Sweden. "Sweden is better than Thailand," he quips, "[not because Swedes drink less] but there is a gender balance among alcoholics. That is, both male and female are equal in being alcoholics" (21). He continues that "the best day for drinking is Midsommardagen . . . there is light all day, so some alcoholics can drink themselves to death. Jesus Christ would probably accept them into heaven, as Jesus himself drinks" (21).

To be sure, the point here is not whether Phra Chamnong could portray 1980s Swedish society as it really was, but his attempts to understand it by creating a contrast. The contrast creates an effect that shows his struggle to come to terms with the new society into which he had just arrived. This contrast, furthermore, is little concerned with real events. As John Berger points out, it was nonetheless important for "strangers" whose lives are situated in the realm that "a future is continually deferred, excludes the present and so eliminates all becoming, all development" (Berger 1990: 152–153).

Therefore, it is not our task to investigate the truth of the following events told by Phra Chamnong: Swedish children belong to the state more than the parents. So, the police can take away the children from their parents based on a neighbour's report of the latter's act of corporal punishment (42–43); Europeans are obsessed with equality, so much that nobody respects each other; children condemn their parents as it is in their rights to do so (39–40); old Swedish people are left to die alone because they never taught their children to be grateful and only seek self-comfort (39–40); and Swedish elderly people commit suicide often. They are successful in this by lying to the doctor so they can get sleeping pills to attempt to commit suicide (49); therefore, Swedish people love pets more than their children, and they spend so much money on having pets. So much so that there was a case when a cat had babies, the kittens were forced down the toilet bowl and flushed (45).

Phra Chamnong's purpose for telling these stories, I must emphasise, is not to relate real events, as he declares clearly from the introduction that they are from his recollections. Rather, they create a contrast which allows a person at the periphery to become relevant. These stories lead Phra Chamnong to find his identity as a missionary monk. He asserts that there is a purpose for him being in Sweden: to communicate the superior teachings of Thai Buddhism to a minority community of Thai Buddhists. Thais, he asserts, grow old happier and not alone (49); Thai women take care of their husbands and parents better than anyone (66–67), and Thai children practise filial piety according to Buddhist principles (43–44). Unlike Buddhism, Christianity conditions help on converting to its faith. If one needs medicine and education, one has to convert to Christianity (48).

The particularity of the historical junctures shown in these three themes in *Ten Years of a Thai Monk in Snowy Lands* reveals the entanglements of interpretation, contestation, memory and narrative. The memoir captures moments rarely recorded, let alone recognised, by the advocates of Official Thai Buddhism or transnational religion in general. It offers a glimpse of enchantment which does not fit in the teleology of rational modernity (Jackson 2022: 4). By reading Phra Chamnnong's memoir for concurrences, these moments appear, even if only for a short while.

Legacies of Phra Chamnong as Luang Ta

A month after his death on 17 June 2003, at the age of 65, the Thai monkhood recognised Phra Chamnong Chuttinattharo as "the Dhamma Missionary in Sweden." The recognition notes that Phra Chamnong helped establish Thai temples in Sweden, Denmark, Norway, Finland and Belgium and renovate a temple in the Netherlands "without financial support from Thailand" (The Sangha Supreme Council of Thailand, 30 July 2003). From this point on, Phra Chamnong's legacies will be capitalised on by the Thai monkhood and the Thai state. He has, in other words, entered a new life as the *Luang Ta* (venerable grandfather) for the Thai community in Sweden.

By the time of his unexpected death, *Luang Ta* had already gained widespread recognition in the Buddhist community in Sweden and Scandinavia. His cremation ceremony was organised on 12 June 2004 by the Thai Buddhist Association in Sweden and patronised by King Rama IX. On the ceremony day, around a thousand people, monks and laymen, participated (Buddharama Temple 2021).

The importance of Luang Ta to the Thai Buddhist community in Sweden and Scandinavia is shown further in the fact that a wax figure of him was placed in the main hall of Buddharama Temple. His wax figure is positioned beside a replica of the Emerald Buddha, one of the most revered Buddha statues in official Thai religious life. Though the act of crafting a wax figure of a highly popular monk is not unusual in Thai Buddhism (McDaniel 2017: 82–130), a wax figure of a diasporic monk, whose popularity is confined within a certain Thai community abroad, is indeed an unusual one.

The Thai Embassy in Sweden began to play an important role in recognising the achievements of *Luang Ta*. Apart from annual Buddhist and Thai national ceremonies, the Embassy takes part in the anniversary of *Luang Ta*'s death, an event of its own kind in the Nordic countries. On 26 June 2021, the embassy took part in the eighteenth anniversary of Luang Ta's death. In the event, apart from the merit making ceremony, the ambassador planted a tree in the name of the Thai embassy to commemorate the event, with a note from the embassy that Thailand "is infinitely grateful to his work" (Tingstam 2021). This departs from the Buddhism that Phra Chamnong himself helped materialise almost two decades earlier, the Buddhism that had folk beliefs at its centre. We see that the narrative of Official "Thai" Buddhism had begun to supersede the rituals and supernatural Buddhism that Phra Chamnong occupied himself with, as "a missionary monk [who] is just like a Thai worker who takes a pilgrimage to sell his labour . . ." (Chamnong Chuttinattharo 1993: 71).

Conclusion

From the early twenty-first century, we can see the narrative of Official Thai Buddhism starting to merge with the story of Phra Chamnong as the Dhamma Missionary. The Buddhism that he advocated through his community work in Sweden transformed into the story of transnational Buddhism under the auspices of the activities supported by the Thai Embassy. His memoir, thus, captured the moment where the lives and voices of concurrent Buddhisms could be heard in Sweden during the 1980s and the 1990s. By looking at his memoir, we are able to see the interplay between Buddhism as a transnational religion and folk Buddhism whose contents are not readily accepted into the pantheon of official Thai religious lives. This is the interplay between *sāsana* and *Buddhasāsana*, according to Obeyesekere.

Phra Chamnong's recognition by the Thai monkhood and his legacies recognised by the Thai state through the embassy show the contestations of the narratives of Buddhism in Sweden and the Nordic countries. In her study of Thai Temples in Fredrika and Bispgården, Katarina Plank mentions that "the cults of saints, kings, and amulets especially are a prominent feature to be found" (Plank 2015: 410). Why is the narrative of enchantment so reluctant to enter into the discussion of Buddhism in the Swedish public sphere, whereas meditation and Zen Buddhism have become an "integral part of the Swedish religious landscape" (Plank 2015: 410)? As Peter A. Jackson contends, "over the past several decades, religious modernity has trended in two apparently opposing directions, with fundamentalisms and magical cults both being equally contemporary phenomena that together reflect inherent divisions and tensions within the modern condition" (Jackson 2022: 3). The interplay between folk Buddhism practised by Thai migrants, on the one hand, and the Buddhism adopted by Scandinavians, on the other, awaits further study.

Acknowledgements

Parts of this article were presented at the workshop on Buddhism and Theosophy in the Nordic Countries, Lund University on 11 May 2022. I would like to thank Kristina Myrvold and Johan Nilsson for organising. I would also like to thank Katarina Plank, Knut A. Jacobsen, Mitra Härkönen, as well as other participants for engaging discussions. Craig J. Reynolds and Matthew Reeder kindly read through the draft and gave valuable comments.

Notes

1 We can compare him to Somdet Phra Buddhakosajarn (Prayudh Payutto), one of the most important intellectual monks in Thai Buddhism, who was born in 1938, the same year as Phra Chamnong. See the study of this figure in Olson (1989).
2 One among recent examples is Björn Natthiko Lindeblad, Caroline Bankler, Navid Modiri (2020) *Jag kan ha fel och andra visdomar från mitt liv som buddhistmunk* (Stockholm: Bonnier fakta). See the survey of receptions of Buddhism in Sweden in Plank (2015).
3 The Dhammaduta College is managed by Mahamakut Buddhist University and Mahachulalongkornrajavidyalaya University, the two major ecclesiastical universities in Thailand. In 1995, the College began its preparation course for monks to be dispatched abroad, which continues to the present (Dhammaduta College, 2022).
4 It is also important to note that the Buddharama Temple was established as a branch of the Maha Nikaya order, which includes the majority of Buddhist monks in Thailand (the other notable order is the Thammayut Nikaya, which was established during the early 19th century and whose members traditionally come from a higher social class and education). In 2016, there were six Thammayut temples and seven Maha Nikaya temples (two of which from the Dhammakāya movement) in Sweden (Plank, 2005: 410; see the discussion about the Dhammakāya movement in Mackenzie, 2007).
5 Unless stated otherwise, the reference page numbers in brackets for this section come from Chamnong Chutinattharo (1993).

References

Primary sources

Chamnong Chutinattharo, Phra. 1993. *Sip pi phra thai nai dawn hima* [Ten Years of a Thai Monk in Snowy Lands]. Bangkok: Lan Asoke Press.
The Sangha Supreme Council of Thailand. 2003.*Phra Ratcharattanarangsi Pratharnsong Wat Puttharam Lae Phra Thammathut Prajam Prathet Sawiden Tueng Moranaphrap* [Phra Chamnong, the chair of Buddharama Temple and Missionary Monk in Sweden, Has passed Away], 30 July 2003.

Secondary sources

Anderson, Benedict and Mendiones, Ruchira. 1985. *In the Mirror: Literature and Politics in Siam in the American Era*. Bangkok: Editions Duang Kamol.

Berger, John. 1990. *Ways of Seeing*. London: Penguin Books.

Buddharama Temple. 2021. [https://sites.google.com/site/worldthaitemple/wad-phuthth-a-ram---buddharama-temple], (accessed 5 Apr 2022).

Chaiyan Rajchagool. 1994. *The Rise and Fall of the Thai Absolute Monarchy: Foundations of the Modern Thai State from Feudalism to Peripheral Capitalism*. Bangkok: White Lotus.

Dhammaduta College, 2022 *"Prawat Khwarm Penma Wittayalai Phra Thammathut"* [The history of Dhammaduta College]. [http://www.odc.mcu.ac.th/?page_id=712], (accessed 5 Apr 2022).

Ferrara, Federico. 2015. *The Political Development of Modern Thailand*. Cambridge: Cambridge University Press.

Ford, Eugene. 2017. *Cold War Monks: Buddhism and America's Secret Strategy in Southeast Asia*. New Haven: Yale University Press.

Fur, Gunlög. 2017. "Concurrences as a Methodology for Discerning Concurrent Histories," In *Concurrent Imaginaries, Postcolonial Worlds: Toward Revised Histories*, edited by Diana Brydon, Peter Forsgren and Gunlög Fur, 33–57. Leiden: Brill.

Guha, Ranajit. 2002. "The Migrant's Time," In *The Small Voice of History: Collected Essays*, edited by Partha Chatterjee, 644–651. Delhi: Permanent Black.

Ishii, Yoneo. 1986. *Sangha, State, and Society: Thai Buddhism in History*. Honolulu: The University of Hawaii Press.

Jackson, Peter A. 1989. *Buddhism, Legitimation, and Conflict: The Political Functions of Urban Thai Buddhism*. Singapore: Institute of Southeast Asian Studies.

Jackson, Peter A. 2022. *Capitalism, Magic, Thailand: Modernity with Enchantment.* Singapore: ISEAS.

Keyes, Charles. 1971. "Buddhism and National Integration in Thailand." *Journal of Asian Studies*, 30(3), 551–567.

Kitiarsa, Pattana. 2010. "Missionary Intent and Monastic Networks: Thai Buddhism as a Transnational Region." *Sojourn: Journal of Social Issues in Southeast Asia*, 25(1), 109–132.

Mackenzie, Rory. 2007. *New Buddhist Movements in Thailand: Towards an understanding of Wat Phra Dhammakaya and Santi Asoke*. London and New York: Routledge.

McDaniel, Justin Thomas. 2017. *Architects of Buddhist Leisure: Socially Disengaged Buddhism in Asia's Museums, Monuments, and Amusement Parks*. Honolulu: University of Hawai'i Press.

Mead, Kullada Kesboonchoo. 2004. *The Rise and Decline of Thai Absolutism*. London: RoutledgeCurzon.

Murashima, Eiji. 1988. "The Origin of Modern Official State Ideology in Thailand." *Journal of Southeast Asian Studies,* 19(1), 80–96.

National Office of Buddhism. 2021. *The list of Thai Temples Abroad*. [https://www.onab.go.th/th/content/category/detail/id/655/iid/6090], (accessed 25 Dec 2021).

Obeyesekere, Gananath. 2006. "Thinking Globally about Buddhism." In *The Oxford Handbook of Global Religions*, edited by Mark Juergensmeyer, 68–83. Oxford: Oxford University Press.

Olson, Grant Allan. 1989. *A Person-Centered Ethnography of Thai Buddhism: The Life of Phra Rajavaramuni (Prayudh Payutto)*. PhD Dissertation, Cornell University.

Plank, Katarina. 2005. "Buddhism i Sverige [Buddhism in Sweden]." In *Det mångreligiösa Sverige: ett landskap i förändring*, edited by Daniel Andersson and Åke Sander, 217–284. Lund: Studentlitteratur.

Plank, Katarina. 2015. "Buddhister och buddhism – asiatisk migration, konvertitbuddhism och sekulär meditation." [Buddhists and Buddhism – Asian Migration, Convert Buddhism and Secular Meditation.] In *Det mångreligiösa Sverige: ett landskap I förändring,* (third edition, revised chapter), edited by Daniel Andersson and Åke Sander, 203–262. Lund: Studentlitteratur.

Plank, Katarina, et al. 2016. "The Temple Mount of Fredrika – Translocality and Fractured Transnationalism of a Visionary Thai Buddhist Retreat Centre." *Contemporary Buddhism*, 17(2), 405–426.

Sangkhatikan. 2021. [https://sangkhatikan.com/monk_view.php?ID=17503].

SCB (Statistiska centralbyrån). 2021. Foreign Citizens, Number By Country of Citizenship, Sex and Year. Thailand, 1984. https://www.statistikdatabasen.scb.se/pxweb/en/ssd/ START__BE__BE0101__BE0101F/UtlmedbR/table/tableViewLayout1/

Sriboonhung, Phramaha Montree. 2007. *Attributive Guideline of the Buddhist Propagation for Overseas Assignment Missionary Monks in the next Decade (BE 2551–2560)*, MA Thesis, Silpakorn University.

Suksamran, Somboon. 1979. *Buddhism and Politics: The Political Roles, Activities, and Involvement of the Thai Sangha*. PhD Dissertation, University of Hull.

Tingstam, Tanya. 2021. "Ake-akararatchathut Thai Khao Ruam Ngarnbun Khrop Rop Moranapharp 18 Pi Khong Phra Ratrattanarangsi (Chamnong Chuttinattharo) Rue Luang Ta Thi Wat Phuttaram Vaemder" [The Thai First Ambassador Participates in the 18 Year Death Anniversary of Phra Ratrattanarangsi (Chamnong Chuttinattharo) or Luang Ta at Bhuddarama Temple, Värmdö] [https://thaiembassy.se/th/เอกอัครราชทูตไทย-เข้าร-3], (accessed 6 Apr 2022).

Winichakul, Thongchai. 1994. *Siam Mapped: A History of the Geo-body of a Nation*. University of Hawai'i Press.

5 Buddhism in Denmark

Institutionalised religion, mindfulness and cool branding

Jørn Borup

Cool Buddha and diversity Buddhism

"The King elevates Buddha above God." This was the headline from a tabloid newspaper the day after King Frederik X's ascension to the throne in 2023.[1] Instead of talking about God, he proclaimed support from "something greater than us." By visibly wearing a popular "Shambala" bracelet, the media went into a frenzy with speculations about possible Buddhist inspiration in the new royal family. The fact that the bracelet was a gift from his children and apparently did not hold special personal symbolism partly reassured the media and the critical Christian voices, who were accustomed to seeing Christianity as the only national religious symbol. For a while, however, the general public was reminded of the popular spread of Buddhism and Eastern spirituality, even in little Denmark. This had been documented a few years earlier. The results from a research institute survey that analysed a representative sample of Danes' responses to the question "How do you assess the significance of the five major religions for humanity?" made it to the front page of a major newspaper: "Buddha is breathing down Jesus' neck." Though the vast majority of Danes (71 per cent) are members of the "Danish People's Church" (the Evangelical-Lutheran Church in Denmark), Buddhism came in second, with almost the same score. Among the eighteen- to fifty-five-year-olds, the urban citizens, the well-educated and the left-wingers, Buddhism was even appreciated more than Christianity. "The Danes are fond of Buddhism," the headlines read.[2] Christian ministers and a former bishop have previously warned against the religion as a challenge to Christianity.

Buddhism's material and aesthetic presence seems to justify its popularity. Buddha figures are on sale in department stores and appear as decorative items in wellness centres. Buddha and Buddhist meditation symbols are used by companies to market their ideas or products through associative correlation of spiritual authenticity and exotic flavour. Citizens with Asian ancestry have long had the honour of being stereotyped as "model immigrants," with Buddhism being a very acceptable foreign religion. Mindfulness has become as fashionable as yoga, and martial arts, which often incorporate or refer to Buddhist elements of Asian cultures, are as popular as ever. The number of officially recognised Buddhist organisations has

DOI: 10.4324/9781003529767-5

increased quite substantially in the last two decades. Media representations and popular culture narratives indeed testify that also in Denmark, Buddhism is considered a nice religion and Buddha is cool (Borup 2016).

As of 2024, there were around forty Buddhist groups in the country, represented by all Buddhist wheels (Theravāda, Mahāyāna and Vajrayāna). Some are very small, with only a handful of participants; others have hundreds of members with regional centres throughout the country. Some of the groups have gained official approval as a recognised religious organisation (see Table 5.1). Such a status does not trigger financial support for the groups, which are self-sufficient and typically supported by donations from their members. Recognition allows the groups to perform marriage ceremonies with legal effect and gives the right to residence permits for foreign preachers, as well as tax benefits and the right to establish cemeteries.[3] Since Karma Kagyu Skolen gained this status in 1988, the number of groups increased to four groups in 2003, and twenty groups in 2024 with almost 5,000

Table 5.1 Buddhist groups in Denmark.

Recognised groups		
Name	*Year of recognition*	*Tradition*
Organisations of mainly migrants and migrants' children		
Den Burmesiske Theravada Buddhistforening Buddha Ramsi	2010	Burmese
Den vietnamesiske Buddhistiske Kulturelle Forening Chua Lieu Quan	no information	Vietnamese
Den vietnamesiske Buddhistiske Kulturforening Quang Huong	2009	Vietnamese
Dhammachaya Buddhist Center Denmark	2022	Burmese
Guan Yin Citta Buddhistiske Kulturforening Danmark	2018	Chinese
Nai Ge Si – Buddhist Union	2023	Chinese
The Buddhist Organisation Dhammakāya in Danmark	2009	Thai
The Natural Forest Monastery in Randers	2022	Thai
Srilankansk-Danske Buddhistiske Religiøse og Kulturelle Forening	2014	Sri Lankan
Wat Dan-Thai	2023	Thai
Watpa Copenhagen (Sunnataram Copenhagen)	no information	Thai
Wat Thai Denmark Brahma Vihara Buddhist Monastery	1993	Thai
Organisations of mainly converts		
Center for Visdom og Medfølelse	2009	Tibetan
Foreningen Stupa Karma Kagyu Buddhistisk Sangha	2012	Tibetan
Foreningen Rangjung Yeshe Sangha	2012	Tibetan
Karma Kagyu Skolen (Diamond Way)	1988	Tibetan
Karmapa Trust Sangye/Tashi Ling	1994	Tibetan
Phendeling – Center for Tibetansk Buddhisme	2005	Tibetan
SGI Danmark	2018	Nichiren
Øsal Ling – Lysets Have	2013	Tibetan

(Continued)

Table 5.1 (Continued)

Non-recognised groups	
Name	Tradition
Organisation of mainly migrants and migrants' children	
Buddha's Light International Association (BLIA)	Chinese
Chua Van Hanh	Vietnamese
Organisations of mainly converts	
Buddhistisk Samfund	Zen
Clear Light Kadampa Buddhist Centre	Tibetan
Dansk Dharmacenter	Japanese
Dzogchen Community	Tibetan
One Drop Zendo	Zen
Samten Tse	Tibetan
Shambala København	Tibetan
Shoubuzenji	Zen
Shugendo Denmark	Japanese
Sōtō Zen Aarhus	Zen
Tarab Institute International	Tibetan
Ten Chi Dojo	Zen
Tergar København	Tibetan
Tilogaard	Tibetan
Triratna Buddhistsamfund Danmark	Theravāda
Zen Buddhistisk Forening	Zen
Vipassana Danmark	Theravāda

members. While the majority of Buddhist communities a few years ago were dominated by convert Buddhists with a primary connection to the Tibetan tradition, today, the groups of migrant Buddhists make up the majority. Thus, there are twelve Buddhist religious organisations with associated temples primarily aimed at Asian Buddhists: five from Thailand; one from Sri Lanka; and two each from Myanmar, China and Vietnam.

Although representing only about a half per cent of the Danish population, Buddhism is rather diverse. There are no cross-sectarian organisations like the Norwegian Buddhistforbundet. The Facebook group Buddhisme i Danmark (Buddhism in Denmark) with almost five thousand (mainly ethnic Danish) members is a forum for Buddhists from different traditions and for people generally interested in its philosophy and teachings, but it does not represent all Buddhist groups. The eclectic umbrella organisation Buddhistisk Forum (Buddhist Forum) lived for only a few years in the early 2000s, with a brief attempted revival in 2014 by the leader of a previously existing group from the Japanese Tendai lineage. Although two centres are open to different groups, and although a cross-denominational Buddhist cemetery offers space for Buddhist urns at Bispebjerg Cemetery in Copenhagen, they share an unmistakable reference to Tibetan Buddhism. It is striking that

Denmark has national representatives neither in the World Fellowship of Buddhists nor in the European Buddhist Union, although individual groups such as Diamond Way and Soka Gakkai International (SGI), with their respective Danish branches, are represented.

Around 30 monks and four nuns residing in the Thai, Vietnamese, Burmese and Sri Lankan temples in Denmark,[4] in addition to a Zen-ordained priest, five lamas,[5] a growing number of "dharma teachers" and an estimated 36,000 Buddhists, presently constitute the broad variety of Buddhists in Denmark.[6] Although the Buddhist groups seem to have challenges in appealing to younger generations,[7] the presence of Buddhist practitioners and Buddhist materiality do indicate a living minority religion having become established after decades of presence in the country. Although some of the temples and centres are rebuilt on preexisting buildings, and seldom with typical Asian aesthetics and architecture, religious characteristics are quite obvious in most of them. Paintings or figures of Buddhas and Buddhist celestial beings as well as photographs of monks and lamas decorate the interior, with outdoor statues and *stūpas* clearly pointing to their religious origin and transnational relations. Such contemporary material representation captures the tangible aspects of a religion shaped by a long historical transformation.

Thinking Buddhism

Christians, poets and scholars

Knowledge about Buddhism in Denmark in the latter part of the nineteenth century and early twentieth century was a conglomerate of circulating ideas of the European cultural elite and Christian responses. Buddhism as a way of life suitable also for modern Westerners is found already in the late nineteenth century as a cross-European ideal among intellectuals. The Theosophical Society also had adherents in Denmark, but it seems that representatives from this esoteric movement were not influential in importing Buddhist ideas as was the case in other countries.[8] Occasional descriptions of this exotic religion appeared in travelogues, magazines and newspapers; in 1852 the "Christian" story of the saints Barlaam and Josaphat was translated into Danish (as *Barlaams og Josaphats Saga*) without mentioning the fact that it was actually a Buddhist legend. Christian theologians and missionaries were, however, well aware of Buddhism. Descriptions of its apparent nihilism and idolatry were based on Christian *othering* and a sense of religious superiority, but were also responses to what appears to have been idealisation of the rational and spiritual religion known in the contemporary discourses of the Romantics. The missionary Jens Kristian Knudsen, from the Mission to the Heathens in Burma (Hedningemissionen i Burma), in 1893 thus angrily accused the "half mad Buddha admiring philosophical bookworms in Europe" (Knudsen 1893, 82–83) of not truly comprehending that the lived folk Buddhism he knew was far from the textualised ideals.[9] Positive relations between Buddhists and Christians subsequently characterised Christian missions, not least the Nordic Christian Buddhist Mission (still existing under the name of Areopagos).[10] In 1927, the politician and poet Christian Reventlow (1867–1954) published an article on Buddhism in Danish literature, concluding that it was

> highly peculiar, that Buddha's message in its core brings the same, as what Christ preached: Open your ears! . . . The European who has not understood this will not be able to write the real book about Buddha.
>
> (Reventlow 1927, 227)

Buddhism as a topic of literary fascination was part of early twentieth-century culture. Not only had Edwin Arnold's famous book *Light of Asia* been translated into Danish (*Asiens Lys*) in 1915, Danish authors also contributed to the genre of "literary Buddhism." The poet and Nobel laureate Karl Gjellerup (1857–1919) was inspired by Richard Wagner and wrote several novels on India and Buddhism. *The Pilgrim Kamanita* (*Pilgrimmen Kamanita*, 1906) was translated into several languages and was used as a textbook in Thailand. To what extent Gjellerup was more than intellectually fascinated with Buddhism is doubtful, but as a response to the Nobel prize's Christian foundation, he responded that he agreed with Christianity wherever it agreed with Buddhism, "But I am Buddhist" (quoted in Nørregård 1988, 174, 242).[11]

Early Buddhologists contributed to the knowledge of the exotic religion. Michael Viggo Fausbøll (1821–1908) became professor at the University of Copenhagen in 1878, introducing Pali studies as an academic discipline. In 1855, he had translated *Dhammapada*, and a seven-volume edition of the *Jataka* came out in the years that followed. The multilinguist Rasmus Rask (1787–1832) had already brought palm-leaf manuscripts from his journey to Ceylon, paving the way for later scholars in the field such as Niels Ludwig Westergaard (1815–1878), Vilhelm Trenckner (1824–1891) and Dines Andersen (1861–1940), the latter two being originators of the ambitious project *A Critical Pali Dictionary*.[12] Early scholarship on Buddhism was based on linguistic analyses of newly discovered Pali texts from classical Theravāda Buddhism, some of them framed in interpretive models comparing it to Christianity. Johannes Edvard Lehmann (1862–1930) in 1900 was the first historian of religion teaching at the University of Copenhagen. His *Buddha* (1907) was primarily written as a defence of Christianity. He was polemical towards Buddhism but also fascinated by Buddha as life philosopher, not least by his "will to life" (as inspiration from Schopenhauer made him reflect). This idealisation of the original message of the rational human Buddha, as against the degraded living Buddhism, was typical in the early reception of scholars, poets and Buddhists.

Christian Frederik Melbye and the first Buddhist group in Denmark

> What is Buddhism? When asked this question, I often reply: It is a certain way of leading one's life. It involves no dogmatism, no definite form of worship; it is not merely a code of morality, not merely a mode of looking at the world, not merely a certain view of life, but above all, it is a certain way of leading one's life. I believe that my Buddhist friends in faraway Ceylon will agree with me in this.
>
> (Melbye 1923–26, 8)

Christian Frederik Melbye (1881–1961)[13] worked as a senior doctor and psychiatric specialist at so-called mental hospitals in Nykøbing Sjælland, Viborg and Nørresundby. Melbye was the first official Buddhist in Denmark. In 1921, he established the Buddhist Society in Denmark (Buddhistisk Samfund i Danmark), the first Buddhist group in the country.

How Melbye became interested in Buddhism remains unknown. Probably his father's Christianity was influential for his existential thoughts and cultural formation, even leading him to identify Jesus and Buddha.[14] He was well read in religious and literary traditions, and he was both knowledgeable and engaged in international currents related to Buddhism. He wrote two books on Buddhism (1926, 1930), and (apart from a few short features) he was the only author of the many articles for the Buddhist magazine *Buddhistisk Budbringer* (1921–1934, from 1939 to 1946 called *Buddhistisk Budskab*, and with the two last issues in 1950 called *Buddhistisk Tidende*). In none of these writings does he expose his own personality; only in passing does he mention his wife (when she dies) and his job. Whether he or the small group consisting of no more than ten people actually met is also doubtful, although he already in 1922 dreamt of a place for practice, a "vihara, where we could meet and celebrate the quiet, solemn . . . Mahābodhi celebration at the Vesak evening in the light of the full moon" (Melbye 1922a: 2). We do know from his writings that he corresponded with well-known international Buddhists such as Paul Dahlke, Paul Carus and D. T. Suzuki and that he was the Danish representative of two of the influential international Buddhist organisations, the Bund für Buddhistische Leben and the Mahābodhi Society.

Anagarika Dharmapala had originally encouraged him to establish the group, and through Dharmapala, his "grand Indian teacher and friend" (1922c: 3), Melbye got a small amount of funding (215 DKK) from Miss Foster's Missionary Fund. If Dharmapala had not had to cancel because of illness, he was planning to visit Melbye on his tour in Europe in 1928.[15] Dharmapala had a large influence on Melbye and his understanding of Buddhism. Melbye was equally inspired by contemporary European and American scholars and practitioners, seeing Buddhism as a high philosophy beyond superstition, and Buddha as a human being rather than a god. He refers to Buddhists as "freethinkers," with the message of seeking life wisdom rather than dogmas. He refers primarily to Pali Buddhism and looks down on the degraded folk religiosity. He takes a sceptical attitude to "pure research," and also to the

> Buddhology and "cadaver philology" manoeuvring with Buddha's thoughts as if manoeuvring with a cadaver on a dissecting room, and not as with thoughts originally born in a living person and since reflected in our hearts.
>
> (Melbye 1925: 3)

He despises the dry science but often refers to Dines Andersen, whose scholarship he admires because of his genuine understanding and apparent sympathetic insights. Melbye was theoretically grounded but also encourages the reader to practical insights.[16] He looked down upon the popular flirting with Buddhist symbols – using Buddha figures as talismans, or using Buddha images and concepts for commercials – that apparently already in the early 1920s was seen in Denmark.[17] This was "just as ridiculous as it is sad" (Melbye 1923: 8). Melbye therefore saw his Buddhist journal also as a channel with a publicly enlightening function. Melbye's Buddhism was typical of what in general terms can be characterised as "modern Buddhism": it is rational, individualistic, humanistic, spiritual and universally applicable in its demythologised form.

Zen, Soka and Danish lamas

Danish convert Buddhists

Postwar economic recovery and new opportunities of travel turned young back-packers East to explore the exotic cultures and religions. In the decades from the late 1960s onwards, a new phase began: Buddhism became a lived religion in Denmark, and the scholarly focus on classical texts now became supplemented by attention to the practised religion.[18]

Theravāda Buddhism was the attraction for some individuals who made their way to Sri Lanka. When in 1969 the French–Danish Denys Jeune was ordained as a novice monk (*sāmaṇera*), he was given the name Ñāṇadīpa ("island of wisdom"), later to become Ñāṇadīpa Bhante after higher ordination as a senior monk. He lived in solitude as a forest monk, with only occasional encounters with other people, before later in life also spending time in monasteries until his death in 2020, leaving behind the legacy of a devoted and respected Western convert monk.[19] Jan Hansen was another Dane pursuing the path of Buddhist seclusion in the remote forests of Sri Lanka. Leaving family and a position as a successful medical doctor and researcher at the University of Copenhagen, he was ordained in 2002 with the name Samahita Thera and spent the next seventeen years as a solitary monk meditating, studying and giving online teachings to his one hundred thousand YouTube subscribers, until he took his own life in 2019 while staying at a Sri Lankan Buddhist temple in Denmark.[20] Westerners seeking experiences in Asian Theravāda monastic settings or meditation centres have adopted especially the *vipassanā* practice, which since the late nineteenth century has become a symbolic manifestation of modern, spiritual Buddhism. *Vipassanā* courses are conducted in several places throughout the country, whether framed as Buddhist or in secular terms. Triratna Buddhist Community, based on the teachings of the British monk Sangharakshita, is also represented in Denmark with a group offering occasional online courses and weekend retreats.[21]

Theravāda had been the main point of entry for Melbye to early Buddhism; several of the contemporary temples with Asian origin also belong to the Theravāda school. But it has not had the same attraction and brand value that Zen and Tibetan Buddhism have had in recent decades. Zen today is known as a concept signalling authenticity, spirituality or simply life quality. Earlier poets such as Dan Turèll, Hans Jørgen Nielsen and Torben Ulrich were influenced by the American beatniks, whose "beat Zen" Buddhist inclinations gave flavour to their literary universes.

A few also went to Japan to actually discover the "square Zen" in the monasteries. Tim Pallis and John Mortensen were two such individuals, who later brought their experiences back to establish Zen practice groups in Denmark. Pallis established and for many years was the lay teacher of the Zen Buddhist Society (Zen Buddhistisk Forening). Mortensen (later using the name Choan Bertelsen Rōshi) was ordained in the American Pine Hill community and later was bestowed the title of *rōshi* by Eido Shimano Rōshi. After having served as abbot in his own temple in the United States for some years, he established a monastic community in Denmark with its own training hall (*dōjō*). In 2024, he chose to resign, transferring the title and responsibility of the monastery to his (female) disciple Seishin Bunyen Osho. Its present name – the Danish Buddhist Society (Dansk Buddhistisk Samfund) – is taken from Melbye's group. Zen is still popular as idea and symbol, but few people practise Zen Buddhism in the established groups. As of 2024, there are six Danish Rinzai and Sōtō Zen groups (Buddhistisk Samfund, Zen Buddhistisk Forening, One Drop Zendo, Ten Chi Dojo, Shoubuzenji, and Sōtō Zen Aarhus), three of them closely related to the lineage of Shodo Harada Rōshi. The (up to) two hundred members are mainly ethnic Danes who meet for periodic meditation (*zazen*) and occasional weekend retreats (*sesshin*).

There was previously a small Tendai group led by a female ordained priest who inspired another female to become ordained in the Shugendō tradition. However, the absolute largest Buddhist group with Japanese origin is Soka Gakkai. The founder of the group in Denmark, Kamio Masaaki (who later changed his name to the more Danish-sounding Mark Kamio), by coincidence ended up in a Danish folk high school (Askov Højskole), where he learned about Danish culture and educational philosophy. This triggered a reconnection to his family's religion back in Japan. The establishment of a Danish group soon attracted other citizens with Japanese origin, mainly women married to Danish men, who met for religious practice and social bridge-building. Soka Gakkai Danmark still has Japanese members, some of whom have socialised their children to belonging to this particular kind of Buddhism. But the majority are ethnic Danes, meeting for religious gatherings at the main centre in Copenhagen (Nordic Culture Centre) or in the seventy local groups across the country. Here they chant the *daimoku* (the Soka Gakkai mantra *namu myōhō rengekyō*) in front of the *gohonzon* (a sacred object containing a painted scroll of the *daimoku*) and read or discuss the thoughts and writings of the charismatic leader Ikeda Daisaku (1928–2023). Some members join international arrangements or go to the main centre in Japan where two summer camps are held. In 2018, SGI Denmark was granted official approval as a recognised religious organisation, being a blueprint for being not only a "true religion" but also authentic Buddhism. SGI Denmark has thus developed from being a small new religious movement consisting mainly of Japanese women having brought their religious identity to Denmark from abroad, to a transnational and religious organisation with Danes of a range of ages.[22] With more than 1,300 members, it is the largest Buddhist group in the country, based on membership numbers.

Another form of Buddhist transnational encounter is related to the Tibetan tradition. Tibet has for most of its history been an unreachable region for most people. Its symbolic role as a container of magic, mystic and authentic purity has been part of Orientalist narratives. Since the Chinese invasion in 1950, the Dalai Lama's forced escape in 1959 and the arrival of Himalayan lamas in the following decades, the images have not grown less positive or even less idealised. If Theravāda was the most favoured kind of Buddhism in the early phase of Buddhist reception in the West, with Zen becoming the ideal in the 1960s and 1970s (with Soka Gakkai following different trajectories), since the 1980s it is the Tibetan kind of Buddhism that has attracted most sympathy and the greatest numbers of convert followers. Books on Tibet and Tibetan Buddhism have been written or translated, Hollywood films have been watched, books by the Dalai Lama and other lamas have been read, Tibetan Buddhist meditation courses have been followed, all by an increasing number of Danes. Individuals with particular interest and fascination have been to the Himalayas to search for, and eventually meet, representatives from the tradition. Others have met some of the many lamas from the different Tibetan schools during their visits to the Denmark.

The Dalai Lama has been in Denmark a few times (most recently in 2015), the Sixteenth Karmapa visited in 1976 and 1977, and the founder and spiritual head of the group Rangjung Yeshe Gomde, Chökyi Nyima Rinpoche, visits the temple every summer to conduct courses with teachings and meditations. Some lamas came as refugees, eventually ending up as Danish citizens and leaders of Tibetan Buddhist groups. Tarab Tulku (1934–2004) worked for thirty years as a research librarian at University of Copenhagen, where he also taught Tibetan language and culture while simultaneously developing the internationally recognised educational Tarab Institute and its "Unity in Duality" programme.[23] Lakha Lama (1942–), a Tibetan monk, was attracted to lay life: on arriving in Denmark in 1976, he began as a cleaning assistant, got married, and had children. After working as a "freelance lama," he established the charity organisation Tibet Charity and his own company Art of Life. Although he has been challenged by age-related illness in recent years, he is still the head of the Tibetan Buddhist group Phendeling in Copenhagen (which is managed daily by the nun and lama Tenzin Drolkar) and of Øsal Ling in Aarhus.

Some Danes who turned to the Buddhist path more deeply were prompted by their encounters with Tibetan culture and teachers. The journalist Erik Meier Carlsen has written on Buddhism for decades, following lamas from the Dzogchen tradition and often functioning as an intellectual voice in the media whenever Buddhist topics are brought up. The Austrian-born Waltraut Küssner (1937–2020) went into a ten-year retreat of total isolation in India, France and Tibet without seeing her family and children. As a nun and lama, under the name Gelongma Palmo, she lived in Aarhus for decades, working until her retirement as a nurse functioning as lama in local Buddhist groups and hospices. Erik Pema Kunsang (Erik Hein Schmidt) has served as a translator for lamas in both Nepal and Denmark. Since establishing his permanent residence at the Gomde retreat centre and conducting popular online teachings which have attracted thousands of international participants, he has played a significant role in transforming the group into a dynamic centre of Danish Buddhism, despite its rural location in Jutland.

Seven of the officially recognised Buddhist organisations belong to the Tibetan tradition, namely, Karma Kagyu Skolen (Diamond Way), the Karmapa Trust Sangye/Tashi Ling, Phendeling – Center for Tibetansk Buddhisme, Center for Visdom og Medfølelse, Foreningen Stupa Karma Kagyu Buddhistisk Sangha, Foreningen Rangjung Yeshe Sangha, and Øsal Ling – Lysets Have. Two of the larger temples (Phendeling in Copenhagen, Øsal Ling in Aarhus) have interior design clearly signalling Tibetan references, but they simultaneously function as cross-denominational centres. Two retreat centres[24] are open to courses and individual retreats aimed at Tibetan Buddhist practice. Other groups (identified as seven)[25] without the official stamp of recognition as Buddhist organisations also contribute to the Tibetan Buddhist landscape in Denmark, attracting a few thousand members and practitioners for meditation, prayers, offerings, chanting and study of (Tibetan) Buddhist teachings.

Lama Ole Nydahl

One particular lama has had a specific impact on Danish Buddhist history, namely Ole Nydahl (b. 1941). Apart from establishing the first Buddhist temple and initiating a generation of lived and practised Buddhism, he also illustrates the quintessential narrative of leaving-as-a-hippie, returning-as-a-lama seen in the early phases of Westernised Tibetan Buddhism. Following their honeymoon in Kathmandu in 1968, Ole and his wife Hannah Nydahl (1946–2007) both returned as practising Buddhists with ambitions of bringing the (to them) newly discovered religion to the West. After meeting lamas in Nepal, they were convinced that the spread of the dharma to the West would change both Buddhism itself and those parts of the Western hemisphere receiving and recontextualising it. Padmasambhava's prophecy that "when the iron bird flies and the fire horse rides and the Tibetans are scattered like ants in the world, then Buddhism will come to the land of the red faces" (Nydahl 1983) is seen as having come true with the Nydahls' endeavours, manifested internationally in their European centre.[26]

Ole and Hannah Nydahl felt deep transformative experiences with, especially, Karma Kagyu lamas Kalu Rinpoche (1905–1989) and the Sixteenth Gyalwa Karmapa (1924–1981). The latter's official recognition as a lama by the institution[27] was both a sign of spiritual approval and (as has sometimes been the case with other Western lamas) a topic of critique.[28] Ole Nydahl's own childhood visions of previous lives in Tibet, and his felt identity as a reincarnation of Mahākāla and a modern version of the yogi Milarepa, may in retrospect have been framed by his initial experiences of how the Tibetan lama Lopon Tsechu Rinpoche (1918–2003) transmitted the lineage power to him through an ecstatic religious experience, an experience that later served as a blueprint for esoteric transmission through spiritual recognition.[29]

In 1972, Ole and Hannah Nydahl established the first Buddhist centre in Denmark. After visits from lamas and a steadily growing number of engaged participants, their financial situation allowed them to later buy a villa (eventually, three villas) in the embassy quarters of Copenhagen. In 1988, their group Karma Kadjy Skolen was approved as the country's first Buddhist religious organisation.[30] Eight national centres and a stable national membership of around five hundred people tell the story of a small Buddhist group with a larger narrative and imprint on the Buddhist scene in Denmark. The "mother centre" in Copenhagen still represents a historical *axis mundi*; in 2019 a "Victory Stupa" was built for Ole and Hannah Nydahl to celebrate their lives and wishing health and long life for Ole.[31] As of 2024, there were more than 650 centres worldwide originating from Ole and Hannah Nydahl's group, today known as Diamond Way Buddhism. Scherer in 2009 estimated there were 15,000 to 70,000 students and casual sympathisers worldwide, with 20,000 persons in Germany regularly visiting the group's centres (Scherer 2009).

What has been characteristic, and undoubtedly also a selling point, for Ole and Hannah Nydahl has been their balancing between experiential insight through personal meditation and tantric rituals in close relation to authorised teachers. Their approach allowed them to negotiate a balance between traditional authority claims and recontextualised authenticity frames. The Nydahls were consciously trying to keep the Tibetan elements alive, with Hannah (sometimes referred to as a "female lama" and by a Danish newspaper as "Mother of Buddhists") being the scholar studying Tibetan and translating for Tibetan lamas,[32] and Ole performing meditation courses and Vajrayāna teachings for Western audiences around the world. At the same time, they have translated and westernised the religion into contemporary relevance, with Ole being the outgoing and self-conscious "white Viking Buddhist," performing, dressing and communicating in a modern style. Apart from recitations in Tibetan, teachings are performed in Danish and English in the centres, and lay teachers rather than monks and nuns have been given authority to conduct meditation guidance for lay practitioners. The group does not identity as "Tibetan Buddhism," but as the more inclusive and universalist name "Diamond Way Buddhism," with lama Ole as the charismatic teacher. In the centres and at the altars of his disciples, there are photos of him next to other lamas of the lineage; when he blesses (with relics given to him by the Sixteenth Karmapa) and gives refuges to his disciples, it is seen as a sign of entering the authentic path of Buddhism. Bee Scherer, a scholar of religion and former member of the Diamond Way, even finds an "Ole normativity" among his disciples, reflecting a tendency to "foster uncritical imitation of Nydahl's hetero-machismo, lifestyle, and political views" (Scherer 2014, 98). The latter refers to controversies in recent years about Nydahl's statements as a freedom-fighting anti-Islam religious warrior with pro-right-wing sympathies,[33] causing the Diamond Way group in 2019 to leave the German Buddhist Union after threats of expulsion.[34] Controversies have also characterised Ole Nydahl's previous career. When the Sixteenth Karmapa of the Karma Kagyu lineage died in 1981 and the right reincarnation was to be recognised some years later, Ole Nydahl was strongly involved in fighting – including physically – for his own candidate (Thaye Dorje) as the Seventeenth Karmapa. Around 1990, this led to a split in the school and divided the Tibetan Buddhists in Denmark into two, with the "Ole Nydahl wing" being increasingly segregated from other Buddhist groups in the country. Some of Nydahl's former friends and acquaintances have since then turned their backs on him; although these incidents are now part of a bygone history that younger generations of followers have probably not even heard of, the group in Denmark still has no relations to any of the other six Tibetan Buddhist groups. Karma Kagyu Skolen has had a stable membership of around 500 for years, preferring with its increasingly international number of practitioners to align itself with the more global Diamond Way Buddhism.

Monks and migrants

The early phases of Buddhism in Denmark were characterised by ethnic Danes "importing" Asian Buddhism as food for thought and as practices, some of which became institutionalised in religious organisations. Before the 1970s, there were likely only a few handfuls of practising Buddhists, some of whom were the relatively few Asians who had come as working migrants or spouses of Danes, as had been the case with Singhalese Buddhists from Sri Lanka. However, with the first waves of Vietnamese "boat people" entering Western countries from 1975 onwards, a new phase of migrant Buddhism appeared. The refugees settled and gave birth to a new generation of descendants, and the diaspora situation eventually changed into more stable forms of transnational belonging, with the establishment of temples and religious communities. Thais, the majority of whom were women, came in larger numbers from the 1980s. They settled, had children, and invited monks to establish Buddhists communities and temples (in already existing buildings), just like the later waves of migrants from China, Myanmar, Nepal, Cambodia and Bhutan. While there have been parallels both in practice and in institutional formation, it is still a distinctive characteristic that the converts and the migrants live and practise relatively distinct kinds of Buddhism.

Jenni and the Vietnamese

Jenni is a young woman born in Denmark to parents who came as refugees from Vietnam. Her family have been Buddhists for generations, and Jenni herself was raised as a Buddhist. She frequently accompanied her parents to the Quang Huong (Quảng Hương) temple near Aarhus for religious services and festivals. Jenni married a fellow Buddhist, and they held a religious ceremony at the temple. Whenever she feels tired or in need of positive thoughts, she confides in the monk. It is not that she believes events occur randomly, as she subscribes to the principle of karma, which asserts that actions have consequences. However, through her engagement with Buddhism, she finds it easier to accept the ways of the world, including her father's recent death.

Jenni primarily offers her prayers at the temple rather than at home, where she has only a Buddha statue as a focal point. She does not meditate at home, finding it too challenging, but she occasionally participates in meditation practices and quiet contemplation at the temple. She also introduced her children to the temple when they were young, but in recent years they have lost interest in joining her, a fact she accepts. As she says, they can also come later when they grow up, a trend she has observed in other families where younger and teenage members lose interest in religion.

Jenni does not identify fully as either Danish or Vietnamese. As a second-generation immigrant, she feels that she exists in between cultures, searching for her own place in life. Buddhism, in her opinion, offers an excellent path for this journey, particularly because it does not rigidly prescribe specific beliefs or practices. In contrast, she notes that Catholicism requires strict adherence to church attendance, rules and religious learning. If you marry a Catholic, you are often expected to convert and to have your children baptised. Some of her friends converted to Catholicism to please their partners, and she is aware of conflicts within families due to religious differences. In the temple, she appreciates the freedom to come and go as one pleases. Jenni does not know of any other Buddhist groups in Denmark, but every summer, she participates in the summer camp for European Vietnamese Buddhists, where monks, nuns and lay Buddhists from all over Europe gather. In fact, she says, "I am glad to be a Buddhist."

Jenni is an individual, with a unique identity. But she is also representative of many of the approximately 10,000 lay Buddhists who are related to the six Vietnamese temples in Denmark.[35] As one of the 6,000 descendants of the 10,000 refugees who arrived in Denmark primarily from 1980 onwards, she is part of the current population of 16,000 residents of Vietnamese origin in the country, 70 per cent of whom have Danish citizenship. As with many other descendants, her cultural identity is not fixed as either "Vietnamese" or "Danish" but rather points to an identity favouring individualist orientation. Jenni's sense of the younger generation being less religious and losing interest in joining their parents for temple visits is typical of much religiosity in Denmark, as are her reflections on the possible return to or change in religious practice in later age. Her description of the differences between Vietnamese Buddhists and Catholics is recognised by others and aligns with findings from a previous study showing Catholics to be more religiously engaged than the Buddhists in terms of belief, moral, practice, attitude and religious upbringing of children.[36] That she does not know of any other Buddhist groups is quite representative of most of the approximately 30,000 migrant or "heritage" Buddhists, who use their religious identities as part of a cultural package closely related to a transnational Buddhism, but with very little crossover to the convert Buddhists.

Jenni is probably more active than many of her fellow Vietnamese Buddhists. Besides visiting the temple at weekends and for religious festivals throughout the year, she strongly identifies as a Buddhist with religious values, and she even participates in meditation and joins the annual summer camps. She has not, however, as some of the spiritually interested Vietnamese Buddhists have, taken part in the mindfulness retreats inspired by the late Thích Nhất Hạnh. These have occasionally been conducted at the Vietnamese temples, as the only activity with ethnic Danes also participating. Other Vietnamese Buddhists could be characterised as more typical "culture Buddhists," interested mainly in being part of a cultural community with its framing of Vietnamese traditions, aesthetics, language and food. As such they are comparable with the majority of Danish "culture Christians," seeing religion as an integrated part of tradition and culture, without the constraints of prescribed ideals for belief and practice.[37] The Vietnamese Buddhist Association in Denmark was established already in 1979 to accommodate the cultural and religious wishes of refugees with a Buddhist background; in 1992, the temple Quang Huong was built. The resident monk there, Thích Giác Tánh, like his five fellow monks and two nuns in the other temples,[38] serves the religious community, who, apart from the very few who show up for daily services, join the temples at weekends and for religious festivals. Thích Giác Tánh, who was in a refugee camp in Thailand before escaping from Vietnam in 1988, came first to Norway and then eventually to Denmark in 1998. As a monk and religious specialist, he has the authority to represent authentic Buddhism as an ascetic full-time priest through charma talks and ritual activities and as administrative chairman of the religious organisation, which also functions as the Danish section of the Unified Buddhist Church of Vietnam (Giáo hội Phật giáo Việt Nam Thống nhất). As such, he is the religious head and patriarch guarding the tradition, with members being ascribed the title of being "Buddha's children" (*phat tu*). Jenni is one of them.

The majority of the Vietnamese immigrants define themselves as ethnic Vietnamese (*việt kinh*), as distinct from the immigrants with ethnic Chinese origin (*hoa*). Chinese from mainland China, Taiwan or Hong Kong might occasionally also visit the Vietnamese temples but also have the opportunity to join the temple at Nai Ge Si Buddhist Union Guanyin Center in Kalundborg (following a Tibetan *rinpoche*), or the small groups Guan Yin Citta Dharma Door and the Buddha's Light International Association (BLIA, associated with Fo Guang Shan) in Copenhagen. All three of these consist of and are aimed at just a few of the 16,000 people of Chinese origin living in Denmark. There are no temples or centres catering to the 1,800 people with South Korean origin or (apart from Soka Gakkai) to the 2,000 people with Japanese origin. Although there are plans to establish a temple in the future, the three Bhutanese lamas serve the two hundred Buddhist members of the Bhutanese Society in Denmark by personal visits to their homes.

South Asian Danish Buddhists

The monk Phra Somsak Gandhasilo lives a quiet life in the Thai Buddhist temple Watpa Copenhagen in Dragør. He originally trained in electrical engineering, but discovered his calling to the monastic life first in Thailand, then in the United States and eventually in Denmark where, after short visits, he established himself as a permanently residing monk. The temple was established in 1991 by Phra Ajahn Yantra Amaro Bhikkhu; it was originally called the Sunnataram Copenhagen Buddhist Meditation Temple, being part of the international Sunnataram Forest

Monastery tradition. Meditation is part of the daily practice for Phra Somsak and the six monks permanently residing in the temple. Their main religious responsibilities are, however, serving the mainly Thai visitors coming to participate in the religious festivals or the periodic ritualised gift (*dāna*) donations.

The Wat Thai Denmark Brahma Vihara Buddhist Monastery in Stenløse (Zealand) offers the same services to their approximately 260 members and two thousand visitors annually. It has no relation to the Watpa temple, and the two in a sense compete for "customers" from the Thai community that supports the temples financially and culturally. Building on support by local Thais, Wat Thai was founded in 1990 and received the status of recognised religious organisation in 1993. The senior monk, Phra Soodthibongse Soodthiwungso, originally invited from a monastery in Bangkok, is still the abbot and leader of the temple, where, as of 2024, two monks are living and nine monks are temporarily residing. The ceremonial building (*bot*) for ceremonies and for the ordination of monks signals its monastic qualities, but Wat Thai is otherwise mainly known as a temple catering to the Thai community with rituals, festivals and social arrangements, such as courses in Thai language, cookery, art, music, massage and football.

Watpa and Wat Thai are typical of traditional Thai Buddhism, belonging respectively to the Dhammayuttika Nikāya and Mahā Nikāya monastic orders. In recent years, smaller temples in Jutland (Randers, Terndrup, Skærbæk, Ribe and Nørresundby) and Lolland (Toreby) have also been established, so Thai communities in other regions now have easier access to practising their religion in the country's total of ten Thai temples. Not all of the 14,000 people of Thai origin are Buddhists, and not all of the estimated 90 per cent of Buddhists are practising, believing, or members of the religious organisations. According to representatives from the temples, however, quite a few of them appear throughout the year, especially for celebrations of religious or cultural holidays, at which the ambassador and visitors from Thailand also typically appear. Eighty per cent of people with Thai origin in Denmark are women; a significant proportion of them are married to Danish men. This demographic trend is readily apparent in gatherings at temples, where, on occasion, some of the spouses participate, with separate areas designated for them.

Dhammakāya, both in Thailand and internationally, has been characterised as a new religious movement. Its relative wealth is based on donations from large numbers of engaged followers. Dhammakāya remains, however, deeply rooted in Buddhism, aligning historical teachings, practices and aesthetics with modern forms that cater also to younger generations who are not bound by traditional norms of religiosity. This is also the case in Denmark, with the two Dhammakāya temples in Juelsminde and Korsør having no affiliations with the other traditional temples. Nine monks and two nuns live there, two of the monks with permanent residence permits and the others with temporary residence permits as religious workers.[39] A total of 850 people are members of these temples, whose aesthetics and homepages clearly illustrate more modern outlooks. In addition to rituals, ceremonies (including ordination ceremonies for temporary monkhood) and cultural activities throughout the year, Dhammakāya is also known for offering lay meditation sessions and courses under the guidance of the monks, or online by monks from Thailand. This also means that more non-Thais (typically ethnic Danes) participate in such practices, in which schools and gymnasium classes are also invited to take part. The temples define themselves as meditation centres with the aim of providing Danish citizens in general with insight into Buddhism.[40]

The Burmese Theravada Buddhist Association Buddha Ramsi (Jutland) and the Dhammachaya Buddhist Centre (Zealand) are two temples catering to the estimated one thousand Buddhists of another South Asian region, namely Myanmar. Both of these have the status of recognised religious organisations; currently there are two monks living in the temples. Neither of the few hundred Nepalese and Cambodian Buddhists have their own temples. Some may visit the Thai temples, or they may participate in the religious activities of the Sri Lankan–Danish Buddhist Religious and Cultural Association, situated in a suburb of Copenhagen. Sixty per cent of the 12,000 residents in Denmark with origin in Sri Lanka are migrants, the remaining 40 per cent descendants. Many of the migrants came as Tamil refugees escaping from the civil war in 1983–2009 and are thus typically Hindu (or Muslims). After the late 1970s and early 1980s, Sri Lanka became a popular holiday destination, and since then, a number of Sinhalese women too have married Danish men, settling in Denmark with permanent residency. Of the estimated 1,500 Singhalese, around 1,200 are Buddhists,[41] and a hundred are members of the Sri Lankan Buddhist temple near Copenhagen, where a monk has been living for years.

Asian migrants and their descendants generally have a positive image in Denmark. They do well educationally, have financial success and are very seldomly portrayed negatively in news or crime statistics. They are often thought of as the "silent others," beyond the radar of media attention and the political ideals of cultural integration. Since the arrival of the Vietnamese as refugees in the mid- and late 1970s, smaller waves of other migrant groups have contributed to an increasingly multicultural society, although in total not exceeding 50,000 people (including both migrants and descendants). In the same period and mainly because of the growing number of migrants, the number of Buddhists with Asian origin in Denmark has increased quite significantly. Today there are twelve groups with the status of officially recognised religious organisation, and fifteen temples with approximately 32,000 individuals who, to varying degrees and types, are associated with Buddhism as believing, belonging or practising. There is no reason to believe that this number and increase in "cultural," "migrant" or "heritage" Buddhists will not continue in the years to come. Youngsters are ordained into "temporary monkhood" in the Thai and Burmese temples, and monks periodically travel to visit; several have received residence permits. Most importantly, Buddhists continue to have children.

Buddhists beyond Buddhism

Lone Overby Fjorback is MD, PhD, psychiatrist and associate professor at Aarhus University. She is also the founder and director of the Danish Centre for Mindfulness, established in 2013 at the same university, where she conducts research and publishes academic articles on mindfulness as an instrumental technique for healing and well-being, mainly within the Jon Kabatt-Zinn inspired tradition of Mindfulness-Based Stress Reduction (MBSR). She has worked for the integration of mindfulness as part of the established Danish healthcare system and has frequently contributed to debates on the topic in public media. One large project aims to train teachers and pedagogues in mindfulness meditation, enabling them to handle stress for children and foster well-being and competences in living a more balanced life. Fjorback acknowledges the Buddhist roots of mindfulness, and she has also used her research as part of Buddhist settings. She has always been religious and, as a child, found the presence of the Christian God in everything. As she has expressed in public media, she does not, however, identify as a Buddhist. Mindfulness she finds mainly to be a path of practice, one that can be followed by Buddhists and non-Buddhists alike.

Fjorback is a specialist and "scholar-practitioner," defining and, in the media, often representing the whole field of mindfulness. As such, she is also representative of the "mindfulness boom" that has reached Denmark especially in the last two decades.[42] The number of mindfulness practitioners has increased significantly; in the city of Aarhus, the number of instructors rose by 75 per cent to 144 in just four years (Borup 2015). There are 270 individuals or companies who have registered in the Central Business Register with "mindful" or "mindfulness," and both book titles and newspaper articles featuring mindfulness have shown a substantial increase, peaking in 2015 and in some ways conceptually overtaking the popular brand of "Zen" (Fibiger & Borup, 2024). A previous investigation showed that some of these mindfulness instructors have personal interests in Buddhism or define themselves as Buddhists, but also that only three per cent referred to Buddhism on their websites to brand their practices, which are typically presented as being conducted by "the clinician" (providing mindfulness as a purely scientific method) or "the spiritualists" (embedding it as an integral part of a broader spiritual or religious worldview) (Borup 2015). Some of the Buddhist groups do use mindfulness meditation as part of the practice repertoire. Mindfulness conceived of as a healing technique of the Self, rather than as a religious or spiritual practice, however, seems more broadly acknowledged; it is sometimes discussed as an illustration of the secularisation of Buddhism in the West. Mindfulness has also been criticised as a diluted form of Buddhism, or as a self-optimising technique in the service of neoliberal individualism. When mindfulness is practised in churches or workplaces, it has also been criticised as a way of sneaking a "foreign" religion in through the back door. Not characterising mindfulness as religion or Buddhism is probably a necessity for Lone Overby Fjorback in applying her research on spiritual well-being to schools and kindergartens (or in providing practice for employees at the university). Seeing mindfulness and Buddhism as nonreligious is, however, also a common trope among many Danish Buddhists, for whom the label "religion" connotes too much institutionalised religiosity. Finding personal lived experience as the main criteria for qualifying authentic knowledge on Buddhism is also characteristic among many convert Buddhists – and also consistent with the ideals of Christian F. Melbye one hundred years ago.

Going beyond institutionalised Buddhism as a "seeker" is another path that has been trodden by spiritually interested individuals who have, in turn, influenced other seekers. Jes Bertelsen is a well-known spiritual teacher whose inspiration from Jungian depth psychology, new age philosophy, Christian mysticism, Buddhist Tantra and esoteric traditions led him to close relations with the Buddhist master Tulku Urgyen Rinpoche, who authorised him to teach Dzogchen meditation. If Bertelsen has attracted thousands of visitors and practitioners to his spiritual retreat Centre for Growth ("Vækstcentret")[43] over the years, then Peter Elsass, clinical psychology scholar, author and globetrotter, has undoubtedly reached out to just as many listeners and readers interested in his personal travels and investigations of lived and practised Buddhism.[44] Some of this audience might also be the many sympathisers or even some of the participants in the annual body, mind and spirit fairs held in the major Danish cities offering practices related to Tantra, Tibetan singing bowls and meditation. Spiritual affinity to Buddhism has been expressed by spirituals, Theosophists and "the nones." Mindfulness and zazen have been offered in Christian churches, with a Christian-based kind of mindfulness ("Christfulness") being an example Buddhist inspiration in also institutionalised Christianity. Buddhism's attraction for celebrities, artists[45] and even business owners[46] is probably related to the generally positive narratives of "cool Buddhism," as expressed also in literature, music,[47] popular culture and brands (Borup 2016). Buddha figures and images in Ikea, health and cosmetic shops, massage parlours, restaurants, magazines and commercials are examples of strategic marketisation using Eastern symbols for communication. But they are also symbolically powerful representations of a cultural domestication of a religion no longer considered strange or exotic. Only traditionalist Christians and the tabloid media are strategically provoked by a king wearing a *shambala* bracelet.

Conclusion: Danish sangha and beyond

In tracing the history of Buddhism in Denmark, the early period was marked by a quest for "original" Buddhism, focusing on Theravāda texts studied by scholars, intellectuals and figures like Christian F. Melbye who founded the first Buddhist group in the country in the early 1920s. In the late 1960s, with the rise of hippies and counterculture experientialists in the late 1960s, Buddhism was imported as a practised religion for the few, exemplified by Ole and Hannah Nydahl, who initiated institutionalised sangha Buddhism. Tibetan Buddhism gained popularity in the 1980s, alongside small Zen Buddhist groups that emphasised meditation as the core practice of modern convert Buddhism. During this same period, Buddhism became further established through the contributions of refugees and migrants from Asia, particularly Vietnamese (as expressed here by Jenny) and Thais, who now constitute the majority of Buddhists in Denmark. Monks, nuns and Tibetan lamas further reflect the transnational nature of the religion. The recent "mindfulness boom" has added a different flavour to Buddhism, even if the practice is not always identified as such. Understanding Buddhism as a peaceful "way of life" aligns with many practitioners' own perceptions, as well as media representations and popular culture narratives of a spiritual path and a silent minority religion.

Buddhism in Denmark is, however, far from homogenous. As in other Nordic countries, it is characterised by diversity, with very little interaction between the converts and the migrant Buddhists. Institutional divides are also common, characterised not least by the exclusiveness of SGI and Diamond Way Buddhism, whose members seldom mingle or practice with Buddhists from other groups. The "Karmapa controversy" from the 1990s may no longer resonate with younger Buddhists, but it continues to influence the Tibetan Buddhist milieu institutionally. Competition between Dhammakāya and Thai temples from the traditional schools is not necessarily acknowledged by practitioners, but hints at underlying tensions. Soka Gakkai's (own interest in self-) exclusion from "the Buddhist family" is another point of discussion, as is the debate over what constitutes true Buddhism versus "new age Buddhism."

Without a central umbrella organisation, there are no representative Buddhist voices in the Denmark. Recognised religious organisations gain symbolic prestige and economic privileges on individual group level, but the authority to represent and perform authentic Buddhism is left to a diversity of individuals and traditions. A main parameter of authority is institutionalised recognition. Sectarian lineages have their structures and procedures of authority claims, represented by the religious experts (monks, nuns, lamas, teachers), rituals (meditation, chanting, prayers, ordinations), symbols (flags, alters, images) and buildings (temples, *stūpa*s, centres, graveyards). In convert groups, individual experience is often seen as the hallmark of authenticity, also for lay practitioners. The teacher as a guide for inspiration showing the way for each individual to accommodate the path for oneself is an ideal for many Buddhists, not necessarily differentiated from the image of the master (guru/lama/roshi/sensei) having achieved suprahuman insights and powers.

As in other Nordic countries, Buddhism in Denmark is characterised by highly transnational networks and connections to global Buddhism. However, translating and interpreting the religion on Danish soil has also posed challenges for both the converts and the migrants, negotiating concepts, practices and institutions to fit both users and suppliers in cultural, economic, social and juridical frameworks. Buddhist groups have had to accommodate the (very much Christian-inspired) regulations from the Danish state in order to get official recognition as a religious organisation. Karma Kagyu Skolen early on decided not to include monastic rules and recitation in Tibetan. Zen groups have been split over the issue of religiosity; to which extent should chanting, incense, bowing be part of Zen practice? A Thai Buddhist temple, on the other hand, has images of the Danish and Thai royal families on the wall, and the Danish national symbol of Holger the Dane (Ogier the Dane, resting as a statue in Kronborg Castle, waiting to defend the country when threatened) enshrined in a spirit house outside the temple. Second-generation "Asian" Buddhists have been brought up as Danes with the Danish language and culture. Balancing between ideals of authenticity and negotiations of authority, all such diverse forms of Buddhism in Denmark can also be seen as cultural representations of a Danish Buddhism (see Figure 5.1)

Figure 5.1 Protector of the temple. The Danish national symbol, Holger the Dane (Ogier le Danois or Oddgeir danski), rests in Kronborg Castle, ready to defend the country in times of need. He is also enshrined in a spirit house outside the Wat Thai temple in Stenløse. During his first visit to Denmark, the senior monk felt the presence of Holger's spirit as a protector of the Danish land and deemed it fitting for him to also safeguard the temple grounds.

Notes

1 Bilstrup 2024: https://ekstrabladet.dk/underholdning/kongelige/danskekongelige/ kommentator-kongen-haever-buddha-over-gud/10094175.
2 https://jyllands-posten.dk/indland/article5284946.ece.
3 The Danish Ministry of Ecclesiastical Affairs can grant this title after a formal application procedure in which the fulfilment of specific criteria (https://www.km.dk/

andre-trossamfund/anerkendelse, Danish only) is acknowledged. The status of recognised religious organisation entitles the groups to perform marriage ceremonies with legal effect under the Danish Marriage Act, it gives the right to residence permits for foreign preachers under the Aliens Act, and it grants a number of tax benefits and the right to establish cemeteries under the Danish Cemeteries Act. A list of officially recognized religious groups can be found at this website from The Danish Ministry of Ecclesiastical Affair: https://www.blkm.dk/andre-trossamfund/trossamfundsregistret/liste-over-anerkendte-trossamfund-og-tilknyttede-menigheder (Danish only).

4 As of 2024, there were eighteen monks; two nuns live in the Thai temples, five monks and two nuns in the Vietnamese temples, two monks in the Burmese temples and one monk in the Sri Lankan temple. Visiting monks typically stay on three-month visas throughout the year.

5 The "lama" title is somewhat fluid in both meaning and use. Sometimes it is interchangeable with other designations of teacher (e.g., Khenpo). Some use the title; others do not. Some lamas are only in the country for specific periods. Seminars or summer retreats occasionally attract participants under the guidance of Buddhist lamas from Himalaya, as has been the tradition at the Buddhist center Gomde, where the spiritual head Chökyi Nyima Rinpoche resides every summer.

6 These are approximate estimates derived from (often imprecise) official figures from the groups, combined with longitudinal and comparative statistics, and with reservations to guard against the illusion of precision. On counting migrant Buddhists in Denmark, see Borup (2016). Statistics Denmark www.statistikbanken.dk is a very usable source of information on population, including migrants and descendants.

7 The Centre for Contemporary Religion at Aarhus University conducted mappings of religions in the city of Aarhus in 2003, 2013 and 2023. In the most recent project, the focus was on religion and youth. In contrast to Islam, among other religious groups there was minimal participation among young people, and in some cases, a decrease was observed. This was also evident within the Buddhist groups, although the figures cannot be said to be representative for the whole country (Centre for Contemporary Religion 2022).

8 H. S. Olcott was never in Denmark to promote the religion, and none of the representatives of Buddhism seem to refer positively to Theosophy. However, some of the well-known Theosophical and esoteric ideas about Eastern religions were presented in publications, some of which were translations from foreign sources. For instance, a Danish translation (which included commentaries, but no translator is mentioned) of the German Theosophist Wilhelm Hübbe-Schleiden's book *Was Jesus Buddhist?* (Andreas Schous Forlag 1895) discusses the popular narrative of Jesus's possible travel to the East. This may have been the book that the author and Catholic monk Johannes Jørgensen had in mind when proclaiming his smiling contempt towards pseudoscientific books in bookseller windows with such speculations (Jørgensen 1896, 14). In 1998 and 1999, a series of articles was still discussing the topic in the Buddhist magazine *Dharma Sol*.

9 Knudsen's contempt for his fellow Europeans' idealization of Buddhism was, however, compensated for by his own personal respect for Burmese and Buddhist culture, described in his book *On Buddha's Ways* (*På Budda's Veje*, 1891).

10 The Norwegian missionary Karl Ludwig Reichelt founded the mission in 1926 (see Jacobsen, this volume). Johannes Prip-Møller, an architect and missionary in Det Danske Missionsselskab (Danish Missionary Society), helped to construct one of its still existing buildings in Hong Kong, Tao Fong Shan. He furthermore wrote the book *Chinese Buddhist Monasteries* (Prip-Møller 1937), one of the classical accounts of pre-communist Chinese Buddhism.

11 Another Danish poet, Valdemar Rørdam (inspired by Edwin Arnold), in 1925, published *Buddha: Lykkens Yndling*. Although not declaring himself a Buddhist, in the afterword, he praises Buddha's teaching for its ability to change white man's culture.

12 The Critical Pali Dictionary was planned as an exhaustive Pali–English dictionary. Three volumes were published, before the project was discontinued in 2011. Poul Tuxen

(1880–1955) was responsible for the project until his death, with Else Margarete Pauly (1918–2000) and Ole Holten Pind (1945–2018) being two prominent scholars of Pali from Copenhagen University contributing to its continuation. An online version is kept by the Data Centre for the Humanities at the University of Cologne, in cooperation with the Pali Text Society (https://cpd.uni-koeln.de/).

13 Christian was the son of Jørgen Peter and Edle Caroline Mathilde. Both his father and his uncle were pastors in Northern Jutland. Christian was married to Jensine Karen Marie Melbye (born Jensen, 1874–1941), with whom he had the adopted son Børge Harry Viggo Melbye.

14 "I, and many other Buddhists with me, see in Jesus a Buddha" (Melbye 1921: 9).

15 Dharmapala had already visited the country in 1904. In Copenhagen, he met the university's president and the Buddhologist Viggo Fausbøll, and was taken to the town hall as if he were a VIP. He was invited to give a lecture at the folk high school Askov Højskole in Jutland. Dharmapala's presence was described in both local and national newspapers, unused to seeing, as the principal Ludvig Schrøder himself wrote in the school's journal, a "beautiful man with dark complexion and strong black hair stand at the podium speaking in his yellow Eastern attire" (Schrøder 1904, 300). The meeting might have been arranged by Gudrun Friis-Holm (1867-?). Friis-Holm was a Danish–American Theosophist and representative of the Mahabodhi Society of California. She lived in the United States from 1896, working with Jacob A. Riis to better the conditions in New York's slum before working at a hospital, later founding her own massage clinic, and eventually returning to Denmark to practice holistic medicine (Kemper 2015, 103ff). Melbye also knew of Friis-Holm. She wrote to the journal from Kamakura in Japan and an Indian ashram where she had stayed. Dharmapala felt attached to her and spoke of her as his "spiritual companion" and "eternal companion." Although she never came to Ceylon as he had hoped, they remained in contact for more than twenty years. To what extent their relationship was merely Platonic may be doubted. As a celibate, Dharmapala naturally had concerns, and described a massage given by her to make him feel "awakened sensations . . . under the clutches of Mara" (Kemper 2015, 103). Among the thirty references to her in his diaries, she is often referred to as Amara, probably referring to the seductive temptation of Mara.

16 "Buddhasasana cannot be learned by reading alone; there must be observance both in bhavana and in action" (Melbye 1922b: 6–7).

17 For most Danes, Buddhism is irrelevant, Melbye thinks. However, "some fuss and dawdle and flirt with it, as when young girls from the bourgeoisie wear a small Buddha figure as a talisman [!], thereby showing that they are completely devoid of any hint of a clue about who and what Buddha was and what he taught. Others use names derived from Buddhism for advertising. There's a 'Buddha powder'; there's a tea that is advertised with a picture of Buddha on the advertisement. There's a substance called 'nirvanol', foolishly named so by people with no reverence, because they have not the slightest idea about what they call 'nirvana'" (Melbye 1923: 8).

18 There are no more chairs and education in Pali, Sanskrit, Indology or Tibetan at Danish universities. In addition to previous philological studies, the *Danish Central Asian Expeditions* (1936–1937, 1938–1939 and 1947–1952) gathered information also on Buddhism, with especially Werner Jacobsen (1914–1979) having deep interest in the religion. In the 1950s, adventurer and ethnographer H.R.H. Prince Peter of Greece and Denmark (1908–1980) gathered material from the Himalayan region, contributing to Tibetan studies in Denmark (Brox 2017). Research on Buddhism has since been conducted by anthropologists and scholars of religion, with the Centre for Contemporary Buddhist Studies at the University of Copenhagen (directed by Trine Brox) illustrating the turn to Buddhism as lived religion in contemporary societies with substantial research projects such as "Buddhism, Business and Believers" and "Waste: Consumption and Buddhism in the Age of Waste." Apart from individual researchers focusing on Asian Buddhism (e.g., Jørgen Østergaard Andersen, Mikael Gravers, Martijn van

Beek, Cameron Warner, Trine Brox, Elizabeth Williams-Oerberg, Jørn Borup, Andreas Doctor), a previous cooperative project at Aarhus University (directed by Martijn van Beek) conducted research on modern Buddhism; in addition, Jørn Borup at the Centre for Contemporary Religion at Aarhus University has since 2003 investigated Buddhism in Denmark (Borup 2005). Christian Lindtner (1949–2020) was a somewhat alternative Buddhologist, both as an Indologist at different universities and as an individual researcher. Through philological analysis, gematria (assigning numerical value to words), "divine geometry," revisionist history and normative speculation, he saw Buddhism as an Aryan religion and Christianity as a misunderstood (and "judaized") imitation of Buddhism (www.jesusisbuddhist.com).

19 Bhikku Hiriko (2020).
20 A documentary on *Samahita* Thera was released in 2023 (*Munken*, "The Monk"). Samahita's urn is buried at Bispebjerg cemetary in Copenhagen.
21 https://triratna.dk/.
22 On Soka Gakkai in Denmark, see https://sgi-dk.org/, on the difference between Zen and Soka Gakkai trajectories in Denmark, see Borup (2025).
23 On Tarab Tulku, see Andersen & Bernstorff 2009 and https://tarab-institute.org/books/.
24 Gomde is the retreat centre owned by Foreningen Rangjung Yeshe Sangha, with Chökyi Nyima Rinpoche as the spiritual leader visiting the centre during summer. Gomde is part of an international network with thirteen centres worldwide. Lolland Buddhist Meditation Retreat Center is part of Karma Kagyu Skolen (Diamond Way), mainly approaching members of this group.
25 In 2024, these groups were identified: Shambala København, Tarab Institute International, Tergar København, Tilogaard, Samten Tse, Dzogchen Community, Clear Light Kadampa Buddhist Centre.
26 The reference to Padmasambhava's prophecy being manifested in the Diamond Way's main centre in Germany can be seen at the group's homepage https://europe-center.org/history/ (accessed 12 October 2023).
27 The official bestowing the title of "lama" to Ole came after the death of the Sixteenth Karmapa by the lineage holder, the Fourteenth Shamarpa. https://www.lama-ole-nydahl.de/dokumente/kenpo_choedrak.htm.
28 Among other arguments, it has been contested that he did not spend the traditionally required three years in a monastery. Ole himself has often referred to the Sixteenth Karmapa's acceptance of this, in accordance with his own wishes for transmitting the dharma. On Ole Nydahl and "the making of a lama," see Scherer 2014, 101–102.
29 Ole Nydahl's own description of this experience was later published in his first book: "Then the lama leaned forward, laid his hands on our heads, and gave us his blessing. He transferred the power of the Kagyupa lineage to us, and I still sweat so many years after just by remembering this: everything became light, and a powerful energy went through us. We shook from head to toe, and everything was perfect" (Nydahl 1983, 38–39, *my translation*).
30 Interestingly, this achievement was accomplished not least with the assistance of Johannes Aagaard, theologian, missionary and director of the anti-cult movement Dialogue Centre (1928–2007), whose "professional friendship" with Ole Nydahl was based on both personalities' interests in defining and representing "true religion" (Borup 2024).
31 The *stūpa* was awarded the Stonemasons Guild's and the Danish Industry's Natural Stone Prize in 2020. Official recognition for their work came in 2015 from another source, when Ole (and posthumously Hannah) received an award for dialogue, coexistence and peace from the UNESCO Association for Intercultural and Interreligious Dialogue.
32 A documentary was made about Hannah Nydahl, *Hannah: Buddhism's Untold Story* (http://www.hannahthefilm.com/en/).
33 Ole has openly revealed that he supports the German right-wing party Alternative für Deutschland as well as the Dutch right-wing politician Geert van Wilders. Some of Ole

Nydahl's disciples have run for election for the Danish right-wing party, Danish Folk Party. A newspaper feature on Ole Nydahl as a "Buddhist warrior" mentions recent controversies (http://kristianlauritzen.dk/wp-content/uploads/Larm-om-Lama-Ole-e7461dd6.pdf).

34 On the "Nydahl controversies," see HTTPS://BUDDHISMUS-KONTROVERS.INFO/?S=NYDAHL.

35 The Vietnamese temples are situated in the cities Aarhus, Odense, Copenhagen, Esbjerg, Aalborg and Horsens.

36 On Vietnamese migration, acculturation and religion in Denmark, see Borup 2011.

37 On Danish "culture religiosity," see Mauritsen et al. 2023.

38 Two Vietnamese Buddhist nuns live in private residences. While not being affiliated to the temples, they do offer religious services to and talks with local Vietnamese Buddhists. Due to some controversies, the monk in Horsens (Dia Tang temple) is not affiliated with any of the other Vietnamese temples.

39 Gaining a temporary permit as a religious worker has become increasingly difficult in Denmark. To keep out fundamentalist Muslim preachers, the law was regulated in recent years, demanding both administrative hassle and financial expenses not realistic to accommodate for smaller religious communities. For regulations, see https://www.nyidanmark.dk/en-GB/Applying/Religious%20workers/Religious%20worker%20etc.

40 https://www.dhammakaya.dk/.

41 Since neither ethnicity nor religiosity is counted in the official data, only estimates based on talks with representatives from Sri Lankan cultural and religious groups are behind these very insecure figures.

42 No mapping or comparative research has yet been made on mindfulness in Denmark. Apart from investigations of the phenomenon in the city of Aarhus (Gottfredsen 2014, Borup 2015) and comparisons of yoga and mindfulness (Fibiger & Borup 2024), Hedegaard's PhD dissertation (2020) is an ethnographic analysis of mindfulness in selected Danish workplaces.

43 https://vaekstcenteret.dk/. On the center's website, information of Jes Bertelsens publications (including books on Tantra and Dzogchen) can be found.

44 Elsass (2011) is an analysis of Buddhist psychology, while Elsass (2016) is an investigation of "the art of being alone," including Buddhist ascetism.

45 Soka Gakkai has been known, both internationally and in Denmark, to attract persons from the art scene. One interesting artist with no relations to any form of institutionalized religion was Ovartaci (Louis Marcussen, 1894–1985). As a patient in psychiatric hospital for most of his adult life, he created art with clear inspiration from Buddhism, and he identified himself as a Buddhist.

46 One example of a successful business owner (and billionaire) using Buddhism in his branding is Christian Stadil of the sports apparel company Hummel. Apart from sponsoring the Tibetan national football team and being an honorary consul for Bhutan, he also uses "company karma" as a part of his business strategy (https://www.hummel.dk/companykarma-home.html). With Steen Hildebrandt, an influential author formerly at Aarhus Business School, he wrote a book with the same title.

47 Buddhism has been used in different ways in popular music. Some musicians are Buddhists or attracted to the religion. Internationally famed jazz musician Niels Lan Doki's tune *Pink Buddha* is a tribute to all the "pink" (non-Asian) Buddhists, some of whom might agree to the ideal of seeing jazz as a way of practising Zen because of its philosophy of "being in the present" (personal communication).

References

Andersen, Jeannie and Anne Sophie Bernstorff. 2009. *Tarab Tulku XI. En tibetansk lama i Danmark*. Cph: Ørnens Forlag.

Bhikku Hiriko. 2020. *The Island Within. The Life of the Hermit Monk Bhante Ñānadipa*. Path Press Publications. https://pathpress.org/wp-content/uploads/2020/12/Bhikkhu-Hiriko-The-Island-Within.pdf (accessed 12 Nov 2024).

Bilstrup, Caroline H. 2024. "Kongen hæver Buddha over Gud." *Ekstrabladet*, 15th January. https://ekstrabladet.dk/underholdning/kongelige/danskekongelige/kommentator-kongen-haever-buddha-over-gud/10094175 (accessed 12 Nov 2024).

Borup, Jørn. 2005. *Dansk dharma*. Højbjerg: Forlaget Univers.

Borup, Jørn. 2011. *Religion, kultur og integration: vietnameserne i Danmark*. Cph: Museum Tusculanum Press.

Borup, Jørn. 2015. "Mindfulness as a Booming, Diverse and (Non) Religious Phenome-non-Mapping and Analyzing Mindfulness in the City of Aarhus." *Religion i Danmark*, 7(2), 1–16. https://tidsskrift.dk/index.php/rid/article/view/23716 (accessed 12 Nov 2024).

Borup, Jørn. 2016. "Branding Buddha-Mediatized and Commodified Buddhism as Cultural Narrative." *Journal of Global Buddhism,* 17, 41–55.

Borup, Jørn. 2024. "Divide and Rule: Strategic Encounters Between A Hippie Buddhist Lama And A Christian Countercult Leader in the Early Phase of Practised Buddhism in Denmark." In *Euro-Buddhism and the Role of Christianity,* edited by Kurt Gakuro Krammer, John O'Grady and Martin Rötting, 71–89. Sankt Ottilien: EOS.

Borup, Jørn. 2025. "Zen for the Elite, Buddhism for the Masses: Religious and Spiritual Circulation Between Japan and the West." In *Sufism and Zen in the West*, edited by Michael Conway and Saeko Yazaki, 209–227. Bloomsbury Academic.

Brox, Trine. 2017. "Tibetologien i Danmark – og tibetanske teksters eventyrlige rejse til Danmark." In *Små fag, store horisonter,* edited by Jakob Skovgaard-Petersen and Tea Sindbæk Tea, 124–41. Institut for Tværkulturelle og Regionale Studier.

Buddhismus Kontrovers https://buddhismus-kontrovers.info/?s=nydahl (accessed 12 November 2024).

Centre for Contemporary Religion. 2022. *Religion i Aarhus*. https://samtidsreligion.au.dk/fileadmin/Samtidsreligion/Religion_i_Aarhus_2022/Kortlaegning_af_Religion_i_Aarhus_0606.pdf (accessed 12 Nov 2024).

Danish Centre for Mindfulness. https://mindfulness.au.dk/en/ (accessed 12 Nov 2024).

Danish Ministry of Ecclesiastical Affairs. https://www.blkm.dk/andre-trossamfund (accessed 12 Nov 2024). https://www.blkm.dk/andre-trossamfund/trossamfundsregistret/liste-over-anerkendte-trossamfund-og-tilknyttede-menigheder (accessed 12 Nov 2024).

Dhammakaya Denmark. https://www.dhammakaya.dk/ (accessed 12 Nov 2024).

Elsass, Peter. 2011. *Buddhas veje. En introduktion til buddhistisk psykologi*. Cph: Dansk Psykologisk Forlag.

Elsass, Peter. 2016. *Kunsten at være alene*. Cph: Gyldendal.

Europe Center. n.d. International Diamond Way Buddhist Center. https://europe-center.org/history/ (accessed 12 Nov 2024).

Fibiger, Marianne Qvortrup and Jørn Borup. 2024. "Yoga and mindfulness as a fluctuating field." *Annual Review of the Sociology of Religion 14*, 180–197.

Gjellerup, Karl. 1906. *Pilgrimmen Kamanita*. Cph: Gyldendal.

Gottfredsen, Rikke. 2014. "Mindfulness – en religionssociologisk analyse." *Religionsvidenskabeligt* Tidsskrift, 61, 55.73.

Hannah: Buddhism's Untold Story. 2024. (http://www.hannahthefilm.com/en/) (accessed 12 Nov 2024).

Hedegaard, Marianne. 2020. *Mindful Work: An Ethnography of Mindfulness and the Sociality of Feeling in Danish Workplaces*. PhD dissertation.

Hübbe-Schleiden, Wilhelm. 1895. *Was Jesus Buddhist?* Cph: Andreas Schous Forlag.

Hummel https://www.hummel.dk/companykarma-home.html (accessed 12 Nov 2024).

Jyllands-Posten. https://jyllands-posten.dk/indland/article5284946.ece (accessed 12 Nov 2024).

Jørgensen, Johannes. 1896. *Beuron*. Kbh: Det Nordiske Forlag.

Kemper, Steven. 2015. *Rescued from the Nation: Anagarika Dharmapala and the Buddhist world*. Chicago, London: The University of Chicago Press.

Knudsen, Jens Kristian. 1891. *På Budda's Veje. Oplevelser og Meddelelser fra Burma.* Cph: V. Pontoppidans Boghandel.

Knudsen, Jens Kristian. 1893. "Lidt Burmesisk Buddhisme." *Højskolebladet* 18, 82–83.

Lama Ole Nydahl. *Kenpo Choedrak*. https://www.lama-ole-nydahl.de/dokumente/kenpo_choedrak.htm (accessed 12 Nov 2024).

Lauritzen, Kristian. 2019. "Larm om Lama Ole." *Weekendavisen*, 19 July. https://www.weekendavisen.dk/2019–29/samfund/larm-om-lama-ole (accessed 12 Nov 2024).

Lehmann, Johannes Edvard. 1907. *Buddha*. Cph: Pios Boghandel.

Lindtner, Christian. https://www.jesusisbuddha.com/ (accessed 12 Nov 2024).

Mauritsen, Anne L., Jørn Borup, Marie Vejrup and Benjamin Grant Purzycki. 2023. "Cultural Religion: Patterns of Contemporary Majority Religion In Denmark." *Journal of Contemporary Religion,* 38, 2, 261–281.

Melbye, Christian F. 1921. "I anledning af den kristne jul." *Buddhistisk Budbringer,* 1(årgang 2), 9–10.

Melbye, Christian F. 1922a. "Vesaktanker." *Buddhistisk Budbringer*, 2(årgang 2), 2–4.

Melbye, Christian F. 1922b. "Buddhistisk samfund i Danmark". *Buddhistisk Budbringer*, 2(årgang 2), 6–7.

Melbye, Christian F. 1922c. "En gave fra Mrs. Fosters missions fond til buddhistisk samfund i Danmark." *Buddhistisk Budbringer*, 2(årgang 3), 3.

Melbye, Christian F. 1923. "Buddhistisk samfund i Danmark." *Buddhistisk Budbringer*, 3(årgang 1), 7–9.

Melbye, Christian F. 1925. "Dines Andersen." *Buddhistisk Budbringer*, 5(årgang 3), 2–4.

Melbye, Christian Frederik. (1923–1926) "Buddha's Holy Way." *Buddhist Annual of Ceylon*, 2, 8–9.

New to Denmark. *Religious Workers*. https://www.nyidanmark.dk/en-GB/Applying/Religious%20workers/Religious%20worker%20etc. (accessed 12 Nov 2024).

Nydahl, Ole. 1983. *Når jernfuglen flyver*. Cph: Borgen.

Nørregård, Georg. 1988. *Karl Gjellerup – en biografi*. Cph.: C. A. Reitzels Forlag.

Pali Text Society. 2024. Pali Text Society. (https://cpd.uni-koeln.de/) (accessed 12 Nov 2024).

Prip-Møller, Johannes. 1937. *Chinese Buddhist Monasteries. Their Plan and Its Function as a Setting for Buddhist Monastic Life*. Copenhagen/Oxford: G. E. C. Gad & Oxford University Press.

Reventlow, Christian. 1927. "Buddhismen i dansk litteratur." *Den Nye Litteratur. Dansk Litteraturtidende* 11, 211–227.

Rørdam, Valdemar. 1925. *Buddha. Lykkens Yndling*. Cph: Aschhougs Forlag.

Scherer, Burkhard. 2009. "Interpreting the Diamond Way: Contemporary Convert Buddhism in Transition." *Journal of Global Buddhism*, 10, 17–48.

Scherer, Burkhard. 2014. "Conversion, Devotion, and (Trans-)Mission: Understanding Ole Nydahl." In *Buddhists: Understanding Buddhism Through the Lives of Practitioners*, edited by Todd Lewis, 96–106. Hoboken, New Jersey: Wiley Blackwell.

Schrøder, Ludwig. 1904. "Et indisk Besøg paa en dansk Højskole." *Højskolebladet* 10, 299–300.

Soka Gakkai Danmark. 2024. Soka Gakkai Danmark. https://sgi-dk.org/ (accessed 12 Nov 2024).

Statistics Denmark. 2024. *Statistics Denmark*. www.statistikbanken.dk (accessed 12 Nov 2024).

Tarab Institute. 2024. Tarab Institute. https://tarab-institute.org/books/ (accessed 12 Nov 2024).

Triratna Denmark. 2024. *Triratna Denmark*. Denmark https://triratna.dk/ (accessed 12 Nov 2024).

6 Buddhism in Norway

The strange story of the rebirth of the Buddha and Sariputra in the early twentieth century and other Buddhist histories and developments

Knut A. Jacobsen

The beginning of Buddhism in Norway

The history of Buddhists in Norway does not start with the arrival of the first migrant Buddhists, a group of forty Tibetan boys who arrived together as refugees in January 1964, or the first meetings of a few people interested in Zen Buddhism taking place in the early 1970s, or the first officially registered Buddhist organisations in the late 1970s. The history of Buddhists in Norway starts in the 1920s and has a strange beginning. It began in 1928 when an Indian Hindu *saṃnyāsin* from Bengal, Sri Ananda Acharya, who lived in Norway from 1915 until his death in 1945 and from 1917 resided in Alvdal in a mountainous area in eastern Norway, announced to his close devotees that he had discovered that he was a rebirth of the Buddha. He pronounced that his soul was the same soul that had lived in Gautama Buddha, that there was only one Buddha in the whole universe and that he was that Buddha who had been born again (Beer 1957: 7, 1960a: 3). In 1932, he announced that he remembered his real name was Tathagata Amoghasiddhi Maitreyya Buddha, who, according to him, was the Buddha that Gautama Buddha had predicted would appear in the future (Beer 1957: 7). He also declared that his main Norwegian disciple, the engineer Einar Beer (1887–1982), was a rebirth of Sariputra, a very close disciple of the historical Buddha. These declarations mark the beginning of Buddhists in Norway.

Sri Ananda Acharya called himself Tathagata Amoghasiddhi Maitreyya Buddha, or Maitreyya Buddha for short, for the rest of his life, and several books were published about Maitreyya Buddha, organised by Einar Beer (Tathagata Amoghasiddhi Maitreyya Buddha 1960, 1967). A stylised photograph of him as Tathagata Amoghasiddhi Maitreyya Buddha was taken and included in the books about him. He died in Alvdal in 1945. For his main disciple Sariputra (aka Einar Beer), Sri Ananda Acharya had from the time of his declaration become the Buddha. Beer published books and shorter papers and lectured on Maitreyya Buddha. One book by Beer about his guru was titled *The Tathagata Amoghasiddhi Maitreyya Buddha*, and another was called *Maitreyya Buddha* and the caption of the photograph in the book of the burial place of his teacher reads "burial place of Maitreyya Buddha"

DOI: 10.4324/9781003529767-6

(Sariputra 1968: 27). Beer wrote a diary, and in his publication *The Tathagata Amoghasiddhi Maitreyya Buddha*, he mentions conversations between his teacher and himself, and in the quotations from his diary he refers to the teacher as "the holy Buddha." In 1931, Maitreyya Buddha supposedly predicted the Second World War and warned that unless many males became *bhikṣu*s (Buddhist monks), war was unavoidable (see Figure 6.1).

The institution that developed from the activities of Maitreyya Buddha, aka Sri Ananda Acharya, and his disciples in Alvdal, today mostly remembers him by his Hindu *saṃnyāsin* name Sri Ananda Acharya and probably regards his period as Tathagata Amoghasiddhi Maitreyya Buddha as a deviation. The current main spokesperson for the institution, Bjørn Pettersen, argues that Sri Ananda Acharya's two different religious identities show that he did not really belong to any religion and that his truth was beyond any such limitations.[1] After the passing of the last

Figure 6.1 Maitreyya Buddha, aka Sri Ananda Acharya who in 1928 announced that he was a rebirth of the Buddha and in 1932 that his real name was Tathagata Amoghasiddhi Maitreyya Buddha and that his main Norwegian disciple Einar Beer was a rebirth of Sariputra, a close disciple of the Buddha, which marks the beginning of Buddhists in Norway. Copyright: The Swami Sri Ananda Acharya Stiftelse. Used with permission.

surviving disciple, Einar Beer in 1982, the institution sought to revive its Hindu background, and it has today no recognisable Buddhist elements. The institution currently uses only the Hindu name of the founding guru.[2]

Tathagata Amoghasiddhi Maitreyya Buddha's original Bengali name was Surendranath Boral (1881–1945) and he was only later known as Sri Ananda Acharya after he had taken *saṃnyāsa* in his youth and had completed his university education. After he announced he had taken the new Buddhist name, he was for some time referred to by that name. People in Alvdal, where Maitreyya Buddha lived and Einar Beer visited, seem to have also referred to them both as Buddhists. As late as the 1960s, Einar Beer would call himself the only Buddhist in Norway and he was also at the time referred to by Norwegian newspapers and state radio as Norway's only Buddhist. In 1967 he was initiated into the Bihar School of Yoga in India by the founder Satyananda Saraswati (a disciple of Sivananda, the founder of Divine Life Society, a Hindu organisation of modern yoga), but that did not change his perception of himself as being a Buddhist. Beer considered this a non-denominational initiation into the ancient Indian *saṃnyāsa* institution and not an initiation into the Bihar School of Yoga as such. Beer's initiation added Swami Acharya to his Sariputra name. He was now Swami Acharya Sariputra (Sariputra 1967: 1). Beer noted that "Sariputra was one of the Buddha's foremost disciples, as I have been Maitreyya Buddha's disciple and try to further his tradition and teaching and guard his sacred memory" (Sariputra 1967: 1).[3] However, the Bihar School of Yoga is part of Modern Yoga (unnoticed by Beer) with a Hindu background and it was one of the early institutions of modern India to initiate Westerners into *saṃnyāsa*. A reviewer of the book *Maitreyya Buddha* in a Norwegian newspaper was so convinced about Einar Beer's Buddhist identity he wrote that Beer was initiated into an "an ancient Buddhist order"[4] where he received the name Swami Acharya Sariputra (Schade n.d.). The institution of the Bihar School of Yoga, however, was neither ancient nor Buddhist.

Buddhism in Norway thus started in a most peculiar way. A Hindu missionary from Hooghly, near to Calcutta in Bengal, had quit his job as teacher of philosophy at Maharaja's College in Burdwan and settled permanently in a cottage in a mountainous area in eastern Norway in 1917 and promoted himself as a Hindu *ācārya*. He had probably been encouraged by his own guru Śivanārāyaṇa Paramahaṃsa to travel to Europe to spread the guru's message (Sarma 1971: xviii). The guru Śivanārāyaṇa Paramahaṃsa was originally from Varanasi, but he was active in Bengal in the last decades of the nineteenth century and had Bengali disciples. He was an idiosyncratic guru, mostly critical of many Hindu teachings and rituals, and was against the worship of *mūrti*s, and he did not belong to any Hindu *sampradāya*. Śivanārāyaṇa Paramahaṃsa taught that God was light, manifesting in the sun and the moon and inside humans as their *ātman*. Śivanārāyaṇa had been compared to Socrates and was even called an Indian Socrates because he believed rational arguments were the most important means of knowledge, and he argued with gurus, priests and yogis at numerous pilgrimage places to convince them of his views, especially about accepting his understanding of a supreme divinity (Chatterjee 1907, 1925). Sri Ananda dedicated many of his books to Śivanārāyaṇa and promoted many views similar to his, but he never presented any specific views as being those of Śivanārāyaṇa. Sri Ananda's idea of divinity, his critique of nationalism and promotion of peace, and ideas of education seem largely inherited from his guru Śivanārāyaṇa Paramahaṃsa (Jacobsen 2025). Sri Ananda's mission to Europe was to spread the message of Indian philosophy, Indian nationalist ideas and the teaching of his guru about peace and education. He wrote books on Indian philosophy and published poetry and plays. His books glorified India as a spiritual and social utopia that was better in all ways compared to the Western world. Sri Ananda's education seems to have been influenced and encouraged by Orientalist romantic views of India as well as emerging Indian nationalism. These views and ideas are very recognisable in his texts.

Tathagata Amoghasiddhi Maitreyya Buddha very likely did not convince many people of his identity as the Buddha apart from his closest disciple. Most individuals who encountered him probably did not even understand what his being the Buddha meant. Maitreyya Buddha and Sariputra did not teach any Buddhist practices, and their Buddhist identities did not lead to further expansion of Buddhism in Norway. Beer published poems and sayings of Tathagata Amoghasiddhi Maitreyya Buddha that promoted Buddhism as he and his guru understood it.

In an issue of the journal *Contemporary Buddhism*, on the topic "Pioneer European Buddhists and Globalizing Asian Networks 1860–1960," the editors noted in their introduction essay that the history of modern Buddhism is too often written about the winners (Turner, Cox and Bocking 2013: 2). The editors encouraged researchers to "consider voices and conversations outside of the standard histories" (Turner, Cox and Bocking 2013: 2). They emphasised looking at interesting failures. The historical twist of Sri Ananda Acharya and his disciple Einar Beer embracing Buddhism seems to have produced what could be considered an interesting failure in the history of Buddhism in the Nordic countries. The story of these first Buddhists, besides its strangeness and its narration of the beginning of a national history of Buddhism, is certainly a story of Buddhist failure. I have never seen their names mentioned in any history of Buddhism in Europe. They did not achieve success in terms of creating a Buddhist lineage or any new Buddhist converts, and their Buddhism is today mainly forgotten. The institution founded by Sri Ananda Acharya and Einar Beer has reverted to its original Hindu connection and none of the many living Buddhist traditions in Norway has any links to these first two Buddhists. No Buddhists visit his *samādhi* (burial place) as far as I know, although some Hindus from South Asia settled in Norway and other Hindu pilgrims do. The two figures cannot even be said to be representative of any mainstream narratives about the expansion of Buddhism in the West or the contemporary world. This highly unusual story is nevertheless of significance as illustrations of what Buddhism was thought to be and to be able to do in the twentieth century, and it highlights a marginal phenomenon and perhaps some forgotten experiences and perspectives in twentieth-century Buddhism.

Two forms of Buddhism succeeded in Norway. First, traditions that offered meditation as a group activity and thus made it possible to develop Buddhist identities and, second, temple Buddhism of migrants. Maitreyya Buddha offered neither meditation as an instructed group activity nor Buddhist temple worship. He was culturally a Hindu[5] and his disciple Einar Beer mainly promoted Buddhism as a habit of the heart.

Sri Ananda Acharya's background

Sri Ananda Acharya was the earliest Hindu guru from India to settle permanently in Europe (Jacobsen 2020). He was a Hindu *saṃnyāsin* who came to Europe, according to the Introduction page of the published book based on the lectures he held at the University of Oslo in the summer of 1915, "in order to make better known to the world the ancient Philosophy of India" (Ānanda Āchārya 1978: iii). Sri Ananda's early education was at a mission school attached to the Bandel Church in Hooghly. His parents were not poor. His guru, Śivanārāyaṇa Paramahaṃsa, did not belong to any *sampradāya* and had no guru but he had a Hindu identity. Sri Ananda therefore did not have a background in a traditional *sampradāya*, which would have made his migration to Europe less likely and probably also his sudden adoption of a Buddhist identity. Sri Ananda left India in 1912 for Europe and arrived in Marseilles the same year, continuing overland to Britain. In Britain, he gave lectures on Sanskrit literature and Indian philosophy. He seems to have struggled to adapt and to be accepted. He depended on patrons, who were mostly British women. In 1914, he left Britain and went to Norway and Sweden. He gave lectures on Indian philosophy at universities in Oslo and Stockholm but then, in 1917, settled permanently in the mountains in Norway in a cottage bought for him by his Norwegian patron Einar Beer, who also became his main disciple. Sri Ananda knew European Indological scholarship and started his lecture at the University of Oslo in the summer of 1915 by recommending "the works of Max Muller and Paul Deussen (etc)" "to those who wish to study" the question "What is an Upanishad" "more deeply" (Ānanda Āchārya 1978: 3). From 1913 to 1928, Sri Ananda published many books but after 1928, the year he made public that he was the Buddha, this hectic publication project stopped. Sri Ananda's book production included several different genres such as philosophy, spiritual diaries, plays and poetry. His first philosophy books were not written by him but were based on notes taken during his lectures, which he held without notes. *Brahmadarsanam, or Intuition of the Absolute: Being An Introduction to the Study Of Hindu Philosophy* was taken from notes from his lectures given at the University of Oslo in 1915 (at that time named the Royal Frederick University) and published by Macmillan in New York in 1917. His lectures at Stockholm University were published in 1922 as *Tattwajnānam: the quest of cosmic consciousness: being public lectures on the metaphysical conceptions of the ancient Aryans of India, delivered in the convocation hall of the University of Stockholm during the winter session of 1915–16*. He published several volumes of fictional spiritual literature such as *The Book of the Cave Gaurisankarguha: Being the Authentic Account of a Pilgrimage to the Gaurisankar Cave, Narrated by the Late Professor Truedream of the University of Sighbridge to His Friends*, published in 1919. His most well-known collection of poems is *Snow Birds*. His British female disciples helped him a great deal with the books published in English, while others assisted him with writings in Swedish and Norwegian. He wrote several spiritual diaries, *Yoga of Conquest* (1924) and *Life and Nirvana* (notes written in 1942–1945 but published by Einar Beer in 1970).

He especially wrote extensively about romantic India, world peace and education, Vedānta and Yoga. His ideas were utopian. Avoidance of war was the main goal in his educational visions. He considered mountains to be appropriate places for learning and suggested establishing educational institutions in mountainous areas around the world as places for the mixing of people from many countries, starting with young pupils who would stay for several years, to form friendships across nations. The idea was to create new human beings who would not feel they belonged to any nations. Romantic ideas about education in India, *gurukul*s and the yogic connection to mountain caves, are detectable in his writings, in addition to his hope of a human global civilisation without war. He believed Indian philosophical and educational traditions could be used to create a better world. The idea of God is central in his teaching as it was in the teaching of Śivanārāyaṇa Paramahaṃsa. The issue of harmony of religions, peace between nations, a rational approach to religion, absence of the worship of *mūrti*s and monotheism were major parts of Sri Ananda's teaching as they were of his guru. They disliked religious institutions.

Einar Beer's Buddha: Tathagata Amoghasiddhi Maitreyya Buddha

After 1928, when Sri Ananda Acharya had realised that he was the Buddha, his publication activity stopped, and it was mainly Einar Beer who wrote and published the Buddhist material. These texts by Einar Beer are used here to analyse their interpretations of Buddhism and how Beer understood Sri Ananda Acharya as the Buddha and himself as his disciple and the only Buddhist in Norway.[6] What did it mean for the Norwegian disciple that his guru suddenly declared himself the Buddha? What did the Buddha do and say and how did the disciple deal with it? Why had the Buddha settled in Norway?

Einar Beer accepted that his guru Sri Ananda really was Tathagata Amoghasiddhi Maitreyya Buddha and called him Buddha or Maitreyya Buddha after being informed about his new identity. However, the two British female disciples, Amy L. Edwards (d. 1947) and Ellen Margaret Jawson (d. 1954), who lived at the *āśram*, apparently did not (Pettersen 2018: 245). Beer tried to make sense of his and Sri Ananda's rejection of Hindu traditions and wrote in a note on 4 April 1931 that Vedānta was really Buddhism, but that the Vedāntins, instead of recognising the Buddha, recognise a divine being who is goodness, which makes, according to him, Vedanta similar to Buddhism:

Vedanta is just a branch of Buddhism. They have no right to call it Vedanta. The Vedas – Rigveda – is devotion, a science of the natural forces like Indra, Agni, etc. – how to gain riches, welfare, good health, etc. While the Vedantins, just like the Buddhists, forsake and believe in spiritual liberation in line with karma's law – good deeds. Instead of the Buddha, the Vedantins accept a God, a divine being whose essence is goodness. How is it different from Buddhism?

(quoted in Pettersen 2018: 244)[7]

For Einar Beer, the guru was superhuman and divine, and for him Maitreyya Buddha and the historical Buddha were the same person. When he writes about the Buddha, the reference is often therefore to his own guru. For him Buddhism was primarily about relating to the Buddha. He seems to have believed that the historical Buddha was a personality that continued to take rebirth in the world and had now been born as Maitreyya Buddha. Beer writes:

> When I try to speak or write about Gotama Buddha or Maitreyya Buddha (Sri Ananda Acharya) it is to me the one and same person, because there is only one Buddha soul in the same way as each of us is only one personality, that is born again, always the same, in that way there is only one Buddha.
>
> (Sariputra 1968: 20–21)[8]

Beer professed to have read books about Buddhism while he studied engineering in Germany. His interpretations are nevertheless unusual, and they illustrate how he tried to make sense of the claims by his guru of being a rebirth of the Buddha. His interpretations of Buddhism seem to be based on what he believed was a direct relationship to the actual Buddha, and not on reading about Buddhism or reading translations of Buddhist texts. Buddha is for him an eternal soul repeatedly being reborn. "It is the same Buddha that Gautama prophesised, but Sri Ananda or Maitreyya Buddha said: 'There is only one Buddha in the universe and I am the same Buddha who has come again.' But this he did not say until long afterwards up here in Tronfjell" (Beer 1960: 2).

In a typed unpublished manuscript by Einar Beer dated to 1968 and now owned by the National Library in Norway, we find more information about Beer's Buddhism (Beer 1968). The manuscript has the title "Swami Sri Ananda Acharya – Maitreyya Buddha" and is a lecture manuscript that also includes questions from students and Beer's answers, which shows it was retyped after the event. In the lecture and in the questions and answers session afterwards, Einar Beer talks about his understanding of Buddhism and his work with Maitreyya Buddha. He presents himself as a Buddhist and Ananda Acharya mostly as Maitreyya Buddha. The text starts with Einar Beer stating his admiration for India and presenting his exceedingly romantic view of the country, in line with Sri Ananda Acharya/ Maitreyya Buddha's missionary views. He then presents Maitreyya Buddha's philosophy of life, his own meeting with him, what he learned from him, and his work with Maitreyya Buddha's books, several of which are based on notes written down by Einar Beer from Maitreyya Buddha's dictation. He functioned as one of the secretaries of Sri Ananda Acharya/Maitreyya Buddha's book publications. The books were published by their own publishing company, The Brahmakul, Alvdal. He then informs the students that in 1927 Sri Ananda claimed that in his last life he had been the famous Ramakrishna (1836–1886) in India and Einar Beer one of his disciples, and it was a year later, in 1928, that he remembered ("erindret") that he was the Buddha and Einar Beer his disciple Sariputra (Beer 1968: 3).

> His conversations – speeches to me, from this time and forward to 1938 – these conversations were of the utmost importance to me. He told me that in

the days of the Buddha I was Sariputra and in the life of Ramakrishna I was also his close friend and disciple through many years. With intervals, in 1929 and the first years of the 1930s, he dictated to me the Buddha book "Cosmic Words of Light" and a number of Buddha poems that were translated.

(Beer 1968: 3)[9]

Beer argues that science and technology lead humanity to destruction and that everyone knows this, and that evil forces are succeeding. Against this only the Buddha can save us:

The Buddha alone has wisdom, has advice. And without break, for many years, the sun of wisdom has been shining over Norway from Tronfjell. Sri Ananda Acharya has created here on Tronfjell a power that the whole of mankind now must learn from, if it wants to avoid war and avoid being annihilated. It has been hard work, his Buddha-work here on Tronfjell for the whole of mankind. Buddha shows the way, an alternative to this self-annihilating life in the world.

(Beer 1968: 3–4)[10]

Humans must give up what they earlier have heard, wished for and wanted. "Then can the peace work – Buddha's peace work – begin" (Beer 1968: 4).[11]

So, what is the teaching of the Buddha, according to this disciple of Maitreyya Buddha? The teaching of the Buddha is identical to the teaching he has heard from Maitreyya Buddha:

Maitreyya Buddha's way is the Way of Friendship to perfect goodness in perfect sacredness. All life is sacred. Spare therefore all life. Be kind. That is the teaching of friendship and mercy. Maitreyya Buddha's message of freedom from desire – from hunger for land, from hatred, war, money, overpopulation, poverty, illness, misery and death.

(Beer 1968: 4)[12]

Everything in the world is a lie, is illusion . . . everything is unreal, becomes unreal, for the person who sees the Eternal, who can lift one's soul to the eternal real life.

(Beer 1968: 4)[13]

A comparison with the historical Buddha and the Norway-based Indian Maitreyya Buddha is made in the text *Interracial Concord*, in which the first ten pages of the book contain a transcription of a radio interview with Einar Beer. His guru Maitreyya Buddha is here considered superior to the historical Buddha, because Maitreyya Buddha had knowledge of philosophy and science. Beer says:

But Gautama spoke to his time, to those who were around him, and Gautama the Buddha did not write because at that time one had to write in the memory of men. So, he spoke quite simple things, but these things have been perfectly gorgeously preserved in Ceylon in the Pali Scriptures as well as in Sanskrit in Northern India, and from there in later centuries they came to China, Korea, Tibet and Japan where they have been preserved. There is a complete conformity, but one may perhaps say that the original teaching of Gautama the Buddha is slightly more brief, a little simpler than this, because now Maitreyya the Buddha came again as a learned philosopher and one who knew all the sciences of the West as well as the sciences of the East – astronomy, astrology and all these sciences of atomic influences from the universe on the human mind – all this lay completely open to him.

(Beer 1960: no pagination)

He explains why he became a Buddhist:

If anyone still asks why I have become a Buddhist – that is, one who seeks truth and awakening to truth, I will answer: because life is so priceless, the most priceless we own. That is why we have to make the best out of it – seek to find and live in truth.

(Beer 1968: 5)[14]

About Buddhism he explains:

Buddhism has in every detail developed a very comprehensive and nuanced system for self-discipline and self-improvement of thought, feelings and action, that every Buddhist has to learn and train. Never do anything wrong, only do what is right and to make the heart pure, that is what all Buddhas teach.

(Beer 1968: 5)[15]

After the lecture, a student, who defines himself as a Christian, asks Beer why he became a Buddhist. Beer answers:

Because I am thankful, because I have conscience, because I love a purity of life and goodness, because I love Norway, this country, therefore I have become a Buddhist.

(Beer 1968: 6)[16]

A student asks him to explain why he mentioned Norway in his answer, and Beer explains:

The Buddha has such a wonderful view of the whole, such wonderful love, such a wonderful heart that embraces everything. Therefore, I love the Buddha. Therefore, I love all I have learned from Maitreyya Buddha, Sri Ananda Acharya – through all the years from 1915 till today. Buddha's religion is the religion of light, the religion of purity. Buddha's teaching is also very secular. It is about making the world pure – make darkness and evil filled with the light of the heart and make them good so that life in the world can be better.

(Beer 1968: 6–7)[17]

That "Buddha's religion is the religion of light" evokes the teaching of Sri Ananda's guru Śivanārāyaṇa Paramahaṃsa, who taught that God is light and becomes manifest in the sun and the moon.

Interestingly, a student asks why the teacher of Beer called himself the Buddha. Beer first gives the obvious answer that if the Buddha had not declared that he was the Buddha, no one would have known. Beer then gives a long answer where he explains the teaching of the Buddha, that all is change leading to *duḥkha*, but that there is a non-changing, eternal reality called *nirvāṇa*, which is not associated with sorrow, and expresses his views about those who joined the Buddha, who are, according to him, mainly the sons of the educated, cultured elite. He says that he is happy to be called Norway's only Buddhist, as some journalists do call him. In the booklet *Maitreyya Buddha: Liv – Sannhet – Lære*, he defines the Buddha as "a human who is born again and again on this earth . . . Buddha means 'the enlightened' – the perfectly enlightened human being. Maitreya Buddha is 'the Buddha of friendship' who teaches unlimited friendship with the pure, goodwill for all life – humans, animals, trees and all nature" (Sariputra 1968: 7).[18]

Maitreyya Buddha seems, during the years of his Buddhist period, to have considered the spread of Buddhism to be his main mission. He wrote in a letter to a neighbour shortly before he died, telling how the world was becoming so much better, that it could now be called the best of all worlds. Democracy, medical science and the arts were improving, and so was the longing for peace, and performance of duties. There was a wave of spirituality and justice and honesty, and the religion of Buddhism was being spread to the whole world and had already won over all thinking and noble people. He saw these as signs of his successful mission. He concluded that the causes of this were that "the prevalence of Sanskrit teachings that bring the sacred texts of the old culture of India, the highest and oldest culture in the world to the West has produced the most beneficial results"[19] but he also noted: ". . . though for egoistical reasons many Orientalists try to destroy its civilizing influence" (in Beer 1975: 39–40), which probably was a response to the criticism he received from textual scholars (see Jacobsen 2020, 2025).[20]

The name Tathagata Amoghasiddhi Maitreyya Buddha has been mostly forgotten, and he is mainly known by his Hindu *saṃnyāsin* name Sri Ananda Acharya and remembered as a Hindu missionary. Sri Ananda Acharya was also the name under which he published many books. His *āśram* institution in Alvdal became hinduised in the late 1980s under new leadership who made connections with a Hindu group in Bengal, Swami Paramananda and the Paramananda Mission, and has more or less erased the Buddhist past of their founding *ācārya* and his disciple. The institution today rejects any Buddhist or Hindu identity and wants to think about Sri Ananda Acharya as a person who transcended all religions.[21]

Some precursors to Buddhism in Norway

An early academic interest in Buddhist texts and traditions, and travel and work in Buddhist countries in Asia preceded the Buddhist awakening of Ananda Acharya and Einar Beer, as well as the growth of Buddhism that happened from the 1970s onwards. This interest can perhaps be considered the precursor to Buddhism in Norway. The first Norwegian to engage himself in knowledge about Buddhism was probably the Indologist Christian Lassen (1800–1876) who was the founder of Pāli studies in Europe together with Eugène Burnouf. He published *Essai sur la Pali* in Paris in 1826 with Burnouf (Burnouf and Lassen 1826), but he worked in Germany and had little influence in Norway. C.A. Holmboe (1796–1882) worked in Norway, and he has therefore probably been called the first Norwegian scholar of Buddhism (Kværne 2022). Holmboe was a philologist with an interest in Asian languages (Persian, Arabic and Sanskrit, possibly the first to teach Sanskrit at a Norwegian University), founder of numismatics in Norway and professor at the University of Oslo (called Royal Frederik University until 1939). Holmboe was one of the first to show the Buddhist origin of the Christian narrative of Barlaam and Josaphat (Kværne 2022). He had an interest in the comparative study of Buddhism, and in the book *Traces de Buddhisme en Norvège* (Holmboe 1857) and in several articles (Holmboe 1862, 1867), he argued for a number of Buddhist influences on the ancient Norse culture. He thought the burial mounds of old Norse religion were based on Buddhist *stūpa*s and that the idea of the sacred trees of the Norse religion came from Buddhist worship of the *bodhi* tree. He also believed that the dividing up of the dead body of the ancient Norwegian king Halfdan the Black into four parts and sharing it between four different villages to provide blessings and a good agricultural harvest, as told in the Old Norse kings' saga *Heimskringla,* was similar to what happened to the body of the Buddha after his death and therefore showed Buddhist influences. He even believed that some of the Norse gods came from Buddhist areas and suggested that the name of a principal god, Odin, was derived from the name of the Buddha (Holmboe 1857). In addition, he attempted to show in his work how these proposed Buddhist influences historically reached Norway. He did not receive much support for these spurious speculations.

Several Norwegians worked for the military in China and encountered Buddhism there and others worked as missionaries and learned about Buddhism by confronting monks and priests with their own Lutheran Christian views. General Johan Wilhelm Normann Munthe (1864–1935) was a general in the Chinese Emperor's army, and after the fall of the empire in 1911, he became an adviser to the Chinese Ministry of War in the early years of the republic. He amassed a vast collection of art, including significant Buddhist material that is today held in several museums around the world, the majority in Bergen, Norway (Haakestad 2018). Texts about Buddhism became available in the early twentieth century, although written from a Christian point of view. A short booklet of twenty-four pages, *Buddhismen, den betydeligste og interessanteste af alle hedenske religioner*, by L. Dahle, was published by a Christian missionary organisation, De unges Missionsforening, in Stavanger in 1911, and is perhaps the first book or booklet on Buddhism in the Norwegian language (Dahle 1911). The Lutheran missionary Karl Ludvig Reichelt (1877–1952) arrived in China in 1903 and spent twenty-five years there before moving his mission to Hong Kong. As his knowledge of China increased, he aimed his mission at Buddhists and especially Buddhist monks. He was interested in "dialogue" with Chinese religions based on knowledge, but with the ultimate purpose of converting them to Christianity where possible. He wrote several books about Chinese religions, with a special interest in Chinese Buddhism, which had become his area of expertise. His book on Chinese religions, published in 1913, included a chapter on Chinese Buddhism (Reichelt 1913: 108–157). Reichelt started this chapter by stating that he assumed his readers knew that Buddha lived in India because the topic of Buddhism had been treated quite widely over the last few years (Reichelt 1913: 108). Reichelt's book *Fra Østens religiøse liv: et indblik i den kinesiske Mahayanabuddhisme*, published in 1922 (Reichelt 1922; English translation: *Truth and Tradition in Chinese Buddhism: A Study of Chinese Mahayana Buddhism*), described lived religion and was his most important book on Buddhism. He founded Den Kristne Buddhistmisjon in 1922. Den Nordiske Kristne Buddhistmission (Nordic Buddhist Christian Mission), still existing under the name of Areopagos, was founded in 1926 by individuals sharing Reichelt's vision (Thelle 2022).[22] An early Indological presentation of Buddhism in Norwegian language was published by Sten Konow (1932).

The growth of Buddhism in Norway

If Einar Beer was the only Buddhist in Norway, as he called himself in the 1960s (being ignorant of, or perhaps disregarding, the forty Tibetan Buddhist boys who from 1964 lived in a camp school in Gjøvik in eastern Norway for several years) and the lineage of Tathagata Amoghasiddhi Maitreyya Buddha was a lost lineage of Buddhism, how did the subsequent growth of Buddhism come about? Who was the second Norwegian Buddhist? This question is not easily answered. Some Norwegian seamen sailing on ships in Southeast or East Asia might have considered adopting a Buddhist worldview or some travellers or tourists to Nepal might afterwards have adopted such a worldview, or there might have been individuals who read Buddhist literature and became convinced about its relevance to their lives, but no information has been found to identify or confirm that this was the case. There might nevertheless have been several individuals who kept their Buddhist views private. A short book on Buddhism, Olaus Høydal's *Buddhismen*, was published in 1963. The book is mostly on Theravāda. He states in the book that at the time there were no Buddhists in Norway (Høydal 1963: 73), which shows that he was ignorant about Eniar Beer, aka Sariputra. Buddhist organisations and people who made an appearance in the public realm can be tracked from the early 1970s when the first Zen study group, "Zenskolen"[23] (Zen School), was organised. The first public Buddhist organisation was created from its gatherings. Its Zen practice was based on reading and discussing books. It was started informally by individuals interested in Zen Buddhism and Arne Tørjesen can be considered its founder. He also placed advertisements in a newspaper in Oslo in which he asked anyone interested in Zen Buddhism to meet. They met in private homes, in schools and in a room in a factory.[24] The Zen School thus started as a study group of Buddhist texts. However, one day Arne Tørjesen suddenly suggested they should sit on the floor and try meditation in practice.[25] They had no encounters with individuals belonging to the living Zen traditions until 1981 when some of them travelled to the United

States to visit Cimarron Zen Center (now Rinzai-ji Zen Center) in Los Angeles and its Mt Baldy Zen Center in the mountains on the outskirts of the city. After that the Zen School followed the tradition of Joshu Sasaki Roshi.[26] However, this led to both disagreements and individuals leaving the group to look for other Buddhist traditions. Den Norske Sotozen Buddhist Orden was established in Kristiansand in 2002 by persons who had experience from Japan and Japanese martial arts and has around 277 members (2023). Karma Tashi Ling buddhistsamfunn also had Norwegian converts and was officially founded in 1975 and followed the Tibetan Kagyu tradition. They started meetings and instructions in 1972 when a lama visited Oslo that year and initiated several converts, many of whom still belong to the group. Karma Tashi Ling continues to be the largest organisation within Tibetan Buddhism.[27] In 2004, a *stūpa* was built in commemoration of the Dalai Lama receiving the Nobel Peace Prize in Oslo that same year. The organisation also owns a retreat centre, Karma Shedrup Ling, in Sørmarka, south of Oslo. Plans for apartment buildings next to the temple in order to create a Buddhist community are currently being promoted.[28] Several other organisations connected to Tibetan Buddhism are also active: Det Norske Buddha Dharma Institutt which follows the Nyingma-tradition of Tibetan Buddhism, Diamantveibuddhisme (Diamond Way Buddhism) in the tradition of Ole Nydahl operates in several cities, and a Kadampa Meditation centre is found in Oslo. Persons interested in *vipassanā* meditation would often go to Sweden where lay *vipassanā* centers had been founded by followers of the teaching of S. N. Goenka.[29] Later instructions in mindfulness became offered by numerous individuals in various settings but some still prefer to go to Sweden. Buddhist retreat centres belonging to the Thai forest tradition, a lineage of Theravāda Buddhist monasticism, have been established, led by convert monks, some of whom have returned to Norway after long periods abroad (Bodhibhumivana Buddhistsamfunn in Lillehammer, Vingrom Buddhist kloster and Skogskloster buddhistsamfunn/Skiptvedt Buddhistkloster in Skiptvedt).

A notable Buddhist individual without connection to any groups in Norway was the leading ecosophist, Sigmund Kvaløy Setreng (1934–2014), who became a Buddhist after visits to Nepal and India. He was educated in philosophy and assisted Arne Naess in developing his Ecosophy (Anker 2011) and organised one of the early non-violent actions for the defence of nature, the Mardal waterfall in 1970. He became interested in the Buddhism of Sherpas in Nepal and later also functioned as an advisor on ecological matters to the King of Bhutan. The poet Jan Erik Vold (b. 1939) became aware of Buddhism through his interest in the literature of the American Beat generation and was inspired in his poetry in both style and content by modern interpretations of Zen Buddhism (Johns 1976). A convert to Theravāda, Kåre A. Lie (b. 1942) has been the most important person for translating Pāli texts into Norwegian. Many of his translations are available in the Norwegian Buddhism e-library.[30] The library, in addition to Lie's many translations, contains several books by Norwegian Buddhists on different aspects of Buddhist teachings. Mali Bagøien wrote a spiritual autobiography, *Issues through the Moss*, which has been published in several languages, about becoming a Buddhist through Buddhist ideas and meeting Buddhism-inspired people (Bagøien 2022). She experienced a deep personal crisis during which she discovered the teaching of the Buddha and finally travelled to Thailand where she came in contact with the Thai forest monk tradition, perhaps one of the earliest Norwegians to encounter it. Bagøien's book describes her struggles and suffering and how Buddhism helped her cope.

The largest number of Buddhists, probably at least 90 per cent of the between 40,000 and 50,000 Buddhists currently living in Norway,[31] are migrants from Asia who brought Buddhist traditions with them as part of their cultural heritage, and children of migrants. The migration started in the 1970s and the numbers have been continually growing. These migrants from countries with strong Buddhist traditions have established temples and monastic institutions of different Buddhist traditions, the largest being Vietnamese Mahāyāna and Thai Theravāda. The Buddhist institutions of the migrant Buddhists organise separate national and ethnic groups and celebrate national origin, cultural and linguistic traditions, traditions of clothing and food cuisine, and so on, as part of their Buddhist heritage (see Table 6.1).

The first group to arrive in significant numbers were the Vietnamese refugees. Many had been rescued by Norwegian ships in Southeast Asia and others came from refugee camps. Not all were Buddhists, but a significant number of them were, perhaps as many as 60 per cent, and they remained the largest group of Buddhists in Norway until the 2010s when Thai Buddhists emerged as the biggest. The Vietnamese arrived as families while Thai Buddhists were mainly women, some with children from previous marriages, who married Norwegian males. While the convert Buddhists established organisations for meditation practitioners, the migrants established temples for worshiping and honouring Buddhas and Bodhisattvas and Buddhist monks and nuns. Celebrations of festivals with a focus on ethnic and linguistic identities became the most important annual events. The motivation for Buddhist practice of the migrants and the converts were often contrary; the migrants were eager to preserve inherited traditions while converts were eager to get away from them.

The first Vietnamese Buddhist temple organisations were established in 1982, and in 1989 the first temple built from the ground in the Vietnamese style opened. Growth of Buddhism was further caused primarily by increased migration from Buddhist countries in Asia and migrants from all the Asian countries with significant Buddhist populations are found in Norway, and many have temple organisations. By far the most numerous migrant temples are Thai. In addition to the many Thai and Vietnamese temple organisations, there are Tisarana srilankisk buddhistforening, founded in 1993, Den burmesiske theravada buddhistforening, Khmer buddhistforening and Buddha's Light International Association (BLIA) with a base in Taiwan.

Buddhism is a well-established religion in Norway with a large number of temple organisations founded mostly by immigrant Buddhists, and meditation organisations founded mostly by Norwegian converts, as well as a significant number of monks and nuns in both types of organisations. The state encourages religious organisations to be officially registered and for them to keep records of their members and submit the details to a public register (see Tablie 6.1 for list of Buddhist groups). Religions and worldview organisations receive economic support from the state (in 2024, NOK 1,419 per member).[32] Buddhist temple organisations that annually receive economic support per member from the Norwegian state had in 2023 a total of 22,126 members.[33] This means that in 2024, the state transferred more than thirty-one million NOK (around three million EUR) to Buddhist organisations. There are five beautiful "display" temples built from the ground in the architectural style of the country of origin in Norway: three Vietnamese Buddhist temples – Khuong Viet temple in Lørenskog, north of Oslo (built in 1989), Liên Hoa Đạo Tràng (Lien Hoa Dao Trang) Buddhist Temple in Smedstua, Jessheim, north of Oslo,[34] and the Chùa Đôn Hậu (Don Hau Pagoda) Vietnamese Buddhist temple in Tiller in Trondheim – and one Tibetan – the Tibetan Buddhist temple Karma Tashi Ling in Bjørndal, southeast Oslo – and one Thai – the Thai Buddhist Wat Thai Norway temple in Frogner, north of Oslo. The temples are partly a result of the generous economic funding of the Buddhist religion by the state but also illustrate the importance for many Buddhists of places of worship, ritual performances and festival celebrations, and the presence of monks.

There is no official account of the number of Buddhist monks and nuns and other religious professionals, but the number has been steadily growing. The increasing number of Thai Theravāda temples need resident monks, and some monks with a Norwegian background have been monks in Asia and have returned to Norway to establish forest retreats/forest monasteries. There were in 2024 probably around eighty-five monks and nuns in Norway but monks and nuns do come and go, so the number is not fixed. The following calculation was made in February 2024.[35] In the largest Thai Buddhist temples (Wat Thai temple, Wat Chinnawong and Wat Ubolmanee), there are eleven monks and five nuns (Maechi or Mae chee), and in addition, there are fifteen Thai-Buddhist organisations and some more temples which each have two or three monks; the Buddhist Sri Lankan temple has two monks; the Burmese temple three monks; the forest monastery has three monks; the Vietnamese temples in Oslo, Bergen, Stavanger, Kristiansand, Moss and Trondheim have all together between thirteen and fifteen monks and nuns; and there are two Tibetan monks and nuns. This strong presence of monks and nuns illustrates that their attendance is necessary for merit making. Another merit making device is the *stūpa*. One *stūpa* has relics of the Buddha and was gifted from Sri Lanka and is taken care of by the Vietnamese Buddhist community in Norway while another commemorates the visit of the Dalai Lama and is looked after by Buddhists that follow Tibetan traditions.

The Buddhist umbrella organisation Buddhistforbundet and the reputation and representation of Buddhism

The Buddhist umbrella organisation Buddhistforbundet was founded by Arne Tørjesen and became active in 1974 (PUKK 1974: 3).[36] Arne Tørjesen was the leader of the Zen-skolen (the Zen School) established in 1972. In 1978, the Zen School took the initiative to register Buddhistforbundet as an official Buddhist religious organisation in order to be able to apply for state funding. The organisation was approved and given official recognition in 1979 by the Norwegian government

Ministry of Church and Education as the first official Buddhist organisation in Norway, and one of the earliest in Europe. Buddhistforbundet invited the Karma Tashi Ling, an organisation of new followers of Tibetan Buddhism founded in 1975 which belongs to the Karma Kagyu tradition, to also join. Buddhistforbundet thus became a Buddhist umbrella organisation with two member organisations, new followers of Zen Buddhism and Tibetan Buddhism. But these two organisations had in 1979 all together only eighteen individual members! The founders of Buddhistforbundet encouraged other Buddhists in Norway to also organise themselves into separate Buddhist organisations and join Buddhistforbundet. Membership to Buddhistforbundet's affiliated organisations started to grow significantly, especially when the third group joined, Den Vietnamesiske Buddhistforening, which was established in 1982. New followers of Theravāda were encouraged to form a group and connect the group to Buddhistforbundet. The purpose was to maximise numbers in order to get state support and public recognition of Buddhism.

Of the more than 22,000 members of Buddhist organisations, 14,699 are members of organisations that are affiliated to the Buddhist umbrella organisation Buddhistforbundet. Around 500 are members of Buddhistforbundet directly without membership in any of its affiliated organisations. As mentioned earlier, some Buddhist temple organisations have chosen for different reasons not to be affiliated with Buddhistforbundet. Buddhistforbundet is an interest organisation that performs services for the Buddhist organisations, especially helping them interact with government bureaucracy. Buddhistforbundet also organises Buddhist confirmation education and rituals for Buddhist youth (Kleive 2022).[37] It represents Buddhists in other organisations such as Samarbeidsrådet for tros-og livssynssamfunn (STL), founded in 1996, an umbrella organisation for religious and worldview groups in Norway.[38] Buddhistforbundet is a member organisation in the European Buddhist Union and in the World Fellowship of Buddhists. With the growth of immigrant Buddhists in Norway, Buddhistforbundet has changed over the years from being an organisation primarily consisting of Norwegian converts to Buddhism to one comprised migrants from Buddhist countries for whom the Buddhist religion is part of a cultural heritage. The interests and understanding of Buddhism in these groups are not identical. The interest in Buddhism of the converts tends to be more oriented towards meditation and texts while the interest of the migrants is oriented around doctrines of karma, rebirth and *puṇya*, cultural heritage, and national and ethnic identities. With increased pluralisation, tensions about representation and presentation of Buddhism have emerged.

An attempt by Buddhistforbundet in 2010 to handle the pluralisation of Buddhism in Norway reveals tensions between convert Buddhism and migrant Buddhism. The case shows Buddhistforbundet making claims that the textual-based convert Buddhism represents the "authentic" teaching of the Buddha while teaching of migrant Buddhism is being criticised as constituting a threat to the reputation of Buddhism in Norway as a minority religion. Buddhism in Norway has in general a good reputation. However, in 2010 Buddhistforbundet reacted to a programme by the Norwegian Broadcasting Cooperation (NRK) that they thought hurt the reputation of Buddhism. The Norwegian journalist and comedian Are

Sende Osen made a series of programmes that year for the NRK where he (supposedly) lived for a few days with families belonging to different religious groups (such as Sikhs, Pentecostals, ISKCON) and then (supposedly) reflected on whether he would consider joining their religion. This Norwegian television programme, called "På tro og Are," included an episode on Buddhism, which was aired on 23 November 2010. It has since also been made available on educational TV intended for use in schools.[39] The main points of the programme were based on interviews about karma, rebirth and gender with second-generation immigrants with a Vietnamese Buddhist background.

In the programme, Sende Osen speaks with his three main informants, who belong to Vietnamese Mahāyāna Buddhism and are worshippers of Amitābha Buddha. Two of the informants are young women living in Trondheim and connected to the Vietnamese temple there and the third is a young monk who lived at that time in the Khuong Viet temple in Lørenskog. One of the women tells Sende Osen that if they remember Amitābha Buddha's name and call upon him for help when they die, Amitābha will come and help them and they will then come to his world, which is much better than this world. She does not name Amitābha's world, but she is obviously thinking of the heavenly world of Sukhāvatī, which is a *buddhakṣetra*, beyond time and space. One of the women is considering becoming a nun and Are Sende Osen asks what happens if she changes her mind after having been a nun for ten years. She answers that men have seven chances to go in and out of monastic life, and women have only one. She follows up to explain why this is so by stating that in Buddhism, women have worse karma than males. Sende Osen is apparently astonished to learn this and asks how she can accept such a view. The other woman answers by giving examples of how we can know women have worse karma. Women get angry more easily, they always nag and they backbite. These are examples that prove that women have worse karma than males, according to these women. Are Sende Osen asks if they have done something wrong in the previous life since they have been born as women, and they confirm that such is the case. He asks them if they really believe this, and the women again confirm this belief. They explain that women have stronger feelings, which is bad, since they have emotional ups and downs. One of the women says she feels more like a man and thinks she will be reborn as a male next time. She says she thinks it is bad being a woman. Are Sende Osen finds it hard to believe and make sense of what they say, obviously because it contradicts contemporary Norwegian values and norms of gender equality. The family of the young women is very supportive of their daughters considering becoming nuns because, they say, many Vietnamese men are not good. Sende Osen comments that apparently then many Buddhists are not good people, which was the opposite of what he had stated at the outset of the programme. Next, the two young women and Are Sende Osen drive together from Trondheim to the Khuong Viet temple outside of Oslo. The topic of karma and rebirth is also talked about during the journey. In the Khuong Viet temple, Sende Osen speaks with a young monk who confirms that according to their Buddhist tradition, men have better karma than women. Sende Osen asks the monk to give examples and the monk replies that women are more jealous than men and they get more easily irritated.

The programme has several sections with background information that uses drawings to try to relate what the interview subjects say about karma, rebirth and women to the historical Buddha and a seemingly "authoritative version of Buddhism." The drawings state that Buddha was against having an order of nuns and that there are around a hundred more rules for nuns than for monks, and that nuns are always subservient to monks. Sende Osen thus makes karma, rebirth and a negative view of women the main issues in his programme and ends by stating how much he dislikes the focus on karma and rebirth in Buddhism, and that life should be about this one life only. In the programmes about other religions, his journalistic angle from the outset was that he disliked them but ended up approving of them. In the case of Buddhism, he started out by mentioning that this is a religion many admire, but found himself disliking it because of the statements by the two women and the monk on karma and gender.

After the programme was aired, the Buddhist umbrella organisation Buddhistforbundet submitted a public protest on 3 January 2011.[40] Since the programme was also made available online for educational purposes by the NRK, Buddhistforbundet has attempted several times to have the programme censored and withdrawn from the broadcaster's online platform.[41]

One possible response from Buddhistforbundet could have been to explain the views of the three Vietnamese Buddhists and to contextualise them in Vietnamese Mahāyāna Buddhism. But instead Buddhistforbundet was mainly interested in defending the reputation of Buddhism. By condemning the views of the programme, they were implicitly also condemning the Vietnamese Buddhists. The Vietnamese Buddhists' views were apparently unacceptable to Buddhistforbundet. Instead of defending them, it made them scapegoats.

Buddhistforbundet, in its response to the NRK, writes that no matter how the Vietnamese Buddhists "have expressed themselves, this in itself cannot prove anything at all about Buddhism's or Buddha's view of women."[42] The letter from Buddhistforbundet seems to imply that the Pāli Canon is more authoritative than any other Buddhist textual tradition. They do not mention any Vietnamese Buddhist textual traditions or texts of Pure Land Buddhism. Buddhistforbundet claims that Vietnam is less developed, and therefore, their Buddhism is also less reliable. Instead of defending the three interviewees, they claim that the programme promotes prejudices about a minority group in Norway. The letter to the Norwegian Broadcasting Cooperation (NRK) is however formulated mainly as a critique of Are Sende Osen's comments. The statements of the Vietnamese Buddhists are not dealt with directly, but through a criticism of Are Sende Osen's remarks. In order to argue against the views of the Vietnamese Buddhists, Buddhistforbundet used textual traditions in Pāli and Sanskrit. It is notable that those who signed the protest letter and those who are quoted as supporting Buddhistforbundet's interpretations are mostly Norwegian males. The views of the Vietnamese Buddhists interviewed in the programme are considered by them to be mistaken and inappropriate and promoting prejudices against themselves as "a minority group in Norway."[43] The paradox that statements of faith made by second generation immigrant Vietnamese Buddhists are thought to promote prejudices against Norwegian convert Buddhists raises the question, who speaks for Buddhists? Are certain views to be censored by the Buddhist umbrella organisation in order to secure the reputation of Buddhist converts (and other) Buddhists in Norway? Instead of explaining the views of Vietnamese Buddhists as expressions of living Vietnamese Buddhism and therefore legitimate representations of lived Buddhist religion, Buddhistforbundet used Buddhist Pāli and Sanskrit texts against them, claiming they represented a backward and underdeveloped Buddhist religious culture. The Norwegian converts, in other words, in this case, claimed the right to define what is proper Buddhism and what is not. It seems the Buddhist views and practices of migrant Buddhists constituted a problem when they were presented in public, outside of the control of Buddhistforbundet.

The plurality of Buddhist migrant communities in Norway means that there is a plurality of lived Buddhism. The Buddhist umbrella organisation led by Norwegian converts seemed to have dismissed the views on karma and rebirth of Buddhists from Southeast Asian countries as part of a Buddhism to which they claimed ownership. Martin Baumann has noted four main types of Buddhists outside of Asia: (1) the first-generation immigrants who continue their culturally embedded Buddhism in a conservative manner; (2) convert Buddhists who try to practise Buddhism as closely as possible to the Asian model; (3) second-generation immigrants who adapt and change established roles, hierarchies, and practices; and (4) convert Buddhists who consciously reform and reinvent Buddhist teachings and practices to align them with Western conditions (Baumann 2012: 127). The strong and persistent protests from Buddhistforbundet are to be understood in this context: the views of the Vietnamese Buddhists on karma, rebirth and gender threatened the project of convert Buddhists to reform and reinvent Buddhist teachings. The views of the three young Vietnamese Buddhists illustrate that second-generation immigrants also continue their culturally embedded Buddhism and represent a fifth type to be added to Baumann's typology of Buddhists outside Asia.

In Norway, those who became Buddhists in the 1970s were interested in doctrines, texts and meditation. It was the migration of Buddhists from Asia that turned Buddhism into a numerically strong minority religion, with a focus on temples and ritual practices. The response of Buddhistforbundet to the NRK programme shows that the difference between convert Buddhism and migrant Buddhism caused confusion and conflict and displayed how a leadership of primarily male convert Buddhists condemned views on karma, rebirth and gender in the lived Buddhism of second-generation immigrants who were followers of Vietnamese traditions of Pure Land. The main reason for their protests seemed to be that it threatened their project of consciously reforming and reinventing Buddhist teachings and practices to align them with Norwegian culture.

Conclusion

The history of Buddhists in Norway analysed here started with an Indian migrant guru who, after having lived in Norway for around fifteen years, became convinced in 1928 that he was a rebirth of the Buddha and that his Norwegian follower was the rebirth of Buddha's disciple Sariputra. I ended the essay by discussing another idea of rebirth, the idea that rebirth as a woman is punishment for bad karma, which is part of the inherited Buddhist traditions of some Vietnamese Buddhists in Norway. This idea was promoted in a television programme in 2010 about Vietnamese Buddhists living in Norway and condemned by the Buddhist umbrella organisation that believed it threatened the reputation of Buddhism in Norway and their project of aligning Buddhist teachings to Norwegian culture. There is a connection between these two events because both, in different ways, disrupt Buddhism as a normative history and project of Norwegian converts to Buddhism. The booklet by Buddhistforbundet, *Buddhismen i Norge*, does not mention Sri Ananda, aka Maitreyya Buddha, and the first Buddhist in Norway, Einar Beer, aka Sariputra, but starts the narrative of Buddhism in Norway with the new followers of the 1970s (Buddhistforbundet 1999). The Buddhism of many of these new followers was textually based and represented modern Buddhism with a focus on doctrines, ethics and meditation, influenced by secular Buddhism and with less emphasis than in many Asian Buddhist countries on ideas of karma and rebirth. Nevertheless, ideas of karma and rebirth are central ideas in the Buddhist religion of many Buddhist migrants in Norway and continue to shape the history of Buddhism in the country.

Table 6.1 Buddhist groups in Norway.

Umbrella organisation and its membership organisations

Name	Membership numbers	Tradition
Buddhistforbundet	14,457	
Organisations of mainly migrants and migrants' children		
Buddha's Light International Association	The numbers of the individual	Chinese
Den burmesiske theravada buddhistforening	organisations are not available but	Burmese
Den Thailandske Buddhistforening	are included in the	Thai
Det vietnamesiske buddhistsamfunn	Buddhistforbun-	Vietnamese
Khmer buddhistforening	det's membership	Cambodian
Thailandske Buddhist Meditasjons Trossamfunn Agder	list.	Thai
Tisarana srilankisk buddhistforening		Sri Lankan
Ubolmanee buddhistforening		Thai theravāda tradition after meditation master Ajahn Chah
Organisations of mainly converts		
Det Norske Buddha Dharma Institutt		Nyingma
Dharmagruppa		Zenmester Thích Nhất Hạnh
Karma Tashi Ling buddhistsamfunn		Tibetan
Oslo buddhistsenter Triratna Norge		Triratna
Oslo Yun Hwa Dharma Sah		Yun Hwa Sangha
Rinzai zen-senter Oslo		Zen
Skogskloster buddhistsamfunn/ Skiptvet Buddhistkloster		Theravāda/Thai
Zen-skolen		Zen

(*Continued*)

Table 6.1 (Continued)

Name	Membership numbers	Tradition
Other Buddhist groups (not affiliated to Buddhistforbundet)		
Organisations of mainly migrants and migrants' children		
Buddhist Bodhiyan Forening	356	Thai
Buddhist Thaikultur Larvik	94	Thai
Buddhist Watpahbodhidhamm Drammen	575	Thai
Den Vietnamesiske Buddhistiske & Kulturelle Foreningen i Trøndelag	768	Vietnamese
Det Norske Dhammakaya Samfunn	364	Thai
Det Vietnamesiske Buddhist & Kultur Senter i Østfold	1,217	Vietnamese
Dhamma Buddhist Trossamfunn Agder	100	Thai
Prakas Puththadhum	314	Thai
Thai Buddhistforening Trondheim	748	Thai
Thai Tempel Hadeland Buddhistforening	178	Thai
Wat Bodhi-Dhamm Buddhistforening i Norge	868	Thai
Wat Buddha Parami Stavanger Foreningen	168	Thai
Wat Buddhapas Samfunn i Haugesund	657	Thai
Wat Luang Phor Sodh – Samfunnet i Norge	94	Thai
Wat Pa Sukjai Harstad	169	Thai
Wat Thai Gardermoen Buddhistforening	354	Thai
Organisations of mainly converts		
Bodhibhumivana Buddhistsamfunn	133	Theravāda/Thai
Den Norske Sotozen Buddhist Orden	277	Zen
Diamantveibuddhisme Karma Kagyu-Linjen, Dkkl	123	Tibetan
Kadampa Meditasjonssenter Oslo	55	Tibetan
Soka Gakkai International	no information	Nichiren
Zen Fredrikstad	57	Zen

Notes

1 E-mail communication with Bjørn Pettersen, 22 May 2023.
2 "Swami Sri Ananda Acharya (1881–1945)," available at https://shantibu.no/en/sri-ananda, accessed 10 October 2024.
3 "Sariputra var en av Buddhas fremste disipler, liksom jeg har vært Maitreyya Buddhas disippel og søker å føre hans tradisjon og lære videre og vokte hans hellige minne" (Sariputra 1967: 1).
4 "Han ble selv for et par år siden under et besøk i India, opptatt i en gammel Buddhistisk brorskapsorden og fikk navnet Swami Acharya Sariputra" (Schade n.d.).

5   Another interesting context for understanding Maitreyya Buddha is the revival of Buddhism in India in the late nineteenth century and in the twentieth.

6   Most of the sources are in Norwegian. I have translated all quotations into English with the original Norwegian text placed in footnotes.

7   "Vedanta er bare en gren av Buddhismen. De har ingen rett å kalle det vedanta. Vedaene – Rig-veda – er tilbedelse, en vitenskap om naturkrefter slike som Indra, Agni, etc., – hvordan få rikdom, velstand, god helse, osv. Mens vedantinerne, akkurat som buddhistene, forsaker og tror på frigjørelse i samsvar med karmas lov – gode gjerninger. Isteden for Buddha anerkjenner vedantinerne en Gud, et guddommelig vesen hvis essens er godhet. Hvilken forskjell er det fra buddhismen?" (quoted in Pettersen 2018: 244).

8   "Når jeg forsøker å tale eller skrive om Gotama Buddha eller Maitreyya Buddha (Sri Ananda Acharya) er det for meg en og samme person, for der er bare en Buddhasjel liksom vi hver av oss bare er én, en personlighet, som blir født igjen, alltid den samme, således er det bare en Buddha" (Sariputra 1968: 20–21).

9   "Hans samtaler – taler til meg, fra denne tid og fremover til 1938 – disse samtaler var av aller største betydning for meg. Han fortalte at i Buddhas dager var jeg Sariputra og i Ramakrishnas liv var jeg også hans nære venn og hengivne ledsager gjennom mange år. Med mellomrom, i 1929 og i de første par av 30-årene, dikterte han til meg Buddhaboken 'Kosmiske Lysord' og en rekke Buddha-dikt som ble oversatt" (Beer 1968: 3).

10 "Buddha alene har visdom, har råd. Og ubrudt, i mange år, har visdommens stille sol skinnet over Norge her fra Tronfjell. Sri Ananda Acharya har skapt her på Tronfjell en makt som hele menneskeheten må ta av og lære av hvis den vil unngå krig og unngå å bli utslettet. Det har vært hand arbeid, hans Buddha-arbeid for menneskeheten her på Tronfjell. Buddha viser en vei, et alternativ til dette selvutslettende liv i verden" (Beer 1968: 3–4).

11 "Da kan fredsarbeidet – Buddhas fredsarbeid – begynne."

12 "Maitreyya Buddhas vei er Vennskaps Vei til fullkommen godhet i fullkommen hellighet. Alt liv er hellig. Skån derfor alt liv. Vær god. Det er vennskaps og barmhjertighetens lære, Maitreyya Buddhas budskap til frihet fra begjær – fra jordhunger, fra hat, krig, penger, overbefolkning, fattigdom, sykdom, elendighet og død" (Beer 1968: 4).

13 "Alt i verden er løgn er sansebedrag . . . alt er uvirkelig, blir uvirkelig for den som ser det Evige, som kan heve sin sjel til det evige virkelige Liv" (Beer 1968: 4).

14 "Hvis noen ennå spør hvorfor jeg er blitt buddhist – d.v.s. en som søker sannhet og opplysning om sannhet, vil jeg svare: Fordi livet er så kostelig, vårt kosteligste eie. Derfor må vi søke å gjøre det beste ut av det – søke å finne og leve i sannhet" (Beer 1968: 5).

15 "Buddhismen har et meget omfattende og i alle detaljer nyansert utarbeidet system til selvdisiplin og selvforbedring av tanke, følelser og handling, som hver buddhist må lære og øve. Aldri gjøre noe galt, bare gjøre det som er riktig og å gjøre sitt hjerte rent, det er det som all Buddhaer lærer" (Beer 1968: 5).

16 "Fordi jeg er takknemlig, fordi jeg har samvittighet, fordi jeg elsker renhet av liv og godhet, fordi jeg elsker Mor Norge, dette landet, derfor er jeg blitt buddhist" (Beer 1968: 6).

17 "Buddha har slikt vidunderlig helhetssyn, slik vidunderlig kjærlighet, slikt vidunderlig hjerte som favner alt. Derfor elsker jeg Buddha. Derfor elsker jeg alt jeg har lært av Maitreyya Buddha, Sri Ananda Acharya – gjennom alle år fra 1915 til den dag i dag. Buddhas religion er lysets religion, renhets religion. Buddhas lære er også meget verdslig. Det går ut på å gjøre verden ren – gjøre mørke og onde hjertelysfylte og gode for at livet i verden kan bli bedre" (Beer 1968: 6–7).

18 "Buddha er et menneske som blir født igjen og igjen på denne jord . . . Buddha betyr 'den opplyste' – det fullkomment opplyste menneske. Maitreya Buddha er 'Vennskapets Buddha' som lærer det ubegrensede vennskap med den rene, gode vilje for alt liv – mennesker, dyr, trær og all natur" (Sariputra 1968: 7).

19 "Utbredelsen av sanskrit lærdom som bringer de hellige skrifter fra den gamle kultur i India, den høyeste og eldste kultur i verden, til Vestens land har frembrakt de mest velgjørende resultater" (Beer 1975: 39–40).

20 ". . . skjønt av selvgode grunner prøver mangen en såkalt orientalist å ødelegge dens siviliserende innflytelse" (Beer 1975: 39–40).

21 "Vismannen på Tronfjell: En kort biografj, available at https://shantibu.no/sites/default/files/docs/BIOGRAFI_0.pdf, accessed 10 October, 2024.

22 "Om oss," available at https://areopagos.no/artikler/les/article/1499647, accessed 10 October 2024.

23 "Zenskolen," available at https://zenskolencom.wordpress.com/historikk/, accessed 10 October 2024.

24 Personal information, Thøger Nordbø, March 2024.

25 Personal information, Thøger Nordbø, March 2024 and Helge Gundersen, June 2024.

26 "Rinzai-ji Zen Center: History" available at https://www.rinzaiji.org/history/, accessed 10 October, 2024: "Rinzai-ji Zen Center: Affiliated Centers," available at https://www.rinzaiji.org/affiliated-centers/, accessed 10 October 2024.

27 Its spiritual leader is the 17th Karmapa Trinley Thaye Dorje.

28 "Karma Tashi Ling buddhistsamfunn," available at https://www.ktl.no/tempelboligprosjektet/, accessed 10 October, 2024.

29 Information proivided by Katarina Plank.

30 "Norsk buddhistisk e-bibliotek," available at https://buddhavithi.webnode.page/kopi-av-bibliotek/, accessed 15 November 2024.

31 "Buddhistforbundet: Over 40.000 buddhister i Norge?," available at https://buddhistforbundet.no/buddhismen-i-norge/, accessed 15 October 2024

32 "Statsforvalteren.no: Tros-og livssynssamfunn," available at https://www.statsforvalteren.no/nb/portal/Folk-og-samfunn/Tros-og-livssynssamfunn/, accessed 17 November 2024.

33 The discrepancy between the two numbers, members of Buddhist organisations (22,126) and the total number of Buddhists (between 40,000 and 50,000) is because the total number includes individuals believed to have a Buddhist heritage but are not members of any organisation or and people who are private Buddhists. Increasingly, Buddhism is also practised as a private religion such as by individuals who do mindfulness meditation often without seeking to join Buddhist communities. Meditation apps are being used but the exact number of users is not known.

34 "Tempelkomplekset i 'Lien Hoa Dao Trang' på Jessheim," available at https://klimaogbygg.no/prosjekt/budhisttempel-jessheim/, accessed 18 November 2024.

35 Email communication with Egil Lothe, 11 February 2024.

36 I thank Helge Gundersen, Peter Koren and Thøger Nordbø for providing copies of PUKK and other important papers and information regarding the early period of Zen Buddhism and the organisation Buddhistforbundet in Norway.

37 "Tilbud om buddhistisk konfirmasjon," available at https://buddhistforbundet.no/tilbud-om-buddhistisk-konfirmasjon/, accessed 17 November, 2024; "Konfirmasjon 2024," available at https://buddhistforbundet.no/konfirmasjon2024/, accessed 18 November 2024.

38 "Medlemmer i STL," available at https://stl.no/medlemsamfunn/, accessed 18 November 2024.

39 "På tro og Are: 6. Episode," available at https://tv.nrk.no/serie/paa-tro-og-are/sesong/1/episode/PRTY12003909, accessed 18 November, 2024.

40 Buddhistforbundet's complaints about the programme and letter to Kringkastingssjef Hans-Tore Bjerkaas with the title "NRK PROGRAM OM NORSK-VIETNAMESISKE BUDDHISTER" is available at https://buddhistforbundet.no/wp-content/uploads/2020/02/1101031.pdf, accessed 18 November 2024.

41 "Buddhistforbundet klager på bruk av program om buddhisme," available at https://buddhistforbundet.no/kringkastingsradet-190307/, accessed 18 November 2024.

42 "Petter Myhr forsøker her innledningsvis å forsvare påstandene ovenfor om buddhismens kvinnesyn ved å si at "de ikke er hentet ut av løse luften" med henvisning til sitater fra de tre intervjuobjektene i filmen. Til det er å si at uansett hvordan de har uttrykt seg kan ikke dette i seg selv bevise noe om helst om buddhismens eller Buddhas kvinnesyn." https://buddhistforbundet.no/wp-content/uploads/2020/02/1101031.pdf

43 The interview subjects also wrote to the NRK to complain about how they were portrayed in the programme. It is mentioned in this letter from Buddhistforbundet, "Buddhistforbundets kommentar til NRKs svar på vår klage på bruk av program på NRKs skoleside," available at https://buddhistforbundet.no/wp-content/uploads/2020/02/1902111. pdf, accessed 18 November 2024.

References

Ānanda Āchārya. 1978. *The Philosophy of The Upanishads: Being a Series of Lectures on the Sacred Writings of India, with Particular Reference to the Brihadaranyaka Upanishad, Delivered at Oslo University, in Autumn 1915.*

Anker, Peder. 2011. "Den store økologiske vekkelsen som har hjemsøkt vårt land." In *Universitetet i Oslos historie* vol. 7, edited by John Peter Collett, 103–171, 461–479. Oslo: Unipub.

Bagøien, Mali. 2022. *Sanningen ger läkning: Elegier genom "mossan."* Original title *Issues through the Moss*. Skiptvet: Lokuttara Vihāra.

Baumann, Martin. 2012. "Modernist Interpretations of Buddhism in Europe." In *Buddhism in the Modern World*, edited by David L. McMahan, 113–135. London: Routledge.

Beer, Einar. 1957. "Forord." In *Tathagata Amoghasiddhi Maitreya Buddha: Kosmiske Lysord Hilsner og Dikt*, 7–25. Brahmakul, Alvdal: Alvdal Bok-og Papirhandel.

Beer, Einar. 1960a. *Inter-racial Concord: The Tathagata Amoghasiddhi Maitreyya Buddha* [Ananda Acharya]. Alvdal. Alvdal Bok-og papirhandel.

Beer, Einar. 1968. "Swami Sri Ananda Acharya – Maitreyya Buddha. Foredrag Holdt d. 11te November 1968 på Tronsvangen Seter for 108 Elever og Lærere fra Elverum Folkehøgskole." Unpublished manuscript. Alvdal.

Beer, Einar. 1975. *Solstreif i Tidens Natt: Maitreyya Buddhas Fredsuniversitet*. Alvdal: Brahmakul Forlag.

Buddhistforbundet. 1999. *Buddhismen i Norge*. Oslo: Buddhistforbundet.

Burnouf, Eugène and Christian Lassen. 1826. *Essai sur le Pali, ou Langue Sacree de la Presqu'ile au-dela du Gange . . . et a Notice des Manuscrits Palis de la Bibliotheque du Roi*. Paris: Librairie Orientale de Dondey-Dupré père et Fils.

Chatterjee, Mohini Mohan. 1907. *Indian Spirituality; or The Travels and Teachings of Sivanarayan*. London: Luzac.

Chatterjee, Mohinimohan. 1925. "The Paramahansa Sivanarayan Swami." *The Calcutta Review*, Volume 16, July-September, 105–112.

Dahle, L. 1911. *Buddhismen, Den Betydeligste og Interessanteste af Alle Hedenske Religioner*. Stavanger: De Unges Missionsforening.

Haakestad, Jorunn. 2018. *Porcelain and Revolution: Johan Munthe and the Chinese Collection in Bergen*. Bergen: Fagbokforlaget.

Holmboe, Christopher Andreas. 1857. *Traces de Buddhisme en Norvége Avant l'introduction du Christianisme*. Paris: S. Raçon.

Holmboe, Christopher Andreas. 1862. "Sammenligning af Stormendsbegravelse Blandt Skandinaver i Hedenold og Blandt Mellemasiens Buddhister." In *Forhandlinger i Videnskabsselskabet i Christiania*, 203–210.

Holmboe, Christopher Andreas. 1867. "Om Flaghaugen på Karmøy og de Buddhistiske Topper i Asien." In *Forhandlinger i Videnskabsselskabet i Christiania*, 146–155.

Høydal, Olaus. 1963. *Buddhismen*. Oslo: Det norske Samlaget.

Jacobsen, Knut A. 2020. "Hindu Traditions in Norway: Gurus, Places and Communities." In *Handbook of Hinduism in Europe*, edited by Knut A. Jacobsen and Ferdinando Sardella, 1241–1264. Leiden: Brill.

Jacobsen, Knut A. 2025. *Hinduism in the World: Migrations and Global Presence*. London: Routledge.

Johns, Ellen. 1976. "'Bak Alle Ansikt er Intet Ansikt': Jan Erik Vold i Lys av Zenbuddhismen." *Norsk Litterær Årbok,* 128–141. Oslo: Det norske samlaget.

Kleive, H. V. 2022. "Buddhistisk Konfirmasjon." In *Møter og Mangfold: Religion og Kultur i Historie, Samti*d *og Skole,* edited by H. V. Kleive, J. G. Lillebø and K.-W. Sæther, 109–128. Oslo: Cappelen Damm Akademisk. https://doi.org/10.23865/noasp.156.ch5.

Konow, Sten. 1932. "Buddhismen." In *Verdensreligioner Utenom Kristendommen,* edited by Sigmund Mowinkel, Wilhelm Schencke and Sten Konow, 164–199. *Universitetenes Radioforedrag,* Serie B. Nr. 5. Oslo: Aschehoug.

Kværne, Per. 2022. "C.A. Holmboe (1796–1882): The First Norwegian Scholar of Buddhism." *Revue d'Etudes Tibétaines,* 64, 344–351.

Pettersen, Bjørn. 2018. *Baral: Vismannen på Tronfjell: Swami Sri Ananda Acharya: En Biografi og en Antologi.* Alvdal: Tronfjell Fredsuniversitet.

PUKK. 1974. *Buddhistforbundets Kontaktorgan,* 30 March 1974.

Reichelt, Karl Ludvig. 1913. *Kinas Religioner: Haandbok i den Kinesiske Religionshistorie.* Stavanger: Det Norske Misjonsselskaps Boktrykkeri.

Reichelt, Karl Ludvig. 1922. *Fra Østens Religiøse Liv: Et indblik i den Kinesiske Mahayanabuddhisme.* København: Gad. (English translation: *Truth and Tradition in Chinese Buddhism: A Study of Chinese Mahayana Buddhism,* Translated by Kathrina van Wagenen Bugge. Shanghai: Commercial Press).

Sariputra, Swami Acharya (Tidligere Einar Beer). 1967. *Meg Selv – og Min Reise til India.* Alvdal: Alvdal Bok-og Papirhandel.

Sariputra, Swami Acharya. (Tidligere Einar Beer). 1968. *Maitreyya Buddha: Liv – Sannhet – Lære.* Alvdal: Swami Ananda Acharyas Venner.

Sarma, K. V. 1971. "Swami Sri Ananda Acharya: A Biographical Sketch." In *Yoga of Conquest:* Sri Ananda Acharya, xvii-xxvi. 1924. Hosharpur: Vishveshvaranand Institute.

Schade, Rolf E. n.d. "Om den indiske vismann som slo seg ned i Alvdal." Review of Einar Beer, *Maitreya – Liv – Sannhet – Lære.* Utgitt av Swami Ananda Acharyas Venner. Newspaper article.

Tathagata Amoghasiddhi Maitreyya Buddha. 1960. *Yoga of Nirvana – Mukti* [by] the Tathagata Amoghasiddhi Maitreyya Buddha, edited with a foreword by Einar Beer. Alvdal: Brahmakul.

Tathagata Amoghasiddhi Maitreyya Buddha. 1967. *Kosmiske Lysord, Hilsener og Dikt.* Brahmakul, Alvdal: Alvdal Bok-og Papirhandel.

Thelle, Notto R. 2022. *Karl Ludvig Reichelt: Misjonær mellom øst og vest.* Oslo: Cappelen Damm.

Turner, Alicia, Laurence Cox and Brian Bocking. 2013. "A Buddhist Crossroads: Pioneer European Buddhists and Globalizing Asian Networks 1860–1960." *Contemporary Buddhism* 14(1), 1–16.

7 Buddhism in Finland

From Kalmyks to engaged activism

Mitra Härkönen

Moving away from cultural uniformity towards Buddhist diversity

Although still a minority religion, Buddhism has gained recognition in Finland in recent decades. The increase in both the number of communities and their membership is a clear indication of the growing popularity of Buddhism: whereas there were an estimated 10,000 Buddhists in Finland in 2010, the number has now increased to around 30,000. Furthermore, in the twenty-first century alone, about 30 new Buddhist organisations, communities and practice groups (see Figure 7.1) have been established in the country (Härkönen 2023b). As anywhere else, the growing popularity of Buddhism in Finland can be attributed to various global trends such as immigration, increased travel, media and social media coverage of Buddhism and its leaders, and the digitisation of communication. Furthermore, the Western interest in spirituality, personal growth and holistic well-being has contributed significantly to the popularity of Buddhism. Finnish Buddhism has thus emerged and developed at different times in line with various international and global trends and currents (Jääskeläinen et al. 2024).

The largest groups of Buddhist practitioners come from Thailand and Vietnam, and their respective Buddhist organisations have the most significant number of followers, boasting hundreds of members and thousands of visitors (Härkönen 2023b). Vietnamese refugees were the first to arrive in the late 1970s, while Thais commonly come to Finland through international marriages with Finnish men (Härkönen et al. 2023; Härkönen 2023a, 2024). Yet, the rise in recognition of Buddhism cannot solely be attributed to immigrants. Many Finns have also turned to Buddhism for ethical, philosophical and mental guidance. Tibetan and Zen Buddhism are particularly popular among people of Finnish background, as in many other Western countries (Härkönen & Sharapan 2023; Cairns & Tikka 2023). These practice communities may be small, but they are diverse due to the variety of schools, lineages and masters their practitioners follow. In addition, various Buddhist-based meditation techniques, such as *vipassanā*, are becoming more prevalent. As a result, Buddhism in Finland has become a multi-ethnic religion and worldview with a wide range of traditions, beliefs and practices.

The influence of Buddhism extends beyond the number of its communities and practitioners in Finland. The popularity of mindfulness is a prime example of

DOI: 10.4324/9781003529767-7

this, as it is practised not only in various mindfulness courses and workshops but also in public spaces such as healthcare institutions, schools and even the Finnish Defence Forces (Husgafvel 2023; Jääskeläinen 2023). It is also worth mentioning that Japanese martial arts, which have ties to Buddhism or cultures influenced by Buddhism, have enjoyed widespread popularity for a considerable amount of time (Cairns 2023). Furthermore, Buddhism has influenced several Finnish artists, and many Finns today read Buddhism-inspired self-help literature or keep a Buddha statue at home (Cairns & Ojanperä 2023b; Bastubacka & Härkönen 2023; Butters & Mallander 2023).

Compared to many other western European countries, Buddhism has taken longer to develop and establish in Finland (Härkönen & Cairns 2023; Baumann 2002; Baumann & Prebish 2002). For a long time, Finland maintained relatively strong religious unity despite the presence of minority religions such as Islam and Judaism, long before gaining independence in 1917. Nevertheless, the number of people migrating to Finland has been increasing only since the 1990s which is later than in many other countries (Illman et al., 2017). Thus, historically, most Finns have belonged to the Evangelical Lutheran Church of Finland, with over 90 per cent being members still in the 1980s. However, in recent years, the number of church members has decreased, and around 65 per cent of the Finnish population and less than 50 per cent of the population in the Helsinki area were members of the Lutheran Church in 2023.[1] Yet, church belonging does not provide a complete understanding of the Finns' Christian faith or religious practice. A significant number of Finns are "culturally religious," and their primary motivation for belonging to the church is to be able to participate in traditional religious ceremonies like Christian confirmation camps or have church weddings. Many people also consider the church's diaconal work to be important (Salomäki et al., 2020).

Although there has been a long history of religious and cultural uniformity, it is worth recognising that Buddhism was present in Finland from a relatively early stage. In the late nineteenth and early twentieth centuries, Buddhism found its way into the country through various channels, such as the growing fascination of the western upper and middle class with spiritualism, eastern philosophies and scientific research, as well as criticism of Christianity. The Finnish elite was not immune to these trends, and they would travel abroad and read international publications. (Jääskeläinen et al., 2024.) The first Buddhist organisation in Finland was also established relatively early, in 1947, and for a brief period in the late 1940s and early 1950s, Helsinki was an international hub for Buddhism (Cairns & Taehye sunim 2023).

Buddhism has been the subject of numerous bachelor's and master's theses in Finland (see Cairns & Ojanperä 2023b). However, it is only in recent years that research on Finnish Buddhism at the doctoral and postdoctoral levels has started to emerge. This research concentrates on contemporary Buddhism in Finland while also delving into the country's earlier and more recent Buddhist history (see Härkönen & Cairns 2023; Husgafvel & Härkönen 2017; Sharapan 2021; Sharapan & Härkönen 2017; Tolvanen 2023a, 2023b; Jääskeläinen et al., 2024). As a result, it is only now feasible to document and feature Buddhism in Finland and include it on the maps of the Nordic countries, Europe and the world.

The chapter begins by discussing the early and more recent history of Buddhism in Finland. It then explores the diversity of Buddhism in present-day Finland. Finally, it delves into Buddhism's place in Finnish society and discusses the future of Buddhism in the country.

Kalmyks, explorers and missionaries

Although the popularity of Buddhism in Finland has increased only in recent decades, Buddhism has been present in the country in some way or another much earlier. During the early Middle Ages, the Vikings engaged in overseas trading, as evidenced by the discovery of Buddha statues in Sweden (see Introduction and Plank in this volume). Along with goods, stories, legends and beliefs were exchanged and carried to the Nordic area. Finland was under Swedish rule from 1150 to 1809, but there is no known evidence of Finns interacting with Buddhism at that time. (Tolvanen 2023a; Gothóni 1981.)

The first group of Buddhists in Finland were likely the Kalmyks, an ethnic Mongolic group. In the eighteenth century, some Kalmyks arrived in Finland alongside Russian Cossacks during the Russian invasion and military occupation of Finland. Their burial customs were recorded in Finnish church records as early as the 1740s. The Turku Wiikkosanomat newspaper introduced the Kalmykian religion with its "Ten Commandments" and "Creed" in 1822, marking an attempt to introduce a foreign religion in a Christian framework and the first mention of Buddhism in a Finnish newspaper. Finnish newspapers and magazines featured articles on the Kalmyks numerous times, with some texts exhibiting hostility towards them. While some folktales also depicted them as brutal killers with animalistic traits, there were also more favourable accounts. For example, in a Finnish dictionary from 1912, the Kalmyks were described as mentally gifted and energetic. The text also mentions that it was precisely the Kalmyks who bestowed the Dalai Lamas secular authority in the leadership of Tibet. Today, a few place names in Finland remain of the Kalmyks and their religion (Tolvanen 2023a).

At the latest in the nineteenth century, Finnish explorers, linguists and missionaries encountered Buddhist peoples, primarily Tibetans. Their experiences were documented in the research literature and travel stories published in Finnish-language newspapers. In 1848, for instance, M.A. Castrén, a Finnish explorer and linguist, wrote a letter to the Suometar newspaper detailing his encounter with a lama at a Buddhist monastery. As an early pioneer in ethnolinguistics, Castrén found it intriguing to encounter a familiar word, "sampo," which was told to mean a secret source of happiness in Mongolian and Tibetan languages and was used for the oldest and most esteemed Buddhist temple. "Sampo" in Finnish mythology, and featured especially in the Finnish national epos, Kalevala, is a mystical device that brings wealth and fortune to its possessor. The discipline of comparative folklore, in addition to comparative linguistics, had become of interest in the country. For example, the story of Barlaam and Josaphat (see Introduction in this volume) was referenced in a doctoral thesis by Kaarle Krohn (1863–1933), a scholar of folk poetry and linguistics, in 1887. As mentioned earlier, at the start of the twentieth century, Finnish dictionaries delved into Buddhism, with three pages dedicated to it in 1909. "Lamaism" was also covered in 1913, described as a religion dominated by priests and superstition, deviating from the Buddha's original teachings. For example, Zen is not mentioned in the dictionaries from that time (Tolvanen 2023a).

A significant event in Finnish Buddhist history involved the meeting of Finnish military leader and statesman Carl Gustav Mannerheim (1867–1951) with the thirteenth Dalai Lama (1876–1933) in 1908. Mannerheim had a strong interest in the "Orient," as evidenced by his extensive library collections and the interior décor of his home, which now serves as a museum in Helsinki. During his service in the Russian Army, Mannerheim undertook a horseback journey to Central Asia from 1906 to 1908. He collected not only military and statistical information but also ethnographic data. On 26 June 1908, Mannerheim met the Dalai Lama and offered him his Browning pistol, acknowledging the need for even a holy man to have one in those times. The Dalai Lama did not agree to be photographed this time but promised a photo next time; after all, they had become good acquaintances with Mannerheim, the Dalai Lama had said. (Tolvanen 2023a; Mannerheim et al., 2008.)

In 1895, the first Finnish missionaries travelled to the Himalayas seeking access to Tibet. They did not succeed but continued to work in different villages in Sikkim and India until the 1970s. Eventually, the missionaries shifted their focus to development cooperation as converting Tibetans proved challenging (Tolvanen 2023a). The Finnish Lutheran Evangelical Association also sent missionaries to Japan in the early twentieth century, but their efforts were relatively unsuccessful, too (Jalagin 2007).

Theosophist and the founding of the first Finnish Buddhist association

Early interactions with Buddhists and Finns were infrequent and scattered, and it was not until the advent of theosophy that Buddhism began to take root locally. Theosophical literature discussing Buddhism arrived in the Grand Duchy of Finland (1809–1917) shortly after its publication. One of the first printed works on Buddhism from that time is a pamphlet titled *Buddha den upplyste och hans lära* ("Buddha the Enlightened One and His Teachings") (1886), authored by Swedish-speaking Lieutenant General Carl Robert Sederholm (1818–1903). The influence of theosophy on the pamphlet is evident, with the appendix Hemligbuddhismen ("Secret Buddhism") bearing a distinct resemblance to Sinnet's "Esoteric Buddhism" (1883). (Jääskeläinen et al., 2024; Tolvanen 2023a.)

The Theosophical Society in Sweden established a library in Helsinki in 1897 named Teosofiska biblioteket i Helsingfors. The Finnish branch of the society was founded ten years later, in 1907. As far as it is known, between First World War and the 1940s, no organised Buddhist activity took place in Finland. However, some influential members of the Finnish Theosophical Society actively promoted Buddhism in the country's early days. One such person was Pekka Ervast (1875–1934), an occultist and theosophist who served as the general secretary of the Finnish Theosophical Society. Among other things, Ervast translated Olcott's collection of Buddhist teachings into Finnish and titled it *Buddhalainen katkismus* ("The Buddhist Catechism") in 1906 (Cairns & Taehye 2023; Jääskeläinen et al., 2024).

Several people played critical roles in establishing Finland's first Buddhist association, with Mauno Nordberg (1844–1956) being the most prominent (see Cairns in this volume). Nordberg was a Finnish cosmopolitan who had served as Finland's consul in Paris for over two decades, where he developed an interest in Buddhism. Upon returning to Finland in 1939, he joined the Finnish Theosophical Society and connected with like-minded individuals who shared his fascination with Buddhism. One of them was Minister of Defense Yrjö Kallinen (1886–1976), a devoted theosophist who had visited the Buddhist Lodge founded by Christmas Humphreys and studied Zen already in the early twentieth century. Among other things, Kallinen gained recognition for being the first and, so far, only pacifist Minister of Defense in Finland (Virtaperko 2023). Other significant contributors to early Finnish Buddhism included actor Jussi Snellman (1879–1969) and Antti J. Aho (1900–1960), author of the book *Gautama Buddha: ihmisenä ja opettajana* ("Gautama Buddha as a man and teacher") (1932) (Cairns & Taehye sunim 2023). Aho's book on Buddhism, the first to comprehensively cover the topic in Finnish, received a harsh review in the Finnish Journal of Theology (Jääskeläinen et al., 2024).

A mutual interest in Buddhism united a group of individuals who eventually established the first Buddhist association. On 10 May 1947, Buddhismin ystävät – Buddhismens Vänner ("The Friends of Buddhism") was founded. The Finnish association's name was directly translated from the French Buddhist association Les Amis du Bouddhisme, of which Nordberg was a member. Jussi Snellman was elected as the first chairman, while Antti J. Aho became the vice chairman and Nordberg the secretary (Cairns & Taehye 2023).

In the beginning, the association had approximately 40 members, and it functioned in both Finnish and Swedish. The members were well educated and came from higher social backgrounds. According to Nordberg, comprehending Buddhist doctrine required at least a high school education due to its complexity. However, this did not prevent the association from publishing and translating numerous books on Buddhism and spreading them to the public audience. Thus, from the beginning, one of the central activities of the association was to distribute Buddhist teachings to different sectors of society, such as public hospitals, lung sanatoriums and prisons. Written works were seen as the most effective way to arouse people's interest in Buddhism (Cairns & Taehye sunim 2023; Jääskeläinen et al., 2024).

The association's primary focus was discussing *Theravāda* Buddhist texts alongside translation and publishing work. It also organised Buddhist festivals, including *Vesak*. Initially, Buddhism was a lodge of the Finnish Theosophical Society, but as the Friends of Buddhism grew, Nordberg aimed to differentiate Buddhism from theosophy due to the latter's "inaccurate" interpretation of Buddhism. Nevertheless, it is possible that many members still identified as Theosophists (Cairns & Taehye sunim 2023).

The Friends of Buddhism engaged in international collaboration from the very beginning. The members visited other Buddhist organisations abroad and corresponded with European Buddhist groups and The Maha Bodhi Society in Calcutta. After three years of its establishment, the Friends of Buddhism became a member of The World Fellowship of Buddhists. Nordberg attended the first Congress in Sri Lanka in 1950 and the third Congress in Burma in 1954 and contributed to international Buddhist publications in English and French. The Friends of Buddhism's international activities helped advance Nordic, Western and global Buddhist development, bringing international influences to Finland early on (Cairns & Taehye sunim 2023).

Buddhism's promising start in Finland was short-lived. The Friends of Buddhism experienced a decline in members and resources as early as the 1950s. They continued to translate Buddhist texts, but the lack of funds made it impossible to publish anything. The original members of the Buddhist community grew older, and it became challenging to attract new, especially younger, members to participate in activities. Norberg reported a similar situation in Sweden, Norway and Denmark. The Friends of Buddhism struggled to sustain their efforts with minimal resources until the 1980s when the last active generation passed away (Cairns & Taehye sunim 2023).

Indigenous and imported Buddhism between the 1970s and 1990s

A quieter phase of Buddhism in Finland followed until the 1970s when it started to revive. In the 1960s and 1970s, individual Finns travelled Europe and Asia, met Buddhist teachers and formed teacher-student relationships with them. One of them was Martti Anttila (born in 1954) who lived as a novice monk in Sri Lanka from 1975 to 1978 (Cairns & Anttila 2023). Yet, it was not until the 1970s that active organising around Buddhism began again.

The first Buddhist association that followed the Friends of Buddhism was the Friends of Western Buddhist Order (FWBO), now known as Triratna. Two Finns, Vajrabodhi Seppo Palosaari and Bodhishri Tarina Lounasmaa, who had previously been ordained as members of the FWBO order in England, brought the teachings to Finland. In the fall of 1973, they started meditation courses and regular evening classes in Helsinki. Notably, the FWBO arrived in Finland relatively quickly after its establishment in England. Namely, the first two branches of the FWBO outside Great Britain were founded around the same time: one in New Zealand and the other in Finland (Sarvamitra et al., 2023).

The Finnish branch of the FWBO closely monitored the activities of their English counterparts. Initially, some members from England came to Finland for varying periods to provide assistance and leadership. Sangharakshita made four visits to Finland between 1974 and 1978, and Finns actively travelled to England to receive initiations into the order. Overall, the brotherhood welcomed nine new Finnish members in the 1970s. Translation of Buddhist texts, publishing activities and community housing experiments were pursued jointly. The association sought financial support from various sources, including growing and selling alfalfa and mung bean sprouts (Sarvamitra et al., 2023; Laaksonen et al., 2003).

While the Finnish FWBO/Triratna has, since its establishment, valued keeping up with the international FWBO community, it also places importance on practising Buddhism in a uniquely Finnish way. The Helsinki centre has, for example, incorporated Kalevala epos notes into their recitations and hosts sauna rituals at their retreat centre, Abhayaloka, which is located under an hour from Helsinki (Sarvamitra et al., 2023; Sillfors 2008).

In the 1970s, also Soka Gakkai International (SGI) was founded in Finland. Soka Gakkai practitioners from around the world arrived in Finland in the 1970s, and the first meeting was held in April 1975. The SGI appointed an executive director for Finland in 1979, and since then, study weekends have been regularly scheduled. Today, there is an active SGI center in Helsinki that engages in active peace work in addition to Buddhist practices (Valkama 2023).

Apart from the aforementioned communities, Tibetan Buddhism especially gained a foothold in Finland's "second wave" of Buddhism. During the midsummer week of 1976, the world conference on transpersonal psychology in Inari, Finland's Lapland, welcomed the first Tibetan Buddhist lamas to Finland. Khensur Pema Gyaltsen Rinpoche, the keynote speaker, was from the renowned Drepung monastery in Lhasa, Tibet. Tarab Tulku Rinpoche, who had moved to Denmark in the 1960s, Gonsar Tulku Rinpoche from Switzerland, and Lakha Thupten Dorje Rinpoche from Dharamsala, India, accompanied him. Along with the conference sessions, the lamas gave Buddhist teachings and started each session with meditation, including reciting mantras. Following the conferences, a few attendees from Inari continued to Vaasa on the west coast of Finland, where the Tibetan lamas hosted a retreat (Tolvanen 2023b). Of the first lamas, Tarab Tulku, also called by some Finns as a "Home Lama," became a significant teacher for numerous Finnish Buddhist practitioners during the early years. Later, in 1998, the Tarab Institute Association Finland was established with a similar objective to other Tarab institutes established in Europe (Härkönen & Sharapan 2023).

On 26 February 1977, another renowned Tibetan lama, Kalu Rinpoche, and his entourage were scheduled to arrive at Helsinki-Vantaa airport from Sweden. The visit was arranged by Ole and Hannah Nydahl, a Danish couple who had become students of both Kalu Rinpoche and the Sixteenth Karmapa during their honeymoon in the Himalayas (see Børup in this volume). Almost two hundred people had gathered in a venue in Helsinki's city centre to see this exotic Tibetan master. However, to their surprise, Kalu Rinpoche did not arrive on the plane as expected but had disembarked during its stopover in Turku. As a result, the teaching session by Rinpoche was rescheduled for the next day. Kalu Rinpoche's visit resulted in establishing a small Buddhist group in Helsinki, to which he donated a Buddha statue (Tolvanen 2023b).

Finnish journalist and author Tuula Saarikoski (1936–2021), who later greatly influenced Buddhism in Finland, was among the individuals who participated in Kalu Rinpoche's visit and who, by chance, ended up interpreting the events. Saarikoski got interested in Buddhism, but as Tibetan lamas rarely visited Finland, she, like some other Finns, often visited Lama Ngawang's centre in Sweden (see Larsson in this volume). During one of her visits, Saarikoski came across a picture of a famous Tibetan Lama, Namkhai Norbu, and invited him to Finland. The visit was eventually arranged in 1981, but it was not until 2011 that the Finnish Dzogchen community, which follows Namkhai Norbu's teachings, was officially registered (Tolvanen 2023b; Härkönen & Sharapan 2023; Saarikoski 2015).

The first Tibetan Buddhist community native to Finland was founded by "Maitreya" Pekka Airaksinen (1945–2019). Airaksinen, who was renowned as an artist, underground musician and poet, began practising Buddhism in 1973 as a member of the FWBO but eventually left the group. Nevertheless, Airaksinen retained the name Maitreya, which was bestowed upon him by Sangharakshita, and he continued to incorporate many practices and teachings from the FWBO. In the year of 1980, Airaksinen and his students established the "Buddhist Dharma Center" (Buddhalainen Dharmakeskus) in Alastaro in southwest Finland. The centre's teachings and practices draw from various Buddhist traditions, with Airaksinen being most influenced by some Tibetan teachers. Airaksinen also developed a meditation practice known as *Odo*, based on the Buddhas mentioned in the ancient Buddhist text Mahāvastu. Today, the Buddhist Dharma Center has two Buddhist centres, including the Samje retreat centre in Siikainen in the Satakunta region and the Tibetan art centre in Alastaro. Finland's first *stūpa*, which is also claimed to be the northernmost *stūpa* in the world, was built in 2001 at the Samje retreat centre, led by Tulku Pema Wangyal, the head of the Songtsen France centre. Tulku Pema Wangyal started visiting Finland in the 1990s and finally established two Songtsen study groups, one in Helsinki in 2000 and the other in Tampere in 2002 (Härkönen & Sharapan 2023).

During the 1990s, two Karma Kagyu Buddhist centres were established in Finland. In Turku, two Russian women who had practised Diamond Way Buddhism in Russia inspired the formation of a community in their new hometown in the late 1990s. Similarly, in Helsinki, the Diamond Way activities started on a larger scale in the spring of 1998 in connection with Ole Nydahl's teaching visit. Despite having a loyal and relatively large group of supporters in Finland, the relationship between Diamond Way Buddhism and other Tibetan Buddhist groups has been tense. This is because of the controversy over two Karmapas and Ole Nydahl's views, which have sometimes been interpreted as homophobic and racist. Notwithstanding the controversies, the Diamond Way community (called Timanttipolku in Finnish) continues to thrive in the country, and it has various satellite centres in different Finnish towns (Härkönen & Sharapan 2023).

In 1997, Ani Sherab Zangmo (formerly known as Pirkko Siltaloppi), a Finnish-born woman, began a Karma Kagyu community called Rokpa Finland with the blessing of her teachers, Akong Tulku Rinpoche and Lama Yeshe. In the early 1980s, Ani Sherab had become acquainted with Helena Kuokkanen, a Finnish woman who spoke fluent Tibetan and had completed a three-year retreat at a Tibetan Buddhist Kagyu centre in Sweden. During her time in Sweden, Ani Sherab was suggested to visit Samye Ling and Akong Rinpoche in Scotland. She eventually chose to stay at Kagyu Samye Ling from 1988 to 1997, where she spent various years in a closed retreat. In 1989, Kenting Tai Situ Rinpoche, the Palpung Sherab Ling Monastery abbot in India, visited the centre and ordained Ani

Sherab as a nun. Later, she was invited to Finland to teach her students. Along with spiritual practices, the activities of Rokpa Finland involved Tara Rokpa therapy and humanitarian work. Today, the spiritual activities continue under the guidance of Kagyu Samye Ling and its spiritual leader Lama Yeshe Losal Rinpoche, now known as Kagyu Samye Dzong Finland, and directed by Ani Sherab (Härkönen & Sharapan 2023).

Danakosha Ling, which follows the Tibetan Buddhist Nyingma school, was established in the late 1990s and visited by esteemed lamas such as Ranyak Patrul Rinpoche and Chimmed Rigdzin Rinpoche. Tulku Dakpa Rinpoche from Mindrolling Monastic University in India was invited to Finland and later settled there permanently. Danakosha Ling had a centre in Helsinki from 2005 to 2014 but later purchased a farm in Jokioinen in Tavastia Proper region in 2016, where they established a Tibetan Buddhist temple and monastery. There is also a newly built *stūpa* at the temple-monastery (Härkönen & Sharapan 2023).

Another renowned teacher who started visiting Finland in the 1990s was Geshe Pema Dorjee, a Geluk teacher and revitaliser of the Tibetan Buddhist *Bodong* tradition. In 2008, his students established a community called Lochen Jangchup Tsemo. Since 2015, they have also run a Lotus Club for children in Helsinki and Oulu. Jangchup Choeling Buddhist Center has operated separately from Lochen Jangchub Tsemo in Ylikiiminki since 2017 (Härkönen & Sharapan 2023).

It is known that some Finns were practising Zen already in the 1970s (or even earlier), and they travelled overseas to meet with teachers and attend retreats. However, organised Zen activities did not become prevalent in Finland until the mid-1980s. The Friends of Buddhism experienced a significant transformation after a Finnish-born monk named Taehye sunim (also known as Mikael Niinimäki and Mahapañña) assumed the role of chairperson in 1985 and shifted its focus towards the Korean Zen/*Seon* tradition and renamed the community as Bodhidharma. Taehye sunim (b. 1952) developed an interest in Eastern philosophies at a young age, despite not knowing any other Buddhists at the time. Later, he pursued religious studies, history and philosophy at the universities of Turku and Helsinki. He also practised Buddhism at the Helsinki FWBO centre and various European Buddhist centres. In 1982, he became a novice monk Mahapañña at Wat Pleng Vipassana monastery in Thailand. However, living as a Theravāda monk in Finland proved quite challenging, so he moved to Sōtō-Zen monasteries in Japan and eventually Korea, where he received the Korean full monk ordination and the name Taehye sunim at Songgwangsa Monastery in 1987. Since then, he has served as the abbot of his Musang Am Temple in Italy. In 1999, he also received the Theravāda *bhikkhu* ordination in Burma from Paññadipa Sayadaw, the master of the World Buddhist Meditation Center. Today, Bodhidharma is a group of a few dozen individuals, with Taehye sunim still serving as its spiritual leader (Cairns & Tikka 2023).[2]

In 1987, the Zenshindojo association was founded by Timo Klemola, marking the first community where Zen practice played a central role. Klemola had previously met Italian Zen teacher Engaku Taino (1938–2021) during his retreats in Orvieto, Italy. Like Taino's centre, the Finnish association practised various activities such as karate-do, *iaido*, taiji, *yiquan*, the go game, rock climbing and meditation. The association was most active during the 1990s to the early 2000s, but its activities gradually declined and ended in 2008 (Cairns & Tikka 2023).

In the early 1990s, some members of the Friends of Buddhism developed an interest in the Vietnamese *Thiền* tradition and eventually formed an association called Valkoinen lumme ("White Water Lily") in 2004. Sister Thieu Nghiem, who came to Finland as a refugee from Vietnam and left for Plum Village in 1995, has been the primary instructor for the Finnish organisation since 2010. Some of the members of the Friends of Buddhism also started travelling to Zengården in Sweden in the early 1990s, strengthening the connections between Stockholm Zen Center, Zengården and their teachers, Sante Poromaa and Kanja Odland. As a result, in 1997, some of these practitioners established the Helsinki Zen Center. Other Zen Centers were subsequently founded in various Finnish towns. Today, the Helsinki Zen Center also has a retreat centre called Sanneji in Karjaa on the southern coast of Finland, and Sangen Salo, who was ordained as a teacher in January 2018, resides permanently in that retreat centre. With a membership of approximately more than a hundred people for the past 15 years, Helsinki Zen Center has a notably higher number of members than other Zen centres in Finland. Zen priest Mitra Virtaperko, who was ordained as a teacher in October 2021, leads Tampere Zen Center and a Zen practice group in Helsinki (Cairns & Tikka 2023).

Buddhist migration

The Wat Buddharama temple is located in the heart of the Finnish countryside and can be reached by car in about one hour from Helsinki. There used to be a Finnish farm where the temple is now located. What is left of the former are a storehouse and an old yellow two-story wooden detached house on the plot, which serves as a residence for the monks and a venue for smaller gatherings. Walking towards the temple, one is surrounded by Finland's national trees, the birches, which give the place a very Finnish appearance. Otherwise, the temple area is surrounded by forests and fields. The landscape changes with the seasons; the lush greenery of summer transforms into the vibrant colours of autumn and the snow-covered scenery of winter.

Despite the Finnish elements, the temple area has a strong connection with Thailand. At the entrance of the temple's large parking area, there is a spirit house, and the pond in the temple courtyard is adorned with Buddha statues in various positions. A new, massive wooden log temple building blends in perfectly with the Finnish landscape, but it still has unique characteristics that distinguish it from typical Finnish architecture. Dozens of shoes are left on the temple's large porch, where wind chimes tinkle in the breeze, inviting guests to enter.

The main hall's interior is truly impressive. Although the wooden walls and vast windows with golden curtains overlooking the field landscape still bear a Finnish touch, the temple's architecture and decoration leave no doubt that one has entered a Buddhist *wat*. The altar is the most striking feature, with the statue of Shakyamuni Buddha at its center. The arrangements of smaller statues, candles, flowers, fruits, and incense surround the principal Buddha statue. On the left side of the altar, there is a long podium for the monks to sit during the ceremonies. The ceiling's border features a series of images depicting the phases of Buddha's life from birth to *parinirvana*, or the nirvana after death. The front of the altar structure is lined with large carpets for laypeople to sit on, with chairs brought out during parties. On the right side, there are sofa groups where visitors can sit. At the other end of the temple complex, one can find a kitchen, storage rooms, social facilities, and an open office space. Between the more mundane and the altar areas, there are tables where the monks' lunch is laid out daily on one round table, while other tables serve laypeople's meals. Most of the temple's items, from altar decorations and statues to furniture and textiles, were imported from Thailand.

(Härkönen 2024, 6–7)

The first Buddhist immigrants arrived in Finland during the 1970s, but it was not until the 1990s that they began to organise themselves. Today, the largest and most vibrant Buddhist communities are the Vietnamese and Thai communities. Their religious life clearly indicates migrant Buddhists' transnational relations and efforts to adapt Buddhism to Finland as described earlier. The Vietnamese "boat refugees" were the initial group of ethnic Buddhists to make Finland their permanent home. In August 1979, the first hundred refugees arrived in Finland. Initially, the Vietnamese practised their religion privately within their families. A monk accompanied the refugees to Finland but later moved to Sweden. In the 1990s, a group of 20 Vietnamese founded (an unnamed) Buddhist group to enhance their spiritual well-being. Initially, the group's activities were informal and involved studying Buddhism from books and *sūtra* texts. The group also organised daylong retreats where they followed the eight guidelines of novice monastics. As the group grew, they expanded their activities, organising *Phật Đản* (*Vesak*) and *Vu Lan* (*Ullambana*) celebrations that were open to everyone. The clubhouse or the school's gymnasium often served as the party venue (Linh 2013; Härkönen et al., 2023).

The group became connected with a monk named Thích Trí Minh, who became responsible for guiding their Buddhist practice. Following the monk's advice, the group began collecting donations from Vietnamese residents in Finland to acquire property for their temple. In 1993, with the funds they raised and a bank loan, they purchased an old, detached house in Loviisa, on the southern coast of the country, which became known as Giác Viên, Finland's first Vietnamese temple. However, the temple's location was deemed too far from the Vietnamese community living in the capital area, and it was ultimately decided to sell the property a few years later (Härkönen et al., 2023).

In 2007, a monk named Thích Hạnh Thông was sent to Finland by the Vietnamese European Congregation Unified Buddhist Association. Having fled to Norway as a refugee in 1994, he had lived with Thích Trí Minh in the Khuông Việt temple in Oslo. Upon arriving in Finland, he initially resided in Turku before eventually relocating to the capital region (Härkönen et al., 2023). In 2008, Vietnamilaisten Buddhalais – Kulttuuriyhteisö ry (the "Buddhist Cultural Community of Vietnamese") was registered. In 2011, the community purchased a detached house in Vantaa, in the capital region, which was transformed into the Phúc Lâm temple. In 2013, Suomen Vietnamilaisten Buddhalaisuus Yhdyskunta (the "Buddhist Community of Finland's Vietnamese"), Chùa Phúc Lâm, serving hundreds of Vietnamese, especially in the capital area, was registered as a religious community (Härkönen et al., 2023).

In 1997, Suomen Vietnamilaisten Buddhalaisten Yhdyskunta (the "Community of Vietnamese Buddhists of Finland") was established in Turku in southwest Finland. Behind the initiative was especially a Vietnamese man called Vĩnh Tuyên, whose dream was to build a Vietnamese temple in Finland. The association achieved a significant milestone when monk Thích Hạnh Bảo, a relative of Vĩnh Tuyên, took the lead in the temple project. Thích Hạnh Bảo, an international trustee and teacher of the *Linji* lineage (*Rinzai*, v. *Lâm Tế*), had previously served as the abbot of the Vạn Hạnh temple in Odense, Denmark, for a decade and was still holding the same position at the Viên Ý temple in Padua, Italy. The Lotus Heart Temple, Chùa Liên Tâm, was completed in 2013 and is now the biggest Vietnamese temple-monastery in Finland, with hundreds of members and thousands of visitors during the most significant Buddhist celebrations (Härkönen et al., 2023).

Alongside those who follow Vietnamese Mahāyāna Buddhism, there are also Vietnamese residing in Finland who practise Theravāda Buddhism. To cater to their needs, the Finnish Vietnamese Buddhadhamma Community, Chùa Đại Thọ, was founded in December 2015 in Kerava close to Helsinki. The temple and community were established by the Vietnamese monk Vijjaviriyo (also known as Thích Minh Tấn), who had initially received a scholarship to study social work in Finland in 2007 (Härkönen et al., 2023). The temple also serves as a temple for a group of Sri Lankan Buddhists who are guided by a Sri Lankan monk.

Currently, Thailand has become one of the most popular travel destinations in the world, and in the Nordic countries, Thailand is one of the most popular travel destinations. According to the statistics, around 150,000 Finns visit Thailand every year (Embassy of Finland 2024). The frequent travel between Finland and Thailand has resulted in many marriages between Finns and Thais. As a result, Thai Buddhism has become the largest branch of Buddhism, largely due to the high number of marriages between Finnish men and Thai women.[3] These Thai women have played a significant role in introducing Buddhism to Finland.

Back in the 1990s, Thai culture was not as familiar to the people of Finland as it is today, and Thai women faced several challenges when it came to integration. Pranom Heinonen was among those Thai women who arrived in Finland relatively early, in 1989, through marriage. Initially, it was a struggle to make friends, but Heinonen gradually connected with other Thai women who used to meet at a Thai restaurant owned by one of the women in Helsinki. During these gatherings, the women bonded over food, took care of their children, shared news, talked about homesickness, and supported each other. These meetings were vital to these women, and Heinonen, who is highly educated and well travelled, came up with the idea of creating a space where Thai people could come together and share their lives, joys, and sorrows. This space would allow women to maintain their country of origin's culture, and Finns could also learn more about them and their culture. Given that Buddhism is a crucial part of Thai culture and identity, there was a proposal to establish a Buddhist temple. In 1994, they founded the Finnish-Thai Buddhist Association (Härkönen 2023a).

In the year 2000, Pra Mahanual Chamnanram was appointed as the first Thai monk in Finland, thanks to the contributions of Thai monasteries in Sweden and

Norway. To provide a residence and meeting place for the monk, a house was rented in Helsinki until 2002, when the community could purchase a property in Sipoo in the Helsinki metropolitan area using the collected funds. Pra Mahanual became the abbot of the newly established Buddharama temple, which, however, soon became too small to accommodate the growing number of Thai attendees. In 2009, a new location in Nurmijärvi was discovered, and the renovated Wat Buddharama temple was officially opened in July 2022 after facing delays caused by the COVID-19 pandemic. The three-day celebration was attended by over a hundred monks and thousands of Thais from various parts of the world (Härkönen 2023a).

Another Thai community, Wat Phutta Tham Finland, which is active in the Turku area, was established in 2006. In the same year, a forest monk named Pra Mahatee Sirijanda was invited to Finland from the Wat Dalarnavanaram temple in Sweden by a Thai woman named Risaraporn Paavola. Due to the lack of a permanent residence permit, the monk initially lived in apartments rented by the association in different places, frequently travelling between Sweden and Finland. In 2011, he finally settled permanently in Finland after the association purchased a detached house close to Turku, which was converted into the community temple known as Wat Phutta Tham that same year (Härkönen 2023a).

The third Thai community, the Wat Asokaram Finland Vipassana Meditation Center following the Thai forest monk tradition, was founded in Lohja in the southern interior of the country. The centre was founded as an initiative by Patcharee Orenius, a Thai woman living in Finland, who had a keen interest in the forest monk tradition. Orenius used to visit the Thai temple in Turku frequently but eventually found it challenging to make regular visits due to the distance. Consequently, the community invited Pra Aja Nak to lead the meditation community (Härkönen 2023a). Some years later, the Wat Pah Buddha Metta Thammataro Finland led by Pra Aja Nak was founded.

In 2000, the first group of Burmese refugees under the quota system arrived in Finland. Finnish authorities have prioritised Christian refugees and as a result, half of the Burmese population in Finland are Christians, while the other half are Buddhists. Furthermore, Burmese refugees in Finland come from a variety of ethnic groups, including Mon, Karen and Bamar. Due to their dispersal throughout the country, it has been difficult for different ethnic groups to maintain their unique traditions. In 2009, the Burmese community established a religious community called Buddha Dhamma Ramsi Finland. Initially, the community had a temple in an apartment in Kuopio in eastern Finland, but in 2018, they purchased a detached house to be used as the Ratnasukha Monastery. The abbot of the monastery is Paññasami, a doctorate monk who lives alone in the temple. Additionally, the Burmese people in the Helsinki area established a temple in Vantaa, which, however, had to be sold due to financial difficulties in 2013 (Cairns & Ojanperä 2023a).

In addition to Vietnamese, Thai and Burmese Buddhists, there is a relatively new but active Finnish-Sri Lankan Buddhist community in the country. There are also some Chinese communities in Finland that practise Buddhism among other activities. However, they do not identify themselves solely as Buddhist communities nor do they collaborate with other Buddhist communities. Although not all

Figure 7.1 Phật Đản (Vesak) marks Buddha's birth, enlightenment and death. Baby Buddha is being bathed during the festival by Vietnamese at Liên Tâm monastery in Turku, Finland. Photo: Mitra Härkönen.

Asians with a Buddhist background have a community of their own, it is common for them to attend temple celebrations and events such as those at Wat Buddharama or Chùa Đại Thọ (see Figure 7.1).

Contemporary diversity

In the twenty-first century, the Buddhist community in Finland has seen a noteworthy increase in numbers. The number of Buddhist practitioners has doubled in just over ten years. This is primarily due to the increase in the number of Buddhist immigrants (Pauha & Martikainen 2022). In addition, over thirty new Buddhist associations, communities and Dharma groups have been formed in the current century alone (see Table 7.1).

Early Buddhism was primarily of interest to a small, well-educated Finnish elite, but this is no longer the case. Since both immigrants and the native population follow Buddhism, it is currently more diverse than ever before. Even in a small country like Finland, with a population of 5.5 million, there are representatives from the three major traditions of Buddhism (Theravāda, Mahāyāna and Vajrayāna), as well as numerous schools and subschools under the main traditions (such as Chan/Zen/Thiện/Seon and Tibetan Buddhism), and their respective lineages of teaching.

There are also distinctive interpretations of Buddhism, including Western interpretations (e.g., Triratna), secular or non-religious interpretations (e.g., *vipassanā* represented by Vipassana Meditaatio as taught by S.N. Goenka and Nirodha Buddhist associations) and engaged Buddhism (e.g., Peacemakers Finland, Green Buddha and Dharma Voices for Animals). Moreover, Buddhist traditions brought by immigrant populations are often shaped by the history, culture and society of their country of origin (e.g., "Vietnamese Buddhism," "Thai Buddhism" and "Burmese Buddhism") while also being internally heterogeneous (Härkönen 2023b).

Tibetan Buddhist communities are the most populous among the various schools of Buddhism in Finland today. As of 2023, there were over twenty Tibetan Buddhist communities, accounting for approximately half of all Buddhist communities in Finland. These communities include those established in the 1990s as well as newer teaching lineages that have been brought to the country later. The newer communities include groups such as Palpung Yeshe Gatshal Finland and Bodhicharya groups, both established in 2007, as well as Palpung Changchub Dargye Ling Finland founded in 2008. The Palpung centres are guided by Tai Situ Rinpoche, who pointed Lama Konchog Chögyal as the spiritual teacher of the centres in 2017. Ringu Tulku Rinpoche guides Bodhicharya group. Of the Kagyu communities, Shambala, founded in 2008, eventually suspended its activities due to the many scandals that plagued the international Shambala community. The Kuopio Bodhi Path meditation group was established in 2011 at the request of Shamar Rinpoche. The Helsinki Bodhi Path Meditation Group was founded in 2018 and is led by Acharya Karma Losal, a former Tibetan monk (Härkönen & Sharapan 2023).

The Tara Liberation Study Group, based on the Geluk tradition of the FPMT center in Europe, was also founded in 2007. A Finnish woman, encouraged by the Kopan monastery in Nepal, established a study group in Finland, blessed and named by Lama Zopa Rinpoche. Suomen Kadampa meditaatiokeskus is led by nun Kelsang Lekmo, a Finnish meditation teacher ordained by Geshe Kelsang Gyatso in 2007 and is one of over 1,200 centres established by Geshe Kelsang Gyatso Rinpoche, the founder of the New Kadampa Tradition (NKT) movement (Härkönen & Sharapan 2023).

Furthermore, there are two active Bön Buddhist communities in Finland, Ligmincha Finland, established in 2007, and Dechen Ritrö, founded in 2016. In addition, there is the Dzogchen Shri Singha Finland, which is a dharma group in Helsinki and online dedicated to preserving and teaching the Tibetan Dzogchen tradition. Probably the most unconventional of the Tibetan Buddhist communities is Amrita Mandala, formerly known as Pemako Buddhism, founded in 2018. The community combines secular and esoteric teachings and practices, seeking insights through tantric yoga and meditation techniques developed by its founder, Finnish Kim Katami also called Amrita Baba (Härkönen & Sharapan 2023).

New Zen organisations based on Japanese traditions have also emerged in the twenty-first century. The first of the new organisations is Kajo Zendo, part of Gudō Wafu Nishijima's Sōtō lineage founded in 2009. Tavallinen Mieli Zendo has its roots in the Ordinary Mind Zen School founded by Charlotte Joko Beck in 1995. In

2011, a Finn, Teemu Kangas, met Karen Terzano during a *sesshin* at the Ordinary Mind Zendo in New York, which led to the first teacher visit in 2012. Today, the community has expanded to include several locations. In addition, in the autumn of 2016, Peacemakers Finland (today known as Helsinki Zen Peacemakers) was established as the third Japanese Zen community. This official regional Affiliate Group of Zen Peacemakers International was founded by Mikko and Maija Ijäs, both artists based in Helsinki. Through socially engaged work, silent reflection and service to the local community, Peacemakers aim to develop forms of engaged Buddhism and integrate activism into Buddhist practice (Cairns & Tikka 2023). In 2022, Ikian Zen Hermitage, continuing the lineage of Japanese Zen masters Harada Daiun Sogaku Roshi and his successor Daisetsu Tangen Harada Roshi, was established.

Furthermore, there are some organisations that advocate for meditation practices. The Nirodha association is centred around the Insight Meditation tradition of Theravāda Buddhism but aims to make it applicable and useful in today's world. The Oulu Mindfulness Association is a meditation group influenced by Toni Packer's approach to meditation. Furthermore, the Center for Mindfulness is a non-religious organisation established by Leena Pennanen, which promotes the MBSR technique across Finland. The latest community, Theravāda Buddhist Dhamma ry, was established in 2024 and is guided by a Finnish monk, Ajahn Mudito.

Some Buddhist groups, like Peacemakers, Green Buddha and Dharma Voices for Animals, fall under Socially Engaged Buddhism. Green Buddha emphasises practising Buddhist principles like compassion and wisdom through practical actions for the environment. Dharma Voices for Animals raises awareness about animal suffering among Buddhists worldwide, providing education, petitions and a vegan mentorship programme (Cairns et al., 2023).

Invisible Buddhists in Finnish society

Buddhists residing in Finland have generally gone unnoticed and have faced more curiosity than hostility towards their beliefs and practices. Most of the time, they have been able to practise Buddhism without disturbance. Nevertheless, during the construction of the Vietnamese temple in Turku, it was burned down, and the culprit was never caught, leaving their motives unknown. Despite the incident occurring on 11 September 2011, the abbot of the temple remains confident that such acts of terrorism would not occur in a safe country like Finland (Härkönen et al., 2023).

Buddhism is widely accepted in Finland not only because of its peaceful reputation but also due to the adaptability of its practitioners to Finnish society. It is worth noting that many Buddhists have a keen understanding of how to navigate society to their benefit. The registration of their organisations as religious communities is one example of this. When Buddhist organisations register as a religious community in Finland, they become eligible for certain benefits, such as financial assistance from the state based on the number of members. Additionally, children who belong to the community have the option to request that Buddhism be included in their religious education at school. Furthermore, the community has the right to perform marriage ceremonies for its members. Interestingly, more Buddhists have registered their organisations as religious communities in recent years, with a sharp increase from twenty-six people in 2000 to 1,834 people in 2021.[4] Though registering serves practical purposes, it also demonstrates the desire of Buddhists to be recognised as a legitimate part of Finnish society.

While Buddhism is known for its ability to adapt to different cultures and societies, it is critical to notice that this flexibility may come at a cost and often requires compromising some of the fundamental principles of Buddhism. A key component of a Buddhist community's prosperity is the presence of a resident teacher (i.e., monks, lamas and sometimes also nuns). However, permanent teachers are often challenging to achieve because of rigorous immigration policies in the country. The Buddhist community must demonstrate sufficient financial support for the permanent teacher, and obtaining permanent residency and especially citizenship is a lengthy process that requires, among other things, fluency in the Finnish language. For example, the Finnish authorities did not fully understand the concept of being a monk when the country's first Burmese monk, Kuladuta, arrived in 2007. As a result, he had to go through several processes, such as registering as an unemployed job seeker and participating in work training. Eventually, Kuladuta was able to relocate to Germany (Cairns & Ojanperä 2023a). It is surprising that Finnish authorities do not always acknowledge the status of ordained monastics, especially since Orthodoxy, another main church in Finland with special privileges as a "state church," recognises monastic life.

While Buddhism is generally accepted, particularly in its secular interpretations, the religiosity of Asian Buddhists is often overlooked. This lack of visibility is evident, for example, in the case of Thai women, who are predominantly viewed as spouses of Finnish citizens rather than as engaged Buddhist practitioners (Härkönen 2023a, 2024). The manifestation of religious blindness is often noticeable in the customs and rituals surrounding death. It is not always possible for a dying person to receive Buddhist death rituals and hospice care within a hospital setting. Furthermore, adhering to Buddhist beliefs may mean that moving the deceased's body within the hospital can interfere with the dying process. In addition, obtaining the necessary permits to construct *pagodas* for housing the deceased's ashes on communal land can be a lengthy and challenging process.

Decision-making in Finnish society often neglects the perspectives and contributions of Buddhists. In recent years, Buddhists have been advocating for their rights. This is done especially through the Buddhist Union of Finland (SBU), which was established in 2009 to promote the visibility of Buddhism in Finland and ensure that the religious needs of Buddhists are met by public institutions, particularly schools and healthcare facilities. The SBU is built on the shared doctrinal foundation of all Buddhist traditions and serves as an overarching organisation for registered Buddhist groups, representing them to society.

Nevertheless, given the diverse nature of Buddhism in Finland, it can prove challenging to identify shared objectives for Buddhist endeavours. For example, the experiences and goals of an urban, educated Finn practising Zen can differ greatly from those of an Asian immigrant. For the former, personal practice and study might be emphasised, and clashes with Finnish society are not a major concern. The latter may place more emphasis on ethnic and cultural customs that are, at times, difficult to adapt to Finnish society. While this division is somewhat over-simplified, it is important to consider the various intersections that shape the status and identity of different Buddhists and impact their challenges and successes in Finnish society. In addition to the lack of human resources, the different needs of Buddhists might thus be one of the reasons for the fact that there were only fourteen member organisations in the SBU in 2024.[5]

For individuals who practise Buddhism and are raising children in the faith, the experience can be challenging, especially for those who have immigrated or entered into transnational marriages. Language plays a crucial role as Buddhist children from migrant backgrounds may struggle with the language skills required to comprehend Buddhist teachings. This can lead to a decline in their ability to practise and understand Buddhism as their primary language skills diminish. To tackle this issue, some Vietnamese Buddhists have established clubs where children and young adults can learn both Buddhism and the Vietnamese language (Härkönen et al., 2023). However, language differences can also create a divide between Buddhists of Finnish and Asian backgrounds. Finnish Buddhists may find it difficult to understand the challenges immigrants face in Finland, not only as Buddhists but also as representatives of a foreign language and culture. Conversely, limited knowledge of the English language may hinder some Finnish individuals from participating. Although Buddhist literature has been extensively translated into Finnish, instructional materials and teacher visits are often conducted in English.

Financial and human resources are scarce in communities with limited size. This issue is particularly impactful for the Buddhist communities with mainly people with Finnish backgrounds, as they do not have the cultural understanding of *dāna* and what is required for maintaining and supporting the community. Despite the aforementioned differences, a common concern among Buddhists in Finland in general is that there is not enough time available in Finnish society for *dharma* practice. It can be very challenging for those who wish to fully devote themselves to the practice, as there is no structural support, for example, if one wishes to take a long retreat.

The future of Buddhism in Finland

The presence of Buddhism in Finland is primarily due to individuals who have introduced the religion and its teachings to the country. As a result, the Buddhist community in Finland is diverse and fragmented. With increased travel and social media connections, the spread of Buddhist influences in Finland is expected to grow. As such, the Buddhist landscape in Finland is constantly evolving and dynamic.

It can be anticipated that immigration will contribute to an increase in the population of Buddhists in Finland in the following years. However, whether the "second" and "third" generations of Buddhist migrants will embrace the religion remains uncertain. Now it seems that Buddhism attracts more young individuals of Finnish origin than those with a migrant Buddhist background. When visiting Buddhist temples belonging to migrant communities, it is noticeable that young people are less present than older generation maybe because they do not find their parents' Buddhist tradition appealing. On the other hand, research conducted on Finnish millennials who define themselves as Buddhists or as Buddhist practitioners indicates that these young adults contemplate deeply life's purpose and for them, Buddhism is not about having "blind" faith but instead a logical, rational and practical worldview. Buddhism thus offers solutions to life's existential questions and obstacles. Furthermore, it provides a framework for interpreting personal experiences and a practical path for individuals to shape their lives and future directions. The abundance of Buddhist traditions available in today's Finland also means that individuals can choose the form of Buddhism that resonates with their own personal way of thinking. And, if someone cannot locate an appropriate community within Finland, they can explore options for communities online or abroad (Härkönen 2022).

It is possible that the climate crisis and ongoing wars and conflicts will also amplify the significance of engaged Buddhism among Finnish Buddhists in the coming years. A study by Härkönen and Cairns (2025) shows that there is a notable divergence in the opinions of Finns with regard to engaged Buddhism. While some think that engaged Buddhism is a welcome and natural development within Buddhism, some are highly cautious. Cautiousness can be explained by Buddhist doctrines, which emphasise equanimity, Finland's geopolitical location between East and West and its complicated relationship with the neighbouring country of Russia. Furthermore, Nordic welfare countries' political, historical and social culture might further promote societal passivity.

Whatever the truth, it is evident that Buddhism has found a permanent place in Finland. There are more individuals who identify as Buddhists and practise Buddhism in Finland than ever before. Moreover, new Buddhist communities are continually emerging, and the far-reaching impact of Buddhism can be observed in various aspects of culture and society. The history of Buddhism and its diversity in present-day Finland reveal that it has been influenced by various global phenomena and movements such as theosophy, Buddhist modernism and cultural influences brought by migrants from their countries of origin. Buddhism has thus arrived in Finland from different parts of the world and has been interpreted and practised transnationally across national borders. Nevertheless, Buddhism and transnational interpretations of it have not moved only between nation-states and across national borders but have also been translocally interpreted and lived (Gottowik 2010; Conradson & Mckay 2007).

Table 7.1 Buddhist groups in Finland.

Name	Tradition
Organisations of mainly migrants and migrants' children	
Buddha Dhamma Ramsi (Ratnasukha monastery)	Burmese
Finnish-Thai Buddhist Association (Buddharama temple)	Thai
Suomalais Thaimaalainen Buddhalainen Yhdyskunta (Buddharama temple)	Thai
Suomalais Vietnamilainen Buddhadhamma Yhteisö (Chùa Đại Thọ)	Vietnamese
Suomen Vietnamilaisten Buddhalaisuus Yhdyskunta (Chùa Phúc Lâm)	Vietnamese
Suomen vietnamilaisten buddhalaisten yhdyskunta (Chùa Liên Tâm)	Vietnamese
Suomalais-srilankalainen buddhalainen yhdyskunta	Sri Lankan
Wat Asokaram Finland Vipassana Meditation Center ry/	
Wat Pah Buddha Metta Thammataro Finland	Thai
Organisations of mainly converts	
Amrita Mandala	non-sectarian
Bodhicharya study group	Tibetan
Bodhidharma ry	Korean Seon
Bodhi Path Meditaatio Helsinki ja Kuopio	Tibetan
Buddhalainen Dharmakeskus	non-sectarian
Buddhalainen yhteisö Triratna ry	Western
Danakosha Finland	Tibetan
Dechen Ritrö ry	Tibetan
Dharma Voices for Animals	non-sectarian
Drala Thang	Tibetan
Dzogchen Shri Singha Suomi	Tibetan
Helsinki Zen Center ry	Japanese Zen
Helsinki Zen – Peacemakers Finland	Japanese Zen
Ikian Zen Hermitage	Japanese Zen
Jangchup Choeling Buddhist Centre	Tibetan
Kagyu Samye Dzong Finland (former Rokpa Finland ry)	Tibetan
Kajo Zendo Helsinki, Lappeenranta Turku	Japanese Zen
Keltainen buddha	Theravāda
Lahti Zen ry	Japanese Zen
Ligmincha Finland	Tibetan
Lochen Jangchup Tsemo buddhalainen yhdyskunta	Tibetan
Nirodha ry: Insight Meditation in Finland	Theravāda
Oulun Mindfulness ry	non-sectarian
Palpung Changchub Dargye Ling Finland	Tibetan
Palpung Yeshe Gatshal Finland	Tibetan
Soka Gakkai International Suomi	Nichiren
Songtsen ry	Tibetan
Sorig Khang Helsinki	Tibetan
Suomen Dzogchen-yhteisö ry	Tibetan
Suomen kadampameditaatiokeskus	Tibetan
Tampereen Dharmaryhmä	Tibetan
Tampere Zen Center ry	Japanese Zen
Tarab Institute Finland	Tibetan
Tara Liberation Study Group	Tibetan
Tavallinen Mieli Zendo – Ordinary Mind Zendo Finland Helsinki, Tampere, Jyväskylä	Japanese Zen
Timanttipolku uskonnollinen yhdyskunta	Tibetan
Valkoinen Lumme ry	Vietnamese Thiền

Notes

1 The Evangelical Lutheran Church of Finland, https://evl.fi/en/.
2 See also https://www.bodhidharma.fi/?p=66.
3 As a result, nearly 83 per cent of Thais currently residing in Finland are female (Statistics Finland 2022).
4 A personal communication of the author with the Statistics of Finland.
5 https://www.sbu.fi/.

References

Bastubacka, Johan and Mitra Härkönen. 2023. "Buddha-kuvat kotona: Buddhalaiset sisus-tuselementit suomalaisissa kodeissa." In *Buddhalaisuus Suomessa*, edited by Mitra Härkönen and Johannes Cairns, 363–378. Helsinki: Finnish Oriental Society.
Baumann, Martin. 2002. "Buddhism in Europe. Past, Present, Prospects." In *Westward Dharma. Buddhism beyond Asia*, edited by Charles S. Prebish and Martin Baumann, 1st ed., 85–105. Berkeley: University of California Press.
Baumann, Martin and Charles S. Prebish. 2002. "Introduction: Paying Homage to the Buddha in the West" In *Westward Dharma. Buddhism beyond Asia*, edited by Charles S. Prebish and Martin Baumann, 1st ed., 1–14. Berkeley: University of California Press.
Bodhidharma. https://www.bodhidharma.fi/?p=66. Accessed 30 Nov 2023.
Butters, Maija and Jan Olof Mallander. 2023. "Buddhalaisuuden materiaaliset ilmentymät: Buddhalaisuudesta inspiroitunut taide ja esinekulttuuri Suomessa." In *Buddhalaisuus Suomessa*, edited by Mitra Härkönen and Johannes Cairns, 341–359. Helsinki: Finnish Oriental Society.
Cairns, Johannes. 2023. "Buddhalaisuus ja taistelulajit Suomessa." In *Buddhalaisuus Suomessa*, edited by Mitra Härkönen and Johannes Cairns, 323–339. Helsinki: Finnish Oriental Society.
Cairns, Johannes and Ari Tikka. 2023. "Chan- ja zenbuddhalaisuus Suomessa." In *Buddhalaisuus Suomessa*, edited by Mitra Härkönen and Johannes Cairns, 215–239. Helsinki: Finnish Oriental Society.
Cairns, Johannes and Martti Anttila. 2023. "Buddhalaismunkkina 1970-luvulla Sri Lankassa." In *Buddhalaisuus Suomessa*, edited by Mitra Härkönen and Johannes Cairns, 87–89. Helsinki: Finnish Oriental Society.
Cairns, Johannes and Matti Ojanperä. 2023a. "Burmalaiset buddhalaiset Suomessa." In *Buddhalaisuus Suomessa*, edited by Mitra Härkönen and Johannes Cairns, 183–186. Helsinki: Finnish Oriental Society.
Cairns, Johannes and Matti Ojanperä. 2023b. "Suomenkielinen buddhalainen kirjallisuus ja buddhalaisuuden tutkimus Suomessa." In *Buddhalaisuus Suomessa*, edited by Mitra Härkönen and Johannes Cairns, 277–300. Helsinki: Finnish Oriental Society.
Cairns, Johannes, Mikko Ijäs and Juha Penttilä. 2023. "Osallistuva buddhalaisuus." In *buddhalaisuus Suomessa*, edited by Mitra Härkönen and Johannes Cairns, 243–265. Helsinki: Finnish Oriental Society.
Cairns, Johannes and Taehye sunim. 2023. "Buddhismin Ystävät – Ensimmäinen buddhalainen yhdistys Suomessa." In *Buddhalaisuus Suomessa*, edited by Mitra Härkönen and Johannes Cairns, 59–86. Helsinki: Finnish Oriental Society.
Conradson, David and Deirdre Mckay. 2007. "Translocal Subjectivities: Mobility, Connection, Emotion." *Mobilities*, 2, 167–174. https://doi.org/10.1080/17450100701381524.
Embassy of Finland. "Finland in Thailand." *Finland Abroad*, Bangkok. https://finlandabroad.fi/web/tha/frontpage. (accessed 9 Oct 2024).
The Evangelical Lutheran Church of Finland. https://evl.fi/en/.
Gothóni, René. 1981. "Buddhismen i Finland." In *Aktuella religiösa rörelser i Finland. Ajankohtaisia uskonnollisia liikkeitä Suomessa*, edited by Nils G. Holm, 133–166. Åbo: Åbo Akademi.

Gottowik, Volker. 2010. "Transnational, Translocal, Transcultural: Some Remarks on the Relations between Hindu-Balinese and Ethnic Chinese in Bali." *Sojourn: Journal of Social Issues in Southeast Asia* 25(2), 178–212.

Husgafvel, Ville. 2023. *Mindfulness-Based Stress Reduction as a Post-Buddhist Tradition of Meditation Practice.* Helsinki: University of Helsinki. [Doctoral dissertation].

Husgafvel, Ville and Mitra Härkönen. 2017. "Buddhalaisuus Suomessa." In *Monien uskontojen ja katsomusten Suomi,* edited by Ruth Illman, Kimmo Ketola, Riitta Latvio and Jussi Sohlberg, 170–181. Kirkon tutkimuskeskuksen verkkojulkaisuja 48.

Härkönen, Mitra and Johannes Cairns, (eds.). 2023. *Buddhalaisuus Suomessa.* Helsinki: Finnish Oriental Society.

Härkönen, Mitra and Johannes Cairns. 2025. "Engaged Buddhism in Finland – Too Cautious to Take Action." *Journal of Buddhist Ethics,* 32, 27–72. https://blogs.dickinson.edu/buddhistethics/2025/02/01/engaged-buddhism-in-finland/

Härkönen, Mitra. 2024. "'A Mini Home Far Away from Home.' The Thai Temple and Women's Sense of Safety in Finland." *Frontiers in Psychology, Sec. Gender, Sex and Sexualities,* 15:1354068. https://doi.org/10.3389/fpsyg.2024.1354068.

Härkönen, Mitra. 2023a. "Elinvoimainen thaibuddhalaisuus." In *Buddhalaisuus Suomessa,* edited by Mitra Härkönen and Johannes Cairns, 167–182. Helsinki: Finnish Oriental Society.

Härkönen, Mitra. 2023b. "Johdanto osaan II." In *Buddhalaisuus Suomessa,* edited by Mitra Härkönen and Johannes Cairns, 127–133. Helsinki: Finnish Oriental Society.

Härkönen, Mitra, Lê Thị Thanh Linh and Ari Vuokko. 2023. "Neljäkymmentä vuotta vietnaminbuddhalaisuutta." In *Buddhalaisuus Suomessa,* edited by Mitra Härkönen and Johannes Cairns, 139–154. Helsinki: Finnish Oriental Society.

Härkönen, Mitra and Maria Sharapan. 2023. "Monien perimyslinjojen tiibetinbuddhalaisuus." In *Buddhalaisuus Suomessa,* edited by Mitra Härkönen and Johannes Cairns, 187–209. Helsinki: Finnish Oriental Society.

Härkönen, Mitra. 2022. "Y-ja Z-sukupolven buddhalaiset: itse valittua ajatonta viisautta ja tekemisen filosofiaa." In *Millenniaalien kirkko: Kulttuuriset muutokset ja kristillinen usko, edited by* Sini Mikkola and Suvi-Maria Saarelainen, 207–228. Helsinki: Kirkon tutkimus ja koulutus 139.

Illman, Ruth, Kimmo Ketola, Riitta Latvio and Jussi Sohlberg, (eds.). 2017. *Monien uskontojen ja katsomusten Suomi.* Kirkon tutkimuskeskuksen verkkojulkaisuja 48.

Jalagin, Seija. 2007. *Japanin kutsu. Suomalaiset naislähetit Japanissa 1900–1941. With an English Summary: Answering the Call: Finnish Missionary Women in Japan, 1900–1941.* Helsinki: Suomalaisen kirjallisuuden seura.

Jääskeläinen, Ari-Pekka, Mitra Härkönen and Johannes Cairns, 2024. "Suomen ensimmäisen buddhalaisen yhdistyksen synty ja ajan ylirajaiset virtaukset." *Uskonnontutkija – Religionsforskaren,* 2, 1–17. https://doi.org/10.24291/uskonnontutkija.148096.

Jääskeläinen, Ari-Pekka. 2023. "Mindfulnessin matka temppeleistä suomalaiseen työelämään." In *Buddhalaisuus Suomessa,* edited by Mitra Härkönen and Johannes Cairns, (eds.), 303–318. Helsinki: Finnish Oriental Society.

Laaksonen, Ari, Anne Vapaa and Bodhishri. 2003. *Helsingin buddhalainen keskus 30 vuotta.* Helsingin buddhalainen keskus.

Lê Thị Thanh Linh 2013. *Buddhist Path – Vietnamese, Thai, and Burmese Buddhists in Finland.* University of Helsinki. [Master's thesis].

Mannerheim, Carl Gustav, translated by Edward Birse, revised by Harry Halén. 2008. *Across Asia from West to East in 1906–1908* (New rev. ed.). Otava: Finno-Ugrian Society.

Pauha, Teemu and Tuomas Martikainen. 2022. "Arvio maahanmuuttotaustaisen väestön uskonnollisesta jakaumasta Suomessa vuosina 1990–2019." *Teologinen Aikakauskirja,* 127(1), 3–23.

Salomäki Hanna, Maari Hytönen, Kimmo Ketola, Veli-Matti Salminen and Jussi Sohlberg. 2020. *Uskonto arjessa ja juhlassa. Suomen evankelis-luterilainen kirkko vuosina 2016–2019.* Kirkon tutkimuskeskuksen julkaisuja 134.

Sarvamitra, Lauri Porceddu, Mitra Härkönen and Johannes Cairns. 2023. "Länsimaisen bud-dhalaisen veljeskunnan ystävät." In *Buddhalaisuus Suomessa*, edited by Mitra Härkönen and Johannes Cairns, 91–101. Helsinki: Finnish Oriental Society.

SBU. https://www.sbu.fi/english-2/. (accessed 1 Dec 2023).

Sharapan, Maria. 2021. *Transculturation of Tibetan Buddhism: Adoption or Adaption?* University of Jyväskylä. *JYU Dissertations*, 454. http://urn.fi/URN:ISBN:978-951-39-8917-0. [Doctoral dissertation].

Sharapan, Maria and Mitra Härkönen. 2017. "Teacher-Student Relations in Two Tibetan Buddhist Groups in Helsinki." *Contemporary Buddhism. An Interdisciplinary Journal*, 1–18.

Saarikoski, Tuula. 2015. *Kaaos ja kirkkaus. Muistelmat*. Helsinki: WSOY.

Sillfors, Mikko. 2008. *Länsimainen buddhalaisuus yksilön ja yhteiskunnan muuttajana. Tapaustutkimus Friends of the Western Buddhist Order-liikkeen veljeskunnasta*. University of Helsinki. [Master's thesis].

Statista. https://www.statista.com/topics/6845/tourism-industry-in-thailand/#topicOverview. (accessed 8 Oct 2024).

Statistics Finland. 2022. *Marriages Contracted*. https://www.stat.fi/tup/maahanmuutto/per-heet/solmitut-avioliitot_en.html. (accessed 28 Nov 2023).

Tolvanen, Kaisa. 2023a. "Buddhalaisuuden varhaisvaiheet Suomessa." In *Buddhalaisuus Suomessa*, edited by Mitra Härkönen and Johannes Cairns, 27–40. Helsinki: Finnish Oriental Society.

Tolvanen, Kaisa. 2023b. "Kun joutsenet saapuivat järvelle: Tiibetinbuddhalaisuus tulee Suomeen." In *Buddhalaisuus Suomessa*, edited by Mitra Härkönen and Johannes Cairns, 103–118. Helsinki: Finnish Oriental Society.

Valkama, Marjatta. 2023. "Soka Gakkai International Suomi: Nichiren Daishōninin buddhalaisuus." In *Buddhalaisuus Suomessa*, edited by Mitra Härkönen and Johannes Cairns, 135–138. Helsinki: Finnish Oriental Society.

Virtaperko, Mitra. 2023. "Suomalaisen zenin varhaisvaiheet: Yrjö Kallinen ja Idän sanoma valaistuksesta." In *Buddhalaisuus Suomessa*, edited by Mitra Härkönen and Johannes Cairns, 45–58. Helsinki: Finnish Oriental Society.

8 Mauno Nordberg and early Buddhism in Finland

Johannes Cairns

Introduction

Mauno Nordberg (1884–1956) was a key founding member and long-term president of the first Buddhist society in Finland, Buddhismin ystävät ry – Buddhismens Vänner r.f. ("Friends of Buddhism"), founded in Helsinki in 1947.[1] After serving for over three decades as Consul General of Finland in Paris, where he had joined the activities of Les Amis du Bouddhisme, Nordberg withdrew to Finland at the commencement of the Second World War, never to return. During this phase of life, he was physically separated from his wife and children who stayed in France, and part-time retirement granted him considerable free time. These conditions allowed Nordberg to dedicate the latter part of his life to his relatively newfound passion for Buddhism.

Facilitated by his elite social status, extensive social network, and unparalleled communication and language skills, Nordberg was able to propel Buddhism from a topic of intrigue among a few Theosophists and Finnish intellectuals into the focus of a decade of organised collective activity. This featured prolific translation and publication work to promote Buddhism in Finland, national and international public presentations, radio hearings, articles in international Buddhist journals, extensive international correspondence with leading Buddhist figures of the time, and visits to key Buddhist events in London and Paris. Among his greatest feats, soon after the founding of the World Fellowship of Buddhists (WFB) in 1950, Nordberg was able to acquire membership for Friends of Buddhism, personally participated in the first (1950) and third (1954) WFB General Conference and became appointed by WFB to oversee Dhamma propagation.

After Nordberg's passing, the Finnish group's level of all activities, especially international ones, dwindled. Nevertheless, during his presidentship, for a moment, Friends of Buddhism in Finland assumed a focal point in the modernisation and westernisation of Buddhism. Nordberg also played a pivotal role in the introduction of Buddhism to Nordic countries, particularly Sweden, whose first Buddhist organisation was named and modelled after Nordberg's example. This chapter explores the activities and impact of Nordberg in detail, focusing on his work to promote Buddhism in Finland and Europe from 1944 to 1956.

DOI: 10.4324/9781003529767-8

Buddhist influences and activities of Nordberg prior to founding of Finnish society

Mauno (Juhana) Nordberg was born in Helsinki on 30 March 1884. He graduated from the Oulun Lyseo upper secondary school in 1902, followed by completing trade school in Helsinki, and in 1904 left abroad. After a year and a half in England, he found himself in France, where he married, had two sons and continued to live for the next thirty-four years. At first, he worked in trade, followed by working for the US Red Cross from 1915 to 1918. The next two decades (1919–1939), until his retirement, he worked as Consul General of Finland in Paris. During 1930–1939, he also worked as Commercial Attaché of the Embassy of Finland in Paris. In France, Nordberg took an interest in Buddhism after becoming widely acquainted with Oriental religious and philosophical traditions.[2]

From an early age, Nordberg had been interested in philosophical questions. In Paris, he was a member of Freemasonry where he advanced to the highest 33rd level, as well as widely exploring different Oriental religious traditions, including studying Sufism under a Sufi master. In 1932, he started to build a library around the theme. In 1936, Nordberg became interested in Buddhism upon reading the book *Le bouddhisme ses doctrines et ses méthodes* by Alexandra David-Néel that had appeared earlier the same year. In the following years 1937–1938, he participated in the activities of the Parisian society Les Amis du Bouddhisme led by G. Constant Lounsbery (1876–1964) from the United States, deepening his understanding on Buddhism. In August of 1939, Nordberg went to Finland on vacation but stayed in the country due to the eruption of the Second World War. His wife also visited Finland but felt uncomfortable because of the cold weather and returned to Paris. Nordberg spent the rest of his days alone in Finland while his wife and two sons, each with families of their own, stayed in Paris. Nevertheless, rather than breaking family connections, Nordberg maintained relations by making yearly trips to Paris to see his wife and sons. At first, Nordberg worked in the French embassy in Helsinki, and upon retirement, he continued to hold a part-time job in the Central Chamber of Commerce due to his French and English language skills.[3]

Upon returning to Finland, Nordberg joined the Finnish Theosophical Society for a few years, looking for an environment where he could continue to pursue his interest in Buddhism, but separated from the Society in 1948. Nevertheless, during this time, he had become acquainted with several Theosophists interested in Buddhism, most notably Jussi Snellman (1879–1969), Yrjö Kallinen (1886–1976), and Hugo Valvanne (1894–1961). Snellman was an actor in the Finnish National Theater and married to Ruth Sibelius, daughter of renown Finnish composer Jean Sibelius (Mäkinen 2001). Snellman was a Theosophist whose main connection to Buddhist philosophy was through his effort in translating into Finnish *The Light of Asia* by Sir Edwin Arnold (1879), a classic poetic account on the life of the Buddha. Snellman was able to get a publishing contract with WSOY, an important Finnish publishing house, and after working on the translation for numerous years, it finally appeared in 1951 (*Aasian valo: runoelma Gautama Buddhan elämästä ja opista*) (Mäkinen 2001).[4] Yrjö Kallinen, who was Minister of Defence and Councellor of Education in Finland, became interested in Indian philosophies already as a youth. As part of his lifelong interest in Theosophy, Kallinen had visited the London Buddhist Lodge and published an early book on Zen Buddhism (*Zen: idän sanoma valaistuksesta* published by the Theosophical Society) in 1944 even before the founding of Friends of Buddhism. Kallinen also had connections to Tammi, another important Finnish publishing house, and potentially through these connections, Tammi was secured as the publisher of a Finnish translation by Nordberg of *What is Buddhism?* by the Buddhist Lodge (*Mitä on buddhismi?* published in 1947) (Kallenautio 2000).[5] Hugo Valvanne was an important Finnish diplomat, including the first Finnish ambassador in India (1949–1956), who translated several Theosophical works into Finnish. He had also studied Sanskrit and Pali under J. N. Reuter at the University of Helsinki. When Nordberg consulted him on his translation of the *Dhammapada* from English-language sources, Valvanne was critical of the seminal work being translated from an intermediate language, which led to a revised translation by him utilising also original Pali sources. The long translation process concluded in the publication of Valvanne's translation by WSOY in 1953 (Karttunen 2017: 33; Harmainen 2010; Heikinheimo 2016).[6]

The Finnish Theosophists interested in Buddhism also connected with other Finnish people interested more specifically in Buddhism. These included Antti J. Aho (1900–1961) and several members of the Hildén family. Antti J. Aho was the son of renowned Finnish author Juhani Aho and had become interested in Buddhism already as a youth. The interest grew during his exchange studies at the University of Columbia in the United States in 1923–1924 as Aho became acquainted with scholars who had lived in India and translated religious texts directly from the original languages into English. This inspired Aho to study Sanskrit and to write a biography of the Buddha. He planned this to be the topic of his doctoral dissertation at the University of Helsinki, but the faculty considered the topic to be unsuitable, which led Aho to have the work published in 1931 by WSOY as a book intended for a general audience. *Gautama Buddha ihmisenä ja opettajana* ("Gautama Buddha as Man and Teacher") was the first book written in Finnish focusing on Buddhism (Niemi 1998; Venny 2021).[7] The Hildén family included father Leo (1876–1945), mother Gina (b. 1881), son Leo (1919–2006), daughter Ilse (1905–1995) and son-in-law Bertel Johansson. Father Leo Hildén had been an influential person in Finnish society, including serving as Member of Parliament in the Social Democratic Party, and had been interested in Buddhism long before marrying Gina in 1904. Although the father experienced an early death in 1945, he had managed to transmit his interest in Buddhism to his wife Gina and son Leo. For instance, Gina translated a German book by Wolfgang Bohn into Swedish, entitled *Buddhismen, läran om befrielsen* ("Buddhism, Teaching on Freedom"), published in 1946 as a self-publishing work[8] (Damsten 1996). While mother Gina was attracted to Buddhism due to its tolerance and message of peace, son Leo was attracted to the logical clarity of the Buddhist teachings. He was inspired by works by the German Theravāda monks Nyanatiloka Mahathera and Nyanaponika Thera and made an effort to study Pali and Sanskrit in order to be able to read and translate Buddhist texts from the original languages. He went on to translate one German work by each of the two renowned monk scholars into Finnish (*Buddhan Sana* by Nyanatiloka Mahathera, 1951; *Satipatthana* by Nyanaponika Thera, unpublished).

Starting from 1943 or 1944, the Theosophists and non-Theosophist Finns interested in Buddhism started to hold gatherings in the homes of Nordberg, Kallinen and Snellman to discuss Buddhist teachings. In addition to the aforementioned persons, early participants included Armas Rankka, Executive Secretary of the Theosophical Society. Hugo Valvanne was appointed as unofficial president of the group. In meetings during the winter of 1945–1946, which were all held in Nordberg's home, there were already twelve to twenty participants. Due to lack of space, the activities were transferred to the facilities of the Theosophical Society in Vironkatu, Kruununhaka, in the autumn of 1946, and the decision was made to establish a society.

Nordberg's activities as secretary and long-term president of Finnish society

The founding meeting of the Finnish society was held on 21 February 1947, and the society was registered on 10 May 1947 with thirty-eight members. The society was named after the Parisian society Les Amis du Bouddhism as Buddhismin ystävät r.y. – Buddhismens vänner r.f. ("Friends of Buddhism"), and the rules of the society were modelled after the rules of the Buddhist Society in London (successor of Buddhist Lodge). The board for the first three-year term of the society included Jussi Snellman (president), Mauno Nordberg (secretary), Anni Yrjänäinen (treasurer), Antti J. Aho, Gina Hildén, son Leo Hildén and Gina's son-in-law Bertel Johnsson. The same board was kept for the two following three-year terms with only a few exceptions. In 1948, Bertel Johnsson requested to be exempted from the board, and diplomat Hugo Valvanne was chosen to replace him. Jussi Snellman left the board in 1949 and was replaced as president by Mauno Nordberg, with Leo Hildén being appointed as secretary. Snellman stated as the reason for withdrawing differences in opinion regarding the direction of the society. The specifics of the conflict remain unclear but could potentially be related to Snellman's interest in interpreting and practising Buddhism in the context of Theosophy, while some other members of the society wanted to focus on Buddhism as a separate philosophy and lifestyle. Despite the conflict, Snellman continued as member of board and presenter in group meetings, was appointed as honorary member in 1950 followed by appointment as honorary president and continued to financially support the group into the 1960s. In 1949, Ines Stenroos also replaced Anni Yrjänäinen as treasurer. Ines Stenroos was the owner of a house Nordberg rented outside of Helsinki in Veikkola in the Kirkkonummi municipality, initially for the summer season and later as permanent residence. Aho acted as vice-president for Nordberg until 1954, withdrawing due to literary obligations and being appointed as honorary member of the society. Norberg continued as president until his death on 22 February 1956 at the age of 72 (see Figure 8.1).[9]

Figure 8.1 Gravestone of Mauno Nordberg at Hietaniemi Cemetery, Helsinki, Finland. The gravestone features Nordberg's diplomatic title "Consul General" (*pääkonsuli*), the wheel of dharma (*dhammacakka*), and the phrase *sabbe saṅkhārā aniccā* (all conditioned things are impermanent), which is the first mark of conditioned things alongside *dukkha* (unsatisfactory) and *anattā* (non-self). Photo: Mikko Koponen.

In 1947, the society received an anonymous donation of 100,000 marks, and in addition to this, in the early years, the society received two 100,000 -mark grants from the Iisakki Räsänen Foundation. Jussi Snellman was on the board of the foundation, and records show he was considered to have influenced at least the latter of the two positive grant decisions. The three large grants were used as a nest egg to fund publishing activities, which included, in addition to the publications mentioned before, the following works:

- *Buddhan opin ydin – Kärnan i Buddhas lära* ("Core of Buddha's Teaching") by Mahathera Nyanatiloka, based on a radio hearing from 1934;
- Neljä jaloa tilaa – De fyra upphöjda tillstånden ("Four Sublime States") by Nyanaponika Thera;
- *Karma ja jälleensyntyminen* ("Karma and Rebirth") by Christmas Humphreys
- *Dhamman Perusaatteet* ("Basics of Dhamma") by Sydney M. Whitaker;
- *Buddhan oppi yleismaailmalliseksi elämänohjeeksi* ("Teaching of Buddha as Universal Guide to Living") by Francis Story; and
- *Buddhan oppi ja länsimainen filosofia* ("Teaching of Buddha and Western Philosophy") by Dr. B. E. Fernando.

All these self-publishing works appeared in 1947–1950, and most of the nest egg was spent in their publication. Despite continuing translation work, additional self-publishing items could not be published due to a lack of additional funding. Moreover, further attempts to obtain publication contracts where a publishing house would cover the costs failed. The last publication with an important publishing house was *Buddhismens budskap* which appeared in 1954 (P.A. Norstedt & Söner in Sweden). Even for *Buddhismens budskap*, the society covered the publication costs itself with a 250-pound donation received from the Union Buddha Sasana Council in Burma. Reasons for the difficulty in obtaining publication contracts included low estimated sales of the items and the lack of professional editors knowledgeable in the field. Because of these reasons, the prolific translation and publication activities that had been a core activity of the society during its early years came to a halt by the mid-1950s.

The society held gatherings every second week. During 1948–1956, about eight gatherings were held in total during each autumn term and eight during each spring term. The programme consisted of a presentation, which was typically a reading of a passage currently being translated by members of the society, followed by a discussion regarding its contents in a spirit of *sine ira et studio* ("without anger and passion"). The main presenters were Mauno Nordberg and Leo Hildén. Occasionally, presentations were also held by other members or invited speakers. These include Terttu Harjanne, who had studied philosophy at the University of Helsinki and written her master's thesis on Buddhist philosophy, and who held two presentations in society meetings in 1951. During 1947–1949, in addition to the Finnish-language meetings in Vironkatu, an equal number of meetings were held in the Swedish language in Mauno Nordberg's home in Mariankatu. However, the Swedish-language meetings were discontinued in the autumn term of 1949 due to poor attendance rates. At first, the Finnish-language meetings had tens of participants, but the number dwindled to only a few persons by the spring term of 1953. Since the autumn term of 1953, the meeting space was changed to the Primula Club Space in the city centre, which caused attendance rates to increase to around twenty persons for the following years. Occasionally, international guests would participate in meetings. In most Mays during the years 1946–1956, a *Vesak* celebration was held to commemorate the birth, enlightenment and death of the Buddha. The event was typically small in scale since there were only few participants due to the approaching summer vacation season. A notable exception was the *Vesak* celebration in 1948, which was held as a public event in the hall of Helsingin Suomalainen Yhteiskoulu ("Helsinki Finnish co-educational school") which was located in Nervanderinkatu at the time. The society had been able to acquire Osvald Sirén (1879–1966), Professor of Art History at Stockholm University, as an invited speaker, and he held a presentation entitled *Vad menas med odödlighet enligt Buddhas Lära* ("What is meant by immortality according to the Buddha's Teaching"). There were as many as 350 participants in the event, including several Professors from the University of Helsinki.[10]

In addition to internal events, starting in 1948, Mauno Nordberg and Leo Hildén held a few Finnish or Swedish language presentations on Buddhism in community colleges. Moreover, Nordberg held presentations at several other national and international events. National events include two presentations in the Small Hall of the University of Helsinki in 1951 regarding his trip to Sri Lanka to attend the first WFB General Conference (a public event arranged by the society) and prohibition of alcohol use in Buddhism (annual meeting of Academic Temperance Federation). Furthermore, Nordberg delivered three speeches on public radio through the Finnish Broadcasting Company in 1952–1953 on the reason for his personal Buddhist conviction, peace work by emperor Aśoka, and Buddhism as a religion of peace (the last one being in Swedish). In 1953, Nordberg held Swedish-language presentations on Buddha as a great Indian freethinker in both Stockholm and Oslo. Newspaper stories were written about him in both cities, and the events resulted in the founding of local Buddhist study groups. In addition to this influence, Nordberg promoted Buddhism in other Nordic countries by maintaining correspondence with various Swedish, Norwegian and Danish Buddhists and producing, publishing and distributing Swedish-language literature. Among others, Nordberg corresponded with sister Amita (Ingrid Wagner, 1910–2001), who had received ordination as a nun in Kathmandu and was the first Swedish Buddhist nun. Through invitation by Nordberg, sister Amita also visited the Finnish society on 4 November 1955. That same year (1955), sister Amita founded a Buddhist society with the same name, Buddhismens vänner, in Sweden, and would continue to be a central figure promoting Buddhism in Sweden for several upcoming decades. Nordberg also held numerous presentations in English and French on the activities of Friends of Buddhism, Buddhism in Nordic countries, and his personal views on Buddhism in events organised by the Buddhist Society and Buddhist Vihara Society in London and Les Amis du Bouddhisme in Paris. Nordberg also held personal memberships in all these societies until his death. The foundation for these activities was laid by the widespread and active international and multi-language correspondence with central Buddhist figures he started in 1945. The correspondence was focused on Nordic countries, London and Paris, but covered the whole globe, including Asia and the United States.[11]

Immediately upon the founding of WFB in 1950, Friends of Buddhism became a member society. Already the same year, Nordberg participated in the first WFB General Conference held in Colombo, Sri Lanka, where he met, among others, B. R. Ambedkar (1891–1956), who a few years later, in 1956, would become renowned for his conversion from Hinduism to Buddhism along with half a million people from the Mahar caste. Nordberg was able to participate because WFB covered half of his travel expenses. Nordberg was officially appointed by WFB to oversee propagation of Buddhism (p. *dhammaduta*), and in 1953, he was appointed member of the executive board of WFB. Due to lack of funds, Nordberg was unable to participate in the second General Conference held in Tokyo in 1952. However, thanks to receiving travel reimbursement again, he was able to attend the next event, the third General Conference held in Burma in 1954. Nordberg also managed to get numerous articles laying out his views to be published in international Buddhist journals including *The Buddhist World*, *The Buddhist*, *Light of the Dhamma*, *News Letter*, *La Pensée Bouddhique* and *Vesak Sirisara*. Furthermore, in the 1950s, several

Finnish newspapers, tabloids, and magazines such as *Seura, Ilta-Sanomat*, and *Nya Pressen* published articles featuring the activities of Friends of Buddhism.[12]

Nordberg's philosophy and practice

Nordberg never felt a connection with Theosophical thinking, nor did he feel that Theosophists understood Buddhism correctly despite acknowledging the founders of Theosophy as Buddhists. In particular, Nordberg considered Theosophists to have difficulties grasping the Buddhist concept of non-self (p. *anattā*), which was a subject of debate among Theosophists interested in Buddhism. The concept of non-self holds that the human individual lacks an unchanging essence, such as a soul that transmigrates from one rebirth to another. Instead, all constituents of what is perceived to be a self, including the mind, are in a constant state of change. Although the Theosophical Society allowed Nordberg to connect with other Finnish people interested in Buddhism and, once the Buddhist society had been established, offered them a meeting space, Nordberg did not consider the activities as a part of Theosophy and wanted to avoid creating this image among participants. On the one hand, the exceptional popularity of Theosophy and Rosicrucianism in Finland could be harnessed to propagate Buddhism. On the other hand, Norberg was uncertain whether comradery with Theosophists and Rosicrucianists would be beneficial in the longer term. Nordberg considered the weakening of the perceived connection with Theosophy as one advantage when the meeting space of the Buddhist society changed from the Theosophical Society in Kruununhaka to another space in the city centre in 1953.[13]

One reason for Norberg to avoid connections with Theosophy was his view that Buddhism represents a logical and rational doctrine that is compatible with contemporary philosophy, natural science, medicine and psychology. In particular, Nordberg saw classical Buddhist core teachings, such as the three marks of existence (p. *anicca, anattā*, and *dukkha*, i.e., impermanence, non-self, and unsatisfactoriness), the four noble truths, the noble eightfold path and the five precepts (abstaining from killing, stealing, sexual misconduct, lying and ingesting alcohol), to represent a rational response to the ethical and spiritual needs of the human being. Christianity had failed in this in terms of rationality, while atheism had failed to provide answers to ethical and spiritual needs. There were also practical considerations regarding the topic. One of the apparent target groups for the propagation of Buddhism in the West, including Finland, were persons who had abandoned Christianity. Nordberg felt that using the word "religion" and religious concepts to describe Buddhism would act as a repellent for this key target group. An experience concerning this had been the decline of Finnish Freethinkers in publishing an advertisement for the Friends of Buddhism in their paper. Nordberg engaged for years in heated debate with some of the most notorious Freethinkers in Finland, trying to convince them that Buddhism is not a religion but rather represents a form of Freethought. He considered the sullen attitude of the Freethinkers towards Buddhism as a sign of a shallow understanding of Buddhism and a narrow-minded conception of Freethought. To avoid mixing Buddhism with religiosity akin to

Christianity, Nordberg wished religious concepts to be avoided in presentations on Buddhism. He delivered speeches and wrote about this topic within the Buddhist world, especially after expanding his networks and influence after the first General Conference of the WFB in Colombo, Sri Lanka, in 1950.[14]

Norberg was curious and tolerant towards different schools of Buddhism despite strongly leaning on the Theravāda tradition himself. He read and collected books from all the main schools. His tolerance was both philosophical and practical. On the one hand, he considered all the main schools to exhibit the same core teachings of Buddhism. Even for Tibetan Buddhism, which Nordberg perhaps was least fond of because of its peculiar external form, Nordberg showed an interest by translating works by Alexandra David-Néel into Finnish. He considered them to have entertainment value, which could be used to draw people to become interested in Buddhism, as well as David-Néel to describe Buddhist core teachings in a very profound and precise manner. On the other hand, Nordberg held that Buddhist communities should be tolerant towards different ways of thought and practice. This also applied to the members of Friends of Buddhism, which included, for example, people specifically interested in Zen Buddhism, and where strict adherence to particular doctrinal stances could drive away a part of the membership, which was small to begin with. Despite his tolerance, Nordberg considered Mahāyāna Buddhism to have drifted away from the original teachings represented by the Theravāda tradition in several ways (e.g., allowing marriage among the Japanese clergy) and called for a return to the original teachings.[15]

To understand and spread the original teachings, it was essential to translate original Pali texts into Finnish, and for such work, it would be helpful to have Finnish Buddhist monks. However, because of the small size and scant resources of the Buddhist community, Nordberg did not believe it would be possible to establish a monastic community in Finland. Nevertheless, he utilised all his diplomatic and Buddhist connections to enable his cousin, sea captain Lauri Parviainen, who was interested in monasticism, to become a monk aspirant under Nyanatiloka Mahathera and Nyanaponika Thera on the monastic island of Dodanduwa in Sri Lanka in 1950. However, Parviainen, who was 52 years old at the time, had considerable struggles with adjusting to life in Sri Lanka in terms of health, culture and social relations already within two weeks of arrival, and he returned to the Nordic countries after only a few months. At the same time, there was also a young member of the society, Oleg Naeboe, who was proficient in many languages and demonstrated some interest in monasticism. Nordberg contacted his networks to further the agenda, but the interest never matured into a firm resolve. Nordberg had wished Parviainen could learn the Pali language and overtake translations from Pali into Finnish and that Naeboe, who was better educated and linguistically capable, could also actively work to promote Buddhism in the West. Nordberg had also himself dreamt of retreating into a monastery in the Far East but felt that his family connections were too strong for him to abandon them and that the environmental conditions, including hot climate and spicy food, were too rough to consider pursuing the dream seriously. These experiences led Nordberg to consider it essential for spreading Buddhism to found a monastery in Europe, and in particular, he sought to promote the long-term project of the Buddhist Vihara Society to set up a monastery in London. Under more suitable conditions, the threshold of becoming a monk would be lower, and monasteries in the West would also allow laypeople to spend time in them and directly receive teachings from Buddhist monks.[16]

Nordberg considered the spread of Buddhism to pertain, first and foremost, to increasing understanding, not to attempt to convert people. After being exposed to Buddhist teachings, receptive individuals would naturally seek to become part of a community and start to enact the teachings in their lives. From this perspective, Nordberg's focus on literary pursuits and presentations does not necessarily reflect an intellectual approach to Buddhism, which Nordberg considered primarily to be a comprehensive lifestyle and practical ethical system. Instead, the aspiration behind these endeavours was to facilitate the understanding of Buddhism in Finland, as it was something alien to the culture, and this would, in turn, lead to a decrease in suffering among those following the teachings as well as more widely in society. Nordberg dedicated himself to the latter cause by distributing publications produced by Friends of Buddhism for several years to numerous libraries, schools, sanitaria, hospitals and prisons.[17]

Nordberg considered insufficient funding a critical bottleneck preventing Buddhism from spreading in the West. This prevented the efficient spread of knowledge, the creation of local monasteries and the arrangement of different events. He saw as the only efficient solution to aquire funding in the West from those Asian countries where Buddhism was a predominant religion and enjoyed considerable local funding. Even though the West was more affluent than Asia, the Western Buddhist community was too small to raise much funding for scaling up its activities, while Asian societies were used to enormous financial investments into Buddhism, illustrated, for example, by the construction of magnificent temple complexes. Even a small proportion of such funding would be of great benefit to the spread of Buddhism in the West. As a practical example, in 1953, after two years of requests, Nordberg managed to acquire 250 pounds from the Union Buddha Sasana Council in Burma. As mentioned before, this allowed the society to publish a Swedish translation of a book by Subhadra Bhikkhu (*Buddhismens budskap*) in Sweden with a reputable publisher (P. A. Norstedt & Söner 1954).[18]

Examples of how Buddhism influenced daily life among members of the society include pacifism, vegetarianism and sobriety, which were practised as part of the Buddhist ethical code, as well as meditation practice. Nordberg had personally been a vegetarian for four years while living in Paris. However, he felt living as a vegetarian in Finland was too difficult since a diverse assortment of vegetables was not available throughout the year, and servants would abandon a household serving only vegetarian food. In general, Nordberg was against fanaticism regarding diet. However, sobriety was close to his heart. He associated alcohol use with the spread of Christianity that favoured it, as well as with serious personal and societal problems (health, social relations, and economy), and argued that abstaining from alcohol should be raised from last to first place among the five precepts. The peace movement was also important to Nordberg. A key reason why Buddhism appealed to him was its non-violence, which could be seen as a lack of religious warfare, adjustment to different cultural settings and peaceful coexistence with other religions and philosophies. A classic example was Emperor Aśoka from the third century BCE who united the Indian peninsula through violent conquests but began to support non-violence after converting to Buddhism. Norberg sought to spread the Buddhist message on peace, for example, by planning to give a speech at the World Peace Congress held in Helsinki in 1955.[19]

Nordberg demonstrated an interest in meditation practice already when starting to build his international Buddhist network in 1945. Buddhist societies in London and Paris were studying texts regarding meditation practice and organising meditation sessions. Nordberg hoped that he or other members of Friends of Buddhism could study these texts and practices and introduce them to the activities of Finnish society as well. Even though Nordberg and other members participated in these types of events already earlier and Nordberg distributed meditation instructions to the members already in 1947, the wish was not fulfilled until years later. Nyanaponika Thera had studied *vipassanā* meditation in Burma and written a book on the classic text *Satipaṭṭhāna Sutta* dealing with mindfulness practice, and in connection with writing the book, he had also written a separate text providing practical advice for meditation practice. The book and the separate meditation instructions were translated into Finnish by the society in the early 1950s, and the society held half-hour meditation sessions based on the instructions from the autumn of 1952 to the spring of 1953. However, in the spring of 1953, the number of participants fell so low that it caused the discontinuation of the meditation practice, although some meditation sessions were held later on, at least in 1956. Nordberg's personal interest in meditation grew after he read about the powerful experiences of a Dutch person who had practised *vipassanā* meditation in Burma under U Ba Khin (1899–1971). U Ba Khin was also the teacher of S. N. Goenka (1924–2013) who was later to spread and popularise *vipassanā* meditation worldwide. While participating in the third General Conference of the WFB in Burma in 1954, Nordberg arranged for himself to attend a ten-day *vipassanā* meditation retreat in the centre of U Ba Khin near Rangoon while other conference attendees were on an excursion. After this, Nordberg continued to correspond with U Ba Khin, whom he addressed as his guru, and to practise meditation during the last year of his life, although his practice was irregular and often took place in the nighttime during periods of insomnia.[20]

Nordberg's legacy

Buddhism became Nordberg's passionate pastime during his retirement. The Second World War may have had a decisive influence on this and for Finland to become the stage. The diplomatic (including the title of Consul General) and linguistic (fluent Finnish, Swedish, French, and English) capacities of Nordberg, combined with his widespread network among elite members of Finnish society and key figures in Western Buddhism, made Helsinki, for a moment at the turn of the 1950s, a focal point of the development of Nordic, Western and international Buddhism.

Nordberg also had an influence on the later developments of Finnish Buddhism. Although the society's activities declined during the presidentship of Nordberg's successor, Leo Hildén, Hildén continued the same basic society model of presentations and discussion focused on Theravāda Buddhism and a rational, modern interpretation of the Dhamma until the termination of his presidentship in 1985. Hildén's successor, Mikael Niinimäki (monk Mahapañña/Taehye sunim) took the society in a different direction as he is a practising Buddhist monk with a background in Theosophy, both Theravāda and Mahāyāna ordinations, and has special interest in meditation practice as well as a more welcoming approach to traditional Buddhist cosmology and devotional rituals. Because of these factors and an increasingly diverse Finnish Buddhist scene, Friends of Buddhism was renamed Bodhidharma Association in 1998, reflecting a shift in focus from modernised Theravāda doctrine to Chan Buddhist meditation practice. Nevertheless, as president, Taehye sunim has also maintained much of the modernistic and rationalistic approach to Buddhism of his predecessors, including having a background as a scholar of religious studies, and has not abandoned Theravāda but instead maintains a Buddhayana approach combining Theravāda and Mahāyāna. The society has also continually taken a central stage in promoting Buddhism and advancing the rights of Buddhists in Finnish society. This culminated in 2009 with the founding of the Finnish Buddhist Union (Suomen Buddhalainen Unioni, SBU), to a large extent, through the initiative and efforts of members of the Bodhidharma Association, taking over many of these tasks. Nevertheless, the historical link to Nordberg remains strong, especially through the continued effort to develop and promote a form of Buddhism that is at once true to its original spirit, respectful to its historical and contemporary manifestations, and relevant to Finnish laypeople and Finnish society today.

Notes

1 This work is largely based on the sections on Mauno Nordberg in a recently published scholarly article written in the Finnish language (Cairns & Sunim 2023). The article examines the history of the Buddhismin ystävät ("Friends of Buddhism") organisation and is part of a compendium on Buddhism in Finland (see Härkönen & Cairns 2023). Previous descriptions on Nordberg's activities are limited to subsections in a couple of short nonacademic works on the history of the organisation by members of the society (Sunim 1988, 1997). I was coeditor of the compendium, lead writer of the article, performed all the investigation on the original sources and wrote all the sections on Nordberg. The main original source in the article is an extensive collection of documents and correspondence by Nordberg, starting from 1944 and lasting until Nordberg's death in 1956, archived by the National Library of Finland (National Library 2007). This work also draws from a Finnish-language article coauthored by me (Jääskeläinen, Härkönen & Cairns 2024). The article analyses the Buddhist views and activities of Nordberg in relation to other important national and international social movements of the time, including Theosophy, Freethought, vegetarianism, pacifism and sobriety. I extracted all the historical documents for the manuscript.

2 National Library 2007: Coll. 753.4 Curriculum vitae, Nordberg 1854-04-18, Coll. 753.5 from Hildén to Lounsbery 1956-04-06.

3 National Library 2007: Coll. 753.1 from Nordberg to Lounsbery 1945-05-01, from Nordberg to Murray 1945-10-02, from Nordberg to Roll 1948-03-17, Coll. 753.5 from Hildén to Lounsbery 1956-04-06.

4 National Library 2007: Coll. 753.1 group history and annual report 1947, annual report 1948; Coll. 753.2 minutes from annual meeting 1949-03-02; Coll. 753.5 minutes from annual meeting 1955-02-17; Coll. 753.8 account book 1962–1980.

5 National Library 2007: Coll. 753.1 group history and annual report 1947, Coll. 753.2 annual report 1950.

6 National Library 2007: Coll. 753.1 from Nordberg to Humphreys 1945-07-26, minutes 1946-01-07, from Valvanne to Nordberg 1946-12-08, from Nordberg to Valvanne 1946-12-15.

7 National Library 2007: Coll. 753.1 text entitled "Buddhismin Ystävät", speech by Nordberg at the Buddhist Vihara Society 1948-12-19, Coll. 753.4 minutes from annual meeting 1954-01-21.

8 Finnish Parliament 2021; National Library 2007: Coll. 753.1 group history and annual report 1947, text entitled "Buddhismin Ystävät", Coll. 753.4 from Nordberg to Kaste 1953-01-02.

9 National Library 2007: Coll. 753.1–753.5 group history and annual report 1947, annual reports 1948–1956.

10 National Library 2007: Coll. 753.1–753.5 group history and annual report 1947, annual reports 1948–1956.

11 National Library 2007: Coll. 753.1–753.5 group history and annual report 1947, annual reports 1948–1956.

12 National Library 2007: Coll. 753.1–753.5 group history and annual report 1947, annual reports 1948–1956, Coll. 753.4 from Nordberg to Y Siri Nyana [Francis Allen] 1953-09-05.

13 National Library 2007: Coll. 753.1 from Nordberg to Humphreys 1945-07-26, from Nordberg to Valvanne 1947-04-16, from Nordberg to Horner 1948-11-20, Coll. 753.2 Speech by Nordberg in London 1949-11-20, Coll 753.4 from Nordberg to Kaste 1953-01-23, from Nordberg to Horner 1953-09-25.

14 National Library 2007: Coll. 753.1 text entitled "Buddhismin Ystävät," speech by Nordberg given at the Buddhist Vihara Society 1948-12-19, Coll. 753.2 from Nordberg to "Hermo-& Mielitautilääkäreille" (Nerve and Mental Health Doctors) in February 1950, from Nordberg to Lau 1950-12-01, from Nordberg to Fernando 1950-12-20, Coll. 753.3 in the attachment from Nordberg to Jayawardena 1951-02-17, from Nordberg to Aaltonen 1952-10-27 and 1952-12-23, from Nordberg to Lounsbery 1952-12-09, Coll. 753.4 annual report 1952.

15 National Library 2007: Coll. 753.2 speech by Nordberg in London 1949-11-20, travel accounts by Nordberg read in meetings 1950-01-20 and 1950-09-08, Coll. 753.4 from Nordberg to Kaste 1953-01-23, Coll 753.5 from Nordberg to Stützer 1954-02-08, from Nordberg to Newton 1955-04-14 and 1955-05-29, from Nordberg to Baker 1955-05-28, from Nordberg to the Buddhist Association of Thailand under Royal Patronage 1955-09-14.

16 National Library 2007: Coll. 753.1 from Nordberg to Roll 1948-01-15, Coll. 753.2 annual report 1949, account of president's trip abroad read 1950-01-20, Coll. 753.2 and 753.3 correspondence between Nordberg and Horner, Nordberg and Nyanaponika, Nordberg and Nyanatiloka, Nordberg and Parviainen, and Nordberg and Valvanne in the years 1948–1951, from Nordberg to Allen 1951-05-11, Coll. 753.3 in the attachment from Nordberg to Jayawardena 1951-02-17, from Nordberg to Horner 1952-01-06.

17 National Library 2007: Coll. 753.1 speech by Nordberg at the Buddhist Vihara Society 1948-12-19, Coll. 753.3 annual report 1951, Coll. 753.5 action plan for 1955, from Nordberg to Newton 1955-04-14.

18 National Library 2007: Coll. 753.2 speech by Nordberg in London 1949-11-20, Coll. 753.3 speech by Nordberg to the Olympic delegations from Burma, Sri Lanka and Thailand 1952-08-04, from Nordberg to Dhebvedhi 1952-10-03, Coll. 753.4 annual report 1953.

19 National Library 2007: Coll. 753.1 text entitled "Buddhismin Ystävät," Coll. 753.2 from Nordberg to Horner 1950-02-22, from Nordberg to Dibelius 1950-03-31, Coll. 753.3 annual report 1950, from Nordberg to Hui 1951-02-01, in the attachment from Nordberg to Jayawardena 1951-02-17, from Nordberg to Horner 1951-05-12, from Nordberg to Y Siri Nyana [Francis Allen] 1952-05-03, Coll. 753.4 annual report 1952, from Nordberg to Gokhale 1953-11-21, Coll. 753.5 annual report 1955, from Nordberg to Story 1954-02-24.

20 National Library 2007: Coll. 753.1 group history and annual report 1947, from Nordberg to Lounsbery 1945-05-01, from Nordberg to the Buddhist Society 1948, Coll. 753.2, travel accounts by Nordberg read in meetings held 1950-01-20 and 1950-09-08, Coll. 753.3 annual report 1951, program for autumn term 1952, Coll. 753.4 annual reports 1952 and 1953, from Nordberg to Story 1953-03-26, Coll. 753.5 from Norberg to U Ba Khin 1954-11-17, 1955-04-09 and 1955-05-01, from Nordberg to Y Siri Nyana [Francis Allen] 1955-06-02.

References

Cairns, Johannes and Tae Hye Sunim. 2023. "Buddhismin ystävät: Ensimmäinen buddhalainen yhdistys Suomessa" In *Buddhalaisuus Suomessa*, edited by Mitra Härkönen and Johannes Cairns, 59–86. Helsinki: Finnish Oriental Society.

Damsten, Margareta. 1996. "Ilse Johnsson." *Genos*, 67, 24.

Finnish Parliament. 2021. "*Leo Hildén.*" *Kansanedustajat.* Available at: https://www.eduskunta.fi/FI/kansanedustajat/Sivut/910478.aspx (accessed 14 June 2021).

Harmainen, Antti. 2010. "*Valvanne, Väinö.*" Kansallisbiografia online publication, Studia Biographica 4. Helsinki: Suomalaisen Kirjallisuuden Seura. Available at: http://urn.fi/urn:nbn:fi:sks-kbg-009612 (accessed 2 Jun 2021).

Heikinheimo, Annika. 2016. *Suomi-neito ja Idän Jätti käyvät tanssiin: Kiinan kansantasavallan ja Suomen välinen kulttuurivaihto 1950-ja 1960-luvuilla.* Master's thesis. University of Helsinki, East Asian Studies, Department of World Cultures, May 2016.

Jääskeläinen, Ari-Pekka, Mitra Härkönen and Johannes Cairns. 2024. "Suomen ensimmäisen buddhalaisen yhdistyksen synty ja ajan ylirajaiset virtaukset. *Uskonnontutkija – Religionsforskaren*, 2, 1–17. https://doi.org/10.24291/uskonnontutkija.148096.

Kallenautio, Jorma. 2000. "*Kallinen, Yrjö.*" Kansallisbiografia online publication, Studia Biographica 4. Helsinki: Suomalaisen Kirjallisuuden Seura. Available at: http://urn.fi/urn:nbn:fi:sks-kbg-000763 (accessed 2 Jun 2021).

Karttunen, Klaus. 2017. "Indian Literature in Finland: A Historical Overview." In *Research on India in Finland: Past, present, future*, edited by Xenia Zeiler, 30–43. University of Helsinki, Etelä-Aasian tutkimus & Intian suurlähetystö Suomessa.

Mäkinen, Helka. 2001. "*Snellman, Jussi.*" Kansallisbiografia online publication, Studia Biographica 4. Helsinki: Suomalaisen Kirjallisuuden Seura. Available at: http://urn.fi/urn:nbn:fi:sks-kbg-001187 (accessed 2 Jun 2021).

National Library. 2007. Archive of Buddhismin ystävät ('Friends of Buddhism') provided to the National Library of Finland in 2007 by the Department of Religious Studies, University of Helsinki, primarily from the years 1944–1958 as well as "*Mauno Nordbergin kansio*" ('*Folder of Mauno Nordberg*') received from the same Department in 1999. Manuscript collection of National Library of Finland, signum Coll. 753. 1–753. 10.

Niemi, Juhani. 1998. "*Aho, Juhani.*" Kansallisbiografia online publication, Studia Biographica 4. Helsinki: Suomalaisen Kirjallisuuden Seura. Available at: http://urn.fi/urn:nbn:fi:sks-kbg-002806 (accessed 2 Jun 2021).

Sunim, Tae Hye. 1988. "Buddhismin ystävät r.y. 40 vuotta." *Elonpyörä*, 1988: 41–48.

Sunim, Tae Hye. 1997. *Buddhismin ystävät (Bodhidharma) ry 50 vuotta.* Unpublished account of history of society, recorded by Jarkko Jokinen on 6 May 1997.

Venny. 2021. *Juhani Ahon pojat.* Yle.fi/Vintti service of Finnish Broadcasting Company. Available at: http://vintti.yle.fi/yle.fi/venny/otsikoissa2b.htm (accessed 23 Jun 2021).

9 Buddhism in Iceland

An overlooked companion

Haraldur Hreinsson

Introduction

The story of how Buddhism took roots in Iceland, a sparsely populated island in the subarctic Atlantic with just under 400,000 inhabitants, constitutes an intriguing chapter in the country's modern history. Compared to many other countries in Northwestern Europe, Iceland was a latecomer to the modern era but after things started to move into that direction in the twentieth century, it happened fast (Karlsson 2000; Hreinsson 2022). In the first part of the century, the shift from rural farming to industrialised fishing caused a socioeconomic transformation around the country. People moved from the countryside to the villages growing along the coastal line and Reykjavík became the island's largest urban centre with educational institutions and a cultural elite (Pétursson 2017). At the same time, the religious field was loosening up: Ideas like religious freedom found their way to the agenda (Hugason 2022) and the religious monopoly of the Lutheran church became religious hegemony (Pétursson and Valdimarsdóttir 2000). In the century's second half, globalising processes began shaping Icelandic society both through emigration and immigration although it was not until the twenty-first century that Iceland could be described as an "immigrant country" with one of the highest immigration rates in Europe (Skaptadóttir and Garðarsdóttir 2020).

Up until the 1980s, Iceland was a religiously homogenous country. As elsewhere in the Nordic countries, the Lutheran majority church dominated the religious landscape and most other religious denominations were Christian as well. In the course of the twentieth century, religious diversity has slowly but gradually increased. In the history of increasing religious pluralism in Iceland, Buddhism enjoys a different place than other major religious traditions as it was introduced earlier and by way of different trajectories (Sigurvinsson 2014). First introduced through writings and translation work of intellectuals in the late nineteenth and early twentieth century, it would later become a topic of special interest in theosophical circles. Well into the second half of the twentieth century, Buddhism would stay a mostly non-practised topic of fascination amongst theosophists, artists and intellectuals. In the late 1970s and 1980s, active interest in Buddhism began to extend itself beyond such circles, leading to the establishing of a number of groups, which had the religious

DOI: 10.4324/9781003529767-9

practice of Buddhism as their main purpose. This change can be explained in light of increased immigration from countries where Buddhism is a majority religion in the late 1970s and the 1980s, most significantly Thailand and Vietnam, but also the attraction of Buddhism to individuals seeking religious answers outside Icelandic mainstream Christianity. Some of these groups have now been discontinued but currently, there are six officially registered Buddhist groups active in Iceland and at least one Buddhist inspired meditation group operating less formally. All of these groups are small, even on Icelandic standards, with the largest one, the Icelandic Buddhist Society, counting 1.066 members in 2024. Other groups have around 200 officially registered members at most.

While this story has its idiosyncratic aspects and peculiar moments, it also follows to a significant extent patterns known from the other Nordics. The well-known model of the "two Buddhisms," for example, which categorises Buddhists in the West into groups of ethnic Asians or "migrant Buddhists" and non-Asian converts or "convert Buddhists" (Numrich 2003), can be applied fairly well to the Icelandic case. Two of the six Buddhist groups registered in Iceland can be categorised as "migrant Buddhist" groups and four as "convert groups" even though one group of these four can be seen to elude the distinction since most of the convert Buddhists in the group are also migrants in Iceland, only not from Asian countries.

The following chapter will provide an overview of Buddhism in Iceland with the intention of mapping a rather unexplored territory. Its source material consists of various types of data. While Buddhism has been addressed as marginal concern in a few research projects (Gunnell 2003; Tran 2015), there is only one single study which has Buddhism in Iceland as its main subject of research. In a pioneering work of research, only available in Icelandic in the form of a master's thesis, Bjarni Randver Sigurvinsson (2014) traced the history of Buddhism in Iceland for the first time on grounds of vast amounts of published material on the topic, both printed and on the web. For the present chapter, Sigurvinsson's study has proven an invaluable source of information but granted how much has happened in the field in the last decade, other sources had to be consulted as well. Thus, the chapter relies to a considerable degree on information collected during field work carried out in 2024 with the intention of including Iceland in a joint mapping study of Nordic Buddhism.[1] In line with such an approach, and reflecting the limited research available on the topic, the chapter is concerned with documenting and describing the field while still at the same time attempting to place the information available in different contexts, local, regional and global.

Early interest

Around the end of the nineteenth century, Buddhism begins to appear, not very frequently though, in the country's emerging public press. Before, Icelandic adventurers had encountered Buddhism on their travels through Asia as early as the seventeenth century but the references to the religious practices they encountered in their travelogues are negative and not very informative.[2]

Among the first Icelandic intellectuals to actively express interest in Buddhism was the pastor-poet Matthías Jochumsson (1835–1920). In his time, Jochumsson was a well-known figure in Icelandic society, an editor of a journal, a playwright, translator and a poet and also at the forefront when it came to offering an alternative to the Lutheran orthodoxy which had dominated the Icelandic religious landscape for centuries. One aspect of this alternative was openness to other Christian denominations and other religions but Jochumsson himself has been shown to have leaned towards Unitarism in his religious thought (Kristjánsson 2020). He is also known to have debated the veracity of Buddhism with his friends (Pétursson 2006). In 1899 he published his translation of the treatise "Karma: A Story of Buddhist Ethics" by the philosopher Paul Carus (1852–1919) in the journal of the Icelandic literary society and an important platform for intellectual exchange in the cultural scene in the nineteenth and twentieth centuries.[3]

The primary venue for introducing Buddhism in Iceland in the early twentieth century was the Theosophical Society (Icel. Guðspekifélagið). The Theosophical Society in Iceland was the fifth biggest in Europe and proportionally larger than in most other places. Since its founding in 1920, Buddhism was a frequent topic in lectures, articles, booklets and books. Hinduism was also regularly discussed but both religious traditions were seen as providing a background to the society's core ideas. Particularly the society's journal, *Gangleri*, was a significant vehicle for introducing Buddhism and the most active proponent was the long-term president of the Theosophical Society, Grétar Fells (1896–1968).

Around the middle of the century, in 1955, a special chapter devoted to the study of Buddhism was founded within the society. As Bjarni Randver Sigurvinsson (2014) has maintained, this group, named Daybreak (Icel. Dögun), can be seen as the first Buddhistic religious group in Iceland. It was led by the journalist Sigvaldi Hjálmarsson (1921–1985) who would in the coming years pen a multitude of article on Buddhism, particularly Tibetan Buddhism. He would also translate Lobsang Rampa's *The Third Eye* (Rampa 1957), long before the book and its author became controversial. In the course of the 1960s, with new authors and editors, most importantly Sverrir Bjarnason (b. 1938), Zen Buddhism would also come to receive attention.

The reception of Buddhism and Buddhist religious discourses in Iceland has not proven controversial although some critical voices were heard from missionary circles and lay groups inspired by the revivalist movements. In his introductory textbook to the world's religions from 1954, Sigurbjörn Einarsson (1911–2008), professor at the faculty of theology at the country's only university at the time, Buddhism was, for the first time, presented from a scholarly point of view. Einarsson, who later became the bishop of the Icelandic national church (1959–1981), had studied classics and comparative religion in Uppsala between 1933 and 1937. Although his text was well received among Buddhist enthusiasts like Sigvaldi Hjálmarsson, the editor of the Theosophical journal *Gangleri*, who even recommended it to his readers, it is also explicitly critical towards Buddhist ethics, as it appears, from a Christian point of view.

Practising Buddhism in Iceland

Before introducing the Buddhist groups active in Iceland, both past and present, a short note on statistics is in order. The statistical information available is provided by the Statistics Iceland (Icel. Hagstofa Íslands), the official institute responsible for all statistics of the Icelandic state, including membership numbers of registered religious groups which receive a part of their members' income tax. While such numbers provide reliable information about the outlines of the religious landscape, they should be taken with the precondition that they do not give insights into the finer developments and less formalised movements in the religious field. With this in mind, the total number of members in the six Buddhist groups in Iceland is 1 659 which amounts to around 0.45 per cent of the Icelandic population (Statistics Iceland 2024). The number of members formally registered in Buddhist religious groups is, however, only one way to account for the number of Buddhists. While no formal research has been carried out on this topic, there are nonetheless good reasons to assume for a higher number of Buddhists in Iceland. Of course, the questions about Buddhist identity, that is as to who ultimately should be counted as a Buddhist, complicates such speculations. Counting people according to religious identity in East Asia is very difficult and does not get easier when counting immigrants (Borup 2016a). However, the fact that the number of people born in largely or predominantly Buddhist countries is double as high as the people registered in the two Thai Buddhist groups in Iceland indicates that the number of Asian Buddhists in Iceland is higher than the official numbers indicate. The number of people born in Vietnam, a country where approximately half of the population is considered Buddhists, living in Iceland in 2024, for example, was 1602, not including their descendants (Statistics Iceland 2024). Unlike elsewhere in the Nordic countries, Vietnamese Buddhists in Iceland have not founded a temple nor organised their religious activities in a formal way. Some of them might be registered in other Buddhist groups but not all of them are.

Migrant Buddhist groups

The members of the so-called migrant Buddhist groups consist predominantly of immigrants from countries in South or Southeast Asia – and often their descendants – where Buddhism is adhered to by a large or an overwhelming part of the population. In the Icelandic context, the larger and more established of the two groups of such nature is the Icelandic Buddhist Society (Icel. Hið íslenska búddistafélag), the members of which are predominantly of Thai origin. For those belonging to such groups, formally or informally, the significance of the group – even if it is a formally registered religious affiliation – is not only religious. Such groups also play an important role for the members' identity in a broader sense as spaces where people can feel a sense of belonging to a "culture" in the sense of shared place of origin, shared language, history and diverse customs.

In 2024, the members of the Icelandic Buddhist Society were 1.066. It operates one Theravada temple in Kópavogur in Reykjavík capital area with four to five monks present at each time. The members are predominantly of Thai origin, but the Temple explicitly welcomes Buddhists of different nationalities, especially mentioning Sri Lankans, Chinese, Vietnamese and Icelanders (Icelandic Buddhist Society 2024). The growth of the Icelandic Buddhist Society goes hand in hand with late twentieth-century social developments like urbanisation and globalisation. While obviously not unique to Iceland, Icelandic society was impacted by these processes in its own way, in particular as the fish industry on the North Atlantic rim was becoming increasingly globalised (Skaptadóttir and Wojtynska 2008). These were the decades when the capital area was growing fast and pulling people away from the coastal towns around the country where fishing industry had been central for the town life. The staff shortage in the fish processing industry was to a significant degree met with labour migration. Immigrants from Thailand have been prominent among the immigrant workers in the fishing industry. The first Thai immigrant settled in Iceland in 1978 and immigration continued steadily through the 1980s and 1990s. A majority of Thai immigrants consists of women who came to the country in order to work in its fast-growing fishing industry or because of marriage relationship to Icelanders (Gisladottir Bissat 2013).

The Icelandic Buddhist Society was founded in 1995 around the growing Thai population with support provided from the Thai-Icelandic Association which had been founded in 1988. Important figures in the founding of the Icelandic Buddhist Society was Andrea Sompit Siengboon (b. 1956), an immigrant from Thailand, and the English Theravada monk Dhammanando Bhikku (b. 1965, née Robert T. Eddisson), who had originally come to Iceland to visit a pen friend of his but decided to stay and support Siengboon and others in the Icelandic Thai community to organise the new Icelandic Buddhist Society.[4] One individual of Icelandic origin has received ordination as a monk although he abandoned monkhood very soon after ordination. A number of people of Icelandic origin also belong to the group but mostly the spouses of people of Thai origin. An explicit function of the society is to make the culture of Theravada Buddhism accessible to immigrants and their descendants (Icelandic Buddhist Society 2024). In addition to regular temple worship, the society offers summer schools for members' children and retreats in a summerhouse owned by the society in Miðhúsaskógur in the South of Iceland. The temple also serves Theravada Buddhists outside the capital area, for example, in the town of Akureyri in the North and the village of Hella in the South. As all formally registered religious groups in Iceland are entitled to applying for a plot of land for their buildings of worship, the municipality of Reykjavík has allotted to the group a plot of land for the building of new land. Currently, however, due to financial reasons, the society does not have any intention of building on the land in the near future.

In 2022, another Thai temple, Wat Phra Dhammakaya Iceland or the Wat Buddha Iceland, was formally registered in Iceland belonging to the Dhammakāya tradition. In 2024 the group had 158 registered members. Without formal statal recognition, the group has been operating longer or since around 2016 in Reykjanesbær in the southwest corner of the country where the temple is also located. As has been pointed out by scholars, the Dhammakāya movement can be understood as part of modernising impulses within Thai Buddhism and has been described εs a new religious movement or a "new Buddhistic movement" (McKenzie 2007). Since the movement's beginning in the 1970s, it has attracted much attention and given rise to controversy both in Thailand and elsewhere, for example, because of its novel approaches to meditation and market-oriented recruitment methods. The Dhammakāya temple in Iceland shows several characteristics of such tendencies, if only when considering the interiors and furnishing of the temple, which is in stark contrast with temples belonging to the more established traditions of Thai Buddhism. The group also advertises meditation courses in a "meditation school" (Icel. Hugleiðsluskóli) open to all.

Unlike Thai Buddhists, Vietnamese Buddhists in Iceland have not engaged in the founding of a temple or, for that matter, formed any formal organisation around their religious activities. Some attempts have been made, through visits of Vietnamese monks, to initiate organised religious activities, but without success. A reason commonly given for the lack of religious organising amongst Vietnamese Buddhists in Iceland is the extent to which their religiosity is restricted to peoples' homes. This element is for example strongly emphasised by ethnologist Terry Gunnell (2003) who interviewed Vietnamese refugees in Iceland in the early 2000s.

Convert Buddhists

There are four convert Buddhist groups in Iceland, all relatively small in size, ranging from a member number of 35 to a number of 207 (Statistics Iceland 2024). These are the Soka Gakkai in Iceland, Zen in Iceland – Night pasture, Tibetan Buddhists and The Icelandic Diamond Way Centre. There is not much interaction between the groups although there are examples of people moving between groups or "trying out" different approaches. Most of the groups have also participated in interfaith work in the context of the Icelandic Interfaith Forum.

The Icelandic branch of the Japanese Buddhist movement Soka Gakkai was founded in 1980. Compared to other Buddhist groups in Iceland, Soka Gakkai has a relatively long history although the group was not formally registered as a religious group in Iceland until 2008. The founder of the group and its current spokesperson is Eygló Jónsdóttir (b. 1957). The first members came into contact with Soka Gakkai in England and while the group has maintained strong ties with the English Soka Gakkai movement, the group has through the years mainly consisted of Icelandic practitioners. Participation of people of diverse origin has increased in the last years, including people from Japan, Brazil, Poland and Lithuania. In accordance with the Soka Gakkai movement's strong emphasis on peace work, the Icelandic group has been active in such operations in Iceland. Thus, it has in cooperation with other groups and institutions, organised large-scale annual peace events like the Reykjavik Peace March on December 23 and a candle-floating vigil on Reykjavík Pond to commemorate the victims of the nuclear bombings in Nagasaki and Hiroshima. Registered members in 2024 are 153. The group has a youth division and several local groups around the country. It has, furthermore, made writings of Daisaku Ikeda (1928–2023), a central figure and the long-term leader of the Soka Gakkai International movement, accessible in Icelandic translation but his book, *One by One: The World Is Yours to Change* (Icel. Baráttan fyrir mannúðlegu samfélagi: Samræður um frið) (Ikeda 2021), was translated by one of the leading members of the Icelandic division, Eyrún Ósk Jónsdóttir (b. 1981).

The largest Buddhist convert group in Iceland, counting 201 members in 2024, is Zen in Iceland: Night Pasture (Icel. Zen á Íslandi: Nátthagi). The beginnings of the group can be traced back to 1985 to a seminar organised by a few people interested in Zen. Before, Zen had been introduced in Iceland by the author Vésteinn Lúðvíksson (b. 1944). Lúðvíksson, who later left the group, is also the translator of Shunryū Suzuki's *Zen Mind, Beginner's Mind* (Icel. *Zen-hugur, hugur byrjandans*), published in Icelandic in 1986. The group was formally registered as a religious group in 1999 and the first official leader of the group was the Chinese American teacher Jakusho Kwong (b. 1935), a disciple of Shunryū Suzuki (b. 1904) and his son Hoitzu Suzuki (b. 1939). Jakusho Kwong has visited Iceland on multiple occasions and actively participated in interfaith activities in Iceland as the leader of Zen in Iceland. Icelandic Zen practitioners have, in turn, also visited Kwong's centre, Sonoma Mountain Zen Center in Northern California. The current teacher of the group is Ástvaldur Traustason (b. 1966) who received dharma transmission from Kwong in 2018 and subsequently became the group's leader. A second teacher at the group and its former leader is Helga Jóakimsdóttir (b. 1940) who received ordination from Kwong in 2011. Zen-Night Pasture has attracted people from the Icelandic cultural scene, painters, writers and musicians. Notable is also that the current group leadership – the group's registered director and one of four ordained priests – includes two internationally recognised businessmen Zen. Nátthagi has appealed to people across religious affiliations including pastors from the Lutheran national church and the group's mediation course offer is specifically directed to people "irrespective of religious affiliation and world views" (Zen Nátthagi, 2024).

Like elsewhere in the Nordics, Tibetan Buddhism has gained ground in Iceland through convert circles. Before actual Tibetan Buddhist groups were organised and established, Icelandic supporters of the fourteenth Dalai Lama had been writing about the Tibetan cause in newspapers and his autobiography was translated in 1990 by Gísli Þór Gunnarsson (b. 1958). Tibetan Buddhism has also been introduced at events organised by the Friends of India Club (Icel. Indlandsvinafélagið) which has now been discontinued. At least one trip to Tibet has been organised by the Chinese Icelandic Culture Club (Icel. Kínversk-íslenska menningarfélagið) in 2006. The first Icelandic individual to visit the Dalai Lama and convert was Þórhalla Björnsdóttir (b. 1950), who attended a month-long meditation course in Tibet in 1975 after finishing her studies in social work in Denmark. Björnsdóttir lived for many years among Tibetan refugees in Nepal and North India and has since then organised visits of Tibetan Buddhist lecturers and led a preparation group for the visit of the Dalai Lama to Iceland in 2009. Furthermore, Björnsdóttir also was a driving force in the building of the only Buddhist *stūpa* in Iceland (see Figure 9.1), which was ordained by her teacher, the Tibetan Buddhist lama Thubten Zopa Rinpoche (1946–2023).

In 2004, a Tibetan inspired mediation group was founded by Dagmar Vala Hjörleifsdóttir (b. 1951), a veterinarian, and her husband Halldór Jónsson (b. 1951),

Figure 9.1 The only stūpa in the North Atlantic. The *stūpa* "Descent from Tushita Heaven" is situated in Kópavogur, Reykjavík Capital area. The building of the stūpa was encouraged by Þórhalla Björnsdóttir and consecrated by Lama Zopa on the 18th of November 1993. Photo: Katarina Plank.

a medical doctor. In her introduction book to meditation (2023), Hjörleifsdóttir has described how she came into contact with Tibetan mediation practice as she and her husband were living and working in development aid in Malawi. There she attended a meditation course with the South African mediation teacher Rob Nairn (1939–2023), a former criminology professor in Cape Town, who would later come to Iceland and give courses. Subsequently Hjörleifsdóttir and Jónsson established further contacts with the Kagyu Samye Ling Monastery and Tibetan Center, north of Lockerbie in Scotland, where Hjörleifsdóttir studied meditation with Chöje Akong Tulku (1939–2013), the monastery's founder. In 2004 they founded a Tibetan Buddhist meditation centre in Iceland, Kagyu Samye Dzong in Reykjavík. Within the confines of the Kagyu Samye Dzong an official religious group has been established, the Tibetan Buddhist Association in Iceland (Icel. Félag Tíbet búddista), counting 46 members in 2024. The group has made relevant reading material accessible in Icelandic, for example, Rob Nairn's *Diamond Mind: A Psychology of Meditation* (Icel. Demantshugur: Sálfræði hugleiðslunnar) (Nairn 2016) and Hjörleifsdóttir herself has composed her own introduction to meditation, *The Rain Drop on the Window: About Meditation* (Icel. Dropinn á rúðunni: Um hugleiðslu) (Hjörleifsdóttir 2023).

Since 2020, a Buddhist group belonging to the originally Danish tradition of the Diamond Way, inseparable with the names of Hannah Nydahl (1946–2007) and Ole Nydahl (b. 1941), has been registered as an official religious group. The group has, however, been active longer, or since 2010 when three people began meeting for meditation under the prescript of the Diamond Way (Buddhist Center Reykjavík, 2024). Unlike other Buddhist convert groups in Iceland, the leadership and active core of the Diamond Way Center in Iceland consists predominantly of immigrants (from Slovakia, Czech Republic, Poland, USA) who converted to Buddhism before they moved to Iceland. The Diamond Way belongs to the Karma Kagyu lineage of Tibetan Buddhism. Thus, in the Icelandic context, the Diamond Way Buddhist Center in Reykjavík can be understood to defy the categorisation between "migrant" and "convert" groups as the "converts" are to a significant also migrants in Iceland, although not from Asian countries. The Diamond Way in Iceland has published a translation of one book by Lama Ole Nydahl, *The Way Things Are: A Living Approach to Buddhism in Today's World* (Icel. *Hvernig hlutirnir eru: Inngangur að fræðum Búdda sniðinn að þörfum nútímafólks*) (Nydahl, 2021). In 2024, the group counted 35 members.

For several years, from 1998 and well into the 2000s, a Buddhist group belonging to the New Kadampa Tradition was actively operating in Iceland, led by the English monk Kelsang Drubchen until 2002 when the nun, Gen Kelsang Ani-la Nyingpo, also English, took over the leadership. The group was called Karuna (Sanskrit for compassion), a name specifically chosen by the founder of the New Kadampa Tradition, Geshe Kelsang Gyatso (1931–2022). Karuna was visible in the public sphere while it operated, organising many events, courses and lectures, publicly advertised in the media and school buildings. In 2001, it organised a blessing ceremony attended by over 100 international guests, including thirty monks and nuns in a layover stop in Iceland on their way to New York in order to participate in a celebration with Kelsang Gyatso. The blessing ceremony was devoted to the Buddhist deity Dorje Shugden which was the source of a major controversy between the New Kadampa Tradition and the Dalai Lama around the turn of the millennium.

Of less organised nature has been the contribution of the Puertorican José M. Tirado (b. 1959), an American Buddhist teacher who has lived in Iceland since 2002. Originally, Tirado identified with Tibetan Buddhism in the tradition of his teacher Dzogchen Pönlop and served as a Buddhist chaplain in hospitals in the United States. After developing a critical stance towards his Tibetan lineage, he changed his allegiance to Japanese Shin Buddhism. After moving to Iceland, the native home of his wife, Tirado began publishing articles in Icelandic newspapers about spiritual matters and furthermore offer a course based on Buddhist meditation called The Path of My Experience. In the 2010s, after enrolling in the University of Iceland's School of Education, where he has submitted his doctoral dissertation, he has led the university's meditation group (Icel. Hugleiðsluhópur Háskólans) which has been allotted a small room in the University's main building and furthermore attracted a considerable following on social media (480 members in June 2024). Tirado's emphasis on meditation, given that Shin Buddhism in Japan traditionally does not lay any weight on meditation, is in line with developments in Western countries, especially the United States, where such practices have become more prominent.

Secular Buddhism and individual explorations

So far, the discussion has been concerned with different forms of organised and collective religious practices, but in this last section, it will be considered how Buddhism has made its impact in Iceland through the explorations and expressions of individuals, both in explicit articulations of their worldview but also in artistic creation and in less elevated modes of self expression, for example, through interior design and garden commodities. It should also be noted that the meditative practice of "mindfulness," with its strong roots in Asian meditation, has, like elsewhere in the Nordics (Enstedt & Plank 2023), found its way into many sectors of Icelandic society: schools, medical institutions, companies and religious organisations like the Lutheran national church.

Like elsewhere in the Nordic countries (Borup 2016b), Buddhism has in the last decades earned a place in Iceland's public sphere for example through depictions of a smiling Buddha in advertisement material or the decorative ornaments of hair salons. As part of the manifestation of religion in the cultural sphere which collectively has been termed "banal religion" (Hjarvard 2012), such representations usually are not intended to convey any direct religious meaning. They exhibit, however, clearly that Iceland is no exception when it comes to the presence of Buddhism through its mediatisation and marketisation in the West (Borup 2016b).

On a more elaborate level, some of Buddhism's central ideas have been consciously employed in artistic creation. While well-known artists like the musician Björk [Guðmundsdóttir] (b. 1961) and comedian and former mayor of Reykjavík Jón Gnarr (b. 1967) have expressed their positive attitude towards Buddhism and (in Björk's case) even personal experience of practising Zen Buddhism, it speaks more for the popular appeal of Buddhism as a "cool" religion (Borup 2016b) than its intentional employment in the artistic creation of these individuals. Other artists have been more explicit in their use of Buddhistic thought in their artistic creation. One example is visual artist Gabríela Friðriksdóttir (b. 1971), a friend of Björk but also a member of Zen Nátthagi and the daughter of one the group's ordained priests mentioned earlier, Helga Jóakimsdóttir. Another example, particularly prominent in recent years, is the visual artist Tolli (Þorlákur Kristinsson Morthens; b. 1953) who has on multiple occasions expressed his enthusiasm for Tibetan Buddhism, especially after his visit to Tibet organised by the Chinese Icelandic Culture Club in 2006. He has, furthermore, been involved in the activities of the Tibetan Buddhist Meditation Center and illustrated a recent publication of the centre's director, Dagmar Vala Hjörleifsdóttir.

Buddhistic thought also found an intriguing and rather unexpected outlet in artistic creation in the films of director Hrafn Gunnlaugsson (b. 1948), who has described his fondness of Zen Buddhism without explicitly identifying as Buddhist. In the course of the late 1980s and early 1990s, he made three films, sometimes referred to as the "Viking-trilogy," where he consciously brings together Zen Buddhism and the story world of the medieval Icelandic sagas.[5] In these films, Gunnlaugsson can also be shown to critically engage with the Christian religion, especially the retributive ethics he associates with the Hebrew Bible, by sometimes reshaping or even replacing the medieval Christian religious background of the period with elements from Buddhism. Thus, scenes taking place in medieval Ireland, an important background context for the settlement of Iceland in the ninth century, portray a cultural context which resembles Japanese Buddhism more than the historically accurate Celtic Christianity (Sigurvinsson, 2014).

Concluding remarks

The many-sided history of Buddhism in Iceland constitutes an overlooked chapter in the modern and contemporary history of a small, insular society in the North Atlantic. While this story contains many distinct and even unique elements, it is also thoroughly intertwined with the sociohistorical processes which within the course of a century transformed Icelandic society into a modern state, shaped by liberal democracy and the global market economy. In its own, unobtrusive way, Buddhism has accompanied Icelandic society over many significant milestones on its way into the modern era.

As soon as the domination of Lutheran Orthodoxy began to loosen up in the late nineteenth century and currents of religious liberty found its way to Icelandic shores, Buddhism attracted the attention of intellectuals and free thinkers in various circles. This was the beginning of the religious individualism which has only grown stronger in the course of the twentieth century and, as some examples in the discussion above have shown, Buddhism has enjoyed a prominent role in the spiritual explorations of Icelanders which furthermore has also found intriguing artistic outlets. It is indicative of Buddhism's role in this development that, apart from Christian denominations, no other religion has as many officially recognised religious groups as Buddhism.

In the last half a century or so, immigration to Iceland has steadily increased and is arguably the social change which has impacted Icelandic society the most in the period. Although it has been part of the history of immigration since the 1970s, when the first Vietnamese refugees arrived in the country, Buddhism has largely remained in the background, in both public discourse and scholarly debate. Also of significance in this context is the extent to which the topic of immigration is interwoven with the socioeconomic shifts related to the transformation of the fishing industry, the country's most important source of revenue in the century. As noted earlier, a significant proportion of the immigrant workers in the fish processing factories came from East Asian countries like Thailand and Vietnam and many of them were practising Buddhists.

Although the present chapter has covered the central components in the history of Buddhism in Iceland, it still only provides the rough outlines of a rich and multilayered story which remains largely unwritten. In one sense, this is a regrettable state of affairs, which can, to a large degree, be explained by the absence of religious studies as a functioning scholarly discipline in Icelandic academia. In another sense, it is exciting as it offers plenty of opportunities for future scholars in all fields of the humanities and social sciences to continue writing the story.

Notes

1 The author thanks Jørn Borup, Mitra Härkönen, Knut Axel Jacobsen, and Katarina Plank for enriching cooperation and conversations during field research in Iceland in February 2024.
2 Both Jón Ólafsson (1594–1679) "the India-Traveller" and Árni Magnússon of Geitastekkur (18th c.) encountered Buddhism in Sri Lanka (Ceylon). In his travelogue, Árni Magnússon describes local customs negatively and the people on the island as "heathens" (Árni Magnússon 1945).
3 Paul Carus, "Karma: Frásaga byggð á skoðunum hinna elztu Buddatrúarmanna," transl. by Matthías Jochumsson, *Tímarit hins íslenska bókmenntafjelags* 20 (1899): 217–234.
4 The documentary *Act Normal* (2006) by Olaf de Fleur (Ólafur Jóhannesson) (b. 1975) is devoted to Dhammanando Bhikku's life course, tracing it from his youth and adolesence in his native England, to places like Thailand, Iceland and Kazakhstan.
5 The films are *When the Raven Flies* (Icel. *Hrafninn flýgur*; 1984), *In the Shadow of the Raven* (Icel. *Í skugga hrafnsins*, 1988), and *The White Viking* (Icel. *Hvíti víkingurinn*, 1991). Because of an artistic disagreement with the producer of the last film, *The White Viking*, director Gunnlaugsson disowned the version, which appeared in 1991. In 2007, his directors-cut version of the film appeared named *Embla*.

Bibliography

Borup, J. 2016a. "Who are these Buddhists and How Many of Them are There: Theoretical and Methodological Challenges in Counting Immigrant Buddhists: A Danish Case Study." *Journal of Contemporary Religion*, 31, 85–100.

Borup, J. 2016b. "Branding Buddha – Mediatized and Commodified Buddhism as Cultural Narrative." *Journal of Global Buddhism*, 17, 41–55.

The Iceland Diamond Way Centre. 2024. *Buddhist Center Reykjavík*. Available at: https://buddismi.is/

Enstedt, D. and Plank, K. (eds.). 2023. *Eastern Practices and Nordic Bodies: Lived Religion, Spirituality and Healing in the Nordic Countries*. Cham: Palgrave Macmillan.

Gisladottir Bissat, J. 2013. "Effects of Policy Changes on Thai Migration to Iceland." *International Migration*, 51, 46–59.

Gunnell, T. 2003. "Vatnið og uppsprettan: Þjóðtrú og þjóðsiðir víetnamskra innflytjenda í Reykjavík," *Skírnir*, 177, 89–108.

Hjarvard, S. 2012. "Three Forms of Mediatized Religion: Changing the Public Face of Religion." In *Mediatization and Religion: Nordic Perspectives*, edited by Stig Hjarvard and Mia Lövheim, 21–44. Gothenburg: Nordicom, University of Gothenburg.

Hreinsson, H. (2022. "Sagas and Secularity: The (Re)Construction of Secular Literature in 20th-Century Iceland." *Working Paper Series of the CASHSS "Multiple Secularities – Beyond the West, Beyond Modernities,"* 24. Leipzig: Leipzig University

Hjörleifsdóttir, D. V. 2023. *Dropinn á rúðunni: Um hugleiðslu*, Reykjavík: Völur.

Hugason, H. 2022. "Þróun trúfrelsis á Íslandi 1874–1915: Umræður og lagarammi." *Studia Theologica Islandica*, 22, 20–43.

Icelandic Buddhist Association (Icel. Búddistafélag Íslands). 2024. วัดไทยไอซ์แลนด์/*búddist Í Íslands*. Available at: http://www.watthaiiceland.net/ (accessed: 23 May 2024).

Ikeda, D. 2021. *Baráttan fyrir mannúðlegu samfélagi: Samræður um frið*. Translated by Eyrún Ósk Jónsdóttir. Reykjavík: Sögur.

Karlsson, G. 2000. *The History of Iceland*. Minnesota: University of Minnesota Press.

Kristjánsson, G. 2020. *Úr hugarheimi séra Matthíasar*. Reykjavík: Ugla.

Nydahl, O. 2021. *Hvernig hlutirnir eru: Inngangur að fræðum Búdda sniðinn að þörfum nútímafólks*. Translated from Danish. Reykjavík: Félag Demantsleiðar Búddismans.

Magnússon, Á. 1945. *Ferðasaga Árna Magnússonar frá Geitastekk: 1753–1797*, edited by Björn K. Þórólfsson. Reykjavík: Heimdallur.

McKenzie, R. 2007. *New Buddhist Movements in Thailand: Towards an Understanding of Wat Phra Dhammakaya and Santi Asoke*. London: Routledge.

Nairn, Rob. 2016. *Demandshugur: Sálfræði hugleiðslunnar*, Translated by Árni Óskarsson. Reykjavík: Völur.

Numrich, P. D. 2003. "Two Buddhisms Further Considered." *Contemporary Buddhism*, 4, 55–78.

Pétursson, P. and Valdimarsdóttir, Þ. 2000. *Til móts við nútímann*. Kristni á Íslandi IV. Reykjavík: Alþingi.

Pétursson, P. 2006. "Deilan um Þyrna Þorsteins Erlingssonar: Guðmundur Hannessson læknir gegn guðfræðingunum Jóni Helgasyni og Haraldi Níelssyni." *Studia Theologica Islandica*, 23, 155–172.

Pétursson P. 2017. *Church and Social Change: A Study of the Secularization Process in Iceland since 1830*, 3rd ed. Reykjavík: Pétur Pétursson.

Rampa, Lobsang T. 1957. *Þriðja augað: Sjálfsævisaga tíbezks lama*. Translated by Sigvaldi Hjálmarsson. Reykjavík.

Skaptadóttir, U. D. and Wojtynska, A. 2008. "Labour Migrants Negotiating Places and Engagements." In *Mobility and Place: Enacting Northern European Peripheries*, edited by Jørgen Ole Bærenholdt and Brynhild Granås. Aldershot: Ashgate, 115–125.

Skaptadóttir, U. D. and Garðarsdóttir, Ó. 2020. "Becoming an Immigration Country: The Case of Iceland 1990–2019." In *Mobility and Transnational Iceland: Current Transformations and Global Entanglements*, edited by Kristín Loftsdóttir, Unnur Dís Skaptadóttir, and Sigurjón Baldur Hafsteinsson, 23–38. Reykjavík: University of Iceland Press.

Sigurvinsson, B. R. 2014. "Búddismi á Íslandi: Einstaklingshyggjutrú og trúarhreyfingar." Unpublished MA-thesis. Reykjavík: University of Iceland.

Statistics Iceland (Icel. Hagstofa Íslands). 2024. *Religious Organisations*. Available at https://statice.is/statistics/society/culture/religious-organisations/

Tran, A. 2015. "Untapped Resources or Deficient 'Foreigners': Students of Vietnamese Background in Icelandic Upper Secondary Schools." Unpublished PhD-thesis. Reykjavík: University of Iceland.

Zen in Iceland (Icel. Zen á Íslandi). 2024. *Námskeið í Zen hugleiðslu*. Available at https://www.zen.is/zen-hugleidsla.html (accessed: 17 May 2024).

10 Conclusion

Jørn Borup, Mitra Härkönen, Knut A. Jacobsen,
and Katarina Plank

How and why the "Helgö Buddha" ended up in Sweden remains unknown. We do know that the small bronze statue, likely made in Northwestern India in the sixth century, is the first known material artefact from the Buddhist religion entering the Nordic countries. The Vikings may not have known its significance, but its material recognisability and portable quality undoubtedly made it valuable. The religious and aesthetic qualities of Buddhist art continued to resonate centuries later, as seen in a small ivory Buddha owned by a Swedish migrant and the sale of Buddha figures as talismans in Denmark in the 1920s.

Buddhism also reached the Nordic countries through other means. *Barlaams og Josaphats Saga* was translated in Nordic languages in the nineteenth century, without Christians realising the fact that it was indeed a Christianised version of the Buddha legend. Images of this "exotic religion" were circulating but also analysed by Nordic scholars already in the late nineteenth century, several of whom became quite influential in the later Buddhology, Indology and History of Religion. Missionaries from the Nordic countries encountered the lived religion of Asia in different ways, sometimes ridiculing their heretic "folk religiosity," sometimes entering into what much later became an ideal of interreligious dialogue. The Nordic Buddhist Christian Mission (Den Nordiske Kristne Buddhistmisjon), founded by persons who shared the vision of the Norwegian Lutheran missionary Karl Ludvig Reichelt, exemplifies such a missionary organisation, still existing under the name of Areopagos with membership associations in Norway and Denmark.

Theosophists and other esotericists interpreted Buddhism into their own religiosities. Some were ridiculed by other founding Buddhists (such as Christian F. Melbye in Denmark). Others were engaged in introducing Buddhism. This was the case in Iceland, and in Finland (as described by Johannes Cairns) Mauno Nordberg was influential in combining Theosophical and Buddhist networks and sources of inspiration. After the Zen beatniks of the 1950s and 1960s had inspired groups of intellectuals, the introduction of lived Buddhism came through two main channels: the hippie generation, some of whom (as the Danish Ole and Hannah Nydahl) travelled to Asia, bringing Buddhism "home," and Asian Buddhists entering the Nordic region as migrants, refugees or missionaries (the latter exemplified by the Tibetan Lama Ngawang, as described by Stefan Larsson).

DOI: 10.4324/9781003529767-10

In parallel with other trajectories, Buddhism in the Nordic region has thus broadly followed the historical backgrounds and recognisable phases with periods of "discovery," recognition, and eventual accommodation, now being an established minority religion.

The Nordic context has had its impact on the religion. As we have seen in all chapters, the status of the Evangelical-Lutheran Church as an absolute majority religion in all Nordic countries has framed the political and legal contexts of Buddhism as well. State recognition gives a symbolic status of being a "real religion" – and in Norway, Sweden and Finland also economic privilege – to a large extent according to Christian ideals. But it is also based on the principles of welfare societies securing the existence of minority religions in countries where both "culture Christianity" and a widespread secular ethos shape also the teaching of Buddhism as a subject in public schools. Buddhism as a spiritual way of life resonates deeply for many Nordic people, several of whom as individuals find alignment with Buddhist values and practice aspects of Buddhism without labelling themselves as Buddhists.

As there are no census data on religion in the Nordic countries, there are no available numbers of self-identifying Buddhists. However, estimates by the scholars in this volume suggest the number could be as high as 200,000, or approximately 0.7 per cent of the total Nordic population, the absolute majority of whom (up to 90 per cent) are migrants from Asian countries and their descendants. Thai Buddhists have become the largest group, the majority of whom are women married to Nordic men. Temples have been built, and the religion has become institutionalised, not least because of Buddhist missionaries such as a Phra Chamnong Chutinattharo (as described by Hongsaton). Dynamic religiosity also depends on engaged lay participants, some of whom (as Härkönen terms it) find their temples as both a wellness centre and a "mini home far away from home." The Vietnamese, arriving in the 1970s as refugees, are the second largest group, with Myanmar, Sri Lanka, Bhutan, Tibet and China being other countries of origin contributing to the plurality of ethnic traditions in the Nordic countries. While influential in importing Buddhism and establishing centres for religious gatherings, the number of convert Buddhists is much smaller, typically with a focus on the Tibetan tradition or on meditation (Zen or *vipassanā*). Numerically, in terms of membership, it is interesting to note that SGI is the largest group in Denmark, significantly outnumbering the SGI groups in other Nordic countries.

The "two Buddhisms" model – differentiating between migrant and convert Buddhists – has been criticised in North American scholarship for being both racist and analytically imprecise. While some of this critique has been ideological, the conceptual impression is obvious. Most converts do not formally convert, and the children of Asian immigrants to the Nordic countries are not migrants. Still, there seems to be a division with parallel congregations, and there is very little overlap between the two groups, which makes it reasonable to use the terms as analytical concepts (and not as emic terms). Converts very seldom visit the Thai, Vietnamese or Chinese temples to participate in ceremonies, offerings, devotional prayers and celebration of cultural traditions, and Asian descendants very seldom go to the convert urban centres to engage in their meditation, dharma talks, courses and retreats. Some interesting overlaps and transitions do, however, occur. As Hreinsson illustrates in his article, the otherwise typical convert group Diamond Way Buddhism in Iceland has a majority of migrant workers from Eastern Europe, illustrating the conceptual porousness. In Denmark, Soka Gakkai was established mainly as a group for ethnic Japanese but has today become globalised with a majority of ethnic Danes as members.

Diversity of religiosity – ways of practising or being Buddhist – is equally highly differentiated throughout the region. The globally recognisable differences of two Buddhisms, between clergy and laity, or between "elite and folk," are also structurally represented in the Nordic religious communities, where a spectrum of minimalist and maximalist religiosity (as conceptualised by Bruce Lincoln) appear as both ideals and realities of different kinds of engagement. The plethora of Buddhist ideas, practices, symbols and identity forms are represented across the groups, allowing individuals to affiliate with membership sangha Buddhism, secular ideas, culture religion or hybrid religiosity.

Diversity can foster flexibility and dynamic possibilities of change. Diversity can also be a result of conflictual developments, as the Karmapa controversies in the late 1980s illustrated in Denmark. The Tibetan Buddhist community was split, and the Ole Nydahl wing isolated itself from other groups who were later fragmented into smaller units, probably being one of the reasons why a Buddhist umbrella organisation has never really caught up in the country. Such organisations are found in Norway (Buddhistforbundet), Sweden (Sveriges buddhistiska gemenskap) and Finland (Suomen Buddhalainen Unioni), giving an institutional foundation and political power, not least in securing and administering state funding for its groups. Functioning as semi-official Buddhist voices, they represent Buddhist authority, which otherwise is acquired and distributed by individual groups and leaders, the charisma and institutional blueprint of which can be object of dispute (as the Karmapa conflicts illustrated). Expressing the Buddhist voice is, however, also a position asking for a balanced awareness. When the "model immigrant" media narrative of the nice religion was questioned in a Norwegian popular TV programme, ridiculing Vietnamese Buddhists for their old-fashioned views of women, the national umbrella organisation did not stand up for their fellow Buddhists. They rather, as Jacobsen explains in his article, used the event to underline the differences between authentic (convert and text-based) and cultural (migrant, lived folk) Buddhism.

Some of the early converts, such as Swedish Nun Amita Nisatta and lay teacher Marcel Sirander, formed a unified Buddhism, emphasising the concept of a unified Buddhism, *Ekayāna*. Lama Ole Nydahl, with his Diamond Way Buddhism, established a new tradition of Western Buddhism in Denmark. In general, however, Buddhists in the Nordic countries are mainly globally oriented, building on already existing transnational networks and traditions. Thais have settled in each of the countries, and many of the women have married men from Iceland, Denmark, Sweden, Norway and Finland. Like migrants and descendants from Vietnam and other Asian countries, they keep in contact with their families of their respective countries of origin. Religious leaders staying on permanent or shorter basis are even more globally oriented as travelling monks. Especially Thai and Vietnamese monks regularly visit each other in the Nordic countries and in some of the larger European or Asian temples. Diamond Way travel teachers visit local groups in the region, and SGI hosts transnational gatherings across the global sphere.

Conflicts with the surrounding society seem to have been extremely few in the Nordic countries. As a religion, it is generally accepted, respected and often portrayed romantically (not least in opposition to a larger minority religion, Islam). Buddhism has never been part of political debates; Buddhists have never been questioned as legitimate citizens. Especially in Sweden, Buddhist organisations' civic engagement has played an important role in crisis preparedness at local, regional and national levels, including spiritual care at healthcare institutions. Buddhist elements have been incorporated into other religious or secular spaces, with mindfulness or Zen being examples of a de-Buddhified practice and conceptual trope having entered the Nordic cultures.

As the articles in this volume have shown, Buddhism has become an established minority religious tradition with a diversity of institutions, practices and interpretations, catering also to the values and narratives beyond religious affiliation in the highly secular and cultural Christian contexts of the Nordic region. With case studies and overall introductions to each of the countries, this volume – the first of its kind – has provided substantial information of Buddhism's existence in Iceland, Norway, Sweden, Finland and Denmark, contributing to the larger narrative of Buddhism in the West. Naturally, this does not mean that the analyses are conclusive. Rather, the volume can be seen as a stepping-stone to further research on also the future Buddhist landscape, exploring some of the questions relevant to Buddhism in the West generally, and specifically to the unique context of Buddhism in the Nordic countries.

Several important questions remain to be investigated (see Figure 10.1): Will the two Buddhisms thesis be relevant in the future? How will mixed marriages contribute to possible double religious identification and practices? Or will the mixed marriages contribute to an increased secularity, since close relationships with a secular partner or parent seem to be the single most important factor to influence individuals self-understanding as being secular? Will the Swedish "Svensson Buddhists" become resources for the temples, without necessarily participating in temple rituals? Will the Vietnamese and their descendants show growing patterns of social mobility, contributing to a religiously convertible capital? Will we see circular migration patterns among the Thais? Will tendencies of de-culturalisation (of mainly migrant Buddhists' transnational ties) and de-secularisation (of mainly converts' modern Buddhism) show different patterns of religiosity? Will Dhammakāya's invitation to non-Thais to meditate in the temples have future cross-fertilising effects, and will further overlaps and social-religious gatherings between the two types be realistic? Will the sectarian divisions continue to be foundational for Buddhist identities, or will further trans-sectarian cooperation and institutional collaboration be a possible scenario? Will legislative frame factors

Figure 10.1 What will the future hold? New Year's celebrations at the Vietnamese temple Phật Quang in Gothenburg, Sweden. The gates to the temple are only opened a few times during the year. The ageing first generation of Vietnamese Buddhist migrants gathers at midnight to enjoy fireworks after a day of meditation, recitation, and ceremonies. Photo: Katarina Plank.

drive different developments in the Nordic countries? Will socially engaged Buddhism become more prominent for Nordic Buddhists, too, including aspects of the religion (beyond mindfulness) in additional domains of society (schools, hospitals, the corporate world)? Will political engagement be in any way realistic for such a small minority religion – or will it bring potential disruption of the ideals of a harmony-seeking spiritual way of life? Will membership religiosity, institutionalised by the governments as a prerequisite for being granted the juridical status of a religious organisation, become a natural feature for more practising Buddhists? Or will "event Buddhism," involving participation in annual retreats and specific experience-oriented arrangements, be better suited in the future to individualised postmodern spirituality than what some will find to be old-fashioned communal religion? And not least: what do the younger generations do, say and identify with? Second-generation (convert and migrant) Buddhists might not appreciate or even interpret the religion in the same way as their parents; potential newcomers might not feel the same kind of appeal as previous generations. Will contemporary identity ideals find an affinity with Buddhist values and practices? Are race, ethnicity, sexuality and gender issues transferable to institutional frames? Could fragments of Buddhist values and practices, reinterpreted within individualised spirituality and way of life beyond (institutionalised) Buddhism, realistically contribute to a potential regenerative configuration of a future Nordic Buddhism?

Index

Note: Page numbers in *italic* indicate a figure, and page numbers in **bold** indicate a table on the corresponding page.

adoption 37, 45, **46**, 88
Advaita Vedānta 52
Akong Tulku Rinpoche 159
Alaska 8, 30
Ambedkar, B. R. 181
Amis du Bouddhisme, Les (Society in Paris) 156, 175–176, 181
Amitābha 143
Andersson, Dan 28
Areopagos 9, 104, 138, 202
Aśoka, Emperor 181, 185

Bagøien, Mali 139–140
Barlaam and Josaphat 9, 104, 137, 154
Baumann, Martin 40, 145
Beer, Einar 127–136, 138, 146
Bengtsson, Pelle 17, 51
Besant, Annie 27
Bhante K. Sri Dhammaratana Maha, Thera 39
bhikkhu ordination 160
Bihar School of Yoga 129
Björk 198
Black Crown Ceremony 33–34, 65
boat refugees 17
Bodhidharma 160
Bodhidharma Association 186
Buddha 1–2, 8, 11–12, 18–20, 202; and Einar Beer 132–136; Denmark 101–107, 116–118; Finland 153–158, 161; Norway 127–145; precursors to Buddhism in Norway 136–138; and Sri Ananda Acharya 131–132; Sweden 26–27, 30–32, 81–83, 92–94; *see also* Helgö Buddha

Buddharama Temple 37, 87, 91–92, 97, 161, 164
Buddhasāsana 82–83, 97
Buddha's Light International Association (BLIA) 114, 140
Buddhism, reputation of 142–146
Buddhismen, den betydeligste og interessanteste af alle hedenske religioner 137
Buddhismin ystävät – Buddhismens Vänner (Friends of Buddhism, Finland) 21, 156, 175, 178
Buddhistforbundet 11, 15, 103, 141–146, 204
Buddhistisk Forum 103
Buddhist Lodge 156, 177
Buddhist modernism 75, 170
Buddhist secularity 41
Buddhist Society (London) 175, 178, 181–182
Buddhist umbrella organisations: Buddhistforbundet 11, 15, 103, 141–146, 204; Suomen Buddhalainen Unioni 186, 204; Swedish Buddhist Community (Sveriges Buddhistiska Gemenskap) 25, 31–33, 45, 49, 52
Burma/Burmese 14–17; and Denmark 104, 116; and Finland 157, 160, 164–168, 180–181, 184–185; and Norway 141; and Sweden 25, 32, 39–40
Burmese Theravada Buddhist Association Buddha Ramsi 116
Burnouf, Eugène 137

Carus, Paul 27, 106, 191
Castrén, Matthias Alexander (M.A.) 154
Center for Visdom og Medfølelse 110
Chamnong Chutinattharo, Phra 19, 81, 83,
    86–87, *89*, 203
Chenrezig 65, 70
Chicago 1–2, 27–29, 86
Chinese 8–9, 16–17, 203; and Denmark
    109, 114; and Finland 164; and Iceland
    193–195, 198; and Norway 137–138;
    and Sweden 25–26, 32–33, 35–37, 40,
    45, 53, 64, 68, 87, 94
Chökyi Nyima Rinpoche 109
Chöpel, Lama 73
Christfulness 52, 118
Christiania 27
Christianity 5, 203; Denmark 101,
    105–106, 118; Finland 153, 182–184;
    Iceland 190, 199; Norway 138; Sweden
    27–31, 43, 50, 82, 96
Chulalongkorn, King Rama V of Siam
    30–31, 38, 84
concurrences 82–84, 88–89, 96
confirmation camps 153
constitutions 4–5, 45
convert Buddhism 11–15, 31–35, 53, 75,
    118, 142, 145
COVID-19 pandemic 164

Daisetsu Tangen Harada Roshi 167
Dalai Lama, fourteenth 25, 34–35, 64–65,
    68–72, 109, 139–141, 195, 197
Dalai Lama, thirteenth 155
Dalström, Kata 10, 28–30
dāna 169; Buddhist *dāna* through taxation
    47, 52
Dansk Buddhistisk Samfund (Danish
    Buddhist Society) 108
David-Néel, Alexandra 176, 183
demographics 25, 37, 44–46, **46**, 52, 115
Den Kristne Buddhistmisjon 138
Den Norske Sotozen Buddhist Orden 139
Den Vietnamesiske Buddhistforening 142
Den vietnamesiske Buddhistiske Kulturelle
    Forening Chua Lieu Quan **102**
Deshimaru, Taisen 35, 50
Dhammachaya Buddhist Center
    Denmark **102**
Dhammakāya 16, 39, **56**, 115
Dhammanando Bhikku 193
Dhammaratana Mahathera, K. Sri 39
Dhammayuttika Nikāya 16, 39, **54**, **56**, 115
Dharamsala 158
dharma 32–35, 70, 110, 114, 169, *179*, 195

Dharmapala, Anagarika 10, 106, 122n15
Diamond Way Buddhism 14–17, 34,
    111–112, 119, 139, 159, 196–197,
    204–105
discrimination 1
Dissenter Acts 4, 10, 30
Dorje Shugden 197

Eastern philosophy 29
economic funding of the Buddhist religion
    141; *see also dāna*
education 5–7, 35–36, 63–64, 108–109,
    130–132, 142–144, 167–168
Ekayana 31, 33, 204
engaged Buddhism 35, 166–167, 170
England 86, 157, 176, 194
Ericsson, Marie 11, 43
Ervast, Pekka 156
European Buddhist Union (EBU) 15,
    104, 142
Evangelical Lutheran Church of
    Finland 153

failures 130
Fausbøll, Michael Viggo 9, 105
Fellingsbro 25, 35, 71, *72*
Finnish Lutheran Evangelical Association
    155
Finnish temperance society 181
Finnish Theosophical Society 155–156,
    176
First World War 155
Fo Guang Shan 114
folk Buddhism 19, 81–83, 97–98, 104
Föreningen Malmö Buddhistcentrum 33
Foreningen Stupa Karma Kagyu
    Buddhistisk Sangha 110
FPMT, Foundation for the Preservation of
    the Mahāyāna Tradition 34, 166
Fredrika 37–38
Fredriksson, Trudy 31–35, 65, 71–74,
    75n3, 76n5
freedom of religion 5, 48
Freethinkers of Finland 182
Friends of Buddhism (Buddhismens
    Vänner) 21, 32, 156–157, 160–161,
    175, 177–178, 181–185
Friends of Western Buddhist Order
    (FWBO), Triratna 157–160, 166
funerals, memorials and cemeteries 33–36,
    47–48, 70, 87, 91–92, 102–103, *179*

Gällmo, Gunnar 31, 42
Geluk 160, 166

gender 4, 41, 46–47, 95, 143–145, 206
generations 11–12, 110–112, 170, 206
Geshe Pema Dorjee 160
Gjellerup, Karl 105
Glassman, Bernie 35
Goenka, S. N. 11, 34, 43, 139, 166, 185
Gothenburg 17, 25, 29, 32–40, 45, 50, 65
Great Britain 45, 49, 157
Guan Yin Citta Dharma Door 114

Hall, Pake 35
Hạnh, Thích Nhất **146**
Harada Daiun Sogaku Roshi 167
hate crimes 48
Helgö Buddha 1, 8, 26, 202
Hildén, Gina 177–178
Hildén, Leo 177–178, 180, 186
Himalayas 11, 109, 155, 158
Hinduism 20, 29, 116, 127–132, 136, 181, 191
Hof, Hans 50–51
Holmboe, C.A. 9, 137
Holst, Harry (Tyagananda) 2, 28–30
Hong Kong 33–37, 114, 137
Humphreys, Christmas 156, 179
Hungary 73

IBPS (International Buddhist Progress Society) 17, 36
immigrant/diaspora Buddhism 15–17, 41, 75, 140–142
India 9–10, 202; and Denmark 105, 109; and Finland 155, 158–160, 177; and Iceland 195; and Norway 129–136, 138–139; and Sweden 29, 32, 35–36, 43, 64–74, 81, 86
Islam 5, 7, 31, 44–45, 82, 153, 205
Italy 160, 163

Jamyangling, Soenam 69–70, 73–74
Japan/Japanese 11–14; and Denmark 103, 108; and Finland 153–155, 166–167, **171**; and Iceland 194, 197–199; and Norway 139; and Sweden 27–28, 36–37
Johansson, Rune E. A. 42
Jönköping 29, 36, 49
Judaism 4, 45, 153

Kalevala 155, 158
Kallinen, Yrjö 156, 176–178
Kalmyks 1, 9, 17, 20, 154–155
Kalu Rinpoche 25, 63–65, 68–73, 110, 158

Kamio, Mark (Kamio Masaaki) 108
Kapleau, Philip 35, 51
karma 28, 112, 142–146
Karma Dechen Ösel Ling (KDÖL) 17, 34, 71, *72*
Karma Kagyu 16–17, 34, 111, 142, 159, 197
Karma Kagyu Skolen (Diamond Way) 102, 110–112, 119
Karmapa, Seventeenth (Thaye Dorje) 73, 112
Karmapa, Sixteenth (Rangjung Rigpe Dorje) 25, 33, 63–68, 73, 109–111, 158
Karmapa controversy 73, 119
Karmapa Trust Sangye/Tashi Ling 110
Karma Shedrub Dargye Ling (KSDL) 63–66
Karma Tashi Ling buddhistsamfunn 139
Karme Tenpe Gyaltsen (KTG) 34, 66, 73
Kathmandu 32, 67, 110, 181
Kelsang Drubchen 197
Key, Ellen 10, 27
Khenchen Lama Sherab Gyaltsen Amipa Rinpoche 34, 71
Kjolhede, Bodhin 35
Klint, Hilma af 28
Korea 36–37, 114, 135, 160
Krohn, Kaarle 155
Kunsang, Erik Pema 109

Lakha Thupten Dorje Rinpoche 109, 158
Lamaism 155
Lama Yeshe 159
Lama Zopa Rinpoche 166
Lassen, Christian 137
legislation 4, 25, 29, 45–49
Lhasa 66–67, 158
Lie, Kåre A. 139
Lindeblad, Björn Natthiko 43–44
Linji lineage (*Rinzai*, v. *Lâm Tế*) 163
Lodru, Lama 65–66
London 28–29, 175–178, 181, 184–185
Lotus Buddhist Order 33
Lounsbery, G. Contstant 176
Lund 31, 35, 42, 98
Lutheran Church 4–7, 21, 101, 153, 189, 203
Lutheran Evangelical Church (Church of Sweden) 25, 29–30, 41, 45–47, 50–52

Maha Bodhi Society, The 157
Mahā Nikāya 16, 39, 115
Mahāyāna 16, 33–3, 39–40, 138, 143–144, 163–165, 186
Maitreyya Buddha 11, 127–130, *128*, 132–136, 138, 146; *see also* Sri Ananda

Acharya; Tathagata Amoghasiddhi
    Maitreyya Buddha
Malmberg, Claes 43
Malmö 17–18, 25, 33–37, 40, 45–47
Mannerheim, Carl Gustav 155
marriage 28, 41, 87–88, 92, 121n3, 163,
    168–169, 205
MBSR, Mindfulness-Based Stress
    Reduction 49, 117, 167
Melbye, Christian Frederik 10, 19,
    105–108, 117–118, 202
Meyer, Gundula 51
Middle Ages 2, 154
migrant Buddhism 11, 14, 20, 112, 142,
    145
migration 1–3, 11–18, 25, 30–31, 140,
    161–165
mindfulness 14–16, 19–20, 205–206;
    Denmark 101, 114, 117–118; Finland
    152–153, 167; Iceland 198; Norway
    139; Sweden 49–5
missionaries 9, 19–20, 104–106,
    136–137, 154–155, 202–203; *see also*
    Missionary, The Thai Dhamma
Missionary, The Thai Dhamma 81–84,
    97–98; history of 85–86; legacies of
    96–97; life and career of 86–88; and
    official Thai Buddhism 84–85; *Thai
    Years of a Thai Monk in Snowy Lands*
    88–96, *89*
Mission to the Heathens in Burma 104
mixed marriages 1, 53, 88, 92, 205
Mongolian 1, 20, 154
monkhood, Thai (*Sangha*) 81–85, 88–90,
    94–97
Mortensen, John 108
Munthe, Johan Wilhelm Normann 9, 137

Nai Ge Si – Buddhist Union **102**
Namkhai Norbu 159
Ñāṇadīpa (Denys Jeune) 107
Narada Thera 33
national epos 154
Natural Forest Monastery in Randers, The
    102
New Zealand 157
Ngawang, Lama 19, 34, 63–66, *72*, 75–76,
    158, 202; impressions of 74–75; life
    before Sweden 66–69; life in Sweden
    69–73
Ngedön Wangchuk, Lama 73, 78n52
Nichiren 36
Nisatta Amita (Ingrid Wagner) 10, 32–33,
    36, 45, 64, 71, 204

Nordberg, Mauno 10, 21, 156, 175, 202;
    legacy 185–186; philosophy and
    practice 182–185; prior to founding
    Finnish society 176–178; as secretary
    and long-term president of Finnish
    society 178–182
Nordic Christian Buddhist
    Mission 104
Nordic welfare 170
Norwegian Broadcasting Cooperation
    (NRK) 142–145
Nyanaponika Thera 177–179, 183
Nyanatiloka Mahathera 177–179, 183
Nydahl, Hannah 11, 65, 110–111, 118, 158,
    196–197, 202
Nydahl, Ole 11, 110–112, 118, 139,
    158–159, 197, 202, 204
Nyingma 139, 160

Odland, Kanja 35, 42, 161
Official Thai Buddhism 81–85, 92, 96
Olcott, Henry Steel 27, 121n8, 156
One Drop Zendo 108
Øsal Ling – Lysets Have 15, 109–110
Osen, Sende 143–144
Oshofors 52
Östersund **55**

pagodas 168
Pallis, Tim 108
Paññadipa Sayadaw 160
Phật Đản (Vesak) 33, 87, 106, 156, 162,
    165, 180–181
Phendeling – Center for Tibetansk
    Buddhisme 15, 109–110
Piadassi, Thera 33
Plum Village 35, 161
pluralisation of Buddhism 142
plurality of lived Buddhism 145
Poromaa, Sante 35, 42, 161
Pra Mahanual Chamnanram 163
Pra Mahatee Sirijanda 164
prison 5, 34–35, 156, 184
Pure Land Buddhism 144

Quang Huong 112, 114

Ragunda 30–31
Rangjung Yeshe Gomde 109
Rask, Rasmus 9, 105
Rättvik 50–51
rebirth 11, 20, 127, *128*, 133, 142–146, 182
refugee 16–17, 202–203; Denmark
    112–118; Finland 161–164;

Iceland 194–195; Norway 140;
  Sweden 25, 36, 64
Reichelt, Karl Ludvig 9, 137–138, 202
religious diversity 7, 189
Reventlow, Christian 105
Rosicrucianism 182
Russia/Russian 1, 9, 154–155, 159, 170

Sakya Changchub Chöling 34, 71
Samahita, Thera (Jan Hansen) 107
sampo 154
Samye Ling 159–160
Sanbō Kyōdan 35, 54
Sangharakshita 43, 157, 159
Sariputra, Swami Acharya 129; *see also*
  Beer, Einar
sāsana 82–83
Sayadaw, Mahasi 32
Scania 25, 34, 36
science and technology 134
Scotland 35, 42, 159, 196
second-generation Buddhists 40, 52, 119,
  143, 145, 206
secularisation 4–7, 25, 41, 45, 49, 52, 117
Sederholm, Carl Robert 155
Seon 160, 165
Setreng, Sigmund Kvaløy 139
Shamar Rinpoche, Fourteenth 73, 166
Shambala 52, 101, 118, 166
Shoubuzenji 108
Shugden 197
Sikkim 65, 68
Sinnet, Alfred Percy 155
Sirander, Marcel (Tao Wei, Acarya
  Shunyata) 10, 31–34, 42–43, 204
Sirén, Osvald 180
Śivanārāyaṇa Paramahaṃsa 129–130,
  132, 136
Sjöström, Henning 43
Snellman, Jussi 156, 176, 178–179
Soka Gakkai International (SGI) 14–18,
  21, 104, 108, 119, 158, 194, 203, 205;
  Denmark 14, 108–109, 114; Finland
  158; Sweden 36
Somsak Gandhasilo 114
Soodthibongse Soodthiwungso 115
Sōtō-Zen 160
Sōtō Zen Aarhus 108
spiritualism 2, 29, 153
Sri Ananda Acharya 127–136; *see
  also* Maitreyya Buddha; Tathagata
  Amoghasiddhi Maitreyya Buddha
Sri Lanka/Sri Lankan 11–19, 25, 203;
  Denmark 103–104, 107, 112, 116;

Finland 157, 163–164, 181–183;
  Iceland 193; Norway 141; Sweden 33,
  37–39, 43–45, 71, 86–87
Srilankansk-Danske Buddhistiske Religiøse
  og Kulturelle Forening **10**
state support of religion 46–47, 142
Stockholm Exhibition 30
Strindberg, August 28
stūpa 17–18, 32–34, 72–73, 110–111,
  137–141, 159–160, 195, *196*
Sugata, Anagarika (Karl-Henrik
  Wagner) 32
supernaturalism, Thai 83
sūtra 162
Suzuki, D. T. 2, 10, 27, 106, 195
Svedal, Hilma 8, 30
Svensson Buddhists 19, 205
Sveriges Buddhistiska Samarbetsråd (SBS)
  33
Swedenborg, Emanuel 1–2, 27–28
Swedish Agency for Support to Faith
  Communities 44, 49
Swedish Buddhist Community (Sveriges
  Buddhistiska Gemenskap) 25, 31–33,
  45, 49, 52
Swedish Buddhist Council (SBC) 71
Swedish Lama Society (Svenska lama
  föreningen) 64
Swedish Tibetan School and Culture
  Society (Svensk-tibetanska skol-och
  kulturföreningen) 7
Switzerland 34, 158

Taehye sunim (Mahapañña, Mikael
  Niinimäki) 160, 186
Tai Situ Rinpoche 159, 166
Taino, Engaku Taino 160
Tantra 52, 118
Tārā 70
Tarab Institute 109, 158
Tarab Tulku Rinpoche 109, 158
Tathagata Amoghasiddhi Maitreyya
  Buddha 127–130, 132–136, 138;
  see also Maitreyya Buddha; Sri Ananda
  Acharya
Ten Chi Dojo 108
Terzano, Karen 167
Thailand/Thai (Dhammakāya, Thammayut,
  Dhammayuttika) 12–21, 203–205;
  Denmark 103–105, 114–116, 119–120;
  Finland 160–168; Iceland 192–194;
  Norway 139–141; Sweden 30–31,
  36–43, 84–88, 91–97; *see also*
  Missionary, The Thai Dhamma

Theosophical Society 9–10, 21; Denmark
104; Finland 155–156, 176–178, 182;
Iceland 191; Sweden 27, 32
Theosophy/Theosophical 8–10, 20–21,
202; Denmark 121n8; Finland 155–161,
175–178, 182; Iceland 189–191;
Sweden 27–28, 31–33
Theravāda 16, 20; Denmark 102, 105–109,
116–118; Finland 156, 160, 163–167,
177, 183, 186; Iceland 192–193;
Norway 138–142; Sweden 31–33,
39–40, 43, 64, 85–87
Thích Giác Tánh 114
Thích Hạnh Bảo 163
Thích Hạnh Thông 162
Thiền 161
three-year retreat 17, 25, 34, 67–68,
71–72, 159
Tibetan 10–11, 14–20, 202–204; Denmark
107–114, 118–119; Finland 152–155,
158–160, 165–166; Iceland 194–198;
Norway 127, 138–142; Sweden 25,
32–36, 43, 63–75, *72*
Tingley, Katherine 27
Tipiṭaka 31
Tolstoy, Nikita and Diana 65–66, 71
Tørjesen, Arne 138, 141
traditional Buddhism 50, 75
Tsultim Rinpoche, Lama 73
Tsurpu Monastery 67–68
Tulku Dakpa Rinpoche 160
Tulku Pema Wangyal 159
two Buddhisms 3, 82, 190, 203–205

U Ba Khin 185
Unified Buddhist Church of Vietnam 114

Vajrayāna 102, 111, 165
Valkoinen lumme ("White Water Lily") 161
Valvanne, Hugo 176–178
Vạn Hạnh 163
Vedānta 132
vegetarianism 184
Vesak 33, 87, 106, 156, 162, *165*, 180–181
Vetterling, Herman (Philangi Dasa) 1–2,
27–28
Vietnam/Vietnamese 7, 13–19, 203–205;
Denmark 104, 112–118; Finland 152,
161–169; Iceland 190–194, 199;
Norway 140–147; Sweden 25, 35–40,
47, 53, 87, 91

Vietnamese European Congregation
Unified Buddhist Association 162
Vijjaviriyo (Thích Minh Tấn) 163
Vikings 1, 8, 26, 111, 154, 198, 202
vipassanā 14–20, 203; Denmark 107;
Finland 152, 160, 164, 166, 185;
Norway 139; Sweden 34, 43, 52
Vivekananda, Swami 29
Vu Lan (Ullambana) 162

Wat Asokaram Finland Vipassana
Meditation Center 164
Wat Buddha Iceland 193
Wat Buddharama 164–165
Wat Chinnawong 141
Wat Dalarnavanaram 164
Wat Dan-Thai **102**
Watpa Copenhagen **102**, 114
Wat Pah Buddha Metta Thammataro
Finland 164
Wat Pah Nanachat 43
Wat Pah Sokjai 48
Wat Phra Dhammakaya Iceland 193
Wat Phutta Tham Finland 164
Wat Piyadhammaram 31
Wat Pleng Vipassana 160
Wat Thai Denmark Brahma Vihara
Buddhist Monastery **102**, 115
Wat Thai Iceland 17
Wat Thai Norway 141
Wat Thai of Los Angeles 86
Wat Ubolmanee 141
Wegemüller, Barbara Salaam 35
World Fellowship of Buddhists (WFB) 10,
32, 104, 142, 157, 175, 181–185
World Peace Congress in Helsinki 185
World's Parliament of Religion 27

Yangpachen 66–67, 69, 73
yoga 5, 19, 25, 49, 52–53, 64, 101, 129,
132, 166

Zen 10–11, 14–21, 202; Denmark
107–109, 118–119; Finland 152,
155–156, 160–161, 166–169, 177, 183;
Iceland 191, 194–195, 198; Norway
127, 138–142; Sweden 27, 33–35, 42,
49–51, 98
Zen Buddhistisk Forening 108
Zengården 17, 35, 42, 161
Zenskolen 138

For Product Safety Concerns and Information please contact our
EU representative GPSR@taylorandfrancis.com Taylor & Francis
Verlag GmbH, Kaufingerstraße 24, 80331 München, Germany